Talks in a Library
with
Laurence Hutton

RECORDED BY

ISABEL MOORE

ILLUSTRATED

G. P. PUTNAM'S SONS
NEW YORK AND LONDON
The Knickerbocker Press

Copyright, 1905
BY
ELEANOR V. HUTTON

Ninth Impression

The Knickerbocker Press, New York

TO

JOSEPH JEFFERSON

THE BEST OF MEN: THE BEST OF FRIENDS: AND THE
ONLY PLAYER IN HIS OWN GROUP

L. H.

INTRODUCTORY NOTE

THE writer of this note was one of those who from time to time enjoyed the privilege of sitting in the library of Laurence Hutton, and of hearing from the lips of his genial host (a man with a genius for friendship and for attracting friends) informal talk concerning the friends with whom Hutton had been associated during a life that, while all too brief, was certainly full and that in many ways, and particularly in this matter of personal relation, was assuredly fortunate. As we moved about between the fascinating collections of the well-furnished shelves and walls of the library in the Princeton country home, one thing and another—portraits, autograph letters, inscribed books, play-bills, menus of old-time dinners—brought to the mind of the host recollections of friends, very many of whom had already "joined the majority." The word of reference, the anecdote or the story, was always kindly and was not only picturesque in itself but doubly interesting in characterising the speaker no less than the person described.

I suggested to my host, as had doubtless often before been suggested, that he ought to put into print his varied memories of men and of things. "Yes," he

Introductory Note

replied, "it would be a pleasant task except for the labour of the writing. I find myself growing lazy in my old age" (he was still, of course, young enough, but, as was afterwards realised, was really growing weaker) "and I cannot now apply myself to any regular task work. If I could talk about my friends into an appreciative and discriminating phonograph, it would be a pleasure to put the reminiscences on record."

The responsibility seemed, therefore, to come to Mr. Hutton's publishing friend for meeting this rather special requirement. The publisher succeeded in finding in the skilled literary worker who has recorded these "Talks in a Library" a "phonograph" that was both sympathetic and discriminating, and it is through her tactful and conscientious service that it has proved possible to preserve in book form this memorial of the genial owner of the library. The volume will, of course, have a personal value for those who knew Hutton, while it should prove of interest also to a wide circle to whom its pages will bring their first impression of his charming personality.

The manuscript was revised by Mr. Hutton before his last illness, but the printing of the record of these Talks was not begun until after his death. The volume stands as his final word to his friends and to the public.

G. H. P.

INTRODUCTION

THE words which here follow were all talked in a Library.

Some of them, elaborated and, since, re-elaborated, have already appeared in periodical form.

The others, during the autumn, winter, and spring of 1903-04, were talked into sympathetic ears, and were recorded by a willing pen, in the talker's own book-room at Princeton. As set down in these pages, they have been submitted to him, and have been the subject of his revision and correction.

He protests that the words are too personal. But he does not see how he can leave himself out and at the same time do full justice to the personal side of his friends.

LAURENCE HUTTON.

PRINCETON, May, 1904.

THE motto of the family of Mr. Laurence Hutton is to the effect that nothing that is human is foreign to them; and the individual note of appreciation was struck by Walcott Balestier who wrote in one of the Hutton Guest Books—that are a record within a record —" To Laurence Hutton: who finds the way to Heaven by doing deeds of hospitality." Had Mr. Hutton ever added to his *Landmarks* series a volume on the Literary Landmarks of New York, he would have had to consider his own home as one of the most notable features connected with such associations, as well as a personification of a most exquisite friendliness of man for man.

That I have been permitted to know the hospitality of Mr. Hutton, and to a certain degree his friendship, as well as something of his literary, dramatic, and artistic interests, will always be to me a gracious memory.

ISABEL MOORE.

NEW YORK, March, 1905.

CONTENTS

CHAPTER I

Stories—Early Days—First Money Earned—Mr. Aldrich — The Strangeness of Coincident — The Colonel — My Barber—First Poetical Efforts 1–31

CHAPTER II

First Published Article — Charles Dickens's Reading — Dickens as an Actor in Liverpool—Florence—Irving as Dombey—The Younger Dickens—An Extraordinary Man 32–57

CHAPTER III

Recollections of the Stage—*Plays and Players*—Frederick Warde — Henry Irving's Generosity — Edwin Booth—The Players Club—Death of Lawrence Barrett 58–89

CHAPTER IV

Joseph Jefferson — Lawrence Barrett — Lester Wallack— Henry J. Montague — "Billy" Florence —John McCullough—Mrs. Keeley—Mrs. Maeder . . 90–118

CHAPTER V

Imaginary "Copy"— Dramatic Criticism—Letters to *The Evening Mail* — The Funeral of Henry Kingsley — "Mothers in Fiction" — Presentation Copies — Authors' Readings — The Professional Critic — Trials of the Literary Life 119–147

Contents

CHAPTER VI

The Collecting of the Death Masks—Benjamin Franklin—Robert Burns—Charles XII. of Sweden—Richard Brinsley Sheridan—Coleridge—John Boyle O'Reilly—Napoleon 148–166

CHAPTER VII

The Collecting of the Death Masks (*Continued*)—Henry Clay—Aaron Burr—Louise of Prussia—Mendelssohn—Beethoven—Cromwell—General Grant—Keats—Wordsworth—Canova—Lawrence Barrett—General Sherman—Cavour—Leopardi—Tasso—Newton—Queen Elizabeth—Shakespeare—Walter Scott 167–197

CHAPTER VIII

The Collecting of the Death Masks (*Concluded*) — Dean Swift—Franklin—George Washington—Robespierre—Marat—Mirabeau—Edmund Keane—Thackeray—Celia Thaxter—Lord Brougham—Laurence Sterne—Lincoln and Booth—Walt Whitman—Liszt—Process of Taking a Life or Death Mask—Casts of Hands That Have Done Things 198–229

CHAPTER IX

Obituary Notices—Professional Readers—Demands upon Authors—The Duties of Editors—The Mistakes of Compositors 230–260

CHAPTER X

The American Actor Series—*Literary Landmarks of London*—Colley Cibber—The Grave of Charles Lamb—Joanna Baillie—Butler—Boswell—The False Making of History—Comparative Rates Paid to Authors and Illustrators—*Literary Landmarks of Edinburgh*—Sir Walter Scott—Dr. John Brown 261–288

CHAPTER XI

The Collectors of Autographs — Begging Letters — The Conscientious Collector and the Pirate—A Dickens Pilgrimage—Mary Anderson 289–310

ILLUSTRATIONS

	PAGE
LAURENCE HUTTON . . . . . *Frontispiece*	
From the painting by Dora Wheeler Keith.	
SILHOUETTE OF MARK TWAIN	6
BROOCH PORTRAIT OF JOHN HUTTON, FATHER OF LAURENCE HUTTON	20
THE DICKENS PLAY-BILL	36
CHARLES DICKENS	40
PEEP O' DAY. LAURENCE HUTTON'S HOME IN PRINCETON, NEW JERSEY	44
THE PEEP O' DAY LIBRARY IN PRINCETON . . .	54
FACSIMILE OF THE BOOTH AND BARRETT PAGE IN THE HUTTON GUEST-BOOK	70
EDWIN BOOTH	74
POSTER PORTRAIT OF J. WILKES BOOTH . . .	84
ORIGINAL "PLAYERS" ON YACHT	86
MRS. G. H. GILBERT	96
LAWRENCE BARRETT	96
WALLACK AND IRVING PAGE IN THE HUTTON GUEST-BOOK	106
SIGNATURES ON THE BACK OF A KINSMEN MENU. IRVING'S BREAKFAST TO BOOTH	114
LAURENCE HUTTON IN THE "MAIL" DAYS . . .	120
THE MAISTER OF "BALDUTHO"	126
HENRY KINGSLEY	126
EDWIN BOOTH, DEATH MASK	212
ABRAHAM LINCOLN, DEATH MASK	212
WALTER SCOTT, DEATH MASK	212

xvi   Illustrations

	PAGE
CAST OF HELEN KELLER'S HAND	226
CAST OF THACKERAY'S HAND	226
CAST OF STEVENSON'S HAND	226
LAURENCE HUTTON'S BOOK-PLATE	258
FRANCIS DAVID MILLET, BY SAINT-GAUDENS	278
PEEP O' DAY, THE HUTTON HOMESTEAD AT ST. ANDREWS, SCOTLAND	282
SIR WALTER SCOTT, DRAWN FROM LIFE BY GILBERT STEWART NEWTON	286
A PAGE FROM THE HUTTON GUEST-BOOK	290
A PAGE FROM THE HUTTON GUEST-BOOK	292
DRAWING BY FREDERICK BARNARD	296
OLIVER HERFORD'S DRAWING IN LAURENCE HUTTON'S COPY OF "THE JINGLE BOOK"	298
A MARK TWAIN LETTER	300
LETTER FROM SAMBOURNE TO ABBEY	304
PART OF THE ORIGINAL MS. OF "SHERIDAN'S RIDE"	306

Attached to the sheet is a knot of horse-hair, as presented in the reproduction.

MARK TWAIN'S PAGE IN THE HUTTON GUEST-BOOK	308
MARY ANDERSON, WILLIAM BLACK, AND JO ANDERSON	312
MONOGRAM, "I. W.," IN WESTMINSTER ABBEY	314
A KINSMEN MENU WITH AUTOGRAPHED DRAWINGS	316
THE PUNCH-BOWL COMPOSITE DRAWING	318
WILLIAM BLACK'S ROOM	320
PEN-AND-INK SKETCH OF LAURENCE HUTTON BY ABBEY	322
SKETCH OF WILLIAM BLACK BY ABBEY	324
"ROSE MEINIE," WRITTEN BY WILLIAM BLACK	326
DRAWING BY CALDECOTT	328
THE KINSMEN "BONE"	330
DRAWING BY ALMA TADEMA	332
AN AUTOGRAPHED KINSMEN MENU	334
AN AUTOGRAPHED KINSMEN MENU	338

Contents

CHAPTER XII

Mary Anderson in London—Dean Stanley—Westminster Abbey and the Izaak Walton Tablet — Stratford-on-Avon — William Winter — William Black — The Kinsmen 311-329

CHAPTER XIII

Alma Tadema — George du Maurier — Charles Reade — George Eliot—Swinburne—Joaquin Miller in England—Locker-Lampson—John Fiske—James Russell Lowell 330-367

CHAPTER XIV

Longfellow—Emerson—Whittier—Celia Thaxter—Louisa M. Alcott — Kate Field — Helen Keller — Charles Dudley Warner — Certain Treasures — Thackeray Drawing of Thackeray — Fitz-Gerald Book-Plate — Signatures with the Hat — The Names of Literary Men—Bret Harte 368-410

CHAPTER XV

Authors Club — Kipling—Tile Club — Vedder — Henry James—Mark Twain and Cable—Mark Twain's Story of Mrs. Stowe — Mark Twain and Corbett — Stockton — Stoddard — George William Curtis — Thomas B. Reed—H. C. Bunner 411-447

Index 449

Illustrations

	PAGE
CARICATURE OF CHARLES READE	342
JOHN FISKE WITH TWO OF HIS CHILDREN	354
From a discoloured photograph.	
HELEN KELLER AND HER DOG	384
Copyright, 1902, by Emily Stokes.	
HELEN KELLER, MISS SULLIVAN, MARK TWAIN, AND LAURENCE HUTTON	398
A CARICATURE OF THACKERAY BY HIMSELF	400
EDWARD FITZ-GERALD	402
THE FITZ-GERALD BOOK-PLATE, DRAWN BY THACKERAY	404
SILHOUETTE OF H. C. BUNNER	406
By courtesy of Keppler & Schwarzmann.	
"TWO GHOSTS OF LAST SUMMER"—MARK TWAIN AND LAURENCE HUTTON	406
LETTER BY JEFFERSON, SENT WITH A NEW HAT FOR LAURENCE HUTTON	408
SIGNATURES SENT WITH A NEW HAT TO LAURENCE HUTTON	412
THE TILE CLUB PORTRAIT OF EDWIN ABBEY	414
PAGE FROM THE HUTTON GUEST-BOOK, WITH PORTRAIT OF MRS. HUTTON BY CARROLL BECKWITH	422
A LETTER FROM R. H. STODDARD	424
A NOTE FROM CHARLES READE	426
INSCRIPTION IN BOOK FROM GEORGE WILLIAM CURTIS	426
A PAGE FROM THE HUTTON GUEST-BOOK	434

They Have Said And They will Say Let Them Be Saying 1720

OLD SCOTCH DOOR LINTEL IN LIBRARY OF PEEP O' DAY

TALKS IN A LIBRARY WITH LAURENCE HUTTON

CHAPTER I

Stories—Early Days—First Money Earned—Mr. Aldrich—The Strangeness of Coincident—The Colonel—My Barber—First Poetical Efforts.

To a club of Seniors at Princeton, before I was connected with the University, I talked one night in the winter of 1896-97, upon a subject selected by them; to wit, my own experiences as a literary man—such as I am! The undergraduates who had journalistic or literary aspirations—and they were in the majority—wanted to know how I began; what was my training; if it had been easy or hard; and what were the net results—if any. No notes were made; I simply told them, for fifty minutes—at a dollar a minute, the first money I ever made in that way, and the easiest money I ever made in any way—how it all came about. I had to talk concerning myself, a subject which is very pleasant to oneself and to nobody else; but if, as Dr.

Holmes has said, "Autobiography is what biography ought to be," I do not see how I could talk about myself, and, at the same time, leave myself out! One incident, or episode, or experience has suggested many others, until I feel myself, as some one has happily put it, in my anecdotage.

I have often been asked to write a story, but I do not possess the gift of invention, and very few of the gifts of expansion and elaboration. All story-telling, I believe, is founded mainly on fact. Thackeray, and Scott, and Dickens, and Balzac, and Zola, and Cervantes, without knowing it, and without meaning it, have told in their stories the essence of the stories of their own lives. And I can only tell the story of my life; the story of the persons, the places, and the things I have known, and seen, and done, since my own life began, a good deal more than fifty years ago. The first decade and a half of it I described in the story of *A Boy I Knew*, which brought me down to the period of long trousers, and out of the influence of dames' schools. Now I am telling about the scenes in which I have been, in which I have acted, and in which I have been acted upon, since I have grown up to man's estate. If I am a part of them, and too large a part of them, I cannot help it. And if I am my own hero, and if my mother and my wife are my heroines, and if my friends—lowly and lofty—constitute my *dramatis personæ*, I feel that I am only doing what other story-tellers have done, and will always do, under a thicker and less transparent veil. I am telling the story of actual persons, of actual places, and of actual things, touching as impersonally as possible, and only in passing, upon the persons who are still in the flesh; dwelling at greater length upon the men and women who were my friends and acquaintances, but who are lost to sight, if still dear to memory.

I never wrote a story. I've told many, but I could never put one into print. That is, a story, a tale, a narrative. Mr. James Harper once gave me two plots, both of them original. But I could never do anything with them. Here they are, for the benefit of some one with the gift of telling short stories.

A man died, in some country town familiar to Mr. Harper or his father. At least the man was supposed by his neighbours and his family—and was declared by himself—to have died. Everything was done to him that is done to the rural corpse, when it was discovered that he was not dead at all but in a trance, and in due course he came back to his earthly self and went about his everyday life. He always contended that his soul had gone on to another and a better world, where he had solved the infinite and had had marvellous and magnificent experiences. What they were—pledged to secrecy by somebody with a capital "S"—he would never tell. At last he consented to write it all down for posterity's benefit, on a paper put into a private drawer of his desk, and not to be seen by mortal eye until he was dead indeed. At the end of ten years or so, his own undoubted end in this world came. It was no trance this time. He was laid out, and "sat-up" with, and the sermon was preached, and the bearers carried him to the family plot, seven and a half miles away, and the last prayer was said, and the grave was covered over, and the sods laid, and then the mourners hurried home to find out the great mystery. But while they were at the cemetery the house had burned to the ground, and everything in it, including the desk and the private drawer and the manuscript, and nobody ever knew what happened to the man who had been dead and then was alive again.

Mr. Harper's second plot was more cheerful in its ending. A valuable letter containing a will or a deed, mailed many years ago, never reached its destination. At last it was found in the lining of an old mail-coach, and it was delivered to the heirs of the person to whom it was originally addressed, the person himself being dead many years. The document seemed to be of value— worth at least a thousand dollars to its latest recipients; and great hopes were raised in the recipients' breast: a thousand dollars was an enormous sum and meant rest and comfort for the end of a weary, poverty-stricken life. A lawyer was employed, deeds were examined, titles were searched, no expense was spared to prove what seemed to be a just and legal claim. But to no end. The case was outlawed, the document was not worth the paper on which it was printed and written, and bitter was the disappointment to all concerned,—

until it was discovered that the postage stamp on the seemingly worthless envelope which contained it was curious and rare, and the stamp was finally sold to an enthusiastic collector of such things for a sum greater than the face value of the deed it was so long in helping to forward.

My own plot for a short story is better than either of Mr. Harper's. It was a fragment of a leaf out of my own experience. After a long, hard journey from the north we came into the railway station at Florence, about sunset, one November evening. As we passed what we would call the baggage car, we saw lifted from the side door, by the tender hands of sympathetic porters and engine drivers, a mite of a boy frightfully pale and weak, eagerly anxious for a familiar face, it seemed to us, but quite alone. He was braced up against the cold, hard wall of the station, two little crutches were put under his arms, and there he was left—to be called for. And then we noticed that one bit of a leg was cut off at the knee, and that he had, without question, just been released from a hospital somewhere out of the town. Nobody paid further attention to him. He waited patiently, and he had no luggage or other impedimenta but the two crutches—and the empty shoe.

In speaking of American story-telling, Mark Twain has often said that the manner is more important than the matter. In the English stories it is altogether different. They can be told at any time and in any way; but ours have to be led up to in order to give the desired effect. Sometimes there is no climax to Yankee stories at all, simply a narration of facts told in a humorous manner—and that is a gift which he has to perfection.

In *Pudd' nhead Wilson*, as first printed in the *Century Magazine*, the narrator says that he had a character of a woman who originally played an important part in the story, but who after a while seemed to fill the whole canvas, and he wanted to get rid of her, so he remarked in colloquial English, "she was drowned in a well"; and there he left her. Afterwards it struck him that it might be a good way to dispose of all his characters,—to drown them all in the same well!

The only thing approaching a book of popular character which I have ever written was the story called *A Boy I Knew and Four Dogs*. I was the Boy, and the Dogs were my own Dogs. It is absolutely biographical, and autobiographical. Every word, every incident is true. It is not based upon fact; it is fact itself. What the Dogs did, and felt, and expressed; where they came from; how they lived; and how they died, in the domestic circle, was set down simply and accurately, without exaggeration or elaboration. They were good Dogs, and I knew them, and I loved them; as they loved and knew me.

The Boy himself was not a bad Boy, and I knew him intimately, and I loved him too. But, curiously enough, as I " wrote him up," he never seemed to be

SILHOUETTE OF MARK TWAIN

myself at all, but some other Boy; perhaps the Boy I lost, and never knew; my own son, into whose feelings, and motives, and sentiments, I entered, in a peculiarly David-and-Jonathan way.

The articles about the Boy and his Dogs upon which the volume was based were written originally for *St. Nicholas*, where they appeared, from month to month, in serial form. And most pleasant reading, to me, were the letters I received concerning them, from the young subscribers to the periodical. Before the closing dog-story, "The Life and Letters of Roy Hutton" was printed, one little girl wrote, from Cambridge, Massachusetts, to ask if I had a dog then; and if so what was his name; and whom did he look like; and would I tell her all about him? Other children wrote to tell me about their dogs, and what they did, and how much they knew. And *apropos* of the Boy, one little chap, from a town in the interior of the State of New York, wrote a long, confiding, epistle, declaring that *his* mother was the eldest of nine children; that *she* was married before she was twenty; that *he* was brought up, as a member of their own generation, by his uncles and aunts; that *his* hair was red, and that *his* nose was long; that *his* aunts and uncles always made fun of *his* red hair, and of *his* long nose; that *he* was constantly falling down; that *he* was invariably dropping things; that *he* was habitually in the way; that *he* cried when girls kissed *him;* that *he* hated to practise on the piano, and to go to dancing-school; that *he*, himself, *must* be the Boy I Knew! And how did I know him so well?

Roy paid for himself—in more ways than one—and in a short time. His original cost, as a puppy—bargained for before he was born—was twenty-five dollars—cash on delivery. His tuition and board, at a private institution of canine learning, added somewhat to the expense; but, from the moment of his joining the family, his eccentricities of deportment and of character readily lent themselves to the production of what is called "copy." I began at once to set down his queer doings and deeds as he did them; all his performances at Onteora, that first summer of his existence, were recorded; his vagaries were noted; his correspondence was carefully preserved; and, when the autumn came, Mrs. Dodge, for *St. Nicholas*, was good enough to give me an hundred dollars for his story, elaborately illustrated, up to that date. This, some three hundred *per centum*, surely was profit enough on the investment; even without the addition of his share of personal percentage in the royalties on the bound volume.

Although it was indirect, one of the most gratifying of compliments was paid to the Dog-and-Boy-book by a perfect stranger, who had no thought of its ever coming to the Boy's ears. Miss Drisler entered a New York up-town bank, one day, leading a bright fox terrier by a chain; a busy clerk, pen in hand, came from behind the high railing and asked, "Is this the

Drislers' Grip?" He was told that it was the Drislers' Grip, and what did he want with the Drislers' Grip? He replied that he simply wished to shake him by the paw; so that he might tell his own boys, at home, that he had met a friend of Roy Hutton's!

The tale of the Boy was written at odd times, and at odd places, in an equally scattering and disconnected way; and it was all based upon the discovery, in an old desk, of the Boy's earliest existent "poem," by Henrietta, the very youngest of the Boy's aunts. The poem, which is in the middle of the book, was an elegy in nine lines, composed before the Boy was nine years of age, and its subject was the untimely ending of the nine lives of a trio of young feline friends of the Boy, and of his Aunt Henrietta. And thus it reads:

Three little kittens of our old cat,
Were buried to-day in this grass plat.
They came to their death in an old slop-pale,
And after loosing their breth they were pulled out by the tale.
These three little kittens have returned to their maker,
And were put in the grave by
     The Boy
      Undertaker.

This, naturally, suggested the death and the solemn funeral of the Cranes' Yellow Cat at Red Hook, in the early fifties; and these suggested other things; and out of these other things grew a little volume published at a dollar and twenty-five cents and yielding its author a fair income of twelve and a quarter cents a copy, for every copy sold, to this day. As the work grew, it was read over and talked about with Aunt Henrietta and the other aunts, and the other companions of the Boy's boyhood. One would say, "Don't forget the little green orange, on the back stoop!" Another would remind me of the day the rough-raiders of the neighbourhood stole my sled; still another advised me to say something about making New Year's calls, and the stewing of the long nose in the hot molasses candy. A playmate in St. John's Park, now a grandfather, reminded me of the smoking beans we smoked, and of the running to fires with the garden-roller. Bob Hendricks recalled the only fight we ever had, which I did not want recalled, because I was entirely in the wrong. And Bob's sister absolutely demanded some account of the valentine I sent to Zillah Crane; because the valentine contained a plain, solid gold ring, and was the greatest thing Zillah and Bob's sister had ever seen— up to that time. And so was evolved the book.

Other bits of literature, far more worthy, and destined to be much more lasting, built up from the middle or from the very bottom, have been evolved in the same manner. Who can say that the soliloquy "To be, or not to be" did not suggest the whole of *Hamlet;* or that the opening lines of the *Æneid*, "Arms and a Man I sing," were not an afterthought of Virgil's? This I know puts the *The Boy I Knew* in the best of all good company; and it may seem very presumptuous indeed on his part. But, insignificant as he is, he cannot help

Certain Inspirations

being made as other Boys are made; no matter how great the other Boys may prove to be!

Mr. John Hay once told me that while listening to a somewhat dull sermon from a preacher with whose views and doctrines he was not altogether in sympathy, it suddenly occurred to him, *apropos* of something he had heard in the discourse, that after all, perhaps

> Saving a little child, and bringing him to his own,
> Is a derned sight better business than loafing 'round the Throne.

And out of this fragment of cloth was cut the *Little Breeches* which are not soon to wear out!

In the same way, he added, that some sentence in a long, impromptu prayer gave him the impression that, may be, in the end,

> Christ ain't going to be too hard
> On a man that died for men.

And on this pedestal was erected the statue of the famous "Jim Bludso" of the steamer *Prairie Belle*, who gave his own life to save the lives of the passengers entrusted to his charge.

To come down to the present, it is said—although I have it not from Mr. Kipling himself—that the famous *Recessional* was based upon three words—"Lest we forget,"—which had impressed its author, years before, and which he had set down in an old notebook, kept for such purposes. A very useful thing to the man who writes is that notebook. If we hear a good thing, if we read a happy thought, let us trust it not to the tablets of our memory—"Lest we forget. Lest we forget!"

It may be remembered that in the Preface to this Dog-and-Boy book—if any one ever read the Preface—there is a brief allusion to the circumstance that the indifferently good Boy of New York and the not altogether bad Boy of Portsmouth were very near neighbours as boys, notwithstanding the fact that neither of them, now, has any recollection of the other then; although as men they have been warm and even intimate friends for upwards of a quarter of a century.

The discovery was made by Mr. Aldrich, when a view of the Hudson Street house of the Boy's grandfather was published in *St. Nicholas*, and a fragment of Mr. Aldrich's own boyhood's home appeared as standing next door. This, naturally, led to reminiscence research into the matter; when it was proven that the fathers and mothers of the boys had known each other well; and, curiously enough, they are now resting almost side by side in the cemetery of Greenwood —near neighbours once more!

While Mr. Aldrich could not recall the Boy himself, he remembered perfectly the Boy's Uncle John, a little nearer to his own age, as the young Scott who was hard of hearing; who went to Billy Forrest's school; who was such a good swimmer; such a fast runner; and the best kite-flyer and the best top-spinner in the Fifth Ward. They were re-introduced, one day, at the end of almost half a century, in the private office of a down-town banking house in New York, and it was very delightful to listen to the stories of their renewed youths. They, too, had skated in the Park, and had run to fires, together; and had had, jointly, a private theatre of their own. And they laughed as they wondered how they lived to tell the tale of their habitual manner of access to each other's garret-rooms; which was by crawling, on their hands and knees, along the gutter, on the edge of the roofs, from dormer-window to dormer-window!

The Boy's Uncle John was a constant reader of the *Atlantic*, and it took a long shelf to hold the row of Mr. Aldrich's works in his library at home. The next time he met his nephew, never realising who his old acquaintance was, he said:

"And so that was little Tom Aldrich! How did you come across him again? I've lost track of him for many, many years; and I never knew what became of him. He seems prosperous enough. What is he doing now for a living?"

I remember, once, after Lawrence Barrett had been acting in Albany, we were going home and noticed a row of unusually large street lights that had been placed before the house Barrett happened to be occupying.

"Those must be Barrett's footlights hanging out to dry," observed Aldrich, as we passed.

Of another friend he once said that he had enough

gout for a centipede. And yet, to aid his imagination, he wrote each set of the *Marjory Daw* letters in a different room, and with different ink and pen on different paper!

To add to the strangeness of coincidences in connection with the early association between these Boys, it was revealed, when *The Boy I Knew* appeared in book form, that the house to which the Aldriches next moved, just a block below, was presented in one of the few new illustrations added by the publishers. And thus, as Mr. Aldrich says, the author builded far better than he thought; for the only topographical pictures in the bound book contain two of the homes of one of the Boys I liked best, and most wished to emulate.

I never had the benefit of a university education, with all that it means, in a social and in an intellectual way. I was too lazy, mentally, to prepare myself. I was too dull in the matter of mathematics and the dead languages to enter any seat of high learning. I went for eight or nine years to one school, that of Dr. James N. McElligott, of blessed memory to me and to many an old boy whom I meet, now and then, in all parts of the world. And I remained under Dr. McElligott until I was about eighteen years of age. His was what he called a " Classical School "; and the tuition was dear. But the chief study was English Composition, interleaved with a little Latin Prose, and to some of his pupils this last was always a stumbling block. McElligott was the author of a very useful book called

The Analytical Manual, of which he was justly proud, but which is now altogether obsolete and neglected. My own well-thumbed copy, in a green pasteboard cover, disappeared long ago. But, as it is recalled now, it was a spelling- and a definition-book combined; full of Rules and Exceptions as to what happens, for instance, on the doubling of final consonants in radical words, and in the addition of a suffix beginning with some particular letter, whose name or whose significance is by me now entirely forgotten. There was a regular composition, on Fridays, after recess, the subjects of which—as "Joan d'Arc," "Is Childhood the Happiest Period of Human Life?" "Contentment Better than Wealth," and the like—were given out a week ahead. But every day—Fridays excepted — before recess, the boys were required to write a slate-ful of what were called "Applications"; namely, a short story or essay upon a topic of their own choosing, in which were to be properly "applied" as many as possible of the words of the morning's lesson. My own great effort in that line, I remember, was based upon words of from three to five syllables, beginning with the letters Al; and was to the effect that "An alliterative and allegorical friend of mine, who was an alchemist, dropped his algebra into an alembic containing alcohol." Dr. McElligott, as long as he lived, never forgot my allegorical and alliterative acquaintance, the alchemist. That alchemist was the only alchemist I ever knew. But the "application" of him, and of others of his kind, has since served me many a good turn in the proper use of words.

Another excellent exercise devised by Dr. McElligott was the translation into English—word by word of the same significance—of certain famous pieces of English prose or verse—such as Gray's *Elegy* or an Oration of Daniel Webster; a most useful but often an absolutely impossible performance for schoolboys, or even for college professors. The *Elegy* was his favourite example, and very queer was the havoc made with it by McElligott's pupils. "The lowing herds wind slowly o'er the lea" one youth rendered "The bellowing bulls meander dilatorily along the meadow"; another gave "heavenly conflagration" for "celestial fire"; but "incense-breathing morn" was entirely beyond us all and was never overcome.

Still another of the good Doctor's admirable methods of teaching readiness in composition was a series of efforts, on the part of his pupils, at the writing and making of history in the form of "reports" of certain important historical events. "The Taking of the Bastille," "The Surrender of Cornwallis," "The Destruction of the Invincible Armada," "The Funeral of Alexander the Great," "The Inaugural of Washington," "The Crossing of the Rubicon," "The Coronation of Queen Elizabeth," were among the various subjects of which we had to treat—as eye-witnesses! We were supposed to be participants in these events, or onlookers, from any point of view; and we were required to set down our impressions—in a certain number of words—as far as possible in the diction, and with the literary style, of the different periods. We were allowed and even urged to "cram" to our heart's content; but not to quote what we had read. All anachronisms were to be avoided; and any amount of invention, provided it did not conflict with possibilities, was permissible. Some of the results were very astonishing, but none of them were without interest in their way. And as a preparation in "special correspondence," with all its romantic possibilities, no training could have been more useful.

My schooldays came to an abrupt and proper end one October morning in the early sixties. I had been particularly lazy and indifferent that month, and my father told me he wanted a serious talk. "You are getting to be a man now," he said, "and, as man to man, and as father to son, I want to ask if you think you are treating me in an altogether fair and honest way. I am paying a great deal of money for your education; are you giving me, in return, a proper equivalent in industry and attention to your studies?" This was a new, but a wholesome, idea of the situation; and for the first time I realised that I was not fulfilling my pecuniary and my intellectual responsibilities; and I resolved to be under no obligation to my father, in a money way, from that hour. I sought, and found, a position as errand-boy—at a salary of four dollars a week—in a large wholesale produce commission house; and there I spent, not unprofitably, except in a money way, another eight or nine years of my life. My first duty was the cleaning out of the office spittoon; my last, the winding up of the affairs of the firm, with nothing to speak of in pocket and a good deal of experience in my head, when it failed in the hop trade in 1870.

I never had any other difference or disagreement with my father, but this peculiar pecuniary relationship between us existed as long as he lived. I asked for, and would accept, nothing from him in the way of money, directly or indirectly.

For many years we had the same tailor, a merchant living next door to our old house on Hudson Street, New York, who had cut my first pair of trousers. He made a suit of clothes for me one autumn, which, as was my inevitable habit then as now, was not ordered until I had the cash in hand to pay for it. When it was finished I asked for the bill and was told that the bill had been settled in advance by my father, who was having an overcoat made in the same establishment. I immediately paid for his overcoat! And the matter was never afterwards alluded to by either of us, although, as was learned from other sources, he was greatly amused and pleased at the transaction.

The four dollars a week was made to go what now seems to have been a very long way. Some fragment of a small domestic allowance was left when I entered the produce trade, and I accumulated two weeks' salary before it was necessary to draw upon my salary at all. That eight dollars—the first money I ever made for myself—was invested in a sentimental way, in the gold-setting, as a finger ring, of a small, shell-cameo profile portrait of the father, cut by a boy of about my own age, with whom I had gone to school for a short time; with whom then I had but slight acquaintance, but who, in later years, has become my very good friend. His name is Augustus Saint-Gaudens. Very many years later a shell-cameo brooch, in what is called a shadow-frame, had its place in the Thirty-fourth Street house, upon the piano in the dining-room; and one night at a large dinner party at which were gathered many distinguished men and women to meet Sir Henry Irving, the box and its contents attracted the attention of a guest who happened to sit opposite to it. In the middle of the symposium he jumped up, grasped the object in both hands, and said:

"Laurence, where did you get this, and who is it?"

"It's my father, given by him to my mother on the twenty-fifth anniversary of their marriage. She wore it a little while, but it was too conspicuous as a personal ornament; and after his death she put it in that frame."

The excited guest exclaimed:

"Your father?"

"Yes, my father."

He then asked in great excitement who did it.

I replied:

"I don't know. It was cut long ago by a little artist in a studio over Brougham's Lyceum, afterwards Wallack's Theatre, on the corner of Broadway and Broome Street. Who he was or what his name was, I do not know, except that he was a clever little Frenchman."

The attention of the whole party was by this time attracted to the dialogue. Looking at the cameo in its case, and his hand shaking a little, the guest said:

"He was a clever little Frenchman, was he, and you don't know his name? Well, I'm the clever little Frenchman, and my name is Saint-Gaudens. It's the earliest piece of my work extant, and when you and Mrs. Hutton get through with it, I want it for Gussie and the boy."

And when we do get through with it they are to have it.

He added afterwards, when his excitement was a little subdued, that he had only a couple of direct sittings from the old gentleman; but had taken him to a shop in the neighbourhood where he had had two ambrotypes made from which to finish the portrait.

Then I went to the end of the room, pulled out a table-drawer, and handed him the two ambrotypes in question, preserved as carefully as was the brooch, during all those years.

That was the evening when Mr. Sherry, then beginning his career as a caterer, presented as a dessert Sir Henry Irving in the character of Becket, most effect-

BROOCH PORTRAIT OF JOHN HUTTON, FATHER OF LAURENCE HUTTON

ively moulded in frozen chocolate, strawberry, and vanilla ice-cream. Irving and the others recognised the likeness at once as an admirable one. When Mrs. Hutton said to the guest of the evening that Mr. Sherry, the artist, was at that moment in the butler's pantry superintending the unveiling of his *chef-d'œuvre*, Mr. Irving jumped up at once without a word and, followed by the entire party, shook hands with the sculptor and congratulated him on the great success of his work, asking him if he would not accept "orders" to see the tragedy of *Becket* the next night.

Mr. Sherry declined with thanks and very politely, saying that what he had done was purely a labour of love and that in making studies for the statue he had spent several evenings at the theatre.

Miss Terry wanted to take the melting figure home with her, but was finally persuaded not to attempt its transportation. And to this day Sir Henry tells his friends in England how in America he had met "a pastry-cook" who was too much of a gentleman to accept a fee!

Ellen Terry was enthusiastic about Eleanor Duse, and remarked that she did very wisely in acting only when she felt like it, so that she always did herself justice. I spoke of how tall she (Ellen Terry) looked on the stage. She said she was five feet seven, but that she never stood on the soles but always on the balls of her feet, and sometimes on tiptoe. She added that it made her feel very much in the air!

An unexpected guest at that dinner was Mr. Clemens. He would certainly have been invited had his presence in the city been known. He had arrived from Hartford late in the afternoon, had discovered from the gossip at the Club that the Huttons were having "a rather unusual dinner-party," was told who were to be present, and decided that it was too good a thing to lose. So he dressed hurriedly, walked in without ceremony just as the feast began, drew up a chair by the side of his hostess, helped himself to her oysters, and for the rest of the evening was the life of the party; one enthusiastic admirer of his confessing, over the coffee and the cigars, that he would give half he possessed if he were intimate enough with Mark Twain to have him drop in at his house in the same delightfully original and Mark Twainey manner.

But to return to that earlier time and the Other Boys whom I knew.

One summer evening I was sitting with my father on the front stoop and we were smoking our pipes together—as was our custom as soon as I was considered man enough to smoke at all—when there came up to us Mr. Haskell, my father's lawyer and warm personal friend. Four youths of about my own age were marching at his heels. He said:

"Hutton, here are several boys of mine just graduated from some of the colleges among the inland towns. They're absolutely fresh to New York, beginning their serious life-work, and naturally with few friends of their own generation. I want Laurie to know them, and I want them to know Laurie. I wonder if he won't take them to the Gymnasium, and give them a hand generally in a social way, and make them feel at home in the great city in which the rest of their years are probably to be spent."

I did take them to the Gymnasium, and I took them into my heart, where they have had a warm place ever since. It was the beginning of a friendship which to me has always been very pleasant, and I am proud that with their brains if not with their muscle they have reflected credit upon the man who put them in the way of handling Indian clubs and dumb-bells in the great metropolis. The first of these boys was Francis Lynde Stetson; the second, Hamilton Mabie (both recent graduates of Williams); the third was Horace Russell, of Dartmouth; and the fourth, Elihu Root, of Hamilton.

In the peculiar financial arrangement between my father and myself, his hospitality with regard to the matter of lodging and board was cheerfully accepted; but in other respects what Burns calls "the glorious privilege of being independent" was, on my part, as cheerfully indulged in.

The weekly stipend was divided into various portions. So much for clothes; so much for theatre-going—not the smallest fraction; so much for stage-fares; and seventy-five cents for dinners. This last amounted to twelve and a half cents—an impossible sum—per diem. On Mondays, Wednesdays, and Fridays, twelve cents were spent for the prandial meal; on Tuesdays, Thursdays, and Saturdays, thirteen; the extra copper being invested in soft brown sugar, spread on the bread and butter, and serving as dessert. I usually dined at an humble little restaurant on the corner of Broad and Pearl Streets, not only because it was cheaper, but on account of the peculiar softness of the brown sugar. My table companions were cartmen, porters, an occasional longshoreman who had not brought his dinner-pail, and errand-boys, like myself. We all wore overalls and huckabuck jackets, and we smelt like horses, when we did not smell like hops. There were no napkins, and nobody ever thought of tipping the waiter, who called most of us by our first names, and who, indeed, was the brother-in-law of Tom Bullen, the second porter, and an ex-policeman. One member of the party had served a short term for manslaughter, and Mr. Bullen, himself, was credited with having had a hand in the shooting of the driver of an outside-car, near the Imperial Hotel at Cork. But they were all very amusing, and the association did no harm to any one.

I never felt that my overalls were very becoming, but I was never ashamed of them; and when a young lady, with whom I had danced the varsovienne one night in Waverly Place, cut me dead the next day in Broad Street, because she saw me—in overalls—rolling a barrel of beans across a pair of "skidds" on to a grocer's wagon, I was ashamed of her!

One of the earliest and pleasantest friends I made in

my business life was my barber. At the close of the very first business day—October 22, 1862—I asked a fellow-clerk where I would find a good shop in which to have my hair cut, wishing to celebrate the interesting and important event, though why I know not, by this tonsorial operation. I was referred to an establishment on the same block, entered it, and of course took the first vacant chair. The artist chanced to be a youth of about my own age, and his work was artistic and eminently satisfactory. His name I discovered was "Charley," and, as I reached the stage of a budding beard which I fancied required shaving two or three times a week, I always put my chin under Charley's deft and sympathetic razor. It was a soft thing for Charley, and consisted chiefly in his wiping off, with a great deal of care and expression, the lather which he had just put on.

Charley and I soon became confidential. I always waited for my "turn" on his chair, and I learned that he was a Swiss-German who studied medicine in his leisure hours, and was madly ambitious to become a doctor. He talked most learnedly and wisely on the subject nearest to his heart, and used professional terms—rightly or wrongly I know not—which would have made my hair curl if there had been the slightest disposition to wave or crink in its composition. I also observed the curious coincidence that he had begun business on the same day that I had; and that I was his very first customer!

When Charles, at a later period, set up in business for himself I followed him to the new seat of trade, and at the end of forty-five years Charles is still my barber and my friend. Every few weeks I called upon him, going a long distance and far out of my way for that purpose, often neglecting my personal appearance when out of town that Charles, and Charles only, should operate upon my gradually thinning locks, hoping as long as I have hair to cut that Charles shall live to cut it.

With Charles I sometimes correspond. He is interested in all I do. He buys my books, and he reads them! He follows my career with interest and with pride, he hangs my picture in his house, he is my guest at my own house, he tells me of his joys and his sorrows, and he still talks medicine and diseases and remedies.

Charles is also devoted to the drama and its literature. He is a constant theatre-goer, but only to the higher class of plays; and he is no mean critic of the tragedians of the city. From Forrest down through Booth, Barrett, McCullough, Irving, to the lesser stars, he has derived much pleasure and profit; declaiming in their style some of the heaviest passages of Shakespeare and of the standard writers of olden times. And he tells me that his recitations and imitations find great favour in his social coterie, and are not infrequently given in a semi-public way at church and other entertainments. On one occasion, more than a quarter of a century ago,

Charles sat in the upper gallery of the old Academy of Music, listening to Parepa, Wachtel, and Santley, while I, in the stalls, was enjoying the same performance. I had left his hands to go home to dress for the performance, and he confided to me the next day that the whole pleasure of the evening was spoiled for him by the professional discovery that my hair was not parted straight.

Associated with Charles for many years was Andrew, a Scottish-American barber, and my friend as well. Andrew, too, reads my books and cherishes my photograph, and even keeps a scrap-book of critiques and paragraphs in which my name appears; often saving me, in my absence from the city, newspaper cuttings containing matters relating to events in which he knows I am interested, and will not in all probability be able to read for myself. If in the course of the winter I did not appear at the shop at the regular period once a month or thereabouts, Andrew, knowing that I was not abroad or they would have heard of it and afraid that I might be ill, would call at the house of a Sunday morning to ask the cause of my absence. I never thought of leaving the country without going in to say good-bye to them, and almost my earliest visit on my arrival at home was a social as well as a professional call upon them.

I was in London in the summer of 1874, when my father died in New York. Their words of sympathy were as sincere and affectionate on my return as any I received, and they told me that on the day of his burial they had gone to the house with the rest of my friends to show their sorrow at my loss, and respect for the dead so near to me. It was only by chance and from others that I learned some time afterwards that on the street door of this little barber shop, at the busiest hour of the day, was a card bearing the inscription: "Closed on account of the death of Mr. Laurence Hutton's father."

Nothing that ever happened to me has touched me more than that affectionate and affecting tribute of these two men,—my friends.

During all that early period, naturally, there was little time left for, and little inclination towards, composition or the improvement of the mind. I read market-reports, and, now and then, I wrote market reports; but not much of anything else, during business hours, at least. I had all the advantages of my father's well-selected library at home; but I did not stay much at home, for, if Davenport was not playing in *The Iron Chest* somewhere, there was skating to do, or a "party" somewhere else. Little besides fiction was read—the modern novels which were talked about—but generally the older novels, those of Dumas, Dickens, Hugo, Cooper, Scott, Thackeray, Marryat, and Miss Mühlbach. And there was unconsciously imbibed from each one of them that indefinable something which, for want of a better term, is called "style." Many letters were written in those youthful days to young women in country towns, who were my seniors in age. And with these recipients of my confidences I suppose I was having a series of mild, epistolary flirtations, although I did not know it at the time! But I did realise, in the composition of those letters, that they bore the impress of the manner of the man in whose work of fiction, or of popular verse, I happened at that moment to be absorbed,—the short, jerky style of Hugo; the confidential, colloquial, "that-reminds-me" style of Thackeray; the "shiver-my-timbers" style of the author of *Peter Simple;* the "Lord-keep-my-memory-green" style of Dickens; or even the "proverbial-philosophical-a-babe-in-the-house-is-a-well-spring-of-pleasure" style of Tupper, and the "civilised-man-cannot-live-without-cooks" style of Owen Meredith; both of which last, by the way, the young ladies from the interior of the State admired particularly. I am not sure that it was the best school of style, but perhaps it was better than the ponderosity of Macaulay, or the bitter dictatorialism of Carlyle, neither of whom, however, were altogether neglected.

The father inquired one night what I was reading. "*The Three Guardsmen.*" "And what is it all about?" "An historical novel, full of romance and incident." "And who are the characters?" "Young, brave, and brilliant soldiers of fortune, beautiful and fascinating ladies of quality, kings, queens, princes of the blood, lords cardinal and temporal, ministers of war and of finance; and, just now, a Duke of Buckingham and one Fenton, who had murdered the Duke in a brutal way." "But how much of it is history, or half-history, and how much of it is pure invention, based upon nothing in real life?" was the further query. It had never occurred to me to sift the true from the false. It seemed to be all true. That Athos was as actual and as much alive as were Mazarin and Colbert, I never doubted. And for many nights thereafter—theatres and skating neglected—father and son studied out, in the encyclopædias and in the histories of England and France, the whole period covered by Dumas in that wonderful series of romances. We learned how much he be-littled, and how much he be-bigged; how much he extenuated; how much he set down in malice. It did not produce an historian or a biographer, but it was enjoyed better than *Rosedale* on Wallack's stage, or even than *Our Mutual Friend* by the open fire of the study. It taught me to dig out my own facts, to verify my own statements, to accept no man's *dictum* as true. And, as a simple and wholesome and effective way of helping education to form the common mind, it is here respectfully suggested to serious students, as well as to those parents and guardians who have mental twigs to bend and who wish to incline the twigs in the right direction.

A poetical effort appeared, but not in print, during the early years of this business life. Like all my efforts, in prose and in verse, it is based upon fact, and it is not impersonal. Thus it reads:

The Last of Hops

        The Hoppist drops
        Into different shops,
        Propping the flopping of hops.
        Bales, bales, bales,
        Of embryo porters and ales,
        Loads, loads, loads,
        Come in by the different roads;
        Till the Bulls declare
        And rear,
        And tear
        Their
        Hair,
        And swear,
        The thing must stop.
        For Hop
        On top
        Of Hop
        Will break the price kerflop,
        Sure pop!

And it did!

The market broke. The house suspended payment, and nothing, in a financial way, was left for any one in the establishment.

CHAPTER II

First Published Article—Charles Dickens's Reading—Dickens as an Actor in Liverpool—Florence—Irving as Dombey—The Younger Dickens—An Extraordinary Man.

THE first published production appeared in 1868 in the columns of the *Red Hook Journal*, a small, inland, weekly periodical, with a very limited and a purely local circulation. The article was devoted to a descriptive criticism of the " Readings of Charles Dickens," then making his second visit to this country. I attended the entire series, enormously interested in the man and in the expression of his conceptions of his own works. I had devoured his stories; his people were mine own people; his characters were my intimate friends. I knew them, of course, by sight and by sound. I had walked with them, I had talked with them, I had laughed and I had cried with them, ever since I could read. I knew every turn of their thoughts, every expression of their faces, every tone of their voices, every incident of their lives. And, lo! when Dickens himself presented them to me they were not my Toots, not my Ham Peggotty, not my Tiny Tim at all ! Yet Dickens must have known them better than I did. But, thanks to Dickens, they were all lost in the crowds at Steinway Hall. And they have never altogether been recovered.

This was the burden of the earliest printed work of the 'prentice hand; and it is not much worse than anything that has been attempted since. It was cruelly treated by proof-reader and type-setter and editor, as represented in the single individual upon the *Journal's* staff; it was signed "Silas Wegg"—I do not know why—and it attracted no attention whatever; not even in Red Hook. Still it was a new and an original view of a subject to which, at that period, columns of newspaper writing were devoted, all over the country. No doubt thousands of listeners were affected in the same way; but nobody else seems to have taken it so much to heart.

Curiously enough, the effort did not turn my head or fill me with ambition. I still paid strict attention to Hops; and my serious attack of what is known as "Literaturitis" did not develop at once. I had sipped from the intoxicating bowl called "Appearance-in-print," and I did not thirst for more; nor was there made any attempt to sip again from the Pierean Spring for a long time. But, when the habit was acquired, it must be confessed that the draughts were deep. A single copy of this "Dickens" article still exists, buried in an old scrap-book of its author's; and, as giving a contemporaneous picture of the man and of his idea of his own characters, it may be of some little interest at the end of all these years.

As recorded at that time Dickens's voice was low,

husky, and monotonous. Sitting in the centre of the hall, I closely watched his face, with a powerful opera-glass, and if I had not been perfectly familiar with his text I would hardly have understood him. Indeed, those who sat in the rear of the room had much difficulty in distinguishing what he said. What is known as the "rising inflection" was marked, and very painfully marked, to American ears. The anticipation in my own case was high. The reputation as a reader which he brought from England was very great. The man was loved by me for the good he had done and for the countless happy hours, perhaps the happiest of my life, spent in the society of Agnes and of Betsy Trotwood, of Esther and of little Miss Flite, of his good Tom Pinch and of his jolly Mark Tapley, of his Dick Swiveller and of the Marchioness, of his Wellers, Tony and Sam, of his Florence Dombey and little Paul, of his Pip and Joe Gargery, of his Dot and his Jennie Wren, and of hosts of others. And I felt that I would rather see the man himself, hear his voice, take him by the hand and call him friend, than almost any man then living. Having all this sentiment of enthusiasm and of hero-worship, I could not confess, as I heard him for the first or the second or for even the tenth time, that his reading was satisfactory. The experience was not regretted then, nor is it regretted now. I would not have missed hearing him for any consideration that could have been offered. But for all that the disappointment was keen.

There were then, and there are now, many students of his works, professional readers and persons who make no pretension to reading, who could have done, and could do, to Charles Dickens far more justice than he did to himself. That he was a great actor, there is no doubt; that in light comedy he was very fine is well known to one who once had the rare good fortune to see him in amateur theatricals in Liverpool, when he delighted an immense audience.

It was in the autumn of 1852, I remember, that we were forced to spend a night in Liverpool, the father and the mother and I, on our way from St. Andrews to New York. I was then nine years old; there was to be an amateur dramatic performance in the town that evening; and the father said—I can hear him now—

"I'll take the boy to the entertainment at Parliament Hall. In fifty years he will be able to boast of having seen Dickens on the stage."

And I have never forgotten that performance. The plays—*Charles XII.*, *Used Up*, and *Mr. Nightengale's Diary*—were nothing to me; but Dickens was David Copperfield himself and I had watched the real David Copperfield in the flesh doing things!

At the end of the fifty years, almost to a day, the old play-bill, overlooked, but in perfect state of preservation, was found in an old portfolio.

It was during one of the provincial journeys of the amateur company of the Guild of Literature and Art, and upon the programme is the announcement that the object of the Society (evidently in Dickens's own words because it sounded *Dickensy*) was " to encourage Life Assurance and other provident habits among authors and artists; to render such assistance to both as shall never compromise their independence; and to found an institution where honourable rest from arduous labour shall still be associated with the discharge of congenial duties."

Among the names of the cast were those of Charles Dickens, John Tennell, Mark Lemon, Augustus Egg, Wilkie Collins, Henry Compton, Frank Stone, Peter Cunningham, Mrs. Henry Compton, and Miss Fanny Young. The scenery was painted by Mr. Pitt, by Clarkson Stanfield, and by Mr. Louis Haghe. The whole was produced under the direction of Mr. Charles Dickens.

A year or two later I was taken by my father under similar circumstances in Manchester, to see Florence, the American comedian, with an English stock company, play Captain Cuttle in a dramatisation of *Dombey and Son*.

At the time of Florence's death, speaking of his extraordinary versatility as a man who could play well more parts of great variety than any other member of his profession, I recalled this performance and added that even to this day the most delightful and memorable feature was the acting of the part of Mr. Dombey. Since that time I have seen almost every dramatisation of the novels of Dickens, from Jefferson's Caleb Plum-

Philharmonic Hall, Liverpool.

Manager, Mr CHARLES DICKENS, Tavistock House, Tavistock Square, in the County of Middlesex.

On FRIDAY EVENING, SEPTEMBER 3rd, 1852,
THE AMATEUR COMPANY
OF THE

GUILD OF LITERATURE & ART;

To encourage Life Assurance and other Provident Habits among Authors and Artists; to render such assistance to both as shall never compromise their independence; and to found a new Institution where honourable rest from arduous labour shall still be associated with the discharge of congenial duties;

WILL HAVE THE HONOR OF PRESENTING
(THIS BEING THEIR LAST NIGHT OF PERFORMANCE,)
THE PETITE COMEDY, IN TWO ACTS, OF

USED UP.

Sir Charles Coldstream, Bart.,	Mr. CHARLES DICKENS.
Sir Adonis Leech,	Mr. COE.
The Honorable Tom Saville,	Mr. JOHN TENNIEL.
Wurzel, (a Farmer)	Mr. F. W. TOPHAM.
John Ironbrace, (a Blacksmith)	Mr. MARK LEMON.
Mr. Fennel, (a Lawyer)	Mr. AUGUSTUS EGG, A.R.A.
James,	Mr. WILKIE COLLINS.
Mary,	Mrs. HENRY COMPTON.
Lady Clutterbuck.	Mrs. COE.

SCENERY.

Saloon in Sir Charles Coldstream's House,	Painted by Mr. PITT.
Distant View of the River,	Mr. STANFIELD, R.A.
Interior of an Old Farm House,	Mr. PITT.

Previous to the Play the Band will Perform an OVERTURE, composed expressly for this purpose, by Mr. C. COOTE, (Pianist to his His Grace the Duke of Devonshire) WHO WILL, ON THIS OCCASION, PRESIDE AT THE PIANOFORTE.

After which, the Historical Drama, in Two Acts, by J. R. PLANCHE, Esq., called

CHARLES XII.

Charles the Twelfth, (King of Sweden)	Mr. FRANK STONE, A.R.A.
General Duckett, (Governor of Stralsund)	Mr. COE.
Colonel Reichel,	Mr. PETER CUNNINGHAM.
Gustavus de Mervelt,	Mr. JOHN TENNIEL.
Major Vanberg, (under the assumed name of Firmans)	Mr. AUGUSTUS EGG, A.R.A.
Adam Brock, (a Wealthy Farmer)	Mr. F. W. TOPHAM.
Triptolemus Muddleworth, (Burgomaster)	Mr. WILKIE COLLINS.
Ulrica, (Daughter of Vanberg)	Miss FANNY YOUNG.
Eudiga, (Daughter of Adam Brock)	Mrs. HENRY COMPTON.

SCENERY.

Public Ground and Inn,	Mr. TELBIN.
A Room in a Village Inn,	Mr. PITT.
Parlour at Adam Brock's,	Mr. PITT.
The Ramparts of Stralsund,	Mr. THOMAS GRIEVE.
Old Tapestry Chamber,	Mr. LOUIS HAGHE.
Another Chamber,	Mr. PITT.
Hall of Audience,	Mr. PITT.

To conclude with, (twenty-third time) an original Farce, in One Act, by Mr. CHARLES DICKENS and Mr. MARK LEMON, entitled

MR. NIGHTINGALE'S DIARY.

Mr. Nightingale,	Mr. FRANK STONE, A.R.A.
Mr. Gabblewig, (of the Middle Temple)	
Charley Bit, (a Boots)	
Mr. Poulter, (a Pedestrian and Cold-Water Drinker)	Mr. CHARLES DICKENS.
Captain Blower, (an Invalid)	
A Respectable Female,	
A Deaf Sexton,	
Tip, (Mr. Gabblewig's Tiger)	
Christopher, (a Charity Boy)	Mr. AUGUSTUS EGG, A.R.A.
Slap, (professionally Mr. Flormiville—a Country Actor)	
Mr. Tickle, (Inventor of the celebrated Compounds)	Mr. MARK LEMON.
A Virtuous Young Person in the Confidence of "Maria"	
Lithers, (Landlord of the "Water Lily")	Mr. WILKIE COLLINS.
Rosina,	Miss FANNY YOUNG.
Susan,	Mrs. COE.

The Proscenium by Mr. CRACE. The Theatre constructed by Mr. SLOMAN, Machinist of the Royal Lyceum Theatre. The Properties and Appointments by Mr. G. FOSTER. The Costumes by Messrs. NATHAN, of Titchbourne Street. Perruquier, Mr. WILSON. Prompter, Mr. COE.

☞ THE WHOLE PRODUCED UNDER THE DIRECTION OF MR CHARLES DICKENS.

The Local Arrangements under the superintendence of Mr. William Sudlow.

Doors open at Six o'Clock. To commence at exactly Seven o'clock; when the whole of the audience are particularly recommended to be seated. Tickets to be had at the Offices of the Philharmonic Society, Exchange Court. Stalls (in the Body of the Hall) and Boxes, 7s. 6d.; Gallery Stalls, 5s. 6d.; Gallery Seats, 3s. 6d.

ENTRANCE TO ALL PARTS OF THE HALL FROM HOPE STREET.

A. IRELAND AND CO., PRINTERS, PALL MALL, MARKET STREET, MANCHESTER.

THE DICKENS PLAY-BILL

mer and Fawcett Roe's Micawber to certain little Emilys and Uriah Heeps, but not one of them had ever entered so completely and so admirably into the spirit of the part as did the evidently young man who had walked the stage as Dombey and whose name was to me quite forgotten if ever known. He looked Dombey, he spoke Dombey, he was Dombey himself! Here I was interrupted by one of my hearers, who said:

"Come, now, old fellow, that won't do. That bit of flattery is altogether too invidious and too apparent. It was almost my first appearance on the stage in anything like an important part, and so far as I can remember it was before I had taken the name of—Henry Irving!"

This is, perhaps, the reason why Sir Henry, at a large banquet at Delmonico's, of which he was the guest, poured some very apparent flattery upon me when he spoke of me as not only one of his best, but as his very oldest, friend in America.

With the elder Dickens I was never brought into personal contact. Of the younger Dickens—Charles—I saw a good deal. We sat next each other at the Rabelais Club dinner in London one night, talking freely, as is the way of men of the same guild when together. I knew who he was, but he had no idea of my identity. He was very much impressed when I told him that I had discovered that his father had made, in *Bleak House*, a curious error, particularly curious for Charles Dickens who was usually so accurate. That he had put Mr. Nemo, the lover of Lady Deadlock and the father of Esther, in a graveyard belonging to a parish in which he had not died,—something impossible under the strict rules of the London churches. No Poor Board ever accepted the ashes of a man for whose interment at their own expense they were not responsible. Mr. Nemo died in the parish of St. Dunstan's and he was buried by the parish of St. Paul's, Covent Garden.

The younger Dickens turned to me, and said:

"You wonderful Americans! You seem to know more about London and certainly more about my father's works, than do all the Londoners put together. That little matter worried him for years, and he was always afraid that his critics would find it out; and for the first time a man from across the Atlantic has dropped upon the fact. He selected Tom All-Alone's because it was picturesque and because it fitted into the story of Jo's devotion and the discovery of Lady Deadlock clasping the gates. There was no possible way of doing it in the proper parish, so he had to carry him to the next one."

An evening or two after, the younger Dickens took me to dine at the ancient Blue Posts Tavern in Cork Street, Piccadilly. It was on a Friday, and we sat where his father always sat on Friday night when he came up from Gad's Hill to see *Household Words* through the press. We had his regular dinner, the waiter recognising his son and speaking affectionately of the father. It seemed to me that this brought me peculiarly close to the man whose novels had impressed me so much for so many years.

When Dickens the younger was in America, I entertained him in my own house,—him and his wife and his daughter. And once I met him abruptly at the door, late one night, at one of the Bohemian clubs in London. Our acquaintance up to that time had been rather formal, but he was so surprised to see me in England that he forgot for an instant that we were not intimate friends, and said:

"Hello, Laurence!"

And I had presence of mind enough to reply:

"How are you, Charles."

After that we were no longer "Hutton" and "Dickens" to each other, but "Charles" and "Laurence" so long as he lived.

As a reader, however, in this country at all events, and in my immature judgment, I was forced to set Charles Dickens the elder down as a failure.

Some of his passages were admirable, but never the pathetic passages. I have shed more tears in my own room over the death of Paul Dombey, before and since, than Dickens brought to my eyes. Of course, he was affecting. The plaintive talk of the old-fashioned child to Florence and Mrs. Pipchin, his "please tell papa that I am better to-day," were certainly touching; his trying in vain to press back the tide which seemed to be bearing him away to the sea; his kind messages on his death-bed to all his friends; his recognition of the mother he had never known as she stood on that shining bank; his last thoughts of his father; his great love for his sister; and his dying there with his cheek pressed against that of Florence, and his little hands clasped in the attitude of prayer,—were very beautiful and very sad. There was, perhaps, not a dry eye in the room. But it was the old, old story over which every eye had been moistened before. It was what he read, not how he read it. It was the matter, not the manner, which moved his audience.

Again in that magnificent tempest scene from *Copperfield*—than which it seems to me there is nothing finer in the whole range of fiction,—the picture of the storm on the wild coast, the sinking of the doomed ship, the noble death of the self-martyred Ham, the tall figure in the red cap, Steerforth lying there in the wet sand with his head upon his arm, as David had so often seen him lie at school, was all very affecting and very effective; but it was the good words of the Dickens who wrote them, not the good reading of the Dickens before us, which so pleased his hearers.

His old men were all alike. His Scrooge and his Justice Stareleigh and Daniel Peggotty and even his juvenile Toots were all the same in tone of voice, although the expression of his face was different. His control of his facial organs was admirable, and this was the redeeming point in the entertainment. But his Squeers was Scrooge with one eye. His John Brodie was Emily's uncle with a slightly different dialect.

CHARLES DICKENS

His Betty, the maid of Bob Sawyer's landlady, who when wanted was always found to be asleep with her head glued to the kitchen table, was the best thing he did; and the intense stupidity of his expression when she opened the door for Mr. Pickwick I have never seen excelled upon the stage. Nevertheless Toots had the same expression, and said "No consequence!" in almost the same tone of voice. My ideas of Toots were all upset. Toots as I had always known him, Toots as he was portrayed by Tom Johnson and by Mr. Jefferson on the stage, was gone and gone for ever. The Toots of Dickens was entirely different, indescribably different, and I cannot even now reconcile myself to the change. It was a revolution in a long-standing and almost intimate acquaintance with Toots which was very dreadful and not to be endured.

So it was with Micawber. Dickens's Micawber was not the stage Micawber of Burton or of John Brougham. Of course, Dickens must have understood his own Toots and his own Micawber better than the actors did. But to have men whom one has known familiarly for years shown up before one in an entirely new light is a severe trial. The light may be the true light and the better light, but the old lights are to be preferred; and Toots and Micawber were never the same again. I was always glad he did not touch upon Miss Trotwood or upon Mr. Dick or upon Bunsby or Cuttle or upon rough and tough old Joey Bagstock or upon Pecksniff or Noddy Boffin or Sampson Brass or Chadband or

Bucket. I could not have stood any more upheavals of old conceptions of good old friends. I was thankful, however, that he did not pass over the elder Weller in the trial scene. His "Put it down with a WE, me Lud, put it down with a WE," was immense! That was Tony's voice indeed; there was no revolution in that case. He was Mr. Weller himself. He would have been recognised anywhere and under any circumstances. But Sam Weller was another and a bitter disappointment. No making-believe very hard, after the manner of the Marchioness with the orange peel and water, could help me to see, in the somewhat overdressed, middle-aged gentleman on the platform of Steinway Hall, Sam Weller in the witness-box, even with the inimitable voice of his respected "parink" ringing in my ears.

Mrs. Micawber was better. Her devotion to Wilkins and her dissertations on coals and the corn-trade were admirably well done; as was the croaking of Mrs. Raddle, Mrs. Pipchin, and Mrs. Chicks. But, as in the case of his old men, his old women were all the same; and he had the tact to avoid anything like the dialogue between Mrs. Gamp and Mrs. Prig.

Perhaps my Great Expectations were too great. But I looked for a good reader, at least, and found a poor one. I thought that everything which Charles Dickens would do or say would be well said and well done. As he once remarked of himself at a London banquet, he was "only human, and very human at that." He was, as the *Tribune* said of him at that period, " the Writer of Writers" but he was not, as the *Tribune* continued, " the Reader of Readers." He showed me no new beauties in his works and he added nothing to my enjoyment of them. On the contrary, he introduced old scenes and old friends in new shapes of which I do not like to think. He killed my Sam Weller and my Micawber. All these years I have mourned doubly for the Ham who was " drownded " in the sea, and taken away from me on the platform. For all these years I have been absolutely Toot-less.

There is in existence, somewhere, a copy of the *Christmas Carol* with the following inscription in its author's handwriting: " To W. M. Thackeray, from Charles Dickens, whom he made very happy once, a long way from home."

One who has been made very happy, very many times, at home and abroad, by Dickens and by Thackeray, hardly knows how to say how happy Dickens has made him or how much the works of Dickens have influenced his life. *David Copperfield* was the first book I ever read; and nothing in its way has ever surpassed it. The second book I read was *Pendennis*—they appeared almost simultaneously, when I was a very immature reader indeed—and the young Arthur nearly rivalled the young Trotwood in my affections. Divided in later years between my allegiance to the creator of Agnes and my allegiance to the creator of Laura, I long felt that Thackeray somehow in a purely personal way was the finer character and the nobler man; perhaps because Thackeray once patted my little red head, long before I had the good fortune to behold Dickens in the flesh; perhaps because Thackeray had had no John Forster to do him injustice with the best of intentions. But when, in 1891–92, I edited the *Letters of Dickens to Wilkie Collins,* through the reading and re-reading of those familiar notes and epistles in manuscript, in galley-proof, in page-proof, for magazine and for book form, I became more and more impressed with their charm and their great interest as literature as well as with the personal charm and even with the personal worth of their writer; and I learned to like the man Dickens better as I knew him better; and began to realise that the world itself is better for knowing the better side of a well-known man.

Although Dickens was emphatically an all-round man, he does not seem to have made as a poet a lasting impression upon the critics. Mr. Stedman, in his *Victorian Poets,* says, " Could Dickens have written verse —an art in which his experiments were for the most part utter failures—it would have been marked by wit and pathos, like Hood's, and by graphic Doresque effects that have grown to be called melodramatic.'' The first and the best known of his rhymes has found a place in Mr. Stedman's *Anthology.* It was written in 1836 or 1837, and it appeared originally in the twelfth chapter of *Pickwick* and was called *The Ivy Green.* Dickens's second poem was written in the Album of Lady Bless-

PEEP O' DAY. LAURENCE HUTTON'S HOME IN PRINCETON, NEW JERSEY

ington, in July, 1843. The third experiment is not to be found in Forster's *Biography*. It was printed in the *London Daily News*, with which journal Dickens was then connected, on the 14th of February, 1846, under the title of *The Hymn of the Wiltshire Labourers*.

The question, "Will Dickens last?" has been asked a hundred times in print since Dickens died; and many times, and in various ways, has the question been answered. All men admit that Sir Charles Grandison has become a bore, where he is known at all; that G. P. R. James's solitary horseman has ridden entirely out of the sight of the present-day reader; that Cooper's Indians and backwoodsmen no longer scalp the imagination of the boy of the period; that Marryat's midshipmen have been left alone and neglected at the mastheads to which he was so fond of sending them; that no one but the antiquary in literature cares now for *Waverley* or *Rob Roy*. But it is too soon yet to say how long it will be before *Bleak House* will become an uninhabitable ruin, or when the firm of *Dombey and Son* will go out of business altogether. *Don Quixote* is as vigorous as he was three centuries ago. *Robinson Crusoe*, born in 1719, still retains all the freshness of youth; who can prophesy how Mr. Samuel Pickwick, the Don Quixote of 1839, will be regarded in 1939, or how Mr. Samuel Weller, his man Friday, will be looked upon by the readers of a hundred years from to-day?

Dickens certainly wrote for his own time, and generally *of* his own time. And during his own time he achieved a popularity without parallel in the history of fiction. But the fashions of all times change; and although Dickens has been in fashion longer than most of his contemporaries, and is still the fashion among old-fashioned folk, there are acute critics who say that his day is over. The booksellers and the officials of circulating libraries tell a different story, however; and when little children, who never heard the name of Dickens, who know nothing of his great reputation, turn from *Alice in Wonderland* and *Little Lord Fauntleroy* to the *Cricket on the Hearth*, loving the old as much as they love the new, it would seem as if the sun had not yet set upon Dickens; and that the night which is to leave him in total darkness is still far off.

A strong argument in favour of what may be called the "staying qualities" of Dickens is the fact that his characters, even in a mutilated, unsatisfactory form, have held the stage for half a century or more, and still have power to attract and move great audiences, wherever is spoken the language in which he wrote. The dramatisation of the novel is universally and justly regarded as the most ephemeral and worthless of dramatic productions; and the novels of Dickens, on account of their length, of the great number of figures he introduces, of the variety and occasional exaggeration of his dialogues, and of his situations, have been peculiarly difficult of adaptation to theatrical purposes. Nevertheless, the world laughed and cried over Micawber, the Marchioness, little Nell, Captain Cuttle, Dan'l Peggotty, and Caleb Plummer, behind the footlights, years after Dolly Spanker, Aminadab Sleek, Timothy Toodles, Alfred Evelyn, and Geoffrey Dale, their contemporaries in the standard and legitimate drama, created solely and particularly for dramatic representation, were absolutely forgotten. And Sir Henry Irving, sixty years after the production of *Pickwick*, drew great crowds to see his Alfred Jingle, while that picturesque and ingenious swindler, Robert Macaire, Jingle's once famous and familiar *confrère* in plausible rascality, was never seen on the boards except as he was burlesqued and caricatured in comic opera.

It is pretty safe to say—and not in a Pickwickian sense—that Pecksniff will live almost as long as hypocrisy lasts; that Heep will not be forgotten while mock humility exists; that Mr. Dick will go down to posterity arm in arm with Charles the First, whom he could not avoid in his Memorial; that Barkis will be quoted until men cease to be willin'. And so long as cheap, rough coats cover faith, charity, and honest hearts, the world will remember that Captain Cuttle and the Peggottys were so clad.

Dickens has been accused of being an irreligious man, and of exhibiting a lack of reverence for sacred and serious things. His Chadband and his Stiggins have been cited as gross libels upon the clergymen of England, by men who forget his Frank Milvey, in *Our Mutual Friend*, and who pay no heed to the fact that he rated severely whatever was bad and reprehensible in the members of every profession. Stiggins and Chadband are no worse than Gradgrind, who was in the hardware line; than Pecksniff, who was an architect; than Ralph Nickleby, who was a money-broker; or than Tackleton, who was a maker of toys.

Dickens was not a church member, or what is called an Orthodox Christian; but he preached many a good sermon for all that; and his text was the Golden Rule, in all its various readings. In many wholesome, reverent ways does the Bible figure throughout his pages. One of the earliest recollections of David Copperfield was the story of the raising of Lazarus, as it was read to him and Peggotty by his mother one Sunday evening. Little Nell used to take her Bible with her to read in the quiet, lovely retreat of the old church. " I ain't much of a hand at reading 'writing-hand,' " said Betty Higden, "though I can read my Bible and most print "; Oliver Twist read the Bible to Mrs. Maylie and Rose Fleming; Pip read the Bible to and prayed with the convict under sentence of death; Scrooge heard Tiny Tim say, "And He called a little child to Him, and set him in the midst "; and when Jo was on his death-bed, Allen Woodcourt asked him:

" ' Did you ever know a prayer, Jo ? '

" ' Never knowed nothink, sir.'

" ' Not so much as one short prayer ? '

" ' No, sir, nothink at all.'

" ' Jo, can you say what I say ? '

"'I 'll say anythink as you say, sir, for I know it 's good.'

"'OUR FATHER'—

"'Our father!—yes, that 's werry good, sir.'

"'WHICH ART IN HEAVEN'—

"'Art in Heaven—is the light a-coming, sir?'

"'It is close at hand. HALLOWED BE THY NAME!'

"'Hallowed be—thy—'

"The light is come upon the dark, benighted way! Dead! . . . And dying thus around us every day."

Upon the morning of the day on which the mortal part of Dickens was laid to rest in the Poets' Corner of Westminster Abbey, June 14, 1870, I printed in the New York *Tribune* the following words of Dickens, taken almost at random from his works. They give his idea of Death, and they seem to prove that he had some faith in a Life to Come:

"Dead, your Majesty, Dead, my lords and gentlemen, Dead, Right Reverends and Wrong Reverends, of every order. Dead, men and women, born with heavenly compassion in your hearts. And dying thus around us every day."—*Bleak House*, Chap. 67.

"The golden ripple on the wall came back again, and nothing else stirred in the room. The old, old fashion, the fashion that came in with our first garments, and will last, unchanged, until our race has run its course, and the wide firmament is rolled up like a scroll. The old, old fashion—Death! Oh, thank God, all who see it, for that older fashion yet, of immortality. And look upon us, angels of young children, with regard not quite estranged, when the Swift River bears us to the Ocean."—*Dombey*, Chap. 17.

"The spirit of the child, returning, innocent and radiant, touched the old man with its hand, and beckoned him away."—*Chimes*, Second Quarter.

"The Star had shown him the way to find the God of the poor; and through humility and sorrow and forgiveness he had gone to his Redeemer's rest."—*Hard Times*, Book III., Chap. 6.

"I felt for my old self, as the dead may feel, if they ever revisit these scenes; I was glad to be tenderly remembered, to be greatly pitied, not to be quite forgotten."—*Bleak House*, Chap. 45.

"From these garish lights I vanish now for ever more; with a heartful, grateful, respectful, affectionate farewell,—and I pray God to bless us every one."—Last Reading, London, March 6, 1870.

"When I die, put near me something that has loved the light, and had the sky above it always."—*Old Curiosity Shop*, Chap. 71.

"Lord, keep my memory green."—*Haunted Man*, Chap. 3.

"'Now,' he murmured, 'I am happy.' He fell into a light slumber, and, waking, smiled as before, then spoke of beautiful gardens, which, he said, stretched out before him, and were filled with figures of men, women, and many children, all with light upon their

faces, then whispered that it was Eden—and so died."
—*Nickleby*, Chap. 58.

". . . died like a child that had gone to sleep."
—*Copperfield*, Chap. 9.

". . . and began the world—not this world, oh, not this world. The world that sets this right."—*Bleak House*, Chap. 65.

". . . gone before the Father; far beyond the twilight judgments of this world, high above its mists and obscurities."—*Dorritt*, Book II., Chap. 19.

". . . And lay at rest. The solemn stillness was no marvel now."—*Curiosity Shop*, Chap. 71.

" It being high water, he went out with the tide."—*Copperfield*, Chap. 30.

I once met a man who was extraordinary in a rather extraordinary way. He was a man of about the usual age,—anywhere between fifty and sixty,—and he did not show his years in his face, in his figure, or in his manner, whatever his years may have been. He came to this country during the middle of the last decade of the nineteenth century, bearing excellent letters of introduction from influential men of the British Isles to certain literary men of our own continent. He was an essayist, a reviewer, a translator, a historian, but not a writer of romance; and he was evidently highly regarded by his many friends in London and in Edinburgh. He had the bearing of a gentleman and the charm of a scholar. He spoke several languages besides his own; he spoke them correctly and fluently;

and what he said bore always the stamp of sincerity and truth. He was put up at the best of clubs, he was met in the best of houses. He never assumed. He was, if anything, rather shy of expressing his views, or his knowledge, concerning men and things. He gave no hint of Münchausenism in his general conversation, and yet he succeeded once in almost paralysing one man who was naturally and proverbially credulous.

We were looking over a private collection of objects of various degrees of art of more or less interest and value,—certainly of more value and interest to their possessor than to anybody else,—when we came upon an indifferent little water-colour drawing of Tom All-Alone's. It contained the steps which the Jo of *Bleak House* kept clean, for the sake of the dear friend whom he had seen thrown roughly into a hole just beyond the iron gates at their top—the steps upon which the prostrate form of Lady Deadlock was found after that long, weary, heartbreaking search by Esther and Mr. Bucket.

The visitor recognised the scene at a glance, and he pronounced the sketch correct and true in all its minor details. He remembered meeting Dickens while the story was appearing in its original serial form. He and the creator of Jo and of Mr. Bucket had been dining one evening with John Forster, in what had been Mr. Tulkinghorn's chambers in Lincoln's Inn Fields, and together they had strolled in the misty moonlight toward Wellington Street and the Strand, stopping to look for a moment or two at the deserted, dreary little graveyard in Russell Court, just off Drury Lane, where the unfortunate Mr. Nemo was to be buried. Dickens explained his great difficulty in finding the proper place for the interment, because Tom All-Alone's was not in the parish in which Mr. Nemo was to die, and because the authorities of one parish will never receive the pauper bones of the man who dies in a parish adjoining.

All this was intensely interesting to me, as the owner of the sketch, and also a great lover of Dickens, and it was a little startling, for Dickens himself had been dead a quarter of a century and *Bleak House* was quite forty years old. But still it might have happened.

The next object which attracted our attention was an engraving entitled "The Last Return from Duty." It represented the old Duke, *the* Duke, the hero of Waterloo, on an old war-horse, perhaps a veteran of Waterloo itself, as leaving the Horse Guards for the last time, and going slowly home, in his ripe old age, to die. The print is not a common one, and to the visitor it had been unknown. He stood before it in an attitude of respectful silence for a moment or two. Making a semi-unconscious military salute, he said: "It is very, very like the Duke, the dear old Duke, the magnificent old Duke, the "ever-grand old Duke," as I remember him so well at Walmer Castle, toward the close of his life. He must have been over eighty then, and his equestrian days were past; but he walked about the grounds unattended, petting the steed he could no longer ride, but still clear of mind, erect of body, quick of step, bright of eye, full of good talk. It is very like him."

This, too, was a little startling, and also very interesting, to me, who had a dim recollection of standing by my father's side as a small boy, in 1852, at a window of Morley's Hotel on Trafalgar Square, and watching the body of the " ever-grand old Duke " carried in great funereal pomp from Chelsea Hospital to St. Paul's Cathedral. But that was a long time ago; and the black-bearded, unwrinkled man beside me, to have been a friend of Wellington's, must have been a good deal older than he looked. But still it might have happened.

And then we stepped up to the library table, upon which, lying in state, was a bronze replica of Dr. Antomarchi's death-mask of the first Napoleon. This of all the things he had seen was to the visitor the most realistic and the most impressive. He had never heard of Dr. Antomarchi or of the death-mask. He inspected it with an intense gaze; he looked at it from all sides and in all lights. He asked permission to take it in his hands, to carry it to the window. He touched it reverently; he put it back in its place with a long-drawn sigh, and he whispered: "It is the very face and head of Bonaparte as I saw him in the flesh!"

This was more than startling. Bonaparte had died in St. Helena in 1821, and here in 1895, seventy-four years later, was a middle-aged man who had seen him in the flesh!

THE PEEP O' DAY LIBRARY IN PRINCETON

The intimacy with Dickens, who had not been in the flesh for five-and-twenty years; the friendship with Wellington, who had been out of the flesh for nearly fifty years, might both be accepted, but not the personal acquaintance with Bonaparte, who had put off his flesh a good many years before the man could possibly have been born. So the man was steered carefully away from a coloured print of Garrick, whose death had eclipsed the gaiety of nations nearly a century before; away from a pencil drawing of the mural tablet to the memory of Tom D'Urfey which Sir Richard Steele had placed on the walls of St. James's, Piccadilly, in 1723; even away from an engraving of St. Jerome, who put the Bible into Latin at the close of the fourth century of the Christian era, for fear the man would tell tales of his personal knowledge of them all. The painful story of the sudden collapse of Ananias was recalled, and it was felt that it would be much more comfortable for all concerned if the present phenomenal economiser of the truth might be permitted to suffer his own inevitable collapse in a public street, or a public conveyance, rather than in a comparatively humble private house.

Therefore, gently but firmly, and, it is to be hoped, imperceptibly to himself, the modern Ananias was conducted from the library to the hall, from the hall to the front door. But, hat in hand, he paused on the threshold, and remarked casually that it had just occurred to him that some of his statements might seem a little surprising to his listener. This was acknowledged with polite hesitation, and the visitor was permitted to come back to explain. It may be stated that the explanation was made in the hall.

It seems that the visitor's family was connected in some way, by marriage, with the family of Dickens, and that he had, naturally, as a young man, seen something in his own house and out of it of the head of the Dickens family. That might have happened.

It also seems that the visitor was the son of an officer who had served on Wellington's staff in the Peninsula; that the Iron Duke had, in consequence, acted as sponsor to the visitor at his christening, and that, spending his childhood at Sandwich, in Kent, near Walmer Castle, the official residence of Wellington as Warden of the Five Ports, he had, as was natural, noticed, and been noticed by, his father's old chief. That also might have happened.

Then followed the most remarkable explanation of all, at the close of which the visitor was once more invited into the library.

It seems that while still a very youthful person he chanced to have been with his father in Paris, in 1840, when, by order of Louis Philippe, the embalmed body of Bonaparte was carried to France to be entombed in the Invalides. Out of pure sentiment, the boy, as a godson of the Duke of Wellington, Bonaparte's conqueror, was permitted to be one of the very few favoured persons who were present when the inner coffin was opened in order to identify the remains. He then saw Napoleon in the actual flesh; and the fact had made an impression upon him, mere child as he was, which he never had forgotten and never could forget.

And that *did* happen!

CHAPTER III

Recollections of the Stage — *Plays and Players* — Frederick Warde — Henry Irving's Generosity — Edwin Booth — The Players Club — Death of Lawrence Barrett.

MY next appearance in print, after the Dickens article, was more successful; it was even a little remunerative, and it settled the whole course of my life. I had gone, in the 'seventies some time, to Booth's Theatre to see the return of the Boucicaults to the New York stage after a long absence. They played *Jessie Brown, or the Siege of Lucknow,* a drama which had stirred up all the young Scotch blood in New York to a remarkable extent when it was originally produced at Wallack's, in the early 'sixties. Many of the members of the first cast were dead; but I set down, in a thousand or two thousand words, all that could be remembered of the original production, and the article was carried to *The Evening Mail*. It was accepted and printed, and paid for,—at the rate of seven dollars a column. It was quoted, and copied, and talked about; and the author was asked for more in the same line. And so I stubbed my toe, as it were, and fell into the arms of a daily journal. The contribution was followed by a long, scattering, irregular series of " Recollections of the Stage," "By a Young Veteran," for which latter I was severely censured on the ground that a veteran must be a man old in years. Which is not true, for there were veteran drummer-boys among my acquaintances then, who had served in the Civil War, who were recognised as veterans and who were younger than I.

The subject-matter selected always related to some current play or event of dramatic interest, the article stating what "The Young Veteran" knew or had seen or had read concerning similar events or plays in the palmy days of the past. If *The School for Scandal* were revived, the story of the comedy was told from the beginning: who wrote it, how, and when; where and when it was first produced in England and in America; how this man played Joseph, how that man played Charles. When Miss Cushman retired, "Last Appearances" were the theme; when Miss Bijou Heron made her *début*, "First Appearances" were talked about, and the "Infant Phenomena"; and when poor Montague received his death-stroke upon the stage, in San Francisco, I dwelt in a reminiscent way upon similar tragedies in real life.

The articles were favourably noticed, except by the actors and actresses who were not themselves noticed; and among the personal letters "The Young Veteran" received upon the subject of reprinting them in book-form was one signed by J. Brander Matthews, who then had never heard "The Young Veteran's" real name, although it has had a familiar, and I am sure not an unpleasant, sound in his ears for more than a quarter of a century since. The book was printed at the author's expense; the edition was limited to five hundred copies, all of which were sold. And the author lost nothing in cash and not much in reputation by the transaction. The title of the work is *Plays and Players*, and rather entertaining is the confusion the name caused in the mind of a Scottish clergyman who wrote that he was glad to think that his young friend had turned his thoughts from the affairs of the theatre to more serious things; and that he hoped soon to be able to read the new book on *Praise and Prayer!*

This work of my 'prentice hand was published in 1875 in a limited edition. For twenty-five years afterwards it was out of print, turning up only occasionally in the sales of collections of *dramatica*. I had searched in vain during quite a decade for a copy of the book, which I wanted for some especial purpose. I had orders in the hands of dealers all over the country and had even advertised for it, when I received a rather peremptory letter from a binder saying that he had in his cellar a number of copies of the work in question which would be destroyed, as was the rule of the house, if they were not taken away immediately. And now I am overloaded with a book, a specimen of which for over a quarter of a century I could not buy at any price. These cost me nothing, finally, but a small matter of expressage. The very first copy ever distributed, by the way, bears the inscription: "To the

Behind the Scenes

Author of the Author's Being, with the Author's love."

I never could understand the fascination possessed by so many persons to visit that strange land called "behind the scenes." Although I have had many experiences within its border, nowhere else have I ever felt so uncomfortably futile and in the way, an idle man among hundreds of busy persons, stage carpenters, scene-shifters, scene-painters, electricians, general managers, stage managers, stars, soubrettes, choruses, supernumeraries, devils, angels,—all having something to do, and all doing it with all their might, while the visitor has nothing whatever to do and does not know how to do it in a graceful way. The contrast between the real and the ideal in stageland is stranger than fiction and sometimes it is impossible to realise which is the truth. In 1879 or 1880, something took me with Kate Field to one of the theatres in Brooklyn to see Adelaide Phillips, who was playing *Pinafore* in the Boston Ideals Company. Contrary to my custom I went behind the scenes and had a long talk with the *prima donna* during one of the waits; resting with her on the long step-ladder which some one had left conveniently lying on its side; "both sitting on one cushion," as Helena says in *The Midsummer Night's Dream*, but not both "warbling of one song." She was the very ideal Buttercup, with a voice perfectly suited to the part.

After the Phillips episode we went into the Park Theatre across the way to see the last two acts of

Othello. Warde, playing Iago, had some trouble which he wished to pour into my ear, and he sent for me to go to the fascinating regions. It was rather a queer experience, after talking music with Buttercup and nonsense with Hebe on the deck of H. M. S. *Pinafore*, to talk of serious affairs with Iago in Desdemona's bedchamber in Cypress while Othello (who happened to be John McCullough), in all the paraphernalia and burnt-cork of the character, was walking about directing the next "set" and asking me, now and then, how long Booth and I stayed together in Saratoga, or some other personal question, and expressing a wish that some English tailor had made *him* an ulster as good-looking as was mine! The Moor of Venice in an ulster seemed to be a long step from the impressive to the grotesque.

There is a very confused and erroneous notion in the lay mind with regard to the actor as a gentleman and as a man; and unfortunately some few of the profession —by the laxity of their morals, and by their curious proneness to divorce—have damaged the reputation of a set of men who are as decent and as respectable as are the members of any profession whatsoever, taken as a whole.

The management of The Players, after years of experience with actors as members of the institution, will certify that the player proper, who is very largely represented in the Club, is as a rule more temperate, better behaved, more prompt in his payments of all indebtedness, than are any other class of men in any other walk of life.

One well-known comedian came in one morning early, absolutely in tears, a man of forty or more and with children of his own. He could n't find his mother! He had been on a long travelling tour, and when he arrived at home he discovered that his mother had suddenly quitted her boarding-house and had for some unknown reason failed to leave her address; and there he was, with his mother looking for him somewhere and he could n't discover her for at least a couple of hours!

I once heard two young members of the profession—so I gathered from their talk, though they were personally unknown to me—discussing an opportunity which had come to one of them to double his salary, to get better parts, and perhaps to establish his growing reputation in a far-away city; but he had concluded not to accept the offer, tempting as it was. His friend said:

"But you can take your wife and the kids with you. You can certainly afford to do that with an extra hundred dollars a week."

"Oh, it is n't the wife and the kids; of course they go wherever I go; but it 's the father and the mother. They want me, and I think they need me here, and I am not going to settle down three thousand miles away from them for any amount of money."

This was not said for the world. It was simply an ordinary expression of the natural filial feeling of a man who honoured the fifth commandment to the very letter. And yet the world thinks that the actor has no feeling for anybody but himself, coupled with a little feeling for his art.

When Frederick Warde, the English tragedian, young, promising, with his undoubted American success not yet fully established, brought his wife and children from London to make their home with him in the new world, he was after various vicissitudes of fortune —most of them discouraging—engaged by Mr. Booth to play leading parts during the coming season. They were to open in Baltimore on a certain Monday evening and Warde was to be Othello to the Iago of the star. The company, long associated with Mr. Booth with this single exception, was not assembled and there could be but one or two rehearsals before the initial performance. Warde had never even seen the play of *Othello*, and had no idea how to dress it,—a very important item to a man who had little money to devote to costumes. There were, of course, professional persons who could have fitted him out from wig to sandal, but to these he could not afford to go. He read the tragedy many times, studied his part till he was what is called "letter perfect," and at the Astor Library he copied many drawings, coloured by his own hand, of the dresses he had to wear. These garments and effects were made out of the cheapest material from his own patterns, cut and sewed by his wife, and for six weeks nothing in that house was thought or talked but

Othello. The young man, realising what it all meant to him, was exceedingly anxious about results, as was his wife. They lived in a poor, humble little apartment and he was to take a midnight train to the scene of his great effort only a day or two before he was to make his *début* in one of the most important and trying parts of the English-speaking drama.

I went with him to the train, and just as we were starting Mrs. Warde came down with her eyes swimming, and said:

"I 've just put the children to bed and I must tell you what Arthur prayed"; Arthur was then a lad not out of his frocks. It seems that the child, kneeling by his little cot, had gone through the regular formula, "Our Father," "Now I lay me," "Please, God, remember papa and mamma and little sister and dear grandmother in England," and had then added, as an impromptu, "and O God, do please help papa through with Othello."

On the Tuesday morning there came to me a telegram from Warde saying, simply, "I think God has heard Arthur's prayer."

I told this story at a dinner one night, as I am trying to tell it now, and was startled by an inquiry from the wife of a well-known New York clergyman who, with wonder and doubt in her voice, demanded,

"Do you mean to tell me that actors' children say their prayers!"

Actors' children do say their prayers. And, as a

class, few better behaved or more dutiful children or more human have come within my ken.

Henry Irving's generosity is unbounded. Because I spoke to him once of an old receipt-book of one of the early Philadelphia theatres as being invaluable on account of the signatures it contained, and said that I would like to own it if the price of the dealer who had it for sale was at all within my limit, he bought the book and gave it to me as a Christmas box.

I have known Irving to devote the whole of a very busy day in New York, neglecting rehearsals and social engagements, to find for an English painter of his acquaintance—clever but unfortunate—some proper and comfortable studio and home where he would be able to do better work in more cheerful and appropriate surroundings. After taking the apartment, paying out of his own pocket three months' rent in advance, he saw that the man of the brush was carefully installed in his new quarters and then rushed away before any thanks could be uttered.

He posed to the same artist in London for his portrait as Hamlet. During one of the sittings there came back from the Royal Academy Exhibition, lately closed, two little landscapes unsold. The disappointment of the painter was expressed very clearly in his face because he had expected by the disposal of the pictures to put himself in very necessary funds. Irving expressed his sympathy and asked the price of the drawings. They were catalogued at one hundred and fifty guineas apiece, but very much less would have been gladly accepted. Irving said:

"Send them down and I'll have them hung in the *foyer* of the Lyceum where they will be seen by men and women, and perhaps attract attention."

This unexpected and kindly offer was eagerly accepted. The pictures would go as soon as they were properly framed and, when properly framed, they went. Mr. Bram Stoker, Mr. Irving's friend and manager, wrote to inquire the price of the frames. This, the painter replied, was his own affair: he was willing to pay half a dozen times the cost of the mounting for the sake of having his work where it was. Mr. Stoker said that Mr. Irving insisted and a bill for ten pound ten was despatched to the Lyceum office. The reply was received by return post and contained Irving's check for three hundred and ten guineas.

A good many years ago, no matter when, while Edwin Booth was playing a successful engagement in one of the leading theatres of the country, no matter where, I dropped into his dressing-room one night during the course of the performance. He chanced to be in a particularly happy and cheerful frame of mind — and he was often cheerful and happy, tradition to the contrary notwithstanding. He was smoking the inevitable pipe, and he was arrayed in the costume of Richelieu, with his feet upon the table, submitting patiently to the manipulations of his wardrobe-man, or "dresser." After a few words of greeting the call-boy knocked at the door and said that Mr. Booth was wanted at a certain "left lower entrance." The protagonist jumped up quickly, and asked if I would stay where I was and keep his pipe alight, or go along with him and see him "lunch the cuss of Rum," quoting the words of George L. Fox, who had been producing just about that time a ludicrously clever burlesque of Booth in the same part. I followed him to the wings and stood by his side while he waited for his cue. It was the fourth act of the drama, I remember, and the stage was set as a garden, nothing of which was visible from our position but the flies and the back of the wings; and we might have been placed in a great bare barn so far as any scenic effect was apparent. Adrian, Baradas, and the conspirators were speaking, and at an opposite entrance, waiting for *her* cue, was the Julie of the evening. She was a good woman and an excellent actress but unfortunately not a personal favourite with the star, who called my attention to the bismuth with which she was covered and said that if she got any of it on his new scarlet cloak he would pinch her black and blue — puffing volumes of smoke into my face as he spoke. When the proper time came he rushed upon the stage, with a parting injunction not to let his pipe go out; and with the great meerschaum in my own mouth, I saw the heroine of the play cast herself into his arms and noticed, to my great amusement, that she *did* smear the robes of my Lord Cardinal with the greasy white stuff he so much disliked. I winked back at the half-comic, half-angry glance he shot towards me over Julie's snowy shoulders. I half expected to hear the real scream he had threatened to cause her to utter. I thought of nothing but the humorous, absurd side of the situation; I was eager to keep the pipe going. And lo! he raised his hand and spoke those familiar lines:

"Around her form I draw the awful circle of our solemn Church. Place but a foot within that hallowed ground and on thy head, yea, though it wear a crown, I'll launch the curse of Rome!" Every head upon the stage was uncovered and I found my own hat in my hand! I forgot all the tomfoolery we had been indulging in; I forgot his pipe, and my promise regarding it; I forgot that I had been an habitual theatregoer all my life; I forgot that I was a Protestant heretic, and that it was nothing but stage-play; I forgot that Booth was my familiar, intimate friend; I forgot everything, except the fact that I was standing in the presence of the great, visible head of the Catholic religion in France, and that I was ready to drop upon my knees with the rest of them at his invocation.

That was Edwin Booth, the Actor!

In 1881 Edwin Booth wrote:

"I hope your dear mother may be spared to you many, many years. *My* dear old mother is not so well as I could wish and my sister Rosalie, her nurse, begins to fail. I'd rather have a cosy home, like yours, with mother, than all the flummery and puffery I 'm wasting my life for."

A few months later he wrote from London:

"I scratch in haste, therefore excuse my incoherence. I am tired in body and brain, my dear Boy. The poor little girl [his second wife] is passing away from us. For weeks she has been failing rapidly; and the doctors have at last refused to attend her longer, unless she follows their directions and keeps her bed day and night. They tell me that she is dying and that I may expect her death at any time. It is very pitiful to see her fading before our eyes. Edwina, deprived of sleep and half dead with sorrow for the only mother she has ever known, and I—worn out with my nightly labors and wretched all the while—sit turn by turn to cheer her. The doctors—Mackenzie and Sir William Jenner—have pronounced her case hopeless. Edwina has written to Mrs. McVickar; and at last Mary knows that she is dying. You can imagine my condition just now; acting at random every evening and nursing a half-insane dying wife all day, and all night too, for that matter. I am scarce sane myself. I scribble this in haste at two in the morning, for I know not when I will have a chance to write sensibly and coherently again. Good-night. And God bless you."

The last portrait for which Booth ever sat was made by Mr. Bradley in black and white and it was reproduced in *Harper's* at the time of Booth's death. It cost the subject a long and weary day's sitting, and it re-

FACSIMILE OF THE BOOTH AND BARRETT PAGE IN THE HUTTON GUEST-BOOK

presents him in his own private room at The Players, surrounded by the inanimate things he loved best. The artist found him in an old-fashioned, commonplace, rep-covered arm-chair of the late Pierce or early Buchanan period, in which he was very anxious to be portrayed; and it was with no little persuasion that he was induced to place himself in another seat much more old-fashioned and much more picturesque. To the artist, who was a stranger to him, he hesitated to give his reason for the queer preference. But it seems that the homely piece of furniture stood in the parlour of Mr. Magonigle's house, in which lived Booth's first wife, and his one love; that it was deeply associated with all the sentiment of their courting days; that after his marriage he had asked Mr. Magonigle for it; that it had gone with him, always, wherever his home had been. And he would have liked, he said, in his ever-gentle way, to have had it in the picture—for "Mary's sake." And then followed many tender, loving words concerning that same Mary whom he had lost thirty years before.

That was Edwin Booth, the Son, the Husband, and the Father!

I can hardly remember when I did not know and admire Booth as an actor. We first met personally on a Long Branch boat in 1865, when I was presented to him by Lester Wallack. We rarely if ever met until ten years later, when, through common friends, we were thrown much together. My mother was in her early widowhood then. Booth and his wife came often to us and we went often to them. A pleasant acquaintance ripened by degrees into an intimate friendship. Booth soon exhibited a very warm feeling for my mother. She came next in his heart to his own mother, he used to say; and he never forgot her. Almost the last time we spoke alone together we spoke of her, years after her death, and in a most sadly tender and prophetic way.

In the summer of 1875 or 1876 the mother and I chanced to find the Booths at the Grand Union Hotel in Saratoga and, at their request, we occupied two vacant rooms in a little suite engaged by them in one of the most retired cottages in the Grand Union grounds. We were together a month or two, dining at the same table and spending most of our waking hours as one family. It was at this period that the second Mrs. Booth, always a nervous invalid, began to show signs of the lack of mental balance which finally sapped her own life and almost broke his heart. During her frequent attacks at Saratoga, and later when the two families met in New York and in London, sometimes she was very trying; but I never knew him to show a sign or utter a word of impatience. He bore meekly with everything she said and did; made excuses for her; concealed her irritability and her irresponsibility as much as possible; held her in his arms as if she were a baby for hours and nights together without a murmur and showed a devotion that hardly can be equalled.

After my mother's death, I went abroad at once with an aunt and her children. We found Booth playing at the Adelphi Theatre in London, and living at an hotel where he was neither satisfied or comfortable. Finally Booth and his daughter moved into the apartments my people had vacated in Clarges Street, Piccadilly. I occupied a bedroom and sitting-room on the upper floor and of course saw Booth daily. He was ill and dispirited. He smoked too much, took too little exercise, was neglectful of his diet, and in a bad physical condition generally. He rehearsed every morning and he played every evening; and his doctor said he *must* live more in the open air and take long walks every day. I was busy and naturally absorbed, but I made it my duty to see that Booth went on foot to and from the theatre every evening, I always going with him. And very pleasant are my recollections of those walks and talks. Down Piccadilly, through the Haymarket, across Trafalgar Square, and along the Strand we went; on through the parks to Whitehall; and home by way of the Embankment. Booth's face was not well enough known to be recognised by all the passers-by as it would have been in an American city and he thoroughly enjoyed the feeling of incognito. Nothing distressed him more than notoriety or public observation. He rarely travelled in a street car or an omnibus on that account and I have seen him shrink like a hyperbashful child at any sign of recognition from strangers.

One perfect night, when the sky was without a cloud

and the full moon was high in the heavens, we wandered home from the theatre along the shore of the Thames; turned into the little square upon which looked the windows of the Banqueting Hall out of which Charles I. stepped to his death; passed through Axe Yard, where Pepys once lived; paused in front of St. Margaret's, where Raleigh's head was buried; gazed at the Abbey; and drifted, by some curious chance of gates being open, into the Cloisters. There we stopped for a long time, with the whole sacred place to ourselves and no sound but the bell of the clock-tower ringing the quarters. The influence of the spot and the hour was upon us, and Edwin spoke of it all in a never-to-be-forgotten way; of Sheridan and Johnson and Cumberland, of Garrick and Newton and Chaucer and the rest of them, sleeping quietly so near us. We were loath to leave, but he dreaded being locked in the place and thereby distressing "daughter" by his non-appearance all night. And we walked back to our own door, almost without a word.

Booth had a keen sense of humour, and among his intimates he was anything but the sad and gloomy man whom the outside world associated, always, with the character of the Melancholy Dane of the stage. His published letters show how bright and cheerful he was, usually, in his familiar correspondence; and this rhyming epistle is an example of his not infrequent efforts in that peculiar line. It came with an engraved portrait, neatly framed:

EDWIN BOOTH

Nonsense Verse

Xmas Eve, '79.
DEAR H.:
   Think not that I forget,
   Or that because the walkin's wet,
   Is why I have n't called as yet
   Fumer la pipe, ou cigarette,
   In your sanctum-sanctorum.
   'T is but because I have to fry
   Some other fish before they're dry;
   This only is the reason why,
   My friends I do not bore 'em.
   So, since I can't *aller chez vous,*
   This dead-head I present, in lieu
   Of the one which here I shoulder,
   Hoping this, too, may likewise call
   Before the New Year learns to crawl,
   Or the old one grows much older.

   But I know not, dear Hutton,
   If you'll care a button
   For this mug o' my own that I send,
   Though 't is told me as truth
   (May be flatt'ry, forsooth)
   By some who are judges—
   That this very mug is
   By far the best phiz
       Of your friend
           Edwin Booth.

P. S.—You may spurn it, or dern it,
   Or dash it, or *dang* it, or burn it,
   Or mash it—by puttin' yer fut on.
   Do anything—rather than hang it,
   If you don't like it, dear Hutton.

In my *Memoir of Booth* I have spoken of his kindness of heart, of his delicacy of feeling, of his thoughtfulness for others, and of his unbounded silent charity. Even the members of his own family and his most intimate friends never heard of half the good he did. Sitting in his room in The Players, when his physical decay was first becoming manifest, I told him of a letter I had just received from the daughter of one of the old comedians in which she offered the club a portrait of her father. Booth had received a letter from her to the same purport; would I write for both of us in reply? Her note was on his desk across the room, that black-bordered one, on the top of a pile of unanswered epistles, he said, just at my hand. I picked it up and read aloud, " My dear Mr. Booth : How can I ever thank you for your great liberality—" "No, no, not that one; the next." The next began, " I do not know what to say to you for your wonderful generosity—" " No, no; not that either "; and he picked up the whole package and threw them into an open drawer, ashamed that I should unwittingly have discovered some of his benefactions.

When an old friend and fellow-player died, Edwin bought a lot for his remains, buried him, placed a handsome monument over his head, purchased a house and furnished it fully for the widow, and gave her a liberal income, continued to her after his own death. He was staying with us—as he often did before he had a city home at The Players,—detained by some mysterious and vexatious business, he said, which kept him, much against his will, from the bedside of his daughter, who was expecting her first confinement in Boston. He was in receipt of long and not very encouraging telegrams from Mr. Grossman every day; and he was visibly anxious. What it was, of course, I never asked, and only knew at last by accident. The widow called one day when Edwin was smoking in the study. The maid reported that there was a reading-class, or a lecture in the library; and the old lady was shown upstairs. I rose to go after the first greeting but she asked me to stay;—perhaps I could help them,—and then the story of the mysterious and important business came out. Booth was arranging for her husband's monument. She thought the pedestal too high, or too low; she could not decide upon the shape of the granite posts or the railing; and she did not altogether like the inscription! And the patient benefactor was waiting in New York, consumed by his paternal anxiety, saying nothing to his old and forlorn friend, who was of course entirely unconscious of his feelings, until she had made up her mind as to what she wanted. I settled everything for them in a few moments, and despatched him to Boston that same evening to make the acquaintance of his new grandchild.

Another old friend of Booth, a superannuated actor and a very aged man, lunched with him one day at The Players. The weather was threatening as he left and his host sent him home in a carriage. The guest was very much affected when they parted and tried to say something, in a half-tearful way, which Booth would not let him utter. After he had gone some one spoke of the gentleness and sweetness of the veteran's character and said that it was to be hoped that he had managed to save enough to keep his body and his soul together for the little time that was left to him here.

"Oh, yes, he's all right!" replied Booth. "He has something to support him comfortably as long as he lives, poor dear. And I'm glad of it."

After Booth had passed away it was learned that the something — more than enough — was furnished by Booth, who had invested nine thousand dollars in an annuity to cheer his fellow-player's declining years. But he did not even hint of such a deed. He simply said, "I am glad of it!"

Many years before that I called upon Booth one afternoon at the Albemarle Hotel in New York, during an engagement of his at the Fifth Avenue Theatre. His wife was dead, his daughter was married and living in a distant city, and he was quite alone and lonely. I brought in to him a little fresh air, something from the outside world, and change of thought; and I was made to feel that my presence was not unwelcome. With the never-missing pipe he sat in an easy chair, restful and content, talking of the old times and old seasons in which he then was beginning almost exclusively to live, when the waiter entered the room and put a visiting-card into his hand. "Tell the lady that Mr. Booth is engaged," was the quiet remark, and he continued the conversation where it had been interrupted. The caller was an influential leader of society in New York and a charming woman personally and I remonstrated with him for not receiving her and her equally charming daughter, who was with her. But he could n't be bothered! In a few moments there came another card—this time that of a prominent man of affairs, a man known honourably throughout the country, a busy man, whose call was a compliment in itself; but " Mr. Booth was lying down." Still another card was presented, two cards, those of a man and his wife whom nobody could afford to refuse to receive. But " Mr. Booth was engaged." At last came a card, followed by the request to " Show the lady up! " I put on my overcoat to leave the room, but was told to wait. The lady was a friend of mine whom I would be glad to see and who would be glad to see me. Curious to discover the identity of the person so distinguished I did wait and Black Betty entered, the old negro servant who had nursed his daughter when she was a baby, who had taken the most tender care of his wife when she was slowly and unhappily dying, and who had been a life-long, devoted, faithful friend to them all. She had left his service after his daughter's marriage and had been married recently herself. She kissed "Massa Edwin's" hand,— she was born a slave,— she shook hands cordially with me, she was placed in the most comfortable rocking-chair, and she began to talk familiarly about her own affairs and his. She could n't afford to go to the theatre " no mo'," she said, but she wanted her husband to see Massa Edwin play; could she have a pass for two for that night? He wrote the pass at once, which she read and returned to him with a shake of the head. They was only niggas; the do'-keeper would n't let no niggas into the orchestra seats; a pass to the gallery was good enough for them! A second paper she received silently but with another and still more decided shake of the head. I saw it over her shoulder and it read, "Pass my friend Betty —— and party to my box this evening. Edwin Booth." And Betty occupied the box!

Still he was too tired to receive the daughter of one of the most distinguished men of science in the country, a judge of the Supreme Court of the United States, or a bishop and his wife!

I remember once asking Booth to put his autograph on an engraving of himself for the daughter of Mr. J. Henry Harper. He asked for the young lady's name in full, and being told that it was Mary Hoe Harper, he said,—punning on the well-known lines from *Pinafore*, then in everybody's mouth,—"What, Ho! the Merry Harper and the Star!"

Marjory Telford, the little daughter of an old friend of Booth, chanced to be born on Booth's birthday. He never forgot her or the fact and, no matter in what part of the world he was, some souvenir of the occasion was sent to the child whom he playfully called his "twin." On one of these anniversaries, when Booth was fifty-six and Marjory was four, a supper-party was given him at The Players. A few of his intimates participated and the table was loaded with flowers, among them being a bunch of red roses "From the Servants of the Club" and a modest little cluster of violets attached to which was the inscription from Marjory Telford: "Dear Mr. Booth. We are sixty to-day."

When the guest of the evening went up to his room that night the only flowers he carried with him were the violets of Marjory Telford and the red roses of the servants of the Club.

Booth was playing an engagement in New York when my mother died suddenly and without warning, in 1882. Mr. Telford, knowing how dear she was to Booth, broke the news to him in his dressing-room at the theatre and he came immediately to the house of mourning, about midnight. He did not ask to see me, he did not want to intrude, he did not even want it known that he was there. He simply felt that he must come. He was taken to my room. I was lying on a sofa, too unhappy to think, realising nothing but the awful fact that I had to meet the greatest sorrow that had ever come to me. Booth sat by my side and kissed the tear-wet cheek — no other man had kissed it for many, many years—and he said simply, "My poor boy; my poor boy!" I tried to tell all this in my *Memoir of Booth*, when my grief at the loss of him was too fresh. I can hardly tell it now.

A short time before his own passing away my mother's name came up in our talk one afternoon at The Players. It was in May, as I remember, and I think it was the anniversary of her death. Booth was very feeble and rather sad and he told how she had helped and comforted him in his trials by her strong nature and by her affectionate womanly sympathy, and how much he loved her. After some moments of absolute silence on his part, and when for an instant we were left alone together in the room, he turned to me abruptly and said:

"I'll see her before you do, dear Boy."

And I replied:

"Give her my love, Edwin; give her my love."

And I am sure he did.

Mr. Booth gave to The Players not only the house and the ground upon which the house was built, but all the furniture and books and objects of art which were in his own home in Boston. In the library he placed his valuable collection of dramatic portraits, from life, of the giants of the stage in the days gone by. The only picture in the room still occupying the place of honour between the front windows which is not of a player is a portrait of Washington, supposed to be from life but not authenticated. It came into Mr. Booth's hands by purchase from an impoverished family in the South who declared and believed that it was the true George Washington from nature. Mr. Booth, a little doubtful of the fact that the artist had ever seen Washington, was too generous to resist the importunities of those who claimed it to be an original, and, in his ready sympathy with all whom he felt to be in want of money and help, bought, at a large price, the doubtful painting.

Apologising once to a party of his friends for its presence in the collection of pictures devoted solely to members of his own profession, he said:

"I don't think it really ought to be where it is."

Whereupon Mr. Thomas Bailey Aldrich comforted the protagonist by remarking that Washington was, at all events, "our leading man."

Booth was certainly a great actor. But it seems to those who loved him best and who knew him best that he was a better man. He was tried by domestic sorrows and by business troubles as few persons have been tried; but he never flinched, he never lost heart, and he never spoke bitterly of those who had wronged him most. His tenderness was exquisitely human.

Mr. Jefferson, his successor in the presidency of The Players and the only man on the American stage today who is worthy to succeed him, spoke of Booth in the club house on the night of his own inaugural in the following words: "But a few years ago Booth although rich in genius was poor in pocket. He had been wealthy and he saw the grand dramatic structure he had reared taken from him and devastated. His reverse of fortune was from no fault of his own, but from a confiding nature. When he again, by arduous toil, accumulated wealth, one would have supposed that the thought of his former reverses would have startled him and that he would have clutched his newly acquired gold and garnered it to himself, fearful lest another stroke of ill fortune should fall upon him. But instead of making him a coward it gave him courage. It did not warp his mind or steel his heart against humanity. No sterility settled upon him. His wrongs seemed to have fertilised his generosity and here we behold the fruit. . . . The walls within which we stand, the art, the books, and the comforts that surround us, represent a life of toil and travel, sleepless nights, tedious journeys, and weary work; so that when he bestowed upon us this club it was not his wealth only but it was himself he gave us. . . . When the stranger comes here and asks us for the monument of Edwin Booth we can truly and significantly say, 'Look around you.'"

It has been said that Edwin Booth was the son of his father; that his reputation as his father's son was not only the foundation, but the greater part, of the reputation he built for himself; that all he knew and all he was came from the father whom he copied so carefully. In his own defence, perhaps, he wrote in an article upon the elder Kean these modest, thoughtful lines: "The word imitation seems to be used as a slur upon the actor alone. The painter and the sculptor go to Italy to study the old masters, and are praised for their good copies after this or that one. They are not censured for imitation; and why may not the actor also have his preceptor, his model? Why should he alone be required to depart from the traditions? True, other

POSTER PORTRAIT OF J. WILKES BOOTH

artists see the work of their predecessors and can retain or reject beauties or blemishes at will; but the actor relies solely on uncertain records of his masters' art and thereby is frequently misled into the imitation of faults rather than into the emulation of virtues. In the main, tradition to the actor is as true as that which the sculptor perceives in Angelo, the painter in Raphael, and the musician in Beethoven; all these artists have sight and sound to guide them. I, as an actor, know that if I could sit in the front of the stage and see myself at work I would condemn much that has been lauded; and correct many faults which I feel are mine and which escape the critics' notice. But I cannot see or hear my mistakes as can the sculptor, the painter, the writer, and the musician. Tradition, if it be traced through pure channels and to the fountain-head, leads one as near to Nature as can be followed by her servant, Art. Whatever Quinn, Barton Booth, Garrick, and Cooke gave to stagecraft, or as we now term it, "business," they received from their predecessors; from Betterton and perhaps from Shakespeare himself who, though not distinguished as an actor, well knew what acting should be; and what they inherited in this way they bequeathed in turn to their art and we should not despise it. Kean knew without seeing Cooke, who in turn knew from Macklin, and so back to Betterton, just what to do and how to do it. Their great Mother Nature, who reiterates her teachings and preserves her monotone in motion, form, and sound, taught them. There must be some similitude in all things that are True!"

And in writing of the elder Booth he said:

"To see my father act, when in the acting mood, was *not* 'like reading Shakespeare by flashes of lightning' which could give but fitful glimpses of the author's meaning; but the full sunlight of his genius shone on every character that he portrayed and so illumined the obscurities of the text that Shakespearians wondered with delight at his lucid interpretation of passages which to them had previously been unintelligible. At his best he soared higher in the realm of Art than any one of his successors have reached; and to those who saw him then it was not credible that any of his predecessors could have surpassed him. His expression of terror and remorse was painful in the extreme, his hatred and revenge were devilish, but his tenderness was exquisitely human."

The history of the conception, the birth, and the baptism of The Players has never been fully told in print. Booth had long desired to do something in a tangible and in an enduring way for the good of his profession; and various schemes were fully discussed during a fortnight's cruise on the steam-yacht *Oneida* in the summer of 1886. The party consisted of Mr. E. C. Benedict, the owner of the beautiful vessel, Mr. Thomas Bailey Aldrich, Lawrence Barrett, Mr. William Bispham, Booth, and myself. Booth's first and original idea was to found and endow some sort of an Actors'

ORIGINAL "PLAYERS" ON YACHT

House or Home, with sleeping-rooms, waiting-rooms, a restaurant, and the like; where strangers in New York could find a lodging; and where residents could assemble whenever they were so disposed; where the old could find a resting-place; the sick could find shelter and a doctor's care; and the poor could find help and comfort. The arguments against this were as many as were those in its favour. It did not seem altogether possible. The difficulties, as they were pointed out to him, were almost insurmountable; and with great reluctance he finally abandoned the idea. The notion of a club for actors was then proposed. Mr. Aldrich with a peculiarly happy inspiration suggested its name, "The Players," and the general plan of the organisation was gradually outlined. Curiously enough the whole thing was based upon the name. The idea was so good that Mr. Booth felt he could not let it pass, and upon the name, which became the corner-stone, was the edifice erected. By no other name could it have smelled so sweet in the donor's generous nostrils; and if Mr. Aldrich had not thought of a name for it before it was thought of itself, The Players perhaps would never have existed; and Booth's beneficence would perhaps have taken some other form. After our return to New York in the autumn a number of Booth's friends were taken into his confidence,—Augustin Daly, Mr. A. M. Palmer, among the managers; Mr. Joseph Jefferson, Harry Edwards, Florence, Mr. John Drew, James Lewis, John A. Lane, among the actors; Mr. Brander

Matthews, Mr. Mark Twain, among the writers; General Sherman, Judge Joseph F. Daly, Mr. Stephen H. Olin, Mr. Charles E. Carryl, among the sympathisers with the stage; and so by them The Players was inaugurated early in January, 1888. Prominent persons in all the kindred professions were nominated as members. The house No. 16 Gramercy Park was purchased by Booth and at his expense it was almost entirely rebuilt under the direction of Mr. Stanford White, one of the original Players. And on the first Founders' Night, the 31st of December, 1888, he transferred it all to the Association, a munificent gift absolutely without parallel in its way. The pleasure it gave to Booth during the few remaining years of his life was very great. He made it his home. Next to his own immediate family it was his chief interest, care, and consolation. He nursed and petted it as it nursed and petted and honoured him. He died in it. And it is certainly his greatest monument.

As he passed away on that sad June night all the electric lamps in the Club House were suddenly extinguished. And we, at The Players, are still in darkness.

The sudden death of Lawrence Barrett was a great shock and a great surprise to Booth. His friend had recovered from the serious operation performed a year or two before and he was seemingly in robust strength, likely long to outlive Booth, who was beginning to become conscious of his own physical decay. They were playing together a successful engagement in New York when Barrett was taken ill one night and was obliged to leave the theatre before the close of the performance. The next night he did not appear and the third night his name was taken out of the bill. Booth, who had no thought of anything serious, asked Mr. Bromley, the manager, to call at the Windsor Hotel and see how " Lawrence was getting on." An hour later Booth was sitting at his supper of bread and milk in the grill-room of The Players when Mr. Bromley entered and said, simply and seriously, " Mr. Barrett has gone." Booth, still suspecting nothing, asked, " Where to?" supposing that Mrs. Barrett had carried her husband off to their home in Boston. He was naturally very much depressed for some time. Indeed, he never fully recovered from the blow. He closed his theatre at once, although he continued the salaries of his company; and finally he played a short engagement in Brooklyn, which proved, as so many of his friends feared it would prove, to be his last.

CHAPTER IV

Joseph Jefferson—Lawrence Barrett—Lester Wallack—Henry J. Montague—"Billy" Florence—John McCullough—Mrs. Keeley—Mrs. Maeder.

IN the spring of 1903, Mr. Jefferson wrote to me:

" MY DEAR LAURENCE:

" When John L. Sullivan, the prize fighter, heard of the death of Edwin Booth, he exclaimed: ' It's a great loss; there are a damned few of us left.'

" This is why I address you as ' Dear Laurence,' and why I would have you address me as ' Dear Joe,' because ' there are a damned few of us left.' I have made a contract with Tom Aldrich to do the same. So many old friends have gone on the long journey that it is pleasant to me to hear myself called ' Joe.'

" Mrs. Jefferson joins me in regards to yourself and Mrs. Hutton.

" Sincerely yours,

"JOE."

Mr. Jefferson is distinguished, as are a good many men of distinction, by his absolute forgetfulness of the names of the many men with whom, in his long career, he has been brought in personal contact. He knows faces—or thinks he does—but it is very difficult for him to apply the appellation to which the face belongs. As he himself says:

"Everybody knows 'Tom Fool,' but how can 'Tom Fool' be expected to know everybody?"

He is fond of telling how, on one occasion, he had a little business to attend to on the top floor of one of the very tall buildings in the lower part of New York City. Entering the descending elevator he found a certain man who greeted him cordially, with whose face he was perfectly familiar but whose name he could not remember. He was peculiarly struck by the fact that the stranger was a stranger to no one else in the car; that everybody looked upon him with a certain respect; and that he was smoking a very strong and black cigar contrary to the printed rules before him. Mr. Jefferson noticed, also, that neither the stranger's hat nor his boots were brushed; that his clothes were not particularly well cut nor well made; and that at the bottom of his trousers hung certain tape strings with which his unmentionable underclothes should have been tied, but which had got loose and were dragging at his heels. He said:

"Mr. Jefferson, you don't remember me?"

"Oh, yes, I remember you perfectly. The last time I saw you was in the far West. We had some talk, but I—really—can't recollect your name."

The stranger said:

"I am General Grant!"

"And then," I asked Mr. Jefferson, when he told me the story, " what did you do then, sir?"

He replied, with the famous little twinkle of his eye: " Why, I got out of the car at the next stop and walked down four flights of stairs for fear I'd ask him if he had ever been in the War!"

Mr. Jefferson said to me once:

" You told me about your magazine articles on the three Italian cities and about the pleasure you had in writing them. You said they were coming out in the Magazine (*Harper's*)—but I have never seen them."

I replied:

" They will appear, Mr. Jefferson, some time during the coming spring."

" But you finished them at least a year ago! Do you mean to tell me that you writing-fellows have got to wait so long for your round of applause? Why, if we acting-fellows don't get a 'hand' when we make our point, we feel that our point is n't made; and we can't understand your sitting for so long a time without knowing, by visible demonstration, whether you've made your hit or not."

A letter dated July 5th, of the same year, was written by him from Buzzard's Bay:

" I regret that I did not know in time that you were taking a trip to England . . . Well, our glorious Fourth of July is over and, thank God, all of my grandchildren are still in possession of their fingers and eyes.

I am fairly patriotic, but I look upon the lively firecracker as an invention of the devil.

"You may sweep up the *débris* as much as you will,
But the scab of the cracker will hang round it still.

" You are sure to see Sir Henry [Irving]. Tell him, if you will, that he is remembered here with much affection and give him my love and respect. I hope that he and I will act together in the other world if not in this.

" And on that last day when we leave those we love
And move in a mournful procession,
I hope we'll both play star engagements above,
For I'm sure they'll 'admit the profession.'
For myself, when I knock at the gate with some fear,
I know that St. Peter will say:
'Walk in, Young Comedian, and act with us here,
But for heaven's sake, get a new play!'

" Ever thine,

"JOE."

Eminently characteristic of Mr. Jefferson's quaint and ready humour was his identification of me at an hotel in Boston. We had arrived at the establishment late one Saturday afternoon; the banks and banking houses were closed; and most of my friends were scattered among the suburbs or at the far end of the town when I discovered that I had not money enough in my pocket to carry me over Sunday; and I asked the clerk of the hotel if he would not cash a check. He said that it was entirely against the rules of the establishment to pass out any money to a man who was not personally known. That, while he had no doubt that my check was a good one, he would lose his situation, even if the draft were honoured. All that was necessary was a personal identification.

At that moment I saw Mr. Jefferson in the lobby and asked if his word would be enough. The reply was emphatically in the affirmative. So I told the genial comedian what the trouble was, and what I wanted him to do. He put his arm over my shoulder and marching up to the cashier's desk, remarked, "I don't know who Laurence says he is, but he's the man!"

Lawrence Barrett, in 1879 or in 1880, wrote *The Life of Forrest* for "The American Actor Series," of which I was the editor. Barrett wrote rapidly, fluently, and eloquently, but very indistinctly and very illegibly. As he travelled about, filling his professional engagements, he sent to me the manuscript of the work chapter by chapter; and by me his "copy" was deciphered and recopied for the printers. One particular paragraph about Forrest's "red-handed democracy"—he was a Democrat in politics—seemed to me to have no meaning. Barrett, then in the far South, was asked by letter to explain it. He replied in a joking way that he could *not* explain it; that it was not his business to explain anything or to make clear what he had written; that such things were solely in the province of his editor. Even when he reached New York and saw his own manuscript he could not interpret the sentence. Finally he was asked to read aloud the entire paragraph that he might gather from the context what he really intended to say; and lo, his "red-handed democracy" was discovered to be his "all-powerful rival Macready!"—the only self-evident letter being the final "y" which is common to both readings.

Barrett was absolutely and entirely self-educated and self-made. He came of simple, plain, honest Irish parents and he was never ashamed of them or of the facts of his birth. He never pretended to be anything more than he was; and he was always ready to speak of his early struggles and disadvantages. A report that his real name was "Larry Brannigan" annoyed him beyond measure. How it originated he never knew, but it was constantly repeated in the newspapers all over the country and no denial on his part could suppress the falsehood. When a *History of the Albany Stage* published the mis-statement, he wrote to the author a dignified letter explaining the matter, and a correction and apology were made at once.

His father, as he often told me, was Patrick Barrett, an Irish emigrant who never rose very high in the social scale. His mother was a hard-working woman, whom he never forgot, and of whom he always spoke with the greatest affection and regard. He was a seven-months' child, with a preternaturally large head which was so heavy that he could not walk until he was quite a lad. He often told his friends and never with the slightest sentiment of shame how his mother wiped the suds from her arms and left her wash-tub to carry him to the little school where he was taught his letters; coming back for him and carrying him home again when the proper time arrived. His father seems to have been a very severe man; and when the lad was ten years old, very slight and frail, he ran away from home, concealing himself under the seat of the "buggy" of a travelling cattle-dealer and not discovering himself until it was too late to send him back. He found employment in a hotel in a Western city and later he became call-boy in a Western theatre. Here he made friends with the property-man, who gave him the ends of the unused candles, which he took to his garret and stuck into nails driven in the floor, because the lights were too short to burn long enough in the bottles which were his only candelabra. By the uncertain flame of these "dips," lying on his stomach on the carpetless planks, he studied an old copy of Webster's *Dictionary*, which formed his entire library. I have heard him tell all this to a President of the United States in the White House and in the presence of foreign Ministers and Secretaries of State and their wives and daughters, as simply as if he were boasting of the claims of long descent. And to prove how familiar he was with his only juvenile book, I have heard him repeat and spell and define obsolete and obsolescent words which the very first page of that dictionary contains.

Barrett was sometimes imperious, hot-headed, impulsive, quick to anger, often unjust; but he was

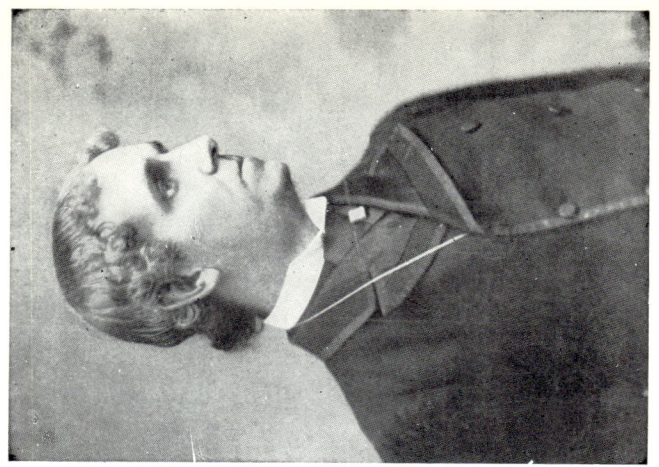
LAWRENCE BARRETT

MRS. G. H. GILBERT

always ready to confess himself in the wrong and to make amends. For years I saw much of him in his own family circle and in mine, at home and abroad, in Paris, London, in Cohasset, in Boston, and in New York, but I saw very little in him that I could not respect and admire. We had but two approaches to a quarrel and each of them very quickly came to naught. In the beginning of our acquaintance Barrett wrote something in his *Forrest* which, as the responsible editor, I could not accept. The author resented what seemed to him to be an unwarranted interference with his manuscript and, after some correspondence, I went to see him in Baltimore where he was then playing. The matter was talked over at breakfast on the morning of my arrival. The editor insisted upon the removal of the obnoxious paragraph; the author insisted upon its retention. He was firm; I was equally firm. He said he would print the chapter exactly as it stood or he would not print it at all. I was sorry, very sorry, but I could not comply. Barrett threw the manuscript upon the table with an impatient exclamation and walked towards the window in suggestive silence. In a moment he came back to where I was sitting, equally silent, and with a half-smile on his face he said, simply: "Old Cassius still!"—held out his hand to me, tore up the disputed pages, and never alluded to the matter again.

He often used to say that there was a great deal of the character of Cassius in his own composition; and that because he *was* Cassius he felt that he played Cassius better than any other part. Mr. Millet's portrait of Barrett as the lean and hungry Roman conspirator has, by the way, a curious history. It was painted in New York and it was exhibited in the Royal Academy in London, where it received no little praise. Barrett proposed to present it to the Garrick Club, of which he was a member (this was long before The Players came into existence), but, as it was being transferred from Burlington House to what was intended to be its final home in Garrick Street, London, it mysteriously disappeared and has never been seen nor heard of since and its present whereabouts have never been traced. The original study for it, a small sketch in oils given to me by the painter many years ago, is still in my possession and is all that is left of the portrait which Barrett intended to be his monument in the Westminster Abbey of British Players.

Towards the very close of Barrett's life came our second serious disagreement. He was dining with us one Sunday evening when he made some severe strictures upon a certain clergyman of New York of whom personally he knew nothing, but whom for some unexplained reason he did not like. I replied at length: "I wish you would not say these things, Lawrence,— they hurt me. The Doctor was a very good friend to me when I most needed friends, and when you were far away. He came to me at the time of the mother's death, although I had no claim upon him whatever, and he was everything that a friend and a clergyman could have been. He buried the mother and I cannot bear to hear you speak of him as you do!"

The subject was dropped at once; but the next morning Barrett called to express his sincere sorrow for his thoughtless remarks. This was the last time he entered our doors. I saw him on the Wednesday of the same week, two days before his death, in his own room at the Windsor Hotel in New York, where he was peculiarly happy and well. He was looking over the settings and designs for the costuming of a new play with Mr. Edward Hamilton-Bell, a native of England. It chanced to be the 17th of March, St. Patrick's Day, and whenever a regiment of soldiers or a benevolent society passed under his window playing the *Wearing of the Green* or some other national Irish air, he would jump to his feet, clap his hands, and shout "Old Ireland forever!" or "Those are the boys to make England quail." He was taken ill that night at the theatre. When I called on the Friday evening to ask about him, he was too ill for me to see him, and he died quietly on his wife's breast before morning. The object of my visit on that Wednesday had been to get him to ask permission from the family of General Sherman to add the death-mask of the old soldier to my collection.

Barrett was a man of very warm and tender affection. Entire harmony existed between him and his family and it was very beautiful to see them together. His affection for and devotion to my mother touched me always as it touched her. He spoke of himself invariably as "One of her boys." Many years her junior he kissed her respectfully and affectionately as they met and parted. He held her hand if by chance they sat together at table or elsewhere ; and of all the letters which came to me at the time of her death none was more tender and sympathetic than Barrett's. The last time she left the house she went to see him play *The Man o' Airlie*, and when after the performance he entered the box he had reserved for her, she handed him to wear in his dress of the character a large silver Scottish brooch on which she had had engraved—"To the Man o' Airlie from the Boy's Mother and the Boy." This brooch, given to me by Mrs. Barrett after her husband's death, is now one of my most cherished possessions. The filial love which Barrett felt for my mother he transferred in a fraternal and, of course, in a less demonstrative way to my wife. He seemed to feel that we belonged to him somehow, and that somehow he belonged to us. He spoke to us in the freest and most confidential manner about his own affairs, personal and professional. We went to see him in Boston very soon after the severe operation for glandular swelling was performed. He was propped up carefully in his bed and he was in the wildest of good spirits at the result, which was entirely successful as he thought, but which we and one or two more of his intimate friends knew was of temporary value only. He told how he had prepared himself for the operation, how he had dreaded it, how he had braced himself up to meet it, how he had met it, how the anæsthetics were applied, how he imagined that they had had no effect until some time afterwards he had found himself in his wife's arms and was told that it was "all right." "And then," he said, "I just put my head on Mollie's [Mrs. Barrett's] bosom and cried like a baby." To those of us who had been told that the trouble would return and ultimately kill him, perhaps in year or two, all this self-congratulation of his was very pathetic. Happily he did not learn the truth and he died suddenly of pneumonia, never realising that the end was near. O for the blessing of the sudden death, against the dangers of which the Churchmen pray!

Barrett and I were in London together one summer when Mrs. Frank Millet was delivered there of a son. The child was to be named " Lawrence" and we went with Mr. Millet to the vestry house of St. Mary's, Kensington, in which parish the child was born, to register the birth. The parish-clerk was a little man, slightly deformed and partly deaf; and we found him perched upon a high stool before a high desk, and with absolutely no experience of the world outside his own parish and the parish work. The usual questions were asked and answered, and finally the name of the child.

"Lawrence," said the father.

"L-a-w-r-e-n-c-e," said Barrett, spelling the word at

length in his most formidable high tragedy voice and with a very strong accent on the " w."

"Pardon me," said I, "L-a-u-r-e-n-c-e, if you please," with the accent on the "u."

"L-a-*w*," shouted Barrett.

"L-a-*u*," insisted I.

And the poor little official laid down his quill-pen in inexpressible amazement. What seemed to him an actual fight was imminent. Such a condition of things he had never experienced or dreamed of before. He felt that such a scene had never occurred in any parish house in all England since the days of the Protectorate, and what it all meant he could not comprehend. Barrett still demanded the "*w*" (his own spelling of the name), I as urgently maintained that the "*u*" must be used (as it is spelled in my name). The clerk was on the point of fainting or calling the police, when Mr. Millet in his quiet way came to the rescue.

"It appears to me," he exclaimed, "that in a case of this kind the father of the child should have something to say. I never interfered with the naming of any of your babies, did I?" Then turning to the clerk, he said, "Spell him with a ' v.' "

And La*v*rence Millet he is by law to this day.

With Barrett and James R. Osgood, the publisher, a dear friend to us both, I spent a very happy week once at Maidenhead on the Thames. We engaged a sitting-room and three bedrooms in a pleasant little inn and thoroughly enjoyed the rest and quiet. On the morning of our arrival our little parlour was invaded by a wild-eyed, queer-mannered personage who played on our piano, although he was informed that the room was private, and who did other offensive and familiar things. Barrett finally ordered him out in his very severest tone and rang the bell to complain to the landlord. The frightened and apologetic waiter informed us that the intruder *was* the landlord, who had had a sunstroke and was not responsible for his actions. Sorry for our brusqueness, Barrett and the rest of us went out upon the lawn after luncheon to make amends to the harmless creature whom we saw busily employed there. As we approached him we discovered that he was twirling around his head a long, heavy, sharp-pointed crowbar, with which, he told us, he was trying to see how near he could come to hitting a certain rose-bush across the bit of lawn. He asked us to join him in his cheerful game. But we scattered as silently and as quickly as possible in every direction except the direction of the rosebush, to join each other an hour later on the banks of the river half a mile away.

During this same season, in the summer or autumn of 1884, while Barrett was playing an engagement at one of the London theatres, I dropped into his dressing-room after an evening's performance and together we went to a theatrical club—the "Green Room," I think —for a bit of supper. We found ourselves seated at a large table, one on each side of Lord Houghton, who presided in an informal way over the symposium. He was then in the last years of his life, garrulous, feeble in body, but perfectly clear in mind. He was in a reminiscent mood that night and he told many stories of the stage as he remembered it in the days of his youth. Most interesting to his two immediate neighbours was his talk until Barrett finally asked which actor, take him all in all, he thought was the greatest he had ever seen; expecting him to reply "Kean," perhaps, or "John Philip Kemble," and thereby evolving a fresh stream of recollections. But he said, "I remember asking Sam Rogers once that very question, and hearing him declare that nobody *he* had ever seen could begin to compare with David Garrick!"

This was startling indeed. There were we drinking in the words of a man who knew the Rogers who had seen Garrick play; and Garrick had died over a century before. And then, to go even further back, Garrick no doubt had seen Barton Booth; Booth was familiar with Betterton; Betterton was in Davenant's company; and Davenant was, perhaps, the son of Shakespeare! We were ourselves a link in a chain only seven links distant from Shakespeare himself.

Barrett, particularly, was enormously impressed. It was the passing along of the famous handshake, in his own case. There were only half a baker's dozen of men between him and the Immortal Dramatist, the Greatest Giant of them all. He was very fond of telling the story, saying sometimes that it was too good to be true.

It *was* too good to be true. Rogers may have seen Garrick, for he was sixteen when Garrick quitted the stage of life, but he never saw Garrick play; and he has told us so himself. In his *Table Talk* there is an account of Garrick's last public appearance as an actor; of the universal sensation the event of his farewell created; of the lad Rogers standing for long hours in the line of patient waiters for admission at the entrance to the pit; of the greatness and the good-humoured roughness of the enthusiastic crowds; and of the boy's very bitter disappointment when the doors were opened to find his poor weak little body hustled out of its place and to find himself left crushed and disheartened in the street without even a glimpse of the inside of the house. He lingered long enough to catch a murmur of applause. That was something. And then he went sadly home.

I never had the heart to tell Barrett that his golden chain was broken. And he has gone now to solve the great problem and, I hope, to meet Shakespeare and Garrick and Rogers face to face.

When Lester Wallack retired from the stage he was asked to write his reminiscences and he consented on the one condition that I should be his editor. The task was not to my liking and I hesitated for some time, finally consenting, at his own and his publisher's urgent request. The old actor took a little suite of apartments in Thirty-fourth Street, New York, so as to be near me, and during the long winter I spent three nights a week in his room. It was discovered in the beginning that he had not put a word to paper, was too feeble to write, and that he had but a vague notion of what he was to say. A stenographer was employed to set down everything that Wallack uttered. I prompted the old actor with a judicious question now and then; and his talk with an old and sympathetic playgoer was as entertaining as any to which I ever listened. But unluckily very much of it could not be transcribed, not because it was improper in any way, but because it could not be used as literature. After each evening the stenographer read his notes and made a type-written copy of what I wished him to preserve. These, after I had gone through with them, were sent to Wallack for final revision. He read and corrected the first article in proof but he died before the second was printed. Fortunately he had dictated enough material for three papers in *Scribner's Magazine*. These I prepared for the press and printed later in book form with an introductory Memoir of Lester Wallack.

I very soon learned to like "The Governor" as he was called on his own stage and in his own family; and I am glad to think, from our personal intercourse and from the few letters he wrote, that the feeling was mutual. His wife, and sometimes his sons and their wives, were present on these evenings; and Mrs. Wallack offered many useful and valuable suggestions as to what he should say concerning his experiences, early

Not exactly to Mrs Hutton

Thy husband's blessed and hath impart
Some pangs to view her happier lot,
But let her not know — Oh. know my heart
Would hate him if he loved thee not.

Lester Wallack. Nov 17th 1887

"I count my life as nothing
else is happy; as in a soul,
remembering my good friend."

Irving. 1887 Nov 28

WALLACK AND IRVING PAGE IN THE HUTTON GUEST-BOOK

and late. He had a sincere affection and respect for his father's memory, and he told many stories of the elder Wallack's life off the stage and on. His great trouble —or his editor's great trouble—was his love for lords; and he was too fond of dwelling on what his father had said to the Duke of Wellington or to the Marquis of Something, to the exclusion of his father's conversation with Elliston or Kean or the other nobility of the stage.

One night, I remember, he had sent us a card for his box at the old theatre, then "Palmer's," at Broadway and Thirtieth Street, to see a revival of *London Assurance*. He had been present at a previous performance and he spent an entire evening in telling how the older actors used to play their parts; giving admirable imitations of all the Dollies and Lady Gays and Sir Harcourts he had known or with whom he had played. Not a word of what he said, of course, could go into the book; but no better talk ever went up a chimney to be lost for ever.

He had a sincere affection for Harry Montague and they were much together. When Montague suddenly died in California, Wallack telegraphed to Mrs. Mann, in London, asking as to what disposition should be made of the body, then on its way to New York. Mrs. Mann — Montague's mother — cabled in reply, "You have been good enough to my boy in life; and I would like him to lie by your side in death." He was buried in the family plot of the elder Wallack in Greenwood. Lester himself rests in the same enclosure.

Wallack's last letter to me is rather pathetic. It is dated April 28 (1888):

"MY DEAR HUTTON:

"If you can look in on me a couple of hours, before your luncheon time to-morrow, we can go through regularly what is already done with a view to the magazine articles. If you cannot come to *me*, I will limp to *you*. Yours always,

"LESTER WALLACK."

I went to him. But very often during those months, in his feeble way, he limped to us; always welcome and always cheerful and lovable. He died in his country home a few months later.

Henry J. Montague was a man of unusual personal charm, off the stage and on. He was sympathetic, gentle, and "sweet,"—a womanly man in a way without being at all unmanly; and he was as popular with men as with the other sex. One Sunday night at Delmonico's, then on the corner of Fifth Avenue and Fourteenth Street, New York, during the first run of the *Shaughran*, he bet dinners for the party that he would the next night whistle the then topical song of the day—*Captain Jenks of the Horse Marines*—instead of *The British Grenadiers*, which the part demanded. We all sat in front and when the young officer crossed the stage at the proper time he gave us a queer little glance and whistled,—*The British Grenadiers!* He confessed afterwards that he had lost his bet voluntarily and for two reasons. In the first place he wanted a chance to pay back some of the hospitality of which he had been the recipient here; and in the second place Mr. Wallack, his manager, had treated him with such uniform kindness and courtesy that he did not feel like taking even so small a liberty upon Mr. Wallack's stage. His last spoken words were curiously prophetic and suggestive: "Ring down the curtain!"

William J. Florence I knew very well and liked very much. Everybody liked "Billy" Florence. His handsome face and his winning smile were absolutely irresistible. In my *Plays and Players* and elsewhere in print I had written something about his dramatic career, and what I wrote was pleasing and gratifying to him. I remembered him from his earliest experiences as an actor. I had watched him closely; I had seen nearly everything he ever did; and as I said of him at the time of his death, I knew of no man on the English-speaking stage who did so many things so well. His versatility was very remarkable and, although he was in nothing great, he was in all things good.

Florence's last joke was one of his best and was also peculiarly pathetic and prophetic. He arrived in New York from Boston at the close of an engagement there and on his way to Philadelphia. At the Fifth Avenue Hotel, where he always stopped, he was told that the barber who had shaved him for many years had died that Sunday morning and was to be buried the next afternoon. Florence's professional engagements would not permit him to attend the funeral, but he would like to do something to show his respect for Fritz and his sympathy for Fritz's family. The boys in the shop had subscribed for a floral tribute and had raised twenty-three dollars for the purpose. "Here are twenty-seven more," said Florence; "make it something handsome!" As the largest contributor he was asked before he left town to suggest an appropriate motto to be fixed in purple violets across the enormous mass of white roses which had been ordered for the occasion; something which everybody would understand, and which Fritz himself would have liked Without a moment's hesitation the actor said "Next!" and the word was accepted and adopted.

"And alas!" said Mr. Jefferson, as he was once telling the story, "poor Billy himself was the next to answer the familiar call!"

He was taken ill in his hotel in Philadelphia at the end of that same week, and died there in the course of a few days. Mrs. Kendal, who was with him during his illness, has told in private many of the particulars of it. He had been in the habit of telegraphing to Mrs. Florence wherever he or she might be, if they chanced to be separated on a Sunday. That last Sunday he worked himself into a fever over the cable message which was to be sent to his wife in London. He did not wish to alarm her, but he knew how ill he was and he did not want to cable what was not true. He sank rapidly the next day and his only desire was that she might reach him before he went into the Awful Future alone. He prayed for her speedy arrival and for his own strength to wait; and Mrs. Kendal says that even until the end he lay with his hands folded in the attitude of prayer, crying almost inarticulately, "O God, keep me until she can come!" But he died before she arrived in this country.

When Florence's body was removed from the hotel to the railway station in Philadelphia, a party of working-men in their Sunday clothes asked permission to carry it through the streets. They were not known to anybody. They said simply that Mr. Florence had afforded them a great deal of pleasure and enjoyment and that they wanted to do something for him in return. Of course their request was granted.

A startling coincidence is connected with Florence's death. I had written a hurried obituary notice of him for *Harper's Weekly*, to receive which the presses were stopped for a few hours. It was to be illustrated with a portrait and with a facsimile of his autograph taken from a letter sent to Franklin Square for that purpose.

On the morning of the funeral, as I was leaving the house, a servant handed me among other mail matter an envelope which contained a note from Florence. It was signed " Yours affectionately "; it was written upon the paper of the Fifth Avenue Hotel, where he was then lying dead; and it bore the date of that very day! Of course it had been written in some previous year; but the shock, naturally, was very great.

Florence, like Booth, occasionally dropped into rhyme. In our Guest Book he wrote:

> When in after years you see
> The page I mutilate for thee,
> Let pearly tears flow fast in torrents
> At thought of yours, forever,
> FLORENCE (W. J.).

Florence was very much interested in The Players from the outset and he was greatly pleased when he was placed on the Governing Board as successor to Lawrence Barrett. He attended but one meeting. He was so full of life and spirits, said so many funny and irrelevant things, that business was greatly interrupted. Booth, who presided, said, "These two boys—Florence and Mr. Jefferson—must be separated!"

And Florence, like the good boy that he was, went over beside the Secretary of the meeting and asked if he might play with the Secretary's watch. He opened it, looked at the works, and wanted to know if he could see the picture of the wife in the locket attached. He was fully aware, however, of what was going on. He made many absolutely pertinent and sound remarks when the occasion warranted; he voted for the proper candidates; then he asked what I (the Secretary) had ever done to merit so good a watch and so good a wife; and he seconded the motion to adjourn.

He never entered The Players again.

John McCullough

I put a nickel in the slot the other day, on the leading thoroughfare of a civilised city, to hear in a phonograph "The Ravings of John McCullough," so advertised in large letters under an old lithograph of the dead tragedian. It was his voice, or a clever imitation of it, from *Virginius*, *Spartacus*, and *Brutus*, and ending each with that dreadful laugh, half insane, half idiotic, which was so distressing to those of us who knew him when his mental infirmities were beginning to make themselves evident.

It was a brutal exhibition. But, startling as it was, it brought up memories of an unusually attractive personality; and it has made me think very often since, pleasantly rather than painfully, of a man of whom I saw not a little in a social way at one time and whom I greatly liked.

I had no knowledge of McCullough's failing physical and mental powers until I met him by chance one Sunday evening in Mr. Millet's studio in New York. McCullough had come in to discuss a costume for *Virginius* which Mr. Millet was designing for him and he talked like his own self until we all walked out together, about ten o'clock. We started toward Sixth Avenue, and when he stopped his car, I said "Good-night, John," and turned to go up the street with Mr. Millet who had come out to exercise his collie dog. John—poor John,—who knew that it was not my way home, thought that I wanted to get rid of him and burst into a torrent of tears. I went with him to his hotel, he holding my hand in the street car; I stopped with him for a while in his room; finally I put him to bed as if he had been a baby and held his hand until forgetfulness came.

There were no ravings on that occasion. He spoke of his past life, professional and personal; of what it had been and of what it might have been; he told me something of his mother, of childish trials and troubles, and he asked affectionately after my mother, forgetting that she was gone. And I think he breathed a little prayer before he went to sleep.

Some time before that I found him sitting with Florence at a small table in Delmonico's *café*. I joined them, when Florence said to him: "John, this boy is going to be married. His engagement is just announced." McCullough replied that he was glad, very glad of it. He knew that I would select none but a good woman. And then he spoke as a bishop might have spoken of the ennobling influence upon any man of a good woman's love. Florence coincided with him in every point; and rarely has woman received a more touching tribute than was paid her by those two play-actors in a public restaurant.

I was told one night some years ago at a large London dinner party, that I was in great luck because I was to act as escort to one of the most beautiful and one of the most charming women in England. And I was in luck. She was everything my hostess had called her, young, lovely, brilliant, and intellectual.

SIGNATURES ON THE BACK OF A KINSMEN MENU
IRVING'S BREAKFAST TO BOOTH

But in a very few moments I forgot all about her! Seated on the other side of me was a lady to whom I had not been presented, whose name I did not hear. She was no longer young, she was no longer pretty, except for that indescribable charm which always accompanies old age; but to me she was very brilliant indeed. She turned to me suddenly and said, "New York must have changed since I saw it, sir." I told her that New York was always changing, always growing; very different had it become in all respects from the city in which I had been born and in which I had spent my early youth; and I asked how long it was since she had known New York. "Let me see," she replied, "I was playing at the Park Theatre with my husband in 1835, or was it 1836? Anyway, it was in midsummer, quite sixty years ago!" And then I knew that my great good luck had given me for a neighbour Mrs. Keeley.

She talked a good deal of New York as she remembered it at the end of all those years and she talked very freely of the American stage and of the British stage in the early days of the century then drawing to a close. She gave me her impressions of the giants whom she had seen play and with whom she had played: Edmund Kean, the elder Booth, Macready, all the Kembles; and she had many questions to ask concerning the stage life and the home life of the men and women who hold the stage to-day on my side of the Atlantic. She wanted to know all about Mr.

Jefferson, and Miss Rehan, and about Mr. Herne and his *Shore Acres;* to all of which I answered as little as possible, in my selfish desire to hear as much as I could. And I felt as if I were turning over the pages of a volume of the most delightful dramatic reminiscences possessed by the modern world.

It has been my good fortune to be able to turn over other equally interesting leaves in that great book of the dramatic past.

One "Ladies' Day" at The Players, when the place was crowded by the fair friends of the club, I was detailed by the chairman of the Reception Committee to do the honours of the house to Mrs. Maeder, a nice, rosy-cheeked, brown-haired little person of what seemed to me to be the usual age of mothers in general. She was much pleased with everything she saw; with the array of pewter mugs in the dining-room, each bearing its owner's name and many of them stamped with great names, which alas, now are only names and memoires; and with all the other objects of rich association. She was very tender and a little tearful as she stood in Booth's empty room and sat for a while in his particular arm-chair, and she spoke of him most familiarly and affectionately as she spoke familiarly and affectionately of his father. She stopped to read some of the more valuable of the autograph letters framed and hanging on the walls and she was particularly impressed by the line of old portraits in the library. She recognised at once Joseph Cowell, John Duff and Mrs

Duff, Cooper, and the rest of the older heroes and heroines of her profession; and when I said, "You seem to be familiar with all these ancient worthies, as they are pictured here, Mrs. Maeder," she replied, "Why, my son, I 'm a contemporary of most of them; I 've been on the stage myself for seventy years and I must go home soon and prepare for my part to-night."

I knew that she was the mother of Mr. Frank Maeder and that she had been an actress; but I did not realise until that moment that she was Clara Fisher—the great Clara Fisher—the most wonderfully successful and the most marvellous of infant phenomena, not even excepting Master Betty, in the whole history of the drama; the Clara Fisher whose own history I had written years before and in the past tense; the "Little Clara Fisher" whose portrait as a child was among the most cherished of my dramatic prints; the Clara Fisher who had carried vast audiences by storm when James Madison was President of the United States and when George III. was King of England; the Clara Fisher who had won all hearts; the Clara Fisher whose name was given to steamboats, and to brands of cigars, and to bonnets, and to neckties long before the fathers and mothers of many of us had the faintest idea what neckties or bonnets were.

Concerning her some local poet wrote, upon her first arrival in New York, in 1827:

> A charming young Fisher a-fishing has come
> From the land of our fathers, her sea-circled home.

She uses no lines, and she uses no hook,
But she catches her prey with a smile and a look.

She caught her prey with the same instruments almost seventy years later.

I was not permitted to monopolise Mrs. Maeder on that occasion. The knowledge of her appearance soon spread over the club, and she was the queen of the afternoon. Every person who had ever heard of her was eager to be presented to her and she began to realise, she said, "the sweet pleasure of not being quite forgotten." Mr. Jefferson, whom she knew as a baby, bowed low over her dear old hand; and Mrs. Drew embraced her heartily. I said, "Here comes another contemporary of yours, Mrs. Maeder; here's Mrs. Drew."

"My son," she cried, with a little laugh,—"my son, I was on the stage before your Mrs. Drew was born!"

And then she turned and kissed on the cheek Mrs. Drew's granddaughter, who was herself on the stage.

CHAPTER V

Imaginary "Copy"—Dramatic Criticism—Letters to *The Evening Mail*—The Funeral of Henry Kingsley—"Mothers in Fiction"—Presentation Copies—Author's Readings—The Professional Critic—Trials of the Literary Life.

MY connection with *The Evening Mail*, slight as it was, naturally brought me into contact with the members of its regular staff, including such men as Major J. M. Bundy, the Managing Editor; Mr. R. R. Bowker, the Literary Editor; and Mr. Bronson Howard, the Dramatic Critic; and I began to write by degrees for the paper all sorts of things upon all sorts of subjects. I attended all important "first nights" at the theatres, noticed books, collected local items, went to fires, and once I assisted in the invention of a peculiarly horrible murder. A "stickful" was wanted by the compositors. A "stickful" is the shop-name for as much type as can be contained in a "composing-stick." It naturally varies in quantity of words according to the size of the type but in space it measures a little more than the length of the palm of a man's hand. Nothing was ready; nobody had a stickful of poetry, literary news, or of anything else, and the murder was devised and invented. Each man contributed some item and

Bundy wrote it all out. The extreme suburbs of Hoboken, New Jersey, were selected as the place; the time was the early morning of that very day; the victim was a hard-working, harmless, worthy wife and mother; the perpetrator was a burly, brutal German called Isaac Ousenblatt, the name being an inspiration of my own. Of course the whole thing was what is called "a fake." There was no murder, there was no victim, there was no Isaac Ousenblatt. But the "Ousenblatt Murder" was reported in the journals of the next morning; its horrors were intensified; it was telegraphed all over the country; and it even came back to America in the "exchanges" from the other side of the Atlantic. So far as the *Mail* knew, the story was never contradicted nor denied. And it has entirely destroyed my own personal belief in anything contained in the papers, no matter what their colour may be.

The next important "fake" I perpetrated was an elaborate operatic criticism. I was "assigned" seats at the Academy of Music, the historical old building on Fourteenth Street and Irving Place. It was to be an ordinary performance and the ordinary "stickful" was requested; a list of the notables present rather than any comment upon the performance or the performers. When I arrived at the door I was saluted by placards stating that the *prima-donna* had the traditional sore-throat, that the bill was changed, and that Signorina Somebody would make her first appearance upon the lyric stage. The importance of the occasion was

LAURENCE HUTTON IN THE "MAIL" DAYS

recognised and the fact that it would give the reporter a chance, perhaps, to get ahead of the other men. An elaborate "Book of the Opera" was bought—score and all—I did not understand a word or a note of it, but that made no difference. I haunted the lobbies, picking up an idea here and there. I besieged my musical friends in the stalls and in the boxes for their impressions. I wormed some sort of a biography of the young *débutante* from a friend of her father; I set down certain technical phrases, as "the second number," "symphonetic," "variety and mastery of expression," "leading themes," "artistic simplicity." I remember saying that "she was a little sharp at the pitch in the beginning, but that she soon overcame the tendency"—whatever that means,—and the result was half a column of sapient wisdom upon a subject concerning which the writer was absolutely and helplessly ignorant. It is recorded that the *débutante*—this was her first and only appearance in anything like a leading part—bought many copies of that evening's paper to send to her friends and that she still preserves it in her scrap-book as the most appreciative and intelligent criticism she ever read.

Such is modern journalism!

Apropos of this it may be confessed that one of the most exhaustive and most comprehensive dramatic notices ever produced was written by my successor on the paper, a young college graduate who had never seen the play before—the play was *Hamlet* and Booth was the Dane—and who had never even read it except in a fragmentary way as it appears in Bartlett's volume of *Familiar Quotations*. Booth did not preserve the article. I doubt if he read it; but the "juvenile" who played Osric and the "old comedian" who played Polonius told me afterwards that the new man understood his business and knew what he was about! The new man later went on to a morning paper and wrote an elaborate notice of a performance which never took place. This brought his career as dramatic critic to an abrupt conclusion. But he was subsequently very successful as a critic on art and as the "Horse Editor" of a daily in Boston. And he died, literally, in harness, years ago.

In my own notices of current dramatic productions more attention was paid to the new players than to the old and I have given to not a few men and women now standing on high ground in their profession the first words of praise they ever received in print. There was nothing new to be written about Wallack's Young Marlow or Gilbert's Old Hardcastle, about Booth's Hamlet or David Anderson's Ghost; but I am glad to think that I saw a good deal of promise in the Diggory of Mr. E. M. Holland and in the Second Gravedigger of Mr. Owen Fawcett and said so, long before any other critic thought them worthy of a line or a word. I recognised the merits and the great possibilities of Miss Clara Morris when she first appeared in a comparatively unimportant part; and when the almost unknown Mrs. G. H. Gilbert played Hester Dethridge in a dramatisation of *Man and Wife*, I prophesied that there had come to us one of the best " old women " the American stage had ever known. The good in play and player was looked for rather than the bad. The desire was to encourage rather than to dishearten—it is much easier to censure than to commend—and, except in cases of indefensible incompetence, indifference, or indecency, silence was maintained rather than damnation or condemnation. This may not be the essence of criticism but it is the spirit of the moral law.

During those *Mail* days I became a man of comparative leisure. Somewhat broken in health, after bearing the burden of that awful load of hops, the father's death had left me modestly, but comfortably, independent in the matter of income, with time on my hands to write a little and to read a great deal. I realised how seriously I had neglected my opportunities in my school-days, and I tried to make up for it by reading everything in a serious vein which came within reach. I had an omnivorous taste; but I preferred history, biography, and autobiography, which, as having man for a subject, I felt to be the proper study of an ignorant member of the genus mankind. *Plutarch's Lives* was the opening chorus; Johnson's *Lives of the Poets*, Pepys, Boswell's *Johnson*, Crabb Robinson, Lockhart's *Scott*, Cumberland's *Memoirs*, Madame D'Arblay, Talfourd's *Lamb*, Moore's *Byron*, and the like, followed in due course; and thereby was made the acquaintance—more or less familiar—of men worth knowing, and of books worth reading.

My mother and I went abroad every summer, making London our centre of travel and seeing something new of the British Isles and of the Continent each year. One season it was the English and the Scottish lakes, the next Holland, perhaps, or Switzerland. The month of August was usually spent upon the large estate of an uncle in Fifeshire, Scotland, and from all these places were written regular weekly letters to the *Mail*. A series of articles upon "Scottish Farm Life" occupied some months. The different grades of agricultural existence, from the Squire who leased land, through the Laird who worked his own land, and the tenant-farmer who tilled the acres rented from the Squire, down to the cotter who worked for yearly wages, were shown. How the labourers were engaged and housed and paid, so much in cash, so much in coals, so many bowls of meal, and so many quarts of milk, *per diem;* how they were cared for when they were ill; the length of their hours of toil; and what happened to them when they were born or married or died,—were all set down. It is a patriarchal existence, slow, but usually sure, and not unhappy. And it is entirely different from the life in rural sections in newer parts of the world. The social line is very strictly drawn. The cotter looks up to the tenant-farmer—who is known as the "Maister." The "Maister" looks up to the Laird; the Laird looks up to the Squire; the Squire, who belongs to the "gentry-class," looks up to the Aristocracy; the Aristocracy looks up to Royalty. And the Almighty looks down on them all!

The Squire's daughter goes to school with the "Maister's" daughter. They study the languages, the arts, and music together, in each other's school-rooms and nurseries, under the same teachers, and out of the same books, on a footing of perfect intellectual equality. But there it ends. The "Maister's" daughter may be more refined, more intelligent, more adaptable, more everything, than is the daughter of the Squire. But she is built of different clay. She recognises the fact; and she accepts it. In the case of any important local social function she will not presume to approach the girl of her own age whose drawings she has corrected and criticised the day before as though they were sisters and peers. She will not dare to sit to-day at the same table with the girl who, yesterday, after the French lesson, spread her bread and butter for her, and shared her jam.

The peculiarities of Scottish local nomenclature are as trying to the eye and to the tongue of the ordinary American visitor as are the Indian names of our own land to the average Scot.

There went one summer to this Fifeshire farm a young lady from Schenectady. Her own personal cognomen, Miss Cunningham, was familiar and easy enough; but

"Miss Cunningham of Schenectady" was beyond the Fifeshire man's powers of utterance. Schenectady to us of the States is as simple as is Albany or Troy or Baltimore; but there was not a person in all that part of the world who could spell or pronounce the word, and most entertaining to Miss Cunningham herself were the attempts at it. "Skinney-faddy" and "Skenk-ter-addy" were as near to it as the most successful of them ever came. To the Laird, particularly, it was most wonderfully perplexing and amusing. He struggled with it day and night, laughing at his own attempts and failures and wondering, in his semi-serious, semi-humorous way, how any sensible, self-respecting Christian could confess to having been born in a place that called itself like that!

In his eyes the orthographic and orthoepic beam of his own titles and appellations was entirely eclipsed by the marvellous mote known as Schenectady; and he never realised that the inhabitants of the counties of Schoharie, Cattaraugus, and Chemung in the State of New York might safely bite their thumbs at the residents of the Shire of Fife in the Kingdom of Scotland, until his eyes were opened somewhat rudely, and his sight was, in a way, restored. "Uncle John," I said to him suddenly one evening when he was in convulsions over Schenectady, "Uncle John, what is the name of your place?" "Baldutho'" ["Balduthy" in the vernacular]. "And of your parish?" "Aroncrauch" [Arron-craw]. "And of your post-office?"

THE MAISTER OF "BALDUTHO"

HENRY KINGSLEY

" Pittenweem " [pronounced as it is spelled]. "And of your railway station?" "Killconguhar" [Kill-nocker]. "And still, Uncle John," I continued, "you, as Laird of Balduthy, Elder of the Kirk of Arron-craw, receiving your letters and papers at Pittenweem, and taking your trains at Kill-nocker, think Schenectady funny!"

Some time during the sixties—I don't remember when—I was in Luzerne, Switzerland, with my mother, and had a great desire to make the ascent of the Rhigi. This was before the days of the railroad to the top of that mountain, when the travel was rough and hard, whether done on foot or on horseback, and involved a good many hours of rough journeying. I started out by a boat to the mountain's foot, with only a small grip in my hand, having arranged by telegraph for accommodation in the little hotel on the top of the mountain. On the way I fell in and foregathered with two American boys of about my own age, as boys are apt to do in a strange land, and when, after some hours of weary labour, we reached our destination we found that there was but one vacant room at our disposal and that one had been promised to each of us. It was a small room and in it was a small single bed. My two companions seemed to have the first claim to it and I was left to sleep upon the floor or upon a billiard table. However, they kindly took me in, had my cot placed in the small apartment, and after much talk we went to our rest, having missed on account of clouds the sunset we had come so far to see. The same fate met us in the early morning, when there was no sunrise visible and no view of anything, and we concluded to telegraph to our several mothers at the Switzerhof in Luzerne the fact that we would give the sun another chance. That day we spent happily together not only among the clouds but above the clouds, which kindly disappeared at the proper time so that at the next sunset and sunrise we saw, as a reward for our patient waiting, one of the most magnificent panoramas in the world.

The following morning, Sunday, we started down the hill together, happy, satisfied, pleased with ourselves and each other. When we reached the level of the lake we discovered that there was no possible boat to take us back to Luzerne for several hours. We sat about contentedly enough, when out of a little hotel in front of us quietly walked a gentleman known to me by sight and the subject, with two exceptions, of my greatest admiration among living Americans. I said:

"Why, there's General McClellan!"

My two unknown companions jumped up, rushed toward the General, who kissed them both—they were only boys—and, after some little surprised talk, took them into the house. In a few moments one of my new-made friends reappeared and said:

"The General has asked us to lunch with him and to bring you with us but we don't know your name and can't introduce you."

I told them what and who I was—not much of anybody—and I said:

"But, I have no idea of your identity."

"Oh," said my interlocutor, "I am Loyal Farragut and the other fellow is 'Bob' Lincoln."

General McClellan treated us most kindly and that was the curious beginning of my acquaintance with him, and my friendship with the sons of the two heroes who, with McClellan, I had most worshipped and revered during the whole course of the Civil War.

In a series of letters from London, subjects from grave to gay were touched upon, as occasion warranted. One entire season I dwelt among and upon the London churches, old and new; from Spurgeon, in his crowded tabernacle, to the rector of some little chapel in "The City" who read his services to a pew-opener, a beadle, a company of choir-boys, and a congregation of five or six. The latter were generally paupers dependent upon the parish and obliged to appear every Sunday under penalty of the loss of the weekly dole of a sixpence or a quartern loaf, left, in perpetuity, by some Lord Mayor, dead and forgotten in the long, long agoes. How the fashionable preachers in the West End preached, and where they preached, and to whom, was one of the themes. A beautiful Sunday was devoted to the Foundling Hospital, where little children come and are not forbidden. Pray do not miss it when you go to London next. It will move to do better and to be better even the men and women who have known no children of their own. Another Sunday was devoted to the chapel of the Charter House, the place of worship of the Poor Brethren so familiar to the friends of Colonel Newcome, where more attention was paid to the reading of the memorial tablets to Thackeray and John Leech, I am afraid, than to the reading of the Gospels or the Lessons. Do not miss that either when you go to London, if it is left intact by the Directors of the Merchant Tailors' School who reign there now.

Another summer was given up to the theatres, particularly to the theatres little known. Still another summer was spent among the coffee-houses, especially among those of literary association: " The Chapter," the home once for a very short time of Charlotte and Emily Bronté; " The Black Jack," in Portsmouth Street, so intimately associated with Mr. John Sheppard, the Highwayman, and with Mr. Joseph Miller, the wit and the player; " The Feathers," in Hand Court, Holborn, familiar to Charles Lamb; " The Salutation and Cat," in Newgate Street, now " The Salutation " only, but very little changed except in name, where Coleridge and Southey had " sat together through the winter nights, beguiling the cares of life with Poesy," and the like. Many were the letters about the squares of London, about the monuments, about the gardens, particularly about those of the Temple; about the Inns of Court and all the memories they brought up; and about such current events as the first visit of the Shah of Persia or the funeral of poor Henry Kingsley. All at seven dollars a column, not regularly paid!

It is a little disgraceful to admit that many of these letters dated in London were written in New York! Not a great deal of European news came in those days to this country by cable; distances were considered too great, and rates too high. But all the foreign exchanges were read as soon as they arrived in the editorial rooms or in the Mercantile Library; and by means of a certain topographical knowledge of the British metropolis, and a familiarity with its inhabitants and their tricks and their manners, it was not at all impossible to give a lucid account of what happened every week. The Queen's "Drawing Rooms" were described, the Lord Mayor's Show; the opening of a new playhouse; the reconstruction of an old club; a great Parliamentary debate; the crowning of a bishop; a suicide from Waterloo bridge; baby-farming; or a birth or a marriage in the Royal Family—with all the accustomed accuracy of an eye-witness— who was three thousand miles away! It is not known that anybody was deceived, but nobody was seriously harmed, and no little practice and experience were gained from it. Still at seven dollars a column!

The funeral of Henry Kingsley I attended in person, moved thereto by feelings of sincere sympathy as well as by professional reasons. I had always admired the works of the man. I still think that there are no heartier, more healthful, more cheerful out-of-door tales than *Ravenshoe* and *The Hillyars and The Burtons*, and no stories were ever more fascinating to me than are the fantastic vagaries of *Oakshot Castle* and *Number Seventeen* in which the majority of the characters are lunatics, amiable or dangerous, and in all stages of eccentric dementia.

I had never seen the man; and nothing could be learned of his nature or individuality. He was not known to the clubs of Literary Bohemia in London, and he seemed to have no friends in town. The little Kentish hamlet in which he had spent the last years of his life was two hours or more from the metropolis on a branch railway, involving many changes. While I was feeling my way to the place in the London Station, asking many questions from railway guards and booking agents, I was accosted by a stranger who said he fancied we were going on the same sad errand, and that if I would enter his compartment he would take me safely to the spot. My business and nationality were told; it was explained that the journey was not taken out of mere idle curiosity nor from a desire to earn the traditional penny-a-line, but from a spirit of pure affection for and admiration of Kingsley's literary qualities. And then it was discovered that the stranger was a near neighbour of the Kingsleys, and the owner of the interesting little old place in which Henry had lived, the Grange, whose garden was the scene of the novelist's own death and of the last tale he wrote. From this gentleman much was learned concerning the man and his life and his surroundings; and all that was learned was good and pleasant to hear and to record. It seemed that the author had put not a little of himself and of his own people in his stories. I learned upon whom the different creations were based and how far they were real and how far elaborated; and I was told that I should meet the original "Hetty," which I did.

My informant took me out of the train at a side-station; drove me, in his own dog-cart, to his own house; shared with me his luncheon; carried me to the quiet, peaceful churchyard in which Kingsley was to rest; and stood by my side as the gentle novelist was laid in his grave. I was introduced to the family doctor and to the rector of the parish, both of whom knew Kingsley well and loved him; and "Hetty" herself it was who picked and handed me the little bunch of rosemary which I laid upon the coffin—for remembrance.

I went back to London with my accidental host and we never met again. When we exchanged cards on parting at the railway terminus I read upon his, engraven, the words, "Samuel Weller, Esquire."

And thus there was a little touch of reminiscent comedy in the tragedy, after all.

I did not confine myself altogether, in those early days, to my generally accepted contributions to the *Mail*. I wrote regularly for the *Arcadian*, a weekly literary and dramatic journal, from which I received nothing in the way of remuneration or salary except as many copies of the paper as I cared to send away by post or to carry away in my pocket; with now and then, thrown in, a new book or a new edition which I had been asked to review. And I wrote essays and stories, grave and gay, which were submitted—aiming high always—to the *Harper's*, *Scribner's*, *The Princeton Review*, *Old and New*, and the like; " return-postage " enclosed. And they invariably came back with the stereotyped note of thanks and regret. It was very discouraging; and the efforts were nearly given up in despair, when a short paper entitled, " Mothers in Fiction," was printed in " The Contributors' Club " of the *Atlantic*, and gave me fresh hope. It attempted to prove that in fiction there are no mothers, to speak of, except step-mothers and mothers-in-law and unnatural mothers or mothers who die young. It gave a long list of leading characters in standard tales who were half-orphans on their mother's side, and it showed that Becky Sharp brought herself up by hand, while Topsey " just growed."

The article excited some little attention and no little consideration. " Mothers in Fiction " was discussed all over the country; and mothers, good, bad, and indifferent, whom I had forgotten or of whom I had never heard, poured in upon " The Contributor's Club " in great quantities.

The general drift of public opinion concerning the Literary Life, and concerning those who live the Literary Life, was vividly shown by a Census-taker who once interviewed me in the interests of the Government of the United States. He asked me the regular questions, all printed in regular rotation, and he inscribed my answers in a very irregular hand. He wanted to know my name, my age, the place of my birth; the names of my father and mother, and the places of their birth. He inquired the number of wives and children I had, or had had, and their names and the places of their birth. He asked if I was white or black and what was my business or occupation. To this last query I replied, with some hesitation, that I was a "Man of Letters." And without a moment's hesitation, or a sign of any change of voice or expression, he asked the next regular question, "Can you read and write?"

It was a fortunate thing, indeed, that I have never been dependent upon my pen for my daily bread. "The writer's cramp" is generally a pecuniary disease. For literary production, even for the best, the prices paid are comparatively low and the beginner works on starvation wages; being lucky, sometimes, to find wages at all. The periodical which offered me a fraction of a cent per word, in the early days, occasionally defaulted altogether or paid in orders upon advertising trades-people who had themselves defaulted. The only remuneration received for what their author considered a rather important series of articles was a suit of clothes which he did not really need and which was made by an English tailor who had not been able to pay for the publication of the fact that, in his own country, he had fitted a valet of the Prince of Wales and had also been permitted to manufacture liveries for the families of the rest of the British aristocracy. He did not seem to appreciate my patronage and he used "farmer's-satin" linings when his contract demanded silk. The collar came too high in the neck, it is remembered; one leg of the trousers was longer than the other; and he absolutely refused to renew a waistcoat button—without extra charge!

In this way I bartered my brains for a number of objects which were neither useful nor ornamental until I was offered a fireplace heater for some months of dramatic criticism — at which I struck. The heater was to be put in its place at my individual expense and I had no place in which to put it. But I enjoyed the life. And I gained in experience.

The subsequent career of some of my rejected manuscripts—then and later—is worth putting on record. One particular article, written to order for *Harper's Weekly*, was rejected in turn by every one of the Harper periodicals and by half a dozen other journals to which it was submitted. It finally appeared in *Kate Field's Washington*, when that bright but unfortunate paper started upon its brief course, and it was accepted in lieu of a year's subscription! It was a semi-traditional, semi-historical, altogether satirical effort to prove that Bacon and Shakespeare, as the sons of Queen Elizabeth, might have been half-brothers, collaborating in defence of their grandmamma, Anne Bullen, as she is portrayed in the tragedy of *King Henry the VIII*. Curiously enough it was accepted seriously and quoted almost in full by one of the editors who had refused it, and, more curiously still, it became the very cornerstone of a volume in the "American Essayist Series" published by the Harpers themselves, upon which the Harpers are still paying a generous royalty.

It may be mentioned, in passing, that the royalties on the first edition of a fairly successful book will, ordinarily, amount to a sum large enough to almost remunerate the author for what he pays for the volumes he gives to those of his friends who expect to receive and sometimes demand "presentation copies"!

With regard to royalties and presentation copies, Mrs. Kate Douglas Wiggin Riggs tells the following little story on herself.

She was reading one night in public, in some faraway and inaccessible town in what are called "the Western wilds," when she noticed in her audience a poorly but neatly clad man in the front row of seats who was watching her intently and was evidently most appreciative and profoundly moved by her own way of expressing, verbally, her own thoughts. At the close of the evening he diffidently approached her, ventured to shake her by the hand and to explain that it had been a great treat to him to hear her; that he and his wife wanted to come to the show, but it was forty miles away from home; that both of them could not leave the house and children for the necessary two days and a night of absence; and his wife had urged him, wifelike, to take the advantage of the outing and the entertainment; and he closed by saying:

"We have read, Mrs. Wiggin, all the books you ever wrote; and," he added impressively, "we've bought *one* of them!"

The calls upon the purse, and the time, of the author, in this and in other respects, are many and great. In my business days I was never asked to contribute a tub of butter to a church fair or a box of cheese to a fresh-air fund. Since my name has appeared now and then upon book-covers and at the bottom of magazine pages, I am frequently—much more frequently than my reputation would warrant—invited to write my name in the inside of a book and to present both the book and the name to a bazar for the benefit of a local charity of which I have never heard and in which I can have no possible personal or local interest. And, harder still, I am requested to prepare articles upon "The Amenities of Literature" or upon "The Higher Education of the Gentler Sex" for the entertainment of the members of a circle of Earnest Women, absolute strangers to me, who meet, fortnightly, in some distant town I have never visited and never expect to visit. For all this nothing is ever given in return. These same Earnest Women might beg a picture from a painter, a recital from a pianist, or a recitation from an actor, but they would hardly think of asking a packer for a tin of pressed beef or their favourite grocer for a pound of tea to be consumed at the fortnightly luncheon which invariably follows the intellectual symposium. And yet the cheering cup and the strengthening meat-extract cost less, last longer, and go farther than does the work of the associates of the Guild of Literature and Art.

The least objectionable of all these performances are what are called "Author's Readings." They cost the performer nothing but a little time, particularly when his expenses are paid, as not infrequently is the case; not uncommonly they tickle the personal pride and vanity which all authors are supposed to possess, and not impossibly they advertise the author and the book which he interprets. The gratuitous, contributed, original article, be it short or long, is a more serious matter. It is a donation of the author's stock in trade which takes the daily bread out of his own mouth and perhaps out of the mouths of those who are dependent upon him. He can rarely afford to give away something which has more than a real money value to him; for if he does not need the money, he needs or he thinks he needs the publicity and the reputation, even the criticism and the accompanying contentment, which are better than wealth!

The professional critic is not so great a trial to the professional author as is generally supposed. The author may have been and may still be a critic himself

—and he knows all about it. He tries to console himself with the thought that somebody once said—I think it was Dr. Johnson: "Conceive a man who has written what he hopes will live, troubling himself about a criticism which he knows will die!" Criticism is sometimes long-lived; but no matter how strong it may be at birth, it does not, except in rare instances, survive the work it commends or condemns. The critic, in return, is a favourite target for the verbal shafts of the author, who often hits the bull's-eye. But the author likes to be shot at all the same, and he would rather be struck by the sharp arrow of the professional critic and wounded in a tender part than not to be made a mark of at all. Disraeli thought that he fired with a deadly aim when he made Mr. Phœbus, in *Lothair* say: "The critics are the men who fail in literature and art"; but that was because Disraeli himself had not been very successful as a critic!

The critic who is apt to hurt the most and to hit the hardest is the domestic or the social critic; the intimate member of the family circle or the familiar acquaintance of the drawing-room or the club, who says frankly, and in what he considers so kindly a way, just what he thinks about one's work. His opinion may be of no critical value—but it hurts! If what he says is complimentary, you fancy that it is perfunctory and sometimes you imagine that it is patronising and it makes no particular impression; but if it is depreciatory you are sure he means it; you look upon it as the average view; you realise that he represents the general public; you feel that if you cannot please him you cannot please anybody else.

Shortly after I had taken charge of the department of "Literary Notes" in *Harper's Magazine* and after my name had appeared upon the cover of the periodical for a few months, I met, by chance in a street-car, a lady with whom I had had for a long time some slight acquaintance. She was a good woman who had never enjoyed the advantages of what we call "a liberal education"; and who, I supposed, never read anything but the daily papers and the signs in the streets. As she made room for me on the seat next to her, she said abruptly and *apropos* of nothing: "Me and my girls have been a readin' of them reviews of yourn. And we come to the conclusion that you done better when you writ books nor when you criticised 'em!" The diction was so peculiar that it burned itself into my memory, and it has remained there; the sentiment was so discouraging that it scarified my feelings; and I still bear the brand. I would no more have respected her *dictum* regarding the literary efforts of anybody else than I would have minded the barking of an honest dog or the whistling of the summer winds; but what she said of my own attempts nearly broke my spirit in twain. She did not even say that "I done well" when I wrote books; but she did say that "I done worse" when I criticised 'em. And it hurt!

I slept very little that night. No comforting speech

of my wife could reduce the inflammation. I repeated the words to my friends—always *verbatim*—and I pretended to laugh over them; but I was almost disheartened, and I even went so far as to tell the Harpers that I feared I had mistaken my vocation and that I would advise them to find some one in my place who could better do the work and give more satisfaction to the great reading public.

All this happened many years ago. I have "noticed" hundreds, if not thousands of books in the meantime. And I am not sure that "I done better" as I went carefully along.

In the winter of 1896-7 I prepared an article for *Harper's Magazine*, upon the personal side and upon the home-life of half a dozen popular actors, as I had seen them and had known them, during many years of intimate personal intercourse. I wanted to show to the world, which only sees the public side of him, that a man can be a good actor, and a good son, a good husband, a good father, a good friend—and a gentleman, as well!

The Players, in the olden days and in the Old World were classed in statute-books with "rogues and vagabonds." In the New World and even in the Old, to-day, they are regarded, when they so conduct themselves, as gentlemen by behaviour if not by birth. In monarchical lands any man may become a gentleman if his sovereign deigns to dub him one; in these United States of ours the only gentleman is the man who respects himself and who respects the feelings of others! Booth, Barrett, McCullough, Florence, Wallack, and Montague respected the feelings of others, and they respected themselves. And I thought the public ought to know it so far as it was in my power and in my right to make it known.

In the article in question I quoted scraps of letters and bits of conversation, generally, as was natural, addressed to me; I showed, as far as was possible and proper, the tender and the affectionate, the humorous and the pathetic nature of these men as I had seen and felt it; I tried to make my readers laugh and I tried to make my readers cry. My anecdotes were all true as I knew by observation, not by hearsay; all the incidents I related were actual occurrences in which I had played some more or less important part, as subject of their speech or deed, or as an eye-witness. My object was, simply, to present my own personal reminiscences of the friends of many years' standing, and this, as well as I could, I did.

When the paper was completed, it was submitted to the kindliest and at the same time the most justly severe of my domestic critics, the fire-tenders of my own hearth; and they pronounced it *too* personal! There was in it, they thought, too much of "me" and "mine"; too much of "I" and "myself." This I myself had feared and had tried hard to avoid. I then proceeded to cut "myself" as loose from the manuscript as possible without destroying the sense or the consequence; and when I was through with the slaughter there was almost nothing left of "mine" and of "me." " I " was eliminated; but so was everything else that would make the paper intelligible or of any worth. I knocked away my foundation and my six stories came tumbling down. There was nothing to be done but to rebuild upon a new plan, and the eight or ten thousand words were taken out of the first person and put into the third, at no small expense of time and trouble and mental strain and to the no little confusion of the persons themselves.

I told my tale, in order to make it seem natural and possible and real, as being the experiences of "A Man I Know." And I seemed to mix up the man I know with the men *he* knew in the most involved way. I went off the track entirely with the impersonal pronoun " one," always a very dangerous figure of speech. " One " recalled this and " one " recalled that, but, in the end, " one " ran away with " one " altogether. With the " him's " and the " he's " it was quite as bad, and not infrequently I myself could not tell whether "he" was Booth or Hutton, whether " him " referred to Montague or to the Man I Know!

But it was licked into something that looked to me like shape, and it was presented to the Editor-in-Chief, who said he would accept it—if I would put it in the " First Person!"

The original copy, altered and twisted out of all shape, had been destroyed as obscure beyond repair.

And an entirely new edifice had to be erected after the primeval model. I put "myself" back, but I left out some of my spirit and interest, and by the time it was finished I was heartily tired of "myself" and almost tired of my six friends—in that connection. And I feared, more than ever, that "me" and "mine" were altogether too much in the foreground, altogether too prominent.

The day the article appeared — it was called "A Group of Players, by Laurence Hutton"—I heard a friendly critic of the club-circle say, as I entered The Players' Reading-room, and evidently for my own hearing, that he had just finished a paper called "A Group of *Laurence Hutton*, by A PLAYER!"

Everybody laughed and I pretended to laugh! It was meant to be funny. It certainly was very clever. It did not mean to be cruel. But I was sure, then, that it was true.

An old ex-sailor man lay dying in his bed, one Christmas Eve, a year or two ago. He had run away to sea when he was a lad of ten; he had worked his hard way up by slow degrees from cabin-boy to captain before he was thirty; he had commanded a brig, called the *British Queen*, sailing from Dundee to New York for a decade or so; when a modest little fortune was bequeathed to him and he retired from the merchant-service, married a wife of about his own age, and settled on shore. In his eightieth year he went back to Scotland to end his days in his native land, and on that Christmas Eve he lay quietly dying—in his bed. He had not known the sea except as an occasional passenger for almost half a century; but in the supreme moment it all came back to him. He had been semi-conscious and quite silent for some hours, the trained nurses had gone off for much-needed rest, and the old captain was sleeping peacefully by the side of his old wife, his feeble old hand in hers. Suddenly he raised himself to a sitting posture, put his hand to his old grey head, pulled his forelock, and in a loud, firm voice he reported himself, in the regulation way, saying, "Come on board, Sir!" For some minutes he gave orders and obeyed them. He "manned the foretop." He "put her helm hard-a-starboard." He hauled sheets; he sang sea-songs; and then, as he fell back on his pillow, he cried "Belay all!" Turning to the old wife, his old hand again in hers, he murmured gently: "My ship's in port, Bess, but she's going out with the tide. I can't take you with me, on this voyage, Bess, but you'll find me waiting for you on the shore, Bess, when you come over!" And, so saying, he died.

The old sailor-man was my uncle, the last of his generation; the old wife—for whom on the shore he is still waiting—is my aunt. And the story is absolutely true. I have set it down here as it was written to me by my cousin, their only child, on that Christmas Day. With a broken voice—my voice always breaks over it

—I once tried to tell it to a certain warm friend of us all. He was, without meaning it, the typical representative of the amiable critic of the social circle. I added: " It seems to me to be a beautiful incident. The ' Come on board, Sir!' and the ' Belay all !' are better than the ' Here!' of Natty Bumpo, or even than the famous '*Adsum !*' of Colonel Newcome, because they are true. It is almost too touching and too sweet a story in its moral lesson to remain unuttered. Some day I 'll put it in print, I think !"

Turning on me savagely, the friendly critic said, his own voice breaking, " You writing-fellows would tear out your heart-strings to tie up a magazine article !"

The rebuke was a harsh one. But, perhaps, it was just. And it hurt. I have never ventured to tell the story, in public, but once before.

CHAPTER VI

The Collecting of the Death Masks—Benjamin Franklin—Robert Burns—Charles XII. of Sweden—Richard Brinsley Sheridan—Coleridge—John Boyle O'Reilly—Napoleon.

THE story of the collecting of the casts from life and death now in the University Library at Princeton is, to me at least, almost as curious as is the collection itself. The first of them came into my life in a purely accidental and unexpected way at which I have merely hinted in *Portraits in Plaster*—my book upon the subject,—and, for some five-and-thirty years now, they have occupied not a small portion of my life's interest and entertainment.

Walking up-town in New York one summer afternoon in the middle sixties, I noticed in a shop window near where the old and original Broadway Theatre used to stand a most grotesquely ugly image of a bulldog done in plaster. Across his pedestal was the legend "Who's afraid?" And in every lineament of his expressive countenance was written the fact that he certainly was afraid of nothing, human or canine. What struck me particularly about his appearance was his astonishing resemblance, notwithstanding his ferocity, to one of the gentlest of all the gentle old ladies of my acquaintance, an old lady known to everybody as "Aunt Jane," who trembled at the sound of her own voice and who shuddered at the sight of her own shadow.

I could not resist the temptation to buy the dog, and while he was being tied up for me a small and ragged boy entered the place and showed to the dealer the cast of a human face, brown with dust and yellow with age, saying : " Is dis wort' anything ? "

The merchant did not seem to think that it was worth anything, but to me it appeared to have a value, and I asked the vendor what he wanted for it and where it came from. Two shillings was the price of it, and for another quarter he would show me where there were a lot more !

It was unmistakably a cast of the face of Benjamin Franklin and it suggested Houdon's famous bust, although it did not seem to be a cast or a copy of that familiar and frequently copied piece of sculpture. I lost my interest in the dog and turned all my attention to the philosopher, following the boy to Second Street opposite the Marble Cemetery where, in a couple of ash-barrels, I found casts of the skulls of Burns and Bruce and of the flesh-covered head of Curran — all labelled,— and of the faces — unlabelled — of a small group of men whom I afterwards thought I had recognised as Washington, Sheridan, Cromwell, Lord Brougham, and others in various exalted walks of life.

I gave the boy the extra quarter for his discovery

and still another twenty-five cents, all in postal-currency, to find for me an express wagon on First Avenue. He came back with the empty cart of a peddler of vegetables and fruits; and I can still remember the sensation I created when I rode up to my own door in that vehicle, sitting by the coatless driver, with my *treasure-trove* — including the image of the dog — packed in cherry-crates behind me. The father, smoking his after-tea pipe, on the "front stoop," fancied that I had lost my senses or my dignity; the live terrier by his side nearly barked his head off at the sight of the sculptured bull-pup I presented to him; and the mother laughed until the tears rolled down her cheeks at the caricature of dear Aunt Jane.

The seniors of the family were, however, quite as much impressed with the acquisition as I was, if not more so; for they knew what death masks were, while I had never even heard of them. My father, who was a student of everything, had studied physiognomy in the pages of Lavater and on the faces of the men and women he met and knew; and after careful comparison with the engraved portraits in our possession we succeeded, as we thought, in identifying all the casts. I was sent the next evening to learn, if possible, the history of the collection; but that particular block on Second Street was literally lined with ash-barrels none of which I could recognise; and I was forced to ring a half-dozen basement bells, meeting with all sorts of discomforting rebuffs, before my question was answered.

Details of the Collecting

At last a sort of housekeeper or upper-servant told me gruffly enough that the master of that particular mansion had lately died; that the masks had been contained in a cabinet in his study, taking up valuable room for many years, and that the lady of the house, always hating the "nasty, ghastly things," had finally given orders to throw them away! Foolishly, as my father told me, I did not think to ask the gentleman's name or his profession; I had not the courage to face the domestic again, and I do not know, to this day, anything about the man or his business.

I gave the matter of original ownership very little thought although I gave much thought to the casts themselves for a quarter of a century. When, in 1889 or 1890, at the suggestion of Mr. James R. Osgood, I began for *Harper's Magazine* the series of articles upon which my book is based, I discovered that there was an absolute dearth of literature upon the subject of that particular form of "Portraits in Plaster"; and my reading for many months was of the most harrowing and melancholy kind, consisting, as it did, almost exclusively, of obituary notices and death-bed scenes. I pored over accounts of lyings-in-state, of post-mortem procedure, and of funeral services; studying carefully the histories of the last sad hours of all sorts and conditions of men from Ben Caunt, the prize-fighter, to Sir Isaac Newton and Frederick the Great, trying to discover if a death mask had ever been made of any of them, and if so by whom and for what purpose.

Very rarely was any allusion made to what seemed to me to be this most important of posthumous performances. The biographers told me fully and in detail who read the services, who were the pall-bearers, sometimes who was the undertaker. "Who saw him die, who dug the grave, who tolled the bell," were all carefully reported, without a word as to who made an impression of the rigid features to be handed down to posterity in exact fac-simile, perhaps the most valuable and correct of all human efforts at portraiture. I received much useful information from the contributors to the British *Phrenological Journal*, published in the thirties, when phrenology was a craze and men were supposed to be known by their bumps alone; but this information was generally of an historical character, as in the accounts, not infrequently by eye-witnesses themselves, of the exhumation of Robert Burns, of Robert the Bruce, of Henry IV. of France, or of the Twelfth Charles of Sweden. At last, in the Library of the British Museum, I came upon a volume of the printed lectures of George Combe, the phrenologist, by which I think I have solved the problem.

This work—long out of print and rarely to be met with—I have had for many years an unlimited order for it in the hands of the British and American dealers of old books — this work was illustrated throughout with rough wood-cuts of the several masks I found in the Second Street ash-barrel. These, in various positions, front face, profile, back of the head, for comparison's sake were frequently repeated. The book contained all these and none others whatever! And the inference so lately and so curiously reached must be, that the man of the cabinet and of the unsympathetic wife was a friend, or a disciple, or an assistant of Combe, who lectured in America in the winter of 1838-9, and that from Combe he had inherited the casts which came so unexpectedly into my hands and which formed the nucleus of the collection now in the Library of the University of Princeton.

While a number of workingmen, in the early part of the last century, under government supervision were making some repairs to the ruined Abbey of Dunfermline in Scotland, they dug up the skeletons of a man and a woman which, from the descriptions of the interment in contemporary records, were identified as those of King Robert the Bruce and his Queen. The bones of the King were unusually large and in an excellent state of preservation. It was seen that the ribs on the left side had been roughly hewn asunder in order to permit of the removal of his heart, which Sir James Douglas, it will be remembered, carried with him to Jerusalem as a pious and a talismanic weapon against the raging infidels. The skull naturally excited an immense amount of interest in Great Britain, particularly among the members of the Phrenological Society who chanced to be holding a meeting at that time in Edinburgh. The Crown gave them permission to make a cast of it before it was reburied; and this cast in the course of events came into the possession of George Combe.

In digging the grave of the widow of Robert Burns, who was to rest by the side of her husband at Dumfries, the skeleton of the poet was disclosed; and Dr. Blacklock, a local surgeon, was permitted to make an anatomical examination of it and to take a cast of the skull, a replica of which was given to Combe by the executors of Mrs. Burns. As I remarked in my book, it is a big head—even for a Scotchman!

The mask of Henry IV. of France was for a long time a matter of uncertainty to me. I had read in contemporary memoirs that a modeller had made a wax cast of the monarch's features immediately after his death and that this wax effigy was displayed at a public funeral, as was the custom in those days; and I knew that a plaster cast of the same dead face was made many years later when the wild Revolutionists sacked the Cathedral of St. Denis, scattered the dust of the Valois and the Bourbons to the winds, and moulded their leaden coffins into bullets with which to murder their descendants. The body of the first and the greatest of the Bourbons had been so well and so carefully embalmed that it was exhibited for a number of days to enormous crowds of curious sightseers.

The Library of St. Genevieve in Paris contains what is claimed to be the " original mask " of Henry, of which this is a copy; and it is the general expert opinion that it was not made at the time of his burial but at the time of his exhumation.

About one hundred and fifty years after his death, the body of Charles XII. of Sweden was disinterred, although in a reverent and proper manner and to satisfy a curiosity which was perhaps justifiable. Historians had differed as to whether he was shot from before or behind, by the enemy or by one of his own soldiers; and they opened his grave to see that the fatal missile had passed entirely through the King's head from left to right, and in a downward direction. In my cast the indentures are plainly perceptible, especially the larger one on the right temple. There is a much finer copy of this mask of Charles in the British Museum, bequeathed to the nation by Charles Christy, who is said to have bought it in Stockholm at the time of the sale of the effects of a famous Swedish sculptor. The museum authorities and others believe that the cast dates only from the occasion of the long-delayed post-mortem examination; but a somewhat rare engraving of it, dated 1823, states that " it was made four hours after he was shot."

The attempt to verify the death mask of Richard Brinsley Sheridan was peculiarly difficult. The cast is unquestionably from nature, and it resembles so strongly in so many facial ways the existent portraits of the author of *The School for Scandal*, particularly the later examples, that it seems to establish its own identity; but, except that it was known to Combe, I have never been able to discover any authority for its existence. Sheridan died in very miserable and painful circumstances. He was deeply in debt, and imprisonment for debt was at that time possible and frequent under the laws of the land. The sheriff's officers were in the place during his last hours; and the already unconscious but still breathing debtor narrowly escaped being carried by force to end his life in what was called a " sponging house" and in a prison bed.

Mention is made by "Tom" Moore, Sheridan's biographer, of the taking of a cast of Sheridan's right hand, but there is no allusion whatsoever to a mould of his head. This cast of the hand, in glaring plaster, was preserved for many years in the house in which the last days of his life were spent in Savile Row, London. The Savile Club, at the beginning of its existence, occupied the premises; it is a literary association, and it was fitting that the fingers which held so facile a literary pen in that spot should have been carefully and reverently portrayed there. They were kept under a glass case upon which some member of the club had inscribed the lines:

> Good at a fight,
> Better at a play ;
> God-like in giving,
> But the Devil to pay !

Telling, in my *Literary Landmarks of London* the story of the passing of Sheridan, I alluded to this fact, and repeated the legend that, in the silent hours of the night and in the rooms in which he did his work, the sound of the scratching of Sheridan's pen was still heard by the fellows of his guild who tried to do good work there at that time. The idea, not mine at all, I thought a rather pretty one; and I myself had fancied over many a late and lonely cigar in that library that I had been able to detect the ghost of the squeak of the master's quill. But I was rudely disillusionised. An author not unknown to fame wrote over his own name to one of the British literary periodicals to state, in all solemnity, that he had been connected with the organisation from its very inception; that he was an officer of the institution; that he had frequented the apartment in question at all hours of the day and night; and that he had never heard, and had never heard of anybody else having heard, the scratching of Sheridan's pen! This, coming from an official source, seemed to settle the matter for all time!

Mr. Kruell, a well-known and a very clever portrait engraver on wood, and naturally an astute physiognomist, was peculiarly interested in the collection then contained in what Mr. Edmund Gosse called my "scullery," and he made more than one semi-professional visit to it during his work upon Lincoln's and other heads. He examined with the eye of an expert—intelligent and quick of apprehension—every face he saw there; recognising some of them at a glance and finding something new, to him, in each of them. Among the warriors he discerned certain marks and lines in common; and he talked most entertainingly upon his subject as he went from Washington to Cromwell, from Charles to Frederick, from Sherman to Grant, from Bonaparte back, always, to Bonaparte.

"And who is this," he said at last, "with the unusual development, next to Sherman?"

"That," was the reply, "is Sheridan."

The surprise was very great.

"Sheridan?" he cried; "Sheridan with that mouth, with that nose, with that chin?"

"Yes," said I, "Sheridan!"

"Why, this man," taking the cast in his hands and carrying it carefully to the window—"this man is a poet and an orator; a man of exceedingly ready wit and quick fancy; a man of slight moral sensibility; a man who does not pay his debts; a man politically ambitious; a rake and a libertine in heart if not in action; a man whose natural weapons are words, not swords."

And in five minutes I was told everything I had read and known of Sheridan by a man, as I afterwards learned, who had never even heard of him. He had, of course, mistaken the playwright for the cavalry-leader; and in the Sheridan before him, protesting constantly that it could not possibly be Sheridan, he found everything that he knew Sheridan was not and nothing that he supposed Sheridan to be. The scene impressed me with the fact that there is a good deal in the science of physiognomy after all!

The gentle Irish poet, who must have been a good

fellow, for all his friends and even the world at large spoke of him—and the world still speaks of him—as "Tom" Moore, says, of course, nothing of the making of his own death mask, nor do any of his contemporaries mention it. It bears the strongest resemblance to all the painted and engraved portraits of the man. It shows clearly the wrinkled forehead, prominent in N. B. Willis's picture of him in *Pencillings by the Way*, and especially the "slightly tossed nose," which, the great American interviewer of seventy or more years ago said, "confirmed the fun of the expression of his face." The experts in portraiture all agree that this is the face of "Tom" Moore. It came from a plaster shop near what is called, in London, "the top of the Brompton Road."

After that curious first visit, Mr. Kruell was fond of comparing the head of Sheridan with that of Coleridge, putting them side by side upon my desk, face to face or back to back, and walking around them in all lights; pouring forth the while a delightful monologue upon the mental differences between them; and ignorant, I am sure, of *The Ancient Mariner* and his author, as he was of *The Rivals* and their creator, but hitting the bull's-eye of their character at every shot!

The Coleridge mask was for a while the subject of much research and much doubt. I found it, in the seventies, in the little shop of a dealer in plaster casts who lived and did business in the Gray's Inn Road, London. He was satisfied that it was Coleridge, but he could tell me nothing of its history; and nothing of its history could I gather in the authorised biographies of the poet. It was like all the contemporary engravings of the man, in his old age, to which I had access; and it bore every mark of being the transcript of the face once described by Coleridge himself as being, unless when animated by immediate eloquence, expressive of great sloth and great, inert, and almost idiotic good nature.

" 'T is a weak carcass of a face, fat, flabby, and expressive chiefly of inexpression!" he said.

Mr. Ernest Hartley Coleridge, the grandson of the poet, told me by letter in 1890 and in reply to my inquiries upon the subject, that he was writing the "Life" of his distinguished progenitor; that in his possession for that purpose were all the family records, journals, and correspondence; that there was a dim tradition among the surviving Coleridges that such a death mask had been made by Sourzheim but that he had been able to find no trace of it whatever. I answered that the object in my possession was unquestionably cast from a mould from nature and after life had left the subject, and that, if it were of Coleridge, it could not possibly have been the work of Sourzheim whom Coleridge had survived for some two years.

I took a large photograph of the mask in profile to the Curator of the British National Portrait Gallery, Sir George Scharf, who was for years the acknowledged leading portrait expert of his country. In an instant he said:

"It's old Sam Coleridge! Look at his ears! They are out of place. The ears of the Coleridges have for several generations been an inch too high."

Armed with this information and with this identification, I sent the photograph to Mr. Ernest Hartley Coleridge, living in some rural spot an hour by rail from London. He telegraphed me, evidently in some excitement, to meet him at his club that afternoon; and when I entered the Reform I saw, crossing the hall, the very realisation of the bit of plaster I had known so well and so long. I spoke to him at once, and he said:

"Of course you recognised me from the extraordinary resemblance. My wife, not knowing anything of our correspondence, opened your package this morning and was absolutely shocked at the startling likeness between the quick and the dead. Now tell me all about it. What a wonderful race you Yankees are! Here we have been searching all England in vain for a family treasure which turns up in a private collection in New York. Everything we particularly need and ought to have drifts, somehow, to the omnivorous States. Tell me where and how you got it!"

And I gave him the address of the little dealer in the Gray's Inn Road, a shilling's cab-fare from where we stood!

In the same little shop in the Gray's Inn Road were

bought, early in the history of the collection, the casts of Sir Richard Owen and Brunel. The Brunels, father and son, were a very remarkable pair of architectural engineers who are frequently mistaken for each other from the similarity of their Christian names and from the fact that they were then at the height of their fame, working together for many years; the elder, a very old man, dying in 1859, the younger dying ten years later.

The mask is of Brunel Junior, the designer of the mammoth steamship *Great Eastern*, which in its day, at the end of the fifties, was looked upon as one of the modern wonders of the world. At the back of the cast, now fractured by careless packers, is the name "Brunel"; but, as in the case of Coleridge, the dealer, who was also a moulder, could not give me any information regarding it. He was of the opinion, and no doubt he was correct, that it was made for Marochetti, the sculptor of the statue of its subject.

Of the story of the Owen mask my Gray's Inn dealer was equally ignorant. It is certainly Owen, and it must be from life, for it came into my hands while Owen was still living. I never dared ask the professor himself about it because, unfortunately, I lack a great deal of the traditional journalistic assurance. But he was an intimate of Thackeray and Tennyson, of Dickens, and of men of that stamp; and when I read that in 1842 Carlyle asked for an introduction to him, I am inclined to ascribe that date to the cast. Owen was then thirty-six, and he looks, in plaster, like a man who had just been introduced to, or was just about to be introduced to, Carlyle.

The mask of the Third Napoleon is a most careful and skilful and successful piece of work. It was made by Brucciani, a London moulder, when the subject did not know whether it hurt him or not. In life the moustache and imperial were always waxed and pointed, and their position in the cast, lying close to the cheeks and chin as they must of necessity do, alters somewhat the appearance of the familiar face. The particular form of beard affected by the Emperor was, by the way, called the " Imperial " in his honour.

In the mask of John Boyle O'Reilly the hairs on the head and the upper lip were covered with greased tissue-paper or thin oiled-silk. This method simplifies the task of removing the matrix, but not infrequently it detracts somewhat from the value of the cast.

John Boyle O'Reilly was a brilliant Irish-American poet and journalist who was banished from his native land for violent revolutionary sentiments, but who, during his life in this country, was one of the most delightful and amiable and gentle of men in all his domestic and social relations.

Mr. Thomas Bailey Aldrich, commenting once upon the trials of Job, remarked that the only proper place to have a boil was between " John " and " O'Reilly."

I well remember O'Reilly's absorbed interest in this Third Napoleon mask. He spoke of its phrenological strength and weakness; he was fond of comparing it with the mask of the First Napoleon, and of questioning if there flowed in the veins of the so-called "nephew of his uncle" a drop of the Bonaparte blood.

The man of destiny who met his fate at Sedan was, certainly, possessed of not one of the facial traits which are so marked in resemblance in the men of that remarkable race. He was, for a time, the head of his house. And he was the only Bonaparte, for four generations at least, who did not look like a Bonaparte.

As little more than a boy myself I can distinctly remember watching the Third Napoleon and his son, the Prince Imperial, as they took their morning walks in the private gardens of the Tuileries. They seemed in their solemn, serious way to be fond of each other—that father and son. But I did not envy them, because my own father told me that he and I, on the *outside* of the iron fence, were having the better and the safer time of it.

What is claimed to be the only and original mask of The Little Corporal is constantly turning up in different parts of the world. It is by no means an uncommon object on either side of the Atlantic, and I have seen and examined not less than a dozen examples of it in plaster and three in bronze. It was taken, of course, at St. Helena and a few hours after the death of the great exile, by Dr. Antomarchi, the Emperor's personal physician. Three or four bronze casts from the mould are certainly known to have been made. One, the property of the French Government, is in the Mint at Paris ; one—well authenticated and signed in the casting—is in the Tussaud Museum in London ; and a third — also well authenticated and signed by Antomarchi—is now the property of a resident of New York, an enthusiastic collector of *Bonapartiana.*

Dr. Antomarchi is known to have been in New Orleans in 1836 and to have died in Cuba in 1838, and it is not at all improbable that he brought with him to this country at least one copy of the mask. In this event it would have been an easy matter for him or for anybody else to have reproduced it, and this would account for its presence in Omaha, in Oswego, in Albany, in New Orleans, and in Ontario, Canada.

The plaster copy in the Princeton Library came with me from Paris in the early seventies, and it is, confessedly, very inferior to the bronze casts in all respects. It is a cast from a copy, no doubt ; but it brings us nearer to the wonderful man than we ever came before.

The statement contained in a number of newspapers lately that there were five bronze casts from the original matrix ; that one is in the British Museum ; that two are in the Louvre, in Paris ; that one is in Omaha, Nebraska ; and that the fifth is " the property of Mr. Laurence Hutton, the editor of the *Century Magazine,*" I am compelled to doubt ; because I have found no trace of such objects either in the Louvre or the British Museum, and because I know that Mr. Laurence Hutton is not the editor of the *Century Magazine*, and that he never owned the Antomarchi mask in bronze.

Nothing in the way of modern sculpture, it seems to me, is more impressive, more touching, more pathetic, and even more tragic in the story it tells than is the marble figure of the dying Bonaparte, studying the map of Europe, waiting patiently or impatiently for the end, and brooding over what might have been. He asked in those last hours that his ashes might be carried to the banks of the Seine, to rest among the people he loved so well. And in Paris, at last, they lie, where the path of glory led them, in the magnificently sombre tomb under the dome of the chapel of the hospital of the sacred veterans of French wars.

CHAPTER VII

The Collecting of the Death Masks (*Continued*)—Henry Clay—
Aaron Burr—Louise of Prussia—Mendelssohn—Beethoven
— Cromwell — General Grant — Keats — Wordsworth —
Canova—Lawrence Barrett—General Sherman—Cavour—
Leopardi — Tasso — Newton — Queen Elizabeth — Shake-
peares—Walter Scott.

ANOTHER occasional caller was an aged gentleman who came one day, some quarter of a century ago, with a letter of introduction from a total stranger to me, stating that he was a sculptor who wished to make a study of my life mask of Henry Clay. I gladly enough gave him free access to it. I learned that he was carving a bust of the silver-tongued Kentuckian for a Kentucky court-house and was anxious to see the cast of the great statesman which, somehow, he heard that I had obtained from the studio of Mills in Washington. I told him that I had bought from the sons of the late Clark Mills casts of the heads of Webster and Calhoun and of the face of Clay; that in the case of Clay the eyes were open; that Mr. O'Donovan, Mr. Saint-Gaudens, Mr. John Scott Hartley, Olin Warner, and other statuary friends of mine were puzzled as to whether it was Clay from nature or from a sculptured bust; that they all agreed that it *was* Clay, but that it had evidently been "worked up"; that although a certain self-conscious rigidity of the muscles of the mouth showed traces of the living and self-conscious face, they could not account for the opening of the eyes, and that it was one of the doubtful masks of the collection.

The other masks left in uncertainty besides Clay, I explained, were Laurence Sterne, Coleridge, Sheridan, Newton, and Aaron Burr. He examined them all, and particularly Burr's, with no little interest; and he said that he could not help me except in the case of Burr. Burr had baffled me, especially; as there are not many existent portraits of Burr in old age or in youth with which to compare it. I had no special admiration for Burr—who once killed a Scotsman,—but I had all the collector's enthusiasm for Burr in plaster and I wanted to think my Burr was Burr. How did he know that the mask was really Burr's? That was easily explained. He had made it himself, going to Staten Island the night after Burr's death for that very purpose! And thus I was able to assure the University of Princeton that Burr has come back to his Alma Mater.

Another mask of Burr, this time from life, was made by Turnarelli, an Italian sculptor in London, in 1808 or 1809. Burr rebelled strongly against the operation, and he wrote to his daughter Theodosia in a half-angry and half-humorous sort of way, that "the infernal mask business" had made a purple mark on his nose which no rubbing or washing would remove; he believed the fellow used quicklime instead of plaster; and he added that he had heaped many curses upon the unfortunate Dago—although he did not call him a "Dago!" I can sympathise with the gifted son of the Princeton president. I have been through the ordeal myself.

Burr is said to have been a very fascinating creature, especially to the ladies, although he does not seem to be particularly attractive as represented in the mask. He was small in stature, but I was surprised to read that he was taller than Hamilton, whom, strangely enough, he so much resembled that they were not infrequently mistaken for each other on the streets. I have no cast of the handsome young Hamilton. If such a thing exists I have never heard of it.

A proud young mother once exhibited to me her new-born and first-born babe, now a blooming and pretty young girl. I was afraid to touch it, of course, and I would not have "held" it for worlds; but I looked at it in the customary admiring way, wondering at its jelly-like imbecility of form and feature. Alas! when I was asked the usual question, "Whom does she favour?" I could only reply, in all sincerity, that it looked exactly like a pink photograph of my death mask of Aaron Burr. And the young mother was not altogether pleased.

I cannot to this day understand how Clark Mills managed to make moulds from life of the entire head of Webster and of that of Calhoun, each so distinct and

so near to nature, without leaving in the casts some
traces of the hair they wore. Their faces were smooth
shaven, but they were both far from being bald. The
occiput must have been carefully and closely covered
with something which left no mark ; but what that
something was I cannot determine. Each cast is
signed by the artist and dated — Calhoun's in 1844,
Webster's in 1849,—and that clearly enough establishes
their identity.

Calhoun's cranium is entirely different in shape, but
both he and Webster—the phrenologists tell us—had
unusually large heads ; and we need no phrenologists
to tell us that there was a good deal in them. The
biggest—in the physical and intellectual sense of the
word, not as the word is slangily applied—the biggest
and the fullest head I ever knew personally was covered
by the hat of Mr. John Fiske; and that hat came down
to my shoulders, extinguishing me completely—in more
ways than one. But I have been told that the size of a
head is not always a criterion of its contents, and I have
found some little comfort in the fact, as stated by Leigh
Hunt in *Byron and His Contemporaries*, that neither
Hunt nor any of Byron's intellectual contemporaries
could put on Byron's hat at all.

The masks of Frederick and Queen Louise, lying in
state, as it were, in the capital city of their kingdom
and coming into my hands as they did, must be accepted without hesitancy as authentic. With the
King's head was moulded the pillow upon which it

rested,—a rather unusual performance. Napoleon III., Thackeray, the Stratford Shakespeare, and General Grant have been placed upon placque backgrounds, designed by the moulders, and artificial; which lend nothing to their value as masks. But in the case of the Great Frederick the background somehow seems to add to the royal dignity of his repose in what is called his "last sleep."

The beautiful Louise of Prussia, the mother of the old Emperor of Germany, the grandmother of the man whom the Germans loved to call "Our Fritz," and the great-grandmother of the present Emperor, whom nobody knows what the Germans call—in their hearts, —must have been very beautiful indeed. With the exception perhaps of the mask of Mendelssohn, hers is the most peaceful and tranquil in the collection.

Her life was not a happy one, and to her, death was a comfort and a relief. She was glad to get rid of the trouble of living; and this is shown in her sweet dead face. It will be observed in examining the cast that a napkin covers her hair and that nothing is presented to reveal the frightful scars on her neck and the ravages of the dreadful disease she inherited and which she handed down to her descendants,— scars which the court painters succeeded so artistically in helping her in life to conceal from the world.

Mendelssohn's death was eminently peaceful. Lampadius, his biographer, in describing the final scene, wrote: "His features soon assumed a glorified expression. So much he looked like one in sleep that some of his friends thought that it could not be death, an illusion which is often given to the eye of love. His friends Bendemann and Huebner," it is added, "took a cast of his features, as he lay."

This is one of the few cases in which there is any contemporary allusion to the making of a death mask. If other biographers had been equally thoughtful of my feelings, I would have been spared much trouble and uncertainty and would have escaped the perusal of not a little melancholy literature.

The story of the Schiller cast is also told in at least one of the *Lives* of the poet. It was made by Klauer, and it was used to identify the skull of Schiller which had been lost for some years and had a curious and wandering existence, resting—uneasily enough— in two or three different cemeteries until it joined the bones of Goethe in the family vault of the Grand Duke of Saxe-Weimar, where it still remains.

There are two masks of Beethoven over which I was much perplexed. One came from Berlin and was official; the other was discovered in Stockholm—in a back street and in a cellar—and it had no history behind it. They are both clearly from nature, they are both unquestionably Beethoven, and they are not entirely alike.

I discovered after a long search that one mask was made by Klein from life in 1812 when Beethoven was in his forty-second year. This the experts consider the better of the two. Klein's bust of Beethoven, taken from it, is a familiar object in the music-halls and music-shops and in the homes of music-lovers the world over.

The second mask was made from death in 1827 by Dannhauer. The eyes, to protect the lashes, were covered with small squares of cloth. In comparing the two, one is struck by the absence of consciousness in the cast from death, and by the decidedly conscious look in the other, as if the original knew he was sitting for his picture and was trying very hard "to look pleasant."

Among the many casts in the museum of the British Phrenological Society in London very few are of individuals of any intellectual note. Beethoven and Sheridan are there almost alone, among a gruesome gang of famous criminals and hydrocephalic monstrosities.

In the case of Cromwell, as in the case of Beethoven, I found two masks—unquestionably of the great Protector—but not from the same matrix. One is in the National Portrait Gallery in London; one is in the British Museum. One is in plaster; one is in wax. Carlyle accepted the plaster cast as genuine, and he owned a copy of it which, through Mr. Charles Eliot Norton, went eventually to Harvard College. It is one of the few things of its peculiar kind which that seat of learning possesses. My replica of it, once the property of George Combe, is now among many others of its genus in Princeton. It is not at all an uncommon object as such objects go, but it is to me of enormous interest.

Of the museum's mask in wax, I have never seen a copy or a replica. Each of the learned institutions of Victoria's capital believed in the verity of its own example, and each of course questioned the authenticity of the other until I solved the problem to their mutual satisfaction. There is plenty of contemporary authority for " the plaster cast of Oliver's face, taken after his death "; but I could learn nothing of the wax cast until I read, in a work called *The House of Cromwell*, written by the Rev. Mark Noble, that " the baronial family of Russell are in possession of a wax-mask of Oliver which is supposed to have been taken off while he was living."

This same Mark Noble tells us that the representative of Ferdinand II. of Tuscany bribed an attendant of Cromwell to permit him to take in secret a mask of the Protector, in plaster of Paris, which was done only a few moments after his Highness's dissolution. A cast from this mould," it is added, " is now (1737) in the Florentine Gallery. It is either of bronze with a brassy hue or stained to give it that appearance." I could find no record of it in the Florentine Gallery, a century and a half later.

The body of Cromwell is supposed to have been buried in the Chapel of Henry VII. in Westminster Abbey. But after the Restoration, with the bodies of Ireland his son-in-law and Bradshaw the Regicide, it—

or what is supposed to be it—was carried to Tyburn, the place of public execution, and there hanged in the public sight; a ceremony which may have given some satisfaction to Royalists but which Cromwell probably did not mind in the least. His favourite daughter, Elizabeth Claypole, was for some unexplained reason permitted to remain among the kings and queens and the knaves and the two-spots in the Abbey—and probably she does not mind it either.

Two moulds from the face of General Grant, another warrior, maker of history, and leader of men, were made almost immediately after his death at Mount McGregor: one without the knowledge or consent of his family, nobody knows by whose connivance; the other, at the request of his family, by Mr. Karl Gerhardt. Both of these, or copies of them, came eventually into my collection. The first is very distressing, and at the request of the present General Grant I have never exhibited it or permitted it to be reproduced in any way. The second was bequeathed to me by Mr. Arthur Dodge, although I have never learned how or from whom he obtained it. It has been put into an allegorical national frame but nothing has been added to its value or its interest thereby.

Mrs. Grant was loath to have the mask in her possession, which she believed to be the only impression in existence, go out of her hands; and it was not until after long correspondence with her and her sons that I finally received consent to have a replica of it made. I went to her house for that purpose and by appointment with Mr. Decomps, one day; all the preparations were made; the cast was before us; when the widow reconsidered her permission and reverently and abruptly and in silence carried it away. Mr. Decomps in the meantime, however, had recognised the fact that it was a cast of the cast which he had made from the original mould, and that it had already been cast by some one else. I have no idea what became of its fellows, unless Mr. Dodge's copy—identical with it except in the matter of the inartistic frame—is one of them.

The "trying-to-look-pleasant" expression is peculiarly noticeable in the life masks of Wordsworth and of Keats; although the former did not altogether succeed, which was not the fault, by the way, of Charles Lamb. Haydon describes the operation in his *Journal*, under date of 1815, and says: "Wordsworth sat in my dressing-gown with his hands folded, sedate, solemn, and still, bearing it like a philosopher." But elsewhere we read that the poet was placed flat on his back on the studio floor, while Lamb capered about him in glee at the undignified absurdity of the proceedings, trying to make the subject grin at his fantastic criticisms and remarks.

Sir Henry Taylor in his *Autobiography* spoke of attending Wordsworth's funeral and of being shown then " a cast of a mask of his face in which was a certain rough grandeur," but he does not say when it was taken; nowhere did I find any reference to a death mask, and what Sir Henry saw and examined in 1850 was no doubt the work of Haydon, done thirty-five years before. It is more like the portraits of Wordsworth in his ripe middle-age than in his declining years.

Mr. John Gilmer Speed, the nephew of Keats, says that the frequently engraved life mask of his uncle was made by Haydon in 1818. Joseph Severn, the friend of Keats, pronounced it " the most interesting as it is the most real portrait of the man in existence "; and he added that it had, or so it seemed to him, "a suggestion of humorous patience in the expression of the mouth." It requires, as I know by actual experience, a good deal of patience, humorous and otherwise, to sit for a "portrait in plaster."

The original of this cast, much more perfect than this and than any other I have seen, was given by Keats himself to John Hamilton Reynolds when Keats left England to die in Rome. It was bequeathed by Reynolds to his sister Charlotte, by whom, with a clear pedigree, it was donated to the Trustees of the British National Portrait Gallery, where it is carefully preserved. Both Charles Armitage Brown and John Taylor speak of "casts of the face, hand, and foot of Keats," taken after death ; but that such things were really made, and that they still exist, I have never been able to learn.

Haydon's own mask, taken after death, is reproduced in the *Memoir* by his son. My copy, purchased in

London after a long search, was carefully packed for shipment and was cruelly broken on its arrival in New York by criminally careless custom-house officials, who opened the case to see that its contents were not contraband and then threw the contents hurriedly back, charging me a heavy duty upon the damage they had done.

The custom-house expenses, brokerage fees, duties, and the like, upon all the foreign masks which I did not bring back with me to this country in my own hands and among my personal luggage, averaged more than one hundred *percentum* on the original cost. As I have said in my book, the heads of my paternal government have taxed me in this matter in order to "protect" the ghosts of bygone plasterers who could not have made the casts if they had wanted to, and who could have found but a poor market for them even if they had been able to make them.

Another valuable mask damaged slightly in the same lawfully-lawless way is that of Bentham, the eccentric jurist and philosopher. George Combe writes of this mask in the *Phrenological Journal* published shortly after Bentham's death in 1832. Although it does not figure in Combe's book, he evidently had a copy of it which he highly prized; but he does not say whether it is a death mask or the life mask known to have been made by the Italian Turnarelli some forty-five years before Bentham died. Bentham it was, by the by, who induced Aaron Burr to submit to the operation at the hands of the same artist.

I have told the gruesome and extraordinary story of Bentham's posthumous fate in another place. It is too long to find room here. Suffice it to say that he bequeathed his skeleton to University College, London, with the request that it should be covered with his own clothes and put, comfortably seated, in the chair he used to occupy. And there, in a commodious glass case, it sits serenely to this day, surmounted by a wax head which this mask closely resembles. Bentham began the study of Latin in his fourth year and he was familiar with the Greek alphabet before he was promoted to trousers. Naturally he had few "conditions" when he entered Queen's College, Oxford, at the age of twelve. For all that he does not seem to have been on any of the existing elevens, and there is no record of his ever having made a touch-down!

The mask of Canova I fractured myself, but happily not to its serious detriment. I accidentally broke its neck while hammering a nail on which to hang the Reverend Thomas Chalmers, one of my father's personal heroes and the "light of the Scottish pulpit."

Concerning the Canova mask might be repeated the saying of Mr. John Fiske's journeyman-carpenter who, when he saw a bust of Voltaire in the Cambridge Library, asked: "Kinder sickly like, warn't he?" Canova certainly looks "kinder sickly like" here. The cast came from Venice, and it was the work of some of the sculptor's devoted pupils, who used it as a model for the medallion bust on the monument in that city, although they glorified and rejuvenated the subject.

I found Dr. Chalmers in George Street, Edinburgh, one day; the only mask or the only thing like a mask which a certain delightful little curiosity-shop contained. And how the dealer came by it he could never explain. He knew all about his old clocks and his ancient warming-pans and his Mary Stuart medals and his antique dirks and helmets and his bawbee pieces and his "Kilmarnock Burns," but he could never tell me "naething about Tom Chawlmers," or where it came from. It cost me half a crown, and I have never regretted its purchase, for that it is Chalmers nobody who ever saw his face or a limning of it can doubt.

For the mask of Lawrence Barrett, made for me, I paid the moulder fifty dollars, the regularly established price for such things. For the casts of Cavour and Pope Pius IX. I paid to a dealer in Rome, Italy, two lire, or forty cents, each. These are the most expensive and the least expensive of the lot.

By a curious coincidence, the last letter which Barrett ever wrote was written at my request and in my presence to Father Sherman, asking his permission to add General Sherman's head to my collection. This was on a Tuesday afternoon. The gentle young priest brought the answer in person, three days later, and he gave it to me in a room in which Barrett lay dead.

This Barrett mask, as I have said before, gave his fellow tragedian a great shock once; and, later, it gave a great shock to me. The copy for *The Players* came one evening when Booth was on the stage, in Brooklyn. It was uncovered by a thoughtless servant and placed on a small table near Booth's bed; and there in all its ghastly whiteness of fresh plaster — almost the man himself—Booth, not knowing of its existence, found it when he turned on the electric lamps at midnight.

When the masks were photographed for *Harper's Magazine*, the work was done for safety's sake in my own house. The conditions were poor and the only proper light was that of an upper guest-chamber. I would not trust the precious objects to careless hands, and I carried them to the operator, one by one, and placed them on the vacant bed; Barrett's head resting by a strange chance upon the very pillow on which I so often had seen it in all the flush of robust health and cheerful spirits.

I had lived so long in intimate intercourse with these things, crowding as they did for a quarter of a century the little room in which so many of my working hours were spent, that I had learned to look upon them with something like a hardened insensibility as to their actual significance. But I realised everything that each one of them had meant—to somebody—when I saw my dear old friend Barrett as I saw him on that gruesome day. It is all very well to discuss the dead faces of Dante or Tasso or of Swift or of Thomas Paine or of the men of other times, but when it comes to the contemplation and examination of the dead faces of the men you have known and loved in the flesh it is a very different matter. John McCullough, Barrett, Harry Edwards, Walt Whitman, John Boyle O'Reilly, Dion Boucicault, General Sherman,—to all of whom I have shown these masks,—have, now, death masks of their own in the collection.

I have spent many an interesting day with Barrett at Stratford-on-Avon. He was a scholar and a ripe and good one; and naturally everything—no matter how vague and misty it might be—which pertained to the personality of Shakespeare appealed to him. His favourite walk was to Ann Hathaway's cottage at Shottery, where Shakespeare's courting was done. We soon became known to the simple old Warwickshire woman who was its occupant and care-taker; and Barrett loved dearly to sit in its great chimney-corner or to ramble among its little garden paths to pick the descendants of the common English domestic flowers of which Shakespeare wrote, and to quote to the ghost of Mistress Hathaway by the hour the words of affection which Shakespeare put into the mouths of the lovers of his creating.

The mask of General Sherman, which came to me with the consent of his family and through Barrett's kindness, is, so far as I can learn, the first and the only cast from the matrix, and is one of the finest in the collection.

The last time I saw General Sherman alive he distinguished me by calling me a "scally-wag" in the presence of three or four hundred men. It was at a public dinner, and it was his own last public appearance. After he had made his happy little speech he left the table, every man in the great room at Delmonico's rising to cheer him and crowding around him to take him by the hand. Both arms were nearly wrung off when he came to me, and he flatly refused to touch my digits. Pushing me back into my chair he cried: "What! shake hands with *you*, you darned scally-wag! I 've shaken hands with you often enough!"

I do not know, exactly, what a "scally-wag" is, but the dear old General seemed to look upon it as a term of affection; and I would rather have been called a "scally-wag" by Sherman than have shaken hands with the Emperor of all the Russias and his court.

Madame Malibran was killed by a fall from her horse, and it is said that her face was disfigured by the accident, although it does not so appear in the mask. Her friend and biographer, the Countess de Merlin, stated that out of respect for Malibran's wishes no posthumous cast or sketch of any kind was made of her. But members of her family, still living, assure me that De Beriot, her husband, did take this cast which helped him to execute that bust of Malibran now in the house of her son in Paris. This was a very unusual performance, as De Beriot was not a sculptor, and he never made anything of the kind before or after. The bust is said to be neither agreeable nor a good likeness; but the mask has been recognised by her friends as unquestionably hers, and the Curator of the British National Portrait Gallery, who knew her personally, asserted that he could see in it plainly, what he had been able merely to trace vaguely in real life, the African type of features which she had inherited from her father, Garcia, who was of Spanish-Moorish descent.

As the open public cab in which we were driving to dine with friends in Rome, Italy, one night some years ago, turned into a little street quite unfamiliar to me, I exclaimed suddenly:

"There's Cavour!"

"Where's Cavour?" asked Mrs. Hutton, greatly interested in the man and forgetting for the moment that he was dead.

But her husband was not by her side. I had leaped from the moving vehicle and was bargaining with a dealer in casts for the masks of Cavour and Pius IX. which I had seen in a plaster-shop window. I brought my purchases back, put them, naked, on the front seat —there was no time to have them wrapped up,—and I took them out to dinner with me.

Why did I not wait until next day? Because next day the shop might be burned or the dealer might have moved away. Anything might have happened. When the true sportsman sees a trout jump within casting distance of him, he does not "wait until the next day!"

Although Cavour was born and buried in Turin he was, naturally, a very familiar figure in the city of Rome; and I have often wondered if he ever passed from the Piazza del Popolo into the little side-street by the convent where Luther lived, to look into the window of the little shop where not very long after his death I found the cast of his own dead face.

The mask of Pius is an unusually fine one. If it is not the first impression from the original matrix, it is assuredly a very early cast. The body lay in state in one of the chapels of St. Peter's for some days, and an eye-witness of the ceremonies said that the face, perfectly visible, had changed very little and that a slight flush even was on the cheeks. This "slight flush" leads me to question if it was not a wax mask of the face which was visible, as a mask of that kind was unquestionably made. Such things, in such exalted and public cases, are often done. But Princeton possesses a replica of the mask, without the flush, and very near to nature indeed.

The mask of Leopardi came to me in Rome and in the same year, directly from the family of the unhappy poet. His deformities of body which so much distressed him not only physically but mentally are of course not apparent in his face. His mind, like that of Alexander Pope (who was similarly disproportioned in person), was more active and more beautiful than was his frame; but it is said that he inspired very little tenderness and affection even in the heart of his own mother. He looks, in cold dull plaster, like one who lacked a mother's love and who missed it. "The man who never shook his mother"—to quote Mr. Mark Twain—is only doing, in his negative way, what all men do; but sad is the lot of the man whom his mother shakes.

From this mask was evolved the engraving of Leopardi on his death-bed, which forms the frontispiece to a volume of his collected works, and is considered the best of the very few portraits of him which exist. If there was any happy period of Leopardi's life it must have been his childhood, spent in Naples, the beautiful and happy place of his birth. Let us hope that for a few years, at least, he was too young and too unobservant to realise the disproportion of his own poor little body or to notice the lack of a mother's love.

The mask of Tasso came from Rome many years earlier. The original, no longer publicly exhibited, is reverently preserved with his bust, his crucifix, his inkstand, and other personal relics of Tasso, in the room of the Convent of San Onofrio in Rome, where he spent the last months of his life and where he died and is buried. Ladies were never admitted into this chamber except upon one day of the year, the anniversary of the poet's death; and, since an earthquake shook its walls and made them unsafe, not even men are permitted to enter at any time.

The card with *Harper's Magazine* engraven upon its front procured for me my interview with Sir Isaac New ton. Portraits of Newton without the flowing wig of his period are rare, and no portrait of Newton that I had seen suggested the mask which I had been assured was his, not even the bust by Roubiliac modelled from it. That Roubiliac had made such a mask, and that it had found its way in the early part of the century into the hands of the Royal Society from the hands of Samuel Hunter Christie, who had purchased it at a sale of Roubiliac's effects, I knew to be a matter of record; and I was naturally anxious to compare mine with the original. The Society's rooms in Burlington House, London, are not open to the public and access is rarely granted to them except for cause. After a good deal of knocking and waiting at their doors, my card was at last taken to a scientific-looking gentleman whose exact position there I could not determine. He allowed me to enter as far as an ante-chamber, where he informed me firmly, notwithstanding the fact that I represented the great periodical, that I could proceed no farther without an order signed and sealed by some great somebody,— I 've forgotten whom. And he added that the great functionary could not sign or seal the order at present because he was dead and his successor had not been appointed.

I was permitted, however, to state the object of my visit and to emphasize what I considered to be its importance, not only to me, but to the magazine-reading public of two continents. My interlocutor, still seeming to regard me as a peculiarly brazen specimen of

American sneak-thief whose object was to steal or to mutilate the relic of the great man, told me that comparison was not only impossible but useless, because I could in no way be possessed of a copy of an object that had never been copied but once and then for Newton's College, Trinity, at Cambridge, and that my specimen must, of necessity, be fraudulent and of no value. He was not a little startled when he examined a photograph of it, and—even without the order sealed and signed—he permitted me to make the comparison I so much desired. The casts were identical, except that the other was the impression from the original mould and naturally better and clearer than mine.

This was a most extraordinary thing! Most astonishing! And mine was really in a private collection in the States? Most astonishing! Most extraordinary!

A committee happened to be sitting that day in an adjoining room. Would I be so good as to go before the committee and show them this most astonishing thing? I *was* so good! And the committee-men in their turn were astounded. But I would not tell them where I got the mask. The modeller employed to make the copy for Cambridge had made two copies, and of these his descendants had sold me one for five shillings sterling in cash—and a quart of beer.

Sir Isaac was buried in the nave of Westminster Abbey beneath a mural monument containing a bewigged bust which looks not in the least like the mask. In all the crowd in what Macaulay calls " that great temple of silence and reconciliation" is no man who ornaments it more than does Newton.

As a matrix is composed of perishable material the first cast is, of course, the most perfect in all respects ; the second is not quite so good ; and the others—when others are made—are apt to be a little more than outlines, although each has its value as a portrait, if only by suggestion. Even the cast from a cast, as is the case of the mask of Newton, is better and in some respects more true to nature than is any other form of portraiture, although it is not so correct as is the original in London ; and the original by the way was not improved in the process of being put into a mould. Of the popular and more common examples, as Dante for instance, casts of casts from copies of copies have been made until very little is left of the famous mysterious head of the Italian poet in the Uffizi Gallery of Florence.

For the illustrations to my book I was fortunate enough to obtain a photograph of the prototype itself. But, as a rule, the Dantes you have seen, while they came from Florence, are cousins of Dante and no man knows how many times removed in plastic relationship. At the side of the Cathedral Square in Florence is still preserved, embedded in the wall of a comparatively modern house, a bit of stone which is highly regarded by those tourists who accept the guide-books as invariable tellers of the truth. This "Stone of Dante" is said to have been a favourite seat of the poet while he watched the building of the Duomo; although why he always occupied the same hard and uninviting resting place and how he could have inspected the erection of a building which at the time of his death had passed nothing but its lower foundation-walls; the guide-books do not explain.

With the exception of the cast of Shakespeare, the only cast in the collection which is not from nature is that of Elizabeth of England; and these two are preserved only because they are both supposed and believed to have been based upon masks from death. The face of Elizabeth is taken from the recumbent figure of the Virgin Queen in Henry VII.'s Chapel in the Abbey of Westminster; and one John de Critz, "famous for his painting," is said to have carved this effigy from the mask in wax which is known to have covered her dead face as she lay in state. This historical waxen object was long preserved in another part of the minster with other similar royal and aristocratic relics. But I have not been able to see it for many years and it has probably gone now the way of wax in general.

The cast of the bust of Shakespeare, I was assured at the time of its purchase in Stratford many years ago, was made direct from the original in the church by a journeyman-plasterer, who did it in the silence of midnight and, of course, by stealth. Mr. Marshall, the antiquary from whom I bought it and long since lying in the Stratford churchyard, had what he declared to be its pedigree,—always promised me but never, alas, forthcoming. This Stratford bust is supposed to have been carved by Gerard Johnson shortly after the funeral and to have been copied from a death mask; but this, like everything else in the story of the personality of Shakespeare, is mere tradition. It was certainly in the church as early as 1623 and while Ann Hathaway Shakespeare still lived, and there is no record of anybody's denying its authenticity as a likeness. It is not identical with the famous Kesselstadt mask which has been the subject of more discussion than any piece of plaster ever made. This latter was found in Germany some time ago; it bears upon its back the initials " W. S.," and the date "1618"; it looks like the alleged portraits of the immortal bard, and the scholars who believe in it believe in it implicitly, while those who do not believe in it do not believe in it at all! It has been photographed and engraved, but no copy of it in plaster or in wax has ever, for its own safety's sake, and very wisely, been permitted. It is said that Chantrey, the sculptor, refused absolutely to accept this head as authentic on the ground that no intelligent human being who ever lived had at the same time a forehead so high and an upper lip so long, but that he changed his views entirely when he saw the mask of Sir Walter Scott and found by actual measurement that Scott was quite as long in the lip and equally high above the eyebrows. And Scott he freely acknowledged to have been a human being of intelligence.

John Aubrey reported Shakespeare as being "a handsome, well-shap't man." The Stratford bust is a rudely carved sample of mortuary sculpture, no better but a little worse than the average examples of its kind and time. It was originally painted, but it was white-washed at the end of the eighteenth century, no one knows exactly why, by Edmund Malone, the Shakespearian commentator. The colours were restored, however, about forty years ago as nearly as they could be distinguished. The eyes are hazel, the hair almost yellow, the jacket is of red under a black stole. The hands, the right holding a quill-pen, rest on a pillow of red, yellow, and green; and the general colour effect is startling.

The Scott mask, from death, in the collection, if it is not from the original mould, is certainly not an early impression. The matrix was made by George Bullock and Bullock and Chantrey both based their busts upon it, while Landseer used it as the model for a painted portrait. It had disappeared for many years, but it was found again by Sir John Steel, the sculptor,—so he told me himself,—in an out-of-the-way corner of Abbotsford while he was at work upon the Lockhart monument at Dryburgh Abbey; and he used it in designing the head of Scott on the statue in Edinburgh, a replica of which ornaments the Central Park, New York. I first saw the original mask at "The Scott Centennial Celebration" at Edinburgh in 1871, when my copy was obtained. But I have never been able to see the life mask of Scott, said to be at Abbotsford and said to have been made in Paris, nobody knows when or for what purpose.

An aged Scotchman, a member of Dr. Wm. H. Taylor's congregation in New York, was exceedingly proud of the fact that he had been the private coachman of the Wizard of the North, and had driven the hearse of Scott from Abbotsford to Dryburgh, that was drawn by a pair of Sir Walter's favourite carriage horses. About half-way on that sad last journey they came to the top of a certain little hill where Scott had been in the habit of stopping for a time to glory in the view of the lands he loved : on one side of him his present home ; on the other side the home that was to be his until eternity began. Here, on the day of the funeral, the horses halted of their own accord, and no persuasion would induce them to move forward until the customary five minutes had passed.

"And so," said the faithful henchman, "the ' Shirra' was able to look around him once again ! "

Perhaps the clearest and most perfect masks in the collection are those of Dion Boucicault, the actor, and Palmerston, the statesman. They are, both of them, the earliest if not the only transcripts. In the Boucicault is seen every line that the face possessed, every crease and wrinkle and indenture of the skin. It is to be regretted that the artist, Mr. J. Scott Hartley, cut off the lower part of the back of the head; but this was necessitated by some imperfection in the mould.

Boucicault was not only very eminent as a player in his peculiar line of eccentric comedy but he was wonderfully prolific as a producer of plays. He was the author, adapter, and translator of more dramatic works than any man of his time and perhaps than any man of any time; and curiously enough nearly all his work was popular and good. The most successful of his dramas was *The Colleen Bawn*, which was taken from a story of Gerald Griffin's called *The Collegians*. The heroine of a play, a young lady always arrayed in a red cloak, would have come to serious grief by falling off a rock in the Lake of Killarney—still bearing her name—if it had not been for the phenomenal efforts of a stage Irishman who, at the risk of his own stage-life, leaped an incredible number of feet—incredible even for an Irishman and on the stage—and carried her, comparatively dry, red cloak and all, through the raging stage billows to the shore. This always brought down the curtain,—and it usually brought down the house.

To the Palmerston mask are still adhering a number of the hairs of the head and the beard which were torn from the flesh in the matrix and then torn from the matrix in the cast. They seem, somehow, to bring one very close to the man himself. And they were the subject of a great deal of excitement and newspaper comment some years ago, when an observing student discovered them, or thought he had discovered them and thereby had established the astounding scientific fact that a plaster bust could raise a human beard. The face of the subject had not been properly prepared for the operation; the hair was torn from the head and the cheeks in removing the matrix, and from the matrix in removing the cast. The cast of Palmerston, hair and all, came from the studio of the sculptor, Mr. Jackson, and I cheerfully paid five pounds sterling for it, because it had never been copied or reproduced and is absolutely unique. It formed the basis of the statue by Jackson now standing in Westminster Abbey.

The Disraeli mask—I can never think of him as Beaconsfield, for I cannot understand how a man who literally made himself, and made himself out of nothing and so great, should have consented to let his sovereign make him so little as the latest of the earls—the Disraeli mask is a cast of the cast from which Sir Edgar Boehm evolved the statue also now standing in the Abbey. I purchased it from an assistant of the sculptor, with the consent of the sculptor's son and heir, and it cost me a guinea — without any beer thrown in. The nose, unhappily, was intentionally broken in the original cast by an irresponsible but enthusiastic admirer of Mr. Gladstone, who hurled a hammer at it in the studio one day because the Grand Old Man of his adoration had been defeated in Parliament by the adherents of his defunct enemy. More than one expert friend of mine has offered to restore the nose from photographs of Disraeli, but I have preferred to keep it as Nature—and the hammer—left it, rather than to call in the aid of the art which was applied to the renovation of Harry Edwards. All the features in the Boehm statue in the Abbey are, of course, intact.

The mask of Edwards was found upon the floor of my study in New York one morning in many fragments, the hook upon which it was hung having been insufficient to hold its weight. Every piece was gathered together and carried to the invaluable Mr. Decomps, who, with the utmost patience and skill, succeeded in making a perfect whole of it, although he could not entirely succeed in concealing the seams and the scars.

"Harry" Edwards, as he was known, was a man of charming personality, of high culture, and of many friends, all of whom respected as well as loved him. He may be remembered as an actor of charming simplicity who succeeded John Gilbert as "leading old man" in Lester Wallack's famous company of comedians; while to many persons who never heard or dreamed of him in connection with the stage he was known as a very distinguished entomologist, a part which not one play-goer in a thousand ever imagined his playing in real life. He was the author of certain standard works upon insects and their natures; of certain sketches and tales—theatrical,—written of course in a lighter vein; and he was happy in the production of occasional verse in the way of prologues, epilogues, and the like. Not one of my friends was more familiar with and more interested in these plaster portraits than was Harry Edwards before his own head was added to the group.

CHAPTER VIII

The Collecting of the Death Masks (*Continued*)—Dean Swift—Franklin — George Washington — Robespierre — Marat — Mirabeau—Edmund Keane—Thackeray—Celia Thaxter—Lord Brougham—Laurence Sterne—Lincoln and Booth—Walt Whitman—Liszt—Process of Taking a Life or Death Mask—Casts of Hands That Have Done Things.

How well I remember John McCullough's coming into the " scullery " one autumn morning, putting his hands in his hearty way on my shoulders, and asking, " How 's the dear mother? "

He had been over the ocean and travelling about our own country for half a year and he had never heard! When I told him " how " he sat down and, literally, he lifted up his voice and wept aloud. The shock of what I had to tell him and of what he felt his innocent query must have meant to me who mourned her recent loss was too much for his already over-sensitive nerves and his already failing mind. After he had recovered himself, in a way, he asked one more question. I know not why. I had never thought of such a thing. Death, for once, had come too near home to me. But he looked around at the casts on the shelves and on the walls, and he asked tremulously:

" Is she here? "

"No, John," I replied, "she is not here!"

And before many months had passed, poor John himself was there.

When Mr. H. H. Kitson, the sculptor, sent me the McCullough mask I hardly recognised it. The changes in his face and expression were so great. And, sometimes, it shakes my faith in the value of these casts as portraits. For it is so unlike the man, sound of brain and of body, whom I had known so well and liked so much. His features as well as his intellect seem, alas, to have gone awry.

Like all the members of his profession, McCullough accepted Shakespeare as the author of Shakespeare's plays, and he literally worshipped the genius of their creator. It was a matter of great pride with him that his most lasting monument was a portrait of himself, hanging in the Shakespeare Memorial Theatre at Stratford, in the erection of which he was so much interested.

A man, great in his own way but very far removed from the American actor in time, in place, in thought, in surroundings, went also awry. The Irish Dean, author of "Gulliver's" famous *Travels*, is supposed to have died in Dublin of softening of the brain. Dr., and, later, Sir William Wilde, the father of Mr. Oscar Wilde, wrote a book once to prove that Jonathan Swift was sane and unusually sane to the end of his life. But Sir Walter Scott, Swift's biographer, thought otherwise. They both of them knew and examined and commented upon the death mask, kept for many years in Trinity College, Dublin. They realised and acknowledged its authenticity. Dr. Wilde compared it with the cast and the drawings of Swift's skull, made when his body was exhumed in 1838, and he accepted it as Swift himself. Whether Swift died "a driveller and a show," matters not. Suffice it to say that the original mask, according to Dr. Wilde, disappeared from Trinity College, Dublin, in 1845 or 1846, and that a copy of it, identical with Dr. Wilde's engraving of it, came into my possession some forty years later through a little dealer in plaster casts in London whom I never found at any hour of the day or evening in a condition of perfect sobriety. He could never explain how he became possessed of it and he did not even know whose mask it was. And so what Trinity College, Dublin, Ireland, has lost forever, the University of Princeton, New Jersey, America, now owns.

Swift and "Stella" were buried side by side in the Cathedral at Dublin, and nearly a century after the Dean's death their coffins were opened by the members of the British Association, then holding its annual meeting in the Irish capital. The skulls were examined and cast, and Dr. Wilde's book contains drawings of them both. Where the original casts of these skulls are now I have never been able to learn.

A mask of Franklin is known to have been made by Houdon in Paris a few months before Franklin sailed from France for the last time and not long before he died. It was sold with the rest of Houdon's effects in 1828 or 1829 and it is supposed to have come into the collection of George Combe.

This Franklin mask has been the subject of some discussion and doubt. Many of the portrait-experts have accepted it as genuine and without hesitation, while others have questioned and even repudiated its authenticity entirely. Among these latter was Mr. Abraham Hewitt, who was the fortunate possessor of the replica of the Houdon bust and who could trace no resemblance between the cast and the sculptured marble. Mr. John Bigelow, on the other hand, the author of a *Life of Franklin*, and naturally very familiar with his face, as it has come down to us in many contemporary paintings from miniatures up to canvases of heroic size, is inclined to believe that mine was taken from life in Franklin's old age and by Houdon.

To satisfy myself and without giving any hint as to who or what I wanted to think it, I showed the object once to Mr. Richard Irwin, a direct descendant of the great philosopher. He had no idea of what was coming, he did not know that such a thing was in existence, but the moment he saw it he exclaimed: " Why, it 's Sophie! "—Sophie being his sister, Miss Sophie Irwin, and a great-granddaughter of Franklin who is said to have perpetuated his own features in hers. Other members of his family have seen and recognised the likeness. This, perhaps, would not have been proof enough in a court of law, but it convinces me in my readiness to be convinced.

Franklin was buried in Philadelphia. His grave, near the back wall of the cemetery, is under the small unpretentious stone which the iconoclasts have not spared. What punishment is meet for the man who would chip a piece off of the monument of Franklin with which to make a paper-weight or to set in a spiral stud?

Franklin brought Houdon to this country in 1785, when he spent some days in the familiar study of Washington's face, and when he made a life mask which he carried back to France and from which he evolved the familiar statue now in Richmond, Virginia. As his stay in America was short and as he was not likely to see Washington again, he manipulated the mask in certain ways, and this will account for the fact that the eyes are open. The original cast belonged to W. W. Story, the artist in words and marble, who had its established pedigree from Houdon's hands. Story always declared that his was the only cast from the mould and that it, itself, had never been moulded. Naturally he doubted the authenticity of my copy and of the copy in the Corcoran Gallery in Washington City; and for that reason his cast, not mine, was with his consent reproduced as the illustration to my book. When I went to Rome last, in the winter of 1892–93, I naturally asked to see the Washington mask. In this Mr. Story could not, at first, gratify me. He knew that it was in his studio; but he could not find it,—at the moment! If a man had confessed to me that he had mislaid his mother-in-law or his second daughter, as if one were an umbrella and the other a lead-pencil, I could hardly have been so greatly shocked. I could no more have mislaid such a treasure than I could have mislaid my own head or my own right hand. But it was found in a forgotten closet after a while and reverently examined. All the texture of the skin was visible and hairs—of Washington—were still attached to the nostrils and to the eyelashes. There had been more hairs, Story told me, but these had been given one by one and only one at a time to be set in rings and brooches by relic hunters whom I envied.

Another mask of Washington was attempted in 1783 by Joseph Wright, but it was broken before it was "set." The fact that the Father of our Country objected, with strong language, on that occasion to submit to a repetition of the performance may prove, perhaps, Mr. Paul Leicester Ford's assertion that while Washington always told the truth, he told it sometimes with pardonable emphasis. This operation by Wright was performed at Mount Vernon and it was one of the few associations connected with his home-life that Washington did not care to dwell upon. The Houdon cast was made in Philadelphia two years later when the subject was about fifty-three years of age.

Finding no very perceptible traces of the fractured jaw-bone in the Robespierre mask, I was in doubt as to its authenticity until I compared it with what is claimed to be the original wax effigy contained in the gallery of the Tussauds in London. Madame Tussaud, the founder of the famous Wax-Works Show, was a French woman of intelligence and veracity who, many years ago, purchased in Paris and carried to the British capital a number of the personal relics of Bonaparte—the bed upon which he died, his toilet articles and the like, including the Antomarchi mask, and she had documents to prove that these with the masks of Marat and Robespierre were what her printed catalogues still declare them to be.

Robespierre, you may remember, attempted or pretended to have attempted to blow off his own head with a pistol bullet before his compatriots should have a chance to cut it off—clean—with the artistic knife invented by Dr. Guillotine. This mask, with those of Marat and Mirabeau, is known to have been made after death " by order of the National Assembly," and the originals of those of Marat and Mirabeau—identical with mine—are in the Musée Carnavalet, the Civic Museum of Paris; Marat in plaster being the exact counterpart of Marat in oils by David, painted from nature immediately after the assassination.

The amiable Miss Corday did a good thing for France and for humanity and for the rights of man when she removed Marat from trials and temptations. And it is to be regretted that she did not begin earlier in her career. There can be very little doubt that the Marat whom she stabbed in the bath, as depicted by David, was the Marat of real life as the cast in my collection embalms him for the inspection of generations yet unborn. Some one has said of him that " he looked like an American Indian with a white skin."

It is said that Mirabeau listened once with complacent eagerness to a certain fine lady of his acquaintance who was making a word-picture of her beau ideal of manly beauty. The description of the face and the figure of the imaginary Adonis entirely coincided with his own notions upon the subject, and when the composite form was completed, the lady paused as if to worship in silence her own creation, and Mirabeau added in a half interrogatory sort of way:

"And a little pock-marked, too, don't you think?"

The signs of the ravages of the dreadful disease on his own face are plainly visible in its replica in plaster.

Mirabeau and Marat were buried for a time in the Pantheon at Paris; but they were soon "de-Pantheonised" by order of the National Assembly. Marat's body was thrown into a common sewer, and the body of Mirabeau was put into an unmarked grave in the criminals' burying-ground. Revenge upon the bones of a dead enemy may be sweet, but it can hardly be savoury.

The Garrick mask, like the cast of the Shakespeare bust, came in 1876 from the shop of Mr. Marshall in Stratford, who wrote its pedigree in pencil upon its back. Unfortunately when the copy was made for *The*

Players in 1888 the writing was effaced and its history I can not now recall. A copy is in the Shakespeare Museum in Stratford; and a third copy I saw in London once, this last being a very early impression and showing conclusively that it was made from nature and probably from life, notwithstanding the fact that a rare engraving of it, not dated, bears an inscription stating that it is "The Mask of Garrick taken from the Face after Death."

There are two alleged death masks of Edmund Kean in existence which do not in the least resemble each other. One is reverently preserved in the rooms of a now degenerate dramatic social club back of the bar of the Harp Tavern near Drury Lane and Covent Garden Theatres in London. Tradition hath it that Kean was a member of this institution, and the mask hangs over the chair in which he is said to have consumed glass upon glass of whiskey after the play and even between the acts; and the surviving members point with great satisfaction at a hole in the wall opposite the mask, made by the quart-cup which Kean threw at the call-boy who ran across the street once to inform him that "the stage waited."

The other mask—my mask—has been accepted as the real Kean by Sir Henry Irving, Edwin Booth, and other lights of their profession; and Sir Henry sees in it a strong likeness to George Clint's hurried sketch of Kean which he now owns and which is supposed to be the only portrait for which its subject ever consented to sit. My own belief is that mine is Kean after death and that the other is perhaps Kean from life—which is very probable,—or perhaps a life or death mask of the younger Kean; or, more likely yet, a death mask or a life mask of somebody else unknown to fame and dead and turned to clay. Kean died and was buried in the town of Richmond on the bank of the Thames. It was hardly the lively Richmond of the present. But not a bad Richmond to die and be buried in for all that. He lies in Old Richmond Church near the bones of Thomson, the poet of *The Seasons*, and not far from the ashes of Burbage, who is said to have been the original representative of Kean's great part, King Richard the Third.

Coming out of the Harp Tavern one day, into which I had gone to inspect this mask and not for any social purpose, I stumbled into the plaster shop of Mr. Brucciani hard by, where I discovered and bought the mask of Thackeray made by Brucciani on that sad Christmas morning at the request of Dr., now Sir Henry, Thompson. It was very distressing to Thackeray's mother and to his daughters, who supposed that the mould and the casts from it had been destroyed as was their strongly expressed wish. Mrs. Anne Thackeray Ritchie, the novelist's surviving daughter, finding to her surprise in 1890 that it still existed and had come into my collection, was good enough, after some natural hesitation, to permit me to have it engraved for my book and later to give it a home at Princeton.

Without this consent of course it would never have met the public eye.

Henry Brougham, the great Lord Brougham, is said to have been possessed of the extraordinary physical accomplishment of being able to waggle his own nose. It was a good nose to waggle. And for years it afforded enormous amusement and no little pecuniary profit to the caricaturists of Great Britain, even to those of his own political party. The description of this famous organ, in a rare book called *Notes on Noses*, is too good to be lost here although I have already quoted it in the *Portraits in Plaster:* " It is a most eccentric nose," says the author; " it comes within no possible category ; it is like no other man's ; it has good points and bad points and no point at all. When you think it is going to the right for a Roman it suddenly becomes a Greek ; when you have written it down cogitative it becomes as sharp as a knife. . . . Verily, my Lord Brougham and my Lord Brougham's nose have not their likenesses in heaven or earth. . . . And the button on the end is the cause of it all." Why the button on the end should mean so much, the author of *Notes on Noses* does not explain. The Brougham mask was one of the original group which found its way from the Second Street ash-barrel into the present collection. Combe seems to have carried it to America while the subject was at the height of his power in England, and so it is therefore, of course, from life.

Another famous nose was the nose of Thomas Paine. Mr. Moncure D. Conway, the biographer of the author of *The Age of Reason*, agreed with me that mine is the mask of Paine, and that it is the work of Jarvis. We compared it carefully with Jarvis's plaster bust of Paine in the rooms of the New York Historical Society and we saw many points of absolute resemblance, especially in the size and the twist of the nose, but it was not until Mr. Conway's *Life* and my own book had gone to press that he found a manuscript journal of Paine's housekeeper which assured us that the mask had been made after death and described the operation. The physiognomists tell us, on the strength of what they find in the cast and in the portrait of Paine, that he was a man of large mental capacity but lacking in thoroughness and correctness; that he was impulsive, self-willed, and arrogant; that he made few personal friends; and that he was not remarkably distinguished for that essential quality of which he wrote so fluently,—to wit, "Common Sense."

I was at Appledore, one of the Isles of Shoals, one dreary grey autumn day in 1894 when Celia Thaxter died. At my suggestion and with the consent of her own people, a mould of her beautifully strong face was made by Mr. Olaf Branner, who also chanced to be at Appledore at that time.

It happened that dear friends of hers and of ours were dining with us on the evening of the day on which the cast came to me. I spoke to them of it and they expressed a wish to see it. I told the butler, John, to bring it down-stairs when he had a moment's leisure. And before we left the table he presented the head—on a silver charger—to each guest in turn. It was a most startling and unexpected act and it precipitated the symposium in a most abrupt manner. Celia always had a wholesome sense of humour, and she would have appreciated the absurdity of the performance, perhaps. But those of us who loved and mourned for her saw only the solemn side of it. It is the first or the second cast from the matrix, and as a "specimen" it is peculiarly strong and fine. Nearly the whole of Mrs. Thaxter's life was spent on one or the other of these beautiful little sea-girt islands off the coast of Maine. She was born, married, and buried among them; there her children were born; there she made and kept her many friends; there she did her work. A veritable queen she was, not only among the humble fisher-folk who were in a way her dependents, but among the cultured summer guests of the hotels, not all of whom were her intellectual peers.

I had so little faith in the so-called mask of Laurence Sterne that I did not put it into my book. No contemporary record of it exists, and I did not see in the peculiarly distressing and unusual circumstances of Sterne's death, how it could possibly have been made. He died in poverty and almost alone. His body-servant, nearly the only friend he had, subsequently told the harrowing story to the world with all its painful details and he mentioned no taking of a mask. The subsequent proceedings were the most gruesome of all. According to tradition, a friend of his, a medical student, going from some festive party to a secret dissecting clinic, found to his horror upon the work-table what was left of Laurence Sterne. He saved the fragments, gathered them up, and buried them in St. George's Cemetery, Bayswater Road, London.

Under these conditions it seems hardly possible that then or earlier a mask could have been made. Nevertheless the face is very like that of the Nolleken's bust, the portraits by Reynolds and Gainsborough, and particularly like the full-length water-colour drawing at Chantilly. But I cannot vouch for it. The world is not so apt to associate Sterne particularly with York Minster, but he was for many years a prebendary of that Cathedral; learning there, no doubt, that the universe was wide enough to hold both him and the poor fly and that God tempers the wind to the shorn lamb, although he could have had there but little actual knowledge as to how terribly our armies swore in Flanders.

Another mask by Brucciani was that of Ben Caunt, the professional prize-fighter and one-time champion of England, although why Brucciani thought the bruiser worthy of a death mask I never quite understood. Mr. Caunt, with a broken nose, retired from the slugging business in the early forties and kept a respectable sporting public-house called " The Coach and Horses " in St. Martin's Lane, London, until he was knocked out forever in 1861. He was highly regarded by the "fancy" for many years; and one of his favourite pupils was Junius Brutus Booth, who presented his son, Edwin, to his sparring master in New York, when Edwin was a lad and enormously impressed by the honour. He had seen judges on the bench and Presidents in the White House; but nobody, he said, ever impressed him so much as did the king of the ring.

Caunt's father, when Caunt was born, was a tenant of Byron's at Newstead Abbey, employed about the grounds in some very humble capacity. The pugilist was fond of declaring that he himself had been a gamekeeper to the author of *Don Juan*. But, as Byron sold Newstead Abbey when Caunt was but three years of age, the latter must have been a very precocious young gamekeeper indeed.

Caunt's was one of the two masks in the collection which affected Booth most. The other, naturally enough, but in a very, very different way, was that of —Lincoln. I shall never forget the first time he saw the Lincoln mask. He asked, innocently enough, whose it was. And when I told him, my heart for a moment stopping to beat, he rose from his seat, took it in his hands, and looked at it for a long time without a word. What it meant to him, we can imagine. The whole awful, awful, business came back to him. The mad, dead brother; the martyred, murdered President. Still, without a word, he put it back in its place, and it seemed to me as he did so that he kissed it with his

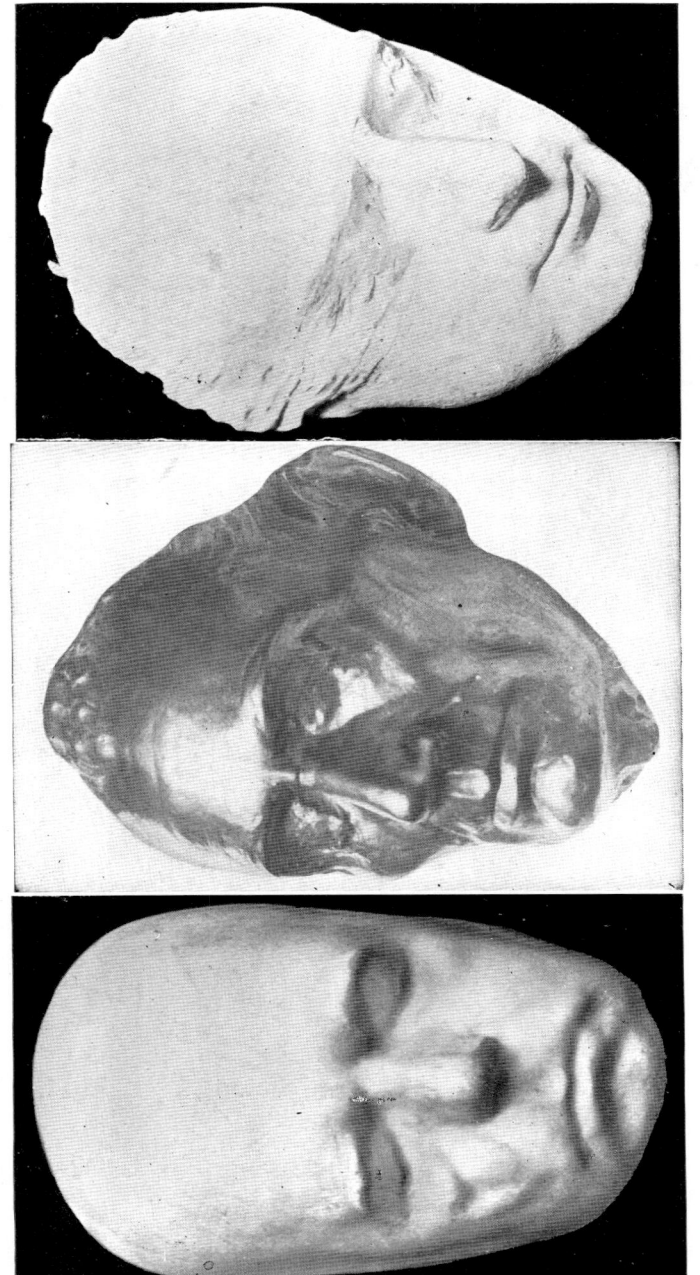

EDWIN BOOTH

ABRAHAM LINCOLN

WALTER SCOTT

DEATH MASKS

fingers. I have seen him in that room look at it silently, over his pipe, many and many a time. But he never touched it or spoke of it again, even to me. What he thought of it, Heaven only knows!

The story that Booth, under similar circumstances, picked up the cast of the hand—not of the head—of Lincoln in the house of Lorrimer Graham, may be and probably is true. But this must have been some years before Booth found the Volk mask in my studio and he never mentioned the incident to me.

Of Lincoln two masks were made, both from life. The first in Chicago in the spring of 1860, by Leonard Volk; the second in Washington some years later by Clark Mills. The Volk mask, without the disfiguring beard, is now in Princeton. The Mills mask belongs to Mr. John Hay, who treasures it very highly. It is so reposeful and peaceful that it has been mistaken for a death mask, even by such expert authorities as Mr. Saint-Gaudens, and the expression of it is very sad. For a long time I could not account for the curious depression in the eyes of my copy of the Volk mask until, in lifting it from its place one day in the library, I unwittingly put my thumbs over the eyeballs and discovered that they fitted the cavities exactly; and I could only infer that some heedless person had done the same thing before the plaster was entirely dry. The mould was made on one piece; and, as it contains both ears, it was removed with difficulty. Mr. Volk described how Lincoln himself assisted in the operation of his own relief by bending his head forward and working it off gradually and gently without injury of any kind to his face or to the mould, notwithstanding the fact that the plaster clung to the high cheek bones and that a few of the hairs of his eyebrows and temples were pulled out by the roots.

Brucciani also made the mask of Rossetti. There are but four casts from the mould. Of one, in the possession of Mr. Hall Caine, that gentleman wrote to me: " I ought, perhaps, to add that it does not give a good impression of Dante. The upper part of the head is very noble but the lower part is somewhat repellent." Mr. William M. Rossetti, from whom my copy came, wrote of it : " I should say that my family and myself do not at all like this vision of my brother's face. In especial, singular as it may sound, the dimensions of the forehead seem wofully narrowed and belied. But, of course, from another point of view the cast tells truth of its own kind."

I can see in the Whitman cast the same wofully narrowing of the forehead. But all the casts tell truth. They must tell truth. They cannot help it. The Whitman mask came to Princeton through me, I am happy to say, from a good Princeton man, the late Mr. Louis C. Vanuxen. But somehow, although it is Whitman, it is not the Whitman I knew. Few men ever impressed me so strongly as did Walt Whitman. It was his personal magnetism that appealed most powerfully to me. It was not his verse, for I did not understand it then, and I do not altogether comprehend it now. It was his wonderful physical beauty. He seemed to be a realisation in the actual flesh of Michael Angelo's *Moses*, or of some of the ancient statues and paintings of Jove himself. I wanted to receive his blessing. As Cervantes said of some one in the translation by Jarvis:

" He had a face like a benediction."

The Whitman mask was made by Mr. Samuel Murray of Philadelphia, assisted by Mr. Eakins. Mr. Vanuxen gave the first cast from the matrix, which included the chest and shoulders, to Mr. H. Buxton Foreman, the editor of Keats and Shelley and a friend and admirer of the American poet. Mr. Foreman has expressed his intention to bequeath his copy to the British Museum. So far as I know there are no others in existence.

I can well remember seeing Whitman before the Civil War—a king-like figure despite his rough clothes —sitting on his favourite throne, the box-seat of the Broadway omnibus of the period. He seemed to spend his whole time in riding up and down that crowded thoroughfare, studying men and things, no doubt, in the glaring light of the *New York Sun*. I knew even then that he was an unique figure in American life, the author of some queer sort of alleged poetry that was already being talked about but which I had not then tried to read. So when an uncle of mine, a youth of about my own age, hailed him once in my presence from a passing omnibus as " Walt ! " I was greatly surprised. I did not suppose that anybody could call him " Walt."

The Liszt mask was the gift of another good Princeton man, Mr. Rudolph Schirmer, whose father brought it to this country from Germany shortly after Liszt died in 1886. As a mask it is an excellent specimen. In the face are seen traces of the unusual resemblance that existed between Liszt and Ole Bull. Mrs. Bull tells of her husband's being frequently mistaken for the harmonious Abbé and of his being the recipient of ovations in public places in Germany which were intended for his double,—demonstrations of popularity which were gratifying neither to the violinist nor to the pianist, each of whom felt himself worthy of applause on his own account.

Edwin Booth gave to The Players the original mask of Burke, and with it a certificate saying that it was made by the especial desire of Queen Caroline; that it came from George IV. to a Mr. Nugent, one of his most excellent Majesty's gentlemen-in-waiting; by whose nephew it was sold in London in 1890 or 1891. The name of its artist is unknown. My copy of it, found in London long before Mr. Booth made his purchase, is probably from the original matrix; but for some unknown reason, perhaps by accident, the moulder scraped the bridge of the nose in the moist plaster, flattening and broading it out of natural shape. It is, in all respects, inferior to The Players cast.

The Curran is one of the Combe masks, the history of the discovery of which I have related. Curran was not distinguished for his good looks. He is described by one observer as being "very ugly indeed, with a thick complexion and a protruding underlip on a retreating face"; and Croker, alluding to his appearance, went so far as to say that he was "like the devil with his tail cut off," which was, no doubt, an exaggeration! But even Sir Thomas Lawrence, who was famous for the flattery he heaped upon his subjects, did not succeed in making Curran a handsome man. One of the best of the existing portraits of Curran serves to establish the identity of the death mask and to show, in the matter of looks, what manner of man was Curran during his life.

Nature made Lawrence himself one of the handsomest men of his time. And this is more evident in the quick than in the dead. A beautiful life mask of him was taken when he was thirty-four, but unfortunately only the rare engraving of this is in my possession. I never saw the plaster and I question if it now exists. The death mask was made by Edward H. Bailey, the sculptor. It does not strike one as being beautiful.

The tail-piece of my published book on the subject of masks is the mask of a living Florida negro boy. The original head was on the shoulders of an humble driver of mules whom Mr. Thomas Hastings, the architect of the Ponce de Leon Hotel at St. Augustine, employed in the building of that famous house. Mr. Hastings gave the subject a dollar to sit for his "portrait in plaster"; and the result was sent to me as representing the lowest intellectual type of present-day humanity, on this continent at least. It is valuable only for comparison's sake.

The process of making a mould of the living face is not quite so agreeable as is sitting for a photograph. I have quoted here very little that is contained in my already printed words on the subject, because I am trying to treat my subject in an entirely different way and from an entirely new point of view. But, from the Introduction to *Portraits in Plaster* I take an eye-witness's account of what happened to a certain Mr. A., in Edinburgh in 1845, which tells the story in full. "The person," we read, "was made to recline on his back at an angle of about thirty-five degrees and upon a seat ingeniously adapted to the purpose. The hair and the face being anointed with a little pure scented oil, the plaster was laid carefully upon the nose, mouth, eyes, and forehead, in such a way as to avoid disturbing the features; and this being 'set' the back of the head was pressed into a flat dish containing plaster, where it continued to recline as on a pillow. The plaster was then applied to the parts of the head still uncovered, and soon afterwards the mould was hard enough to be removed in three pieces, one of which, covering the occiput, was bounded anteriorly by a vertical section immediately behind the ears, and the other two, which covered the rest of the head, were divided from each other by pulling a strong silken thread, previously so disposed upon the face, on one side of the nose." The further remark was made that

"Mr. A. declared that he had been as comfortable as possible all the time!"

This last statement, judging from my own experiences, I am strongly inclined to doubt. An artist friend, who said he knew how to do it, kindly volunteered to perform the operation upon me, and I was anything but "comfortable all the time" or for some time afterwards. I was placed flat upon my back on the laundry table in my own house; my head was put upon an empty soap-box; around my neck and behind my ears was built what was called a "dam" of softish clay; and quills were inserted into my nostrils that I might breathe freely. I was buttered all over, literally, no pure scented oil being available; a pad and a pencil were placed in my hands that I might describe my sensations and give the alarm of impending suffocation if necessary; and the plaster was applied. I do not know how long a performance it was, but it seemed to me to be a year and a day before the thing was pronounced "set," and the heavy burning weight was ready to be removed. And then the trouble began. The operator had not thought the strong silken thread essential; the mould—it was of the face only—was in one piece as in the case of the Lincoln mask; and it would not come off! The butter on the upper lip had not been spread thick enough, and the long hairs of a not very sparse moustache were imbedded in the fixed plaster much more firmly than in the spot of their natural growth. The filaments yielded at the roots and beneath the roots and small fragments of their native soil yielded with them; but the plaster gave up nothing. I was willing to sacrifice my moustache for the cause of science, but it was impossible to loosen the matrix sufficiently to insert a pair of scissors or a razor beneath it. It was finally broken with a hammer as gently as possible, which was not very gently, and it was consequently absolutely ruined as a mould.

The artist was good enough to offer to do it again. But I declared then and there that no other mask of me should be taken until I had passed into a condition of total indifference to worldly things.

I have been asked, frequently, how I became possessed of all these masks of men and women so varied in character, in nationality, and in social position.

How does the angler catch his fish; how does the hunter bag his game? By close study of its dispositions, its habits, by a thorough knowledge of its homes and its haunts. The first cast, as I have shown, was the result of what is called "a fluke." I baited my hook for a bullhead and I killed and landed a salmon, which is the king and the most gamey of all the fish that swim. In my journeyings about the world, on the continents of America and Europe and in fractions of Asia and Africa, for many years I have fished and hunted for masks. I went to the studios of sculptors, to the public museums, and to the plaster shops. Of these last I made a list—from the Trades' Directories—whenever I entered a strange town; and I visited them all, sometimes with success, more often without. In Rome I procured three casts; in Berlin I found four or five; in Paris, half a dozen; in London, eight or ten. Robert Browning and Richard Wagner with a half-forgotten Doge or two are treasured in the City-built-on-piles, but no influence or persuasion of mine could put them into my basket or my bag. The capital of the German Emperor was more generous and obliging. In the Hohenzollern Museum there is the largest but not the most interesting collection of such things in the world. They are purely local and national—"portraits in plaster" of royal personages and of civic or state dignitaries little known or little honoured outside of their own country.

Of these I cared only for the Great Frederick, for the beautiful Louise of Prussia, for Schiller, Mendelssohn, and Beethoven. They are kept in a great hall, in a series of boxes, looking like the desks of a public-school, and each by itself is revealed by the opening of a lid, as if one were inspecting in succession a row of coffins and was permitted to gaze for a moment upon each pallid face in turn—by no means a cheerful or an exhilarating experience. This ghastly effect I have tried as far as possible to avoid in arranging my galaxy of genius in the University Library of Princeton. I want the collection to attract, not to repel; to instruct, not to disgust.

The authorities of the Hohenzollern Museum granted me replicas of the casts I wished upon the assurance that they were not to be used by me for commercial but purely for scientific and educational purposes, and upon the strength of valuable letters of introduction.

The general notion of the money value of these masks is very vague. The newspapers all over the country not long ago stated gravely that I had refused thirty thousand dollars for the collection. I was never offered any amount of money for it or for any part of it, and its actual cost to me—in cash, not in time—was a very much smaller sum.

A gentleman wrote to me once that he had the mask of Madame Malibran, the opera-singer; that he could vouch for its authenticity because it was made by his father; and that he would sell it to me, in the circumstances, for a thousand dollars. I replied that I had a written certificate from Malibran's son, declaring that his own father had made it; and that for my copy, an early one, I had paid fifty cents.

I received, at The Players, one day, a letter from a well-known sculptor saying that he had taken a cast of an equally well-known man of the brush, recently dead; that he had not been successful in finding a market for the bust, based upon it; and that he would sell me the mask for twenty-five hundred dollars. I read the epistle aloud to the group of sympathising members of the club with whom I chanced to be sitting, all of whom knew the artist and his subject, and I remarked that "when the time came to take a mask of the sculptor there would not be plaster enough to cover his cheek!"

This observation, never intended to be made public of course, found its way into print; and it very nearly forced me to become the defendant in a suit for libel.

The collection of casts of hands that have done things has been an interesting side issue to my quest, although of sufficient value to be considered a pursuit in itself. In my Princeton library I have hung the contrasting hands of Voltaire and Walt Whitman side by side. Similar casts of the former are common objects in the plaster shops of Paris, and the original cast is generally accepted as made from nature, although there seems to be no authentic record to this effect. Above it in my library is the written motto, translated from a letter of Voltaire to Cardinal de Berins in 1761: "There are truths which are not for all men, nor for all times." And above the cast of Walt Whitman's hand is the inscription, taken from his *Leaves of Grass*: "One world is away and by far the largest to me, and that is myself. And whether I come to mine own to-day or in ten thousand or ten million years, I can cheerfully take it now or with equal cheerfulness I can wait."

This cast was made by a friend of Walt Whitman's who contributed it to the collection. My first meeting with Walt Whitman recalls exceptionally pleasant reminiscences. I was taken to call upon him in 1877 —Whitman at that time being fifty-eight years old—by Mrs. Mary Mapes Dodge, of whom he was very fond; and in that way I got closer to him than I could have done in a dozen casual meetings. His talk was plain, homely, and tinged with an unexpected vein of "that most uncommon sense of all, common sense." After he went back to Camden he sent me two volumes of his poems—in exchange for a ten-dollar bill—with an autograph inscription. I prize the books highly, although I never read them. I saw him a short time before his death, looking like a god as painted by one of the old masters, and again I came under his peculiar magnetic influence. He drew me down upon the arm of the chair in which he was sitting and held my hand while he talked with me. This, no doubt, was his way with all men, but he made me feel as if I were so distinguished above the rest, and in spite of myself I became an enthusiastic worshipper of Walt Whitman —the man.

The casts that I own of the hands of Lincoln, Thackeray, and Goethe are casts from casts, and as such are none of them so communicative of "the touch of a vanished hand." They are also less clear in detail and less perfect of outline. That of Goethe was found in a plaster shop in Berlin many years ago.

The original of Thackeray's hand was owned by Augustin Daly and was sold at the auction of his effects for the exorbitant sum of $110 to Dean Sage. There is an account in Daly's letters of the manner in which possession of the cast of Thackeray's hand was obtained. As will be remembered, Thackeray died in great pain, and the fingers are noticeably clinched into the flesh as they were found that sad Christmas morning by the mother of the novelist who, as Dickens said, blessed him not only in his first sleep but in his last.

The hands of Lincoln—whom I never saw but once, and that was when he was making a speech on the steps of the Astor House in New York on his way to Washington—were taken by Leonard W. Volk in Springfield, Ill., on the Sunday following Lincoln's nomination in 1860. Mr. Volk was the first Chicagoan to congratulate Lincoln, and at the same time he made an engagement for the following day to obtain a cast of Lincoln's hands. Later that same afternoon, thousands marched to Lincoln's home, passing through the house in single file, each citizen giving Lincoln a vigorous hand-shake. The swollen muscles that resulted from this reception are quite noticeable in the cast. The originals are of bronze and are in the National Museum; but they had disappeared and were virtually forgotten until Mr. Saint-Gaudens found them by accident in a vault adjoining either the Smithsonian Institute or the Patent Office. This was not known to me till I was told quite recently about it by Mr. Saint-Gaudens himself.

The only bronze cast I own is that of the hands of the Duke of Wellington. They are crossed, and not upon the hilt of a sword, and there is supposed to be no other copy of the cast in America. I do not know by whom it was made, but think it was originally done for a statue of the Duke.

Sir Edgar Boehm made the cast of Carlyle's hands

that was loaned to the Carlyle Museum in Chelsea, where I saw it in 1899. Upon learning that they had been loaned by a sculptor whose studio was in the neighbourhood of Cheyne Row, I went to the address given, where I was told that the owner was taking a holiday on the Continent. On the way out of the little courtyard, I noticed the shop of a manufacturer of plaster casts, and found an Italian inside who spoke very little English and who was eating his luncheon. Several specimens of famous statuary were produced, such as are used by pupils who are studying black and white in the art schools. "No," said I, "I want the real hands of famous folk."

The man had nothing but the hands of Carlyle, cast with the mask, after death, in Carlyle's house. These he was ready to sell, but felt that he could not part with the cast for less than two shillings, or fifty cents. After some apparent hesitation we agreed to this price: my real feeling being that it was well worth $50 to me. The man offered to pack the cast and send it after the purchaser, but I carried my new treasure off in a silk handkerchief, and from Chelsea to Princeton virtually held it in my lap. So far as can be ascertained, no other replicas exist.

A gift from William M. Rossetti was the cast of the hand of his brother, Dante Gabriel Rossetti, that was made at the same time as the death mask.

Yet another gift was the plaster hand of Robert Louis Stevenson,— with the forefinger between the

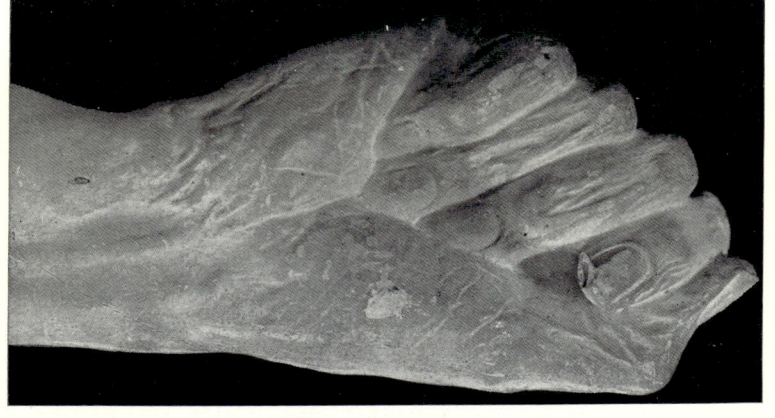

CAST OF THACKERAY'S HAND

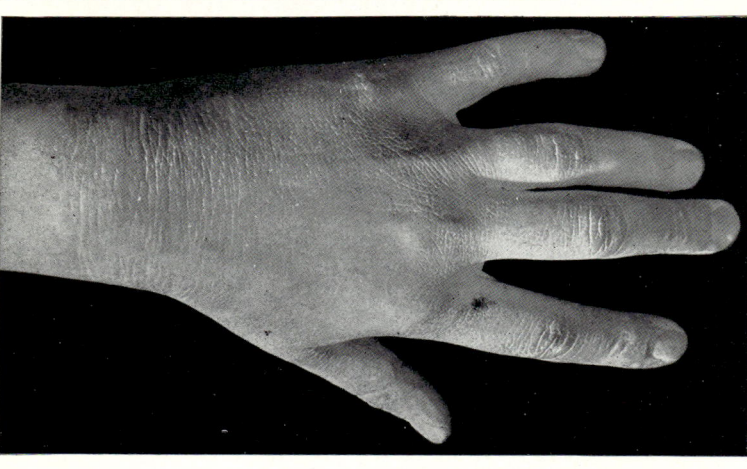

CAST OF HELEN KELLER'S HAND

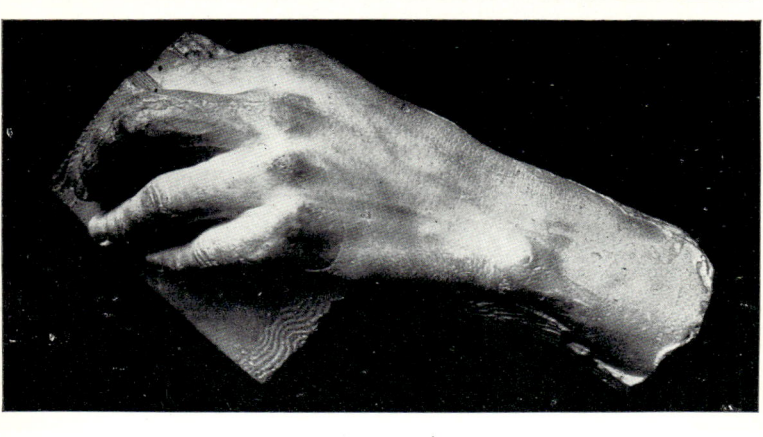

CAST OF STEVENSON'S HAND

leaves of a book,— cast by Mr. Saint-Gaudens as a guide for the large upright medallion now built into the mantelpiece of the library in the house of Mr. George Armour in Princeton. A replica of this medallion was made and sent by Mr. Saint-Gaudens to Stevenson in Samoa, but it never reached its destination nor could it be traced. Mr. Saint-Gaudens afterwards made a second copy of the original which is now in the San Francisco home of Mrs. Stevenson.

How the cast of Whittier's hands came into my possession I cannot remember; but I do remember how, on one occasion, they were put into the lap of the wonderful Helen Keller, of whom Mrs. Hutton is guardian. She instantly recognised the hands as those of Whittier, but said:

"Take them away, take them away! they are so hard and cold and dead, — not the responsive and affectionate hands of dear Mr. Whittier whom I knew so well! Take them away! Please take them away!"

Of all the casts I ever saw, I consider that of Helen Keller the most perfect one taken from nature. It was made about two years ago, and it is of her left hand, the hand by which she reads the raised letters of the electrotyped page before her. Under it, as it hangs in the library, is written:

> She is deaf to the sounds all about us,
> What she sees we cannot understand,
> But she hears with the tips of her fingers,
> And her sight 's in the touch of her hand.

Why the cast of the hand of the artist, William Hunt, is also the left instead of the right, no one knows. It may be that Mr. Hunt was left-handed, or it may be that his right hand was injured at the time of his death.

No cast of Charles Dudley Warner's hands was thought of when his mask was taken after death; and so much did I regret this that Mrs. Warner had made an enlargement of a small picture in which Mr. Warner's hands were prominent, and gave it to me. Failing an autograph inscription, there is a note attached to the frame of the picture, containing the following words:

"HARTFORD, Dec. 2, '94.
"DEAR LAURENCE AND HIS WIFE,
    "BOTH BELOVED:
"We go down Friday morning and shall spend the night with Mrs. Youmans, corner 5th Avenue and 28th Street, and I shall go round to see you if I can. We sail on *La Champagne*, Pier 4, foot of Morton Street, Saturday noon. If we do not see you, you will know that we love you, and love is enough.
    "Yours affectionately,
        "CHARLES DUDLEY WARNER."

Upon the back of the photograph of the Chopin cast is written:

"The cast of Chopin's hand was formerly the property of A Gentleman. By him it was given in 1880 to Countess Castelvecchio, then residing in Florence, and it came to me direct from a member of her family in 1898.

"The drawing of Chopin by Winterhalter was also formerly in A Gentleman's possession, and is dated May 2, 1847.

"(See Weeks's *Life of Chopin*, p. 344.)

"ED. HENNELL."

This is supposed to be the only cast of Chopin's hand in existence. Mr. Hennell, a diamond merchant of Bloomsbury, at whose house are to be met many interesting people, gave it to me.

One of my treasures is the hand of an Egyptian mummy,—no cast this, nor photograph, but the veritable hand,—bought just outside the Tombs of the Kings from an Arab who produced it, with great secrecy, from the folds of his single garment, and who accepted for it just exactly ninety per cent. of the price he originally asked. On its being unpacked with many other rare possessions in the Thirty-fourth Street house, an old family servant asked what it was.

"The hand of an Egyptian princess," I told her, "a princess of the time of the Exodus—it may be the hand of Pharaoh's daughter herself."

Whereupon the woman called in some excitement to a little serving-maid of the house:

"Come here, Maggie: I want you to shake hands, Maggie, with the hand that may have shaken hands with Moses!"

CHAPTER IX

Obituary Notices—Professional Readers—Demands upon Authors—The Duties of Editors—The Mistakes of Compositors.

THE most trying and most nerve-tearing work I ever did was the writing of the obituary notices of my own personal friends before their deaths. It is hard enough to learn to talk of those we love in the past tense when the tense is past; but when one is forced thus to write of men still in the flesh, of men with whom, perhaps, one is still brought into daily, intimate contact, the task is sometimes heart-breaking. Not a few tears have I shed, of a morning, over men with whom I have laughed the night before, and with whom I hoped to laugh for many years to come. They knew of the laughter. But they never heard of the tears,—at the time. Perhaps when that eternity is reached where they are to shed no more tears they will learn all about it.

The first of these ante-mortem requiems was my "Memoir of Booth," written for *Harper's Weekly* when it was seen that the fatal hour which his friends dreaded, but which he, himself, did not dread, was so soon to come. He told me one night, when I occupied

one of his rooms at The Players, and as I helped to
undress him and to "tuck him" into his bed, that his
only fear was a long, helpless invalidism, involving
weeks and months of a rolling chair or a sofa ; was to
be fed and waited on by others ; to be a nuisance to
himself and to his people. And he added that he
would lay his head on his pillow and go to sleep with
perfect contentment if he were sure that he would
awake in "The Mysterious Somewhere-Else," to which
he was not afraid to go. When I looked at him the
next morning, that beautiful head resting upon his
arm, his eyes closed, his face in absolute repose, his
breathing hardly perceptible, I thought for a moment
that the hour he hoped for had come ; and I was almost
glad, for his own dear sake.

That day, and not until that day, did I consent to do
what my editors wished. They thought that I knew
more of his inner life, more of the man as a man, and
not as an actor, than did any other available writer ;
and the sorrowful task was performed, to be put away
for a few short months and published, alas, too soon.

I wrote, in the same sad, anticipatory way of poor
Barrett, of Bunner, of Kate Field, as I saw them or as
I heard of them slowly dying. I wanted the world to
know, so far as I could tell it, what I knew of the good
that was in them ; and, hard as it was, I realised that
what I had to say could not be said by me under the
pressure of personal, present grief.

I have, carefully housed in editors' safes, long obituary notices of two men, still living, who are very dear to me. And they both know it. What I am to put on record concerning Mr. Joseph Jefferson when he joins the enormous majority will be said with his knowledge, in a way, and partly at his own suggestion. What I said about Mark Twain when the report came to us, happily to be contradicted, of his lying at the point of death in some far-away, strange city, during his memorable journey around the world, I would permit Mark to read, if I were not, man-like and Scotch-like, ashamed to let him understand how much I love him, how dearly I prize his affectionate friendship. May they rest unread, carefully stowed away in the editors' safes—those two brief chronicles—for many years to come.

I spent on one afternoon late in November, 1898, some ten minutes or so in Mr. Jefferson's room at the Holland House, New York. He had been quite ill for some weeks, but that day he was very bright, and full of hope and of interest in things mundane; and as we talked and laughed together I had — all the while, weighing me down like a lump of ice—that obituary of him in my pocket! I did not expect to see him; I did not think of the horrible bit of manuscript as I sent my card to him, until suddenly its presence flashed upon me,—and I felt like a literary ghoul!

The general reading-public must be astonished sometimes at the prompt and exhaustive notices which the daily journals contain of important personages, who are cut off suddenly or prematurely in the midst of their life-work. Long and immediate articles appear concerning some great warrior killed at the head of his army or on the deck of his ship; of some political ruler shot by the hand of an assassin; of some author or artist found dead in his bed, or thrown from his wheel. But these articles are often prepared long years before they are used, and are kept "up to date" by men whose business it is to set down each one of his subject's public acts or notable achievements. If ex-President Harrison marries; if ex-President Cleveland moves to Princeton; if President McKinley signs a declaration of war with Spain, it is all noted under the proper head and with the correct date; and when the supreme earthly hour comes, the editor has but to press the button and the compositor, and the printer, and the proof-reader, and the newsboy do the rest. It happens, now and then, that the obituary-writer has the weird experience of reading his own or her own obituary notice—so far as it goes! Miss Gilder, detailed to tell the sad story of the taking off of John Gilbert, the actor, properly pigeon-holed under the alphabetical *Gil*, was curious to look a little beyond the consonant *b* for the consonant *d*; and there she found what was to be said of *Gilder, Jeannette*, the morning before her funeral.

Of all the manuscript — poetry, sermon, history, romance, essay, sketch, story, grave or gay, long or short, wise or foolish—that is submitted to publishers of books or periodicals, it is estimated that but ten *per centum* is worthy of serious consideration and that not three *per centum* is likely to see the light of print. "Professional readers," like all other men, are of course not infallible; and some serious mistakes are make in the best regulated of establishments; but the verdict is generally just and according to the evidence. Sad is it, though, to think of the hours and days and weeks and months and even years spent in the production and in the elaboration of so many unavailable articles; of the care given to them, of the life and heart put into them; and of the bitter mortification and disappointment which are the only results.

There once came to me as a publisher's "reader," from a town in the far north-east of these United States, the manuscript of a story which was fully twice as long as *Vanity Fair* or *The Pickwick Papers*. Its manual part was the perfection of neatness. It was written with the utmost care in a hand beautifully clear and distinct; it was the hand of a slow and laboured writer, and it was the hand of a refined and probably a youngish woman. Every *i* was dotted; every *t* was crossed; every comma was in its place; the French and the Italian words and the English italicised sentences, which were many, were underlined by means of a ruler and with a coarser pen; the thousands of pages of heavy foolscap were numbered in red ink; the chapter-heads were engrossed in Old English text, and it was dated on the last leaf, "Christmas Day, 183—."

The Publisher's Reader 235

As a story it was without interest, sequence, sometimes without sense. Its acceptance was utterly out of the question. One reader, who had not heard my "opinion," condemned the work in two words as "no good!" And when I saw it packed to be returned to its creator I felt as if I were an executioner attending the funeral of some widow's only child, my own victim; as if I were a murderer, standing by a casket holding nothing but the ashes of dead hopes!

The publisher's reader works in the dark and in profound secrecy. He or she, very frequently she, is not permitted to exchange views with the other readers until the final judgment is put on record; sometimes is not supposed to know who the other readers are; and is rarely permitted to know the name of the author whose work is to be read. I accepted—without reading it at all—a certain story called *Their Pilgrimage* because I recognised, at the first glance, the handwriting of Mr. Charles Dudley Warner and because I had heard, from Mr. Warner himself, that it had been ordered and accepted and paid for in part already! It was submitted to me, I presume, as a test and because I had some time before rejected emphatically, as lacking in everything, a romantic tale which had since been accepted and published by another house, had been universally praised by press and public, and had sold enormously. I do not care much for the matter or the manner of it, to this day!

On the other hand, I urged the acceptance of a

serious book which, as I understood later, every other reader on the staff had condemned. It seemed to me to fill every practical want, to have all the merits and few of the faults of its kind, and to have, above all, the not common merit in books of its kind—to wit, the promise of popularity. I am glad to say that it was accepted, and I am proud to say that it is now universally regarded as a standard work, although it was a first effort of its maker. It has been followed by many more, written at the publisher's request, and forming now a very valuable library of their own. I met the author once at a dinner party; but I never mentioned the fact that I had had, by chance, the great good fortune to be the first to discover him.

The professional reader's lot in life is not always a particularly happy one. At a salary ranging from fifteen to twenty-five dollars a week, he is expected to examine into the worth or the worthlessness of from three to six examples of literary manufacture a day; the amount of his wages depending upon the quality of his examples; the number of his examples depending upon their length. He must know what the publisher wants, which is what the public wants; for the publishers, no matter how much they may like it themselves, cannot afford to put upon the markets, at considerable cost of production, any article which is not likely to sell. And the reader must know why it is wanted. Style and subject may be admirable, but if the subject is hackneyed no amount of style will give it a trade-value. In considering translations, the reader must try to discover if the work has ever before been rendered into English and, if so, by whom, under what name, how, when, and where. Before the passage of the American International Copyright Law, he had to find out if any British work submitted to him had already been printed in this country, or had been imported in printed form, and the size of its edition. He must have a knowledge of books and of their makers; a familiarity with standard and ephemeral literature of all kinds sufficient to admit of his being able to detect plagiarisms of plot, of expression, and even of ideas. He must overcome his own personal prejudices. He must keep ever in his mind the fact that, even if he is not cultivating the public taste, it is at least his bounden duty to see that the public taste is not vitiated by bad language, bad English, bad manners, and bad morals.

He must write and sign on all occasions a carefully prepared "opinion," as it is technically called, giving as concisely and as clearly as possible his verdict upon the particular piece of work in question and his reasons for delivering that verdict. These "opinions" are written upon uniform paper; they are marked, numbered, and dated; they are folded always in a certain way; they are put into cases made for the purpose; they are indexed under three heads—the name of the author, the name of the reader, and the title of the work; and they are kept for many years. Some of these "opinions" are literature in themselves although never to see the light of print, and they are often most interesting reading when looked at in the light of subsequent results. But not so often are they agreeable reading to the reader whose "opinion" is shown to have been wrong.

Above all, the reader must devote a good many precious hours to the perusal of countless pages which cannot interest him, which often bore him, and which sometimes shock him, at a stipend of from two and a half to four dollars a day. It must not be inferred that he is dissatisfied with his pay. If he resigns or is removed, there are many others ready and eager to take his place; for he is a lucky workingman of letters who can earn, readily and surely, the daily wages of a plumber's assistant or the gas-man's apprentice.

The "*special* reader" is paid by the piece; usually five dollars for each work submitted to him. He reads occasionally and only the subjects relating to his own particular line of thought and study. As an expert in mathematics, let us say, or geology or music or the arts or in maritime construction, or in anything else, his opinion is of course valuable. Not regularly attached, he not infrequently reads for more houses than one, and as books are passed from firm to firm of publishers, it happens, now and then, that the "special reader" is paid six times for saying to half a dozen different establishments that a certain work, on "Ancient Hymnology," for instance, he cannot conscientiously recommend. That is almost the only kind of reading which the professional reader thoroughly enjoys.

Prominent among the troubles and trials of the professional writer are the amateur papers, in prose and verse, which he is asked to read and to criticise and sometimes to find a market for. They come from friends whom he would like to help and to encourage; and they come from utter strangers who have no claim whatever upon his time or his attention. The strangers do not understand how much they are asking and the friends are rarely satisfied with the results of their requests. To tell a young man, who thinks he has ideas and the gift of expressing them, that his ideas are not new and that his manner of expression is not particularly happy is an exceedingly unpleasant and thankless task. Nevertheless the young man wants to be told "the whole truth and nothing but the truth," and he does not believe it is the truth when he hears it. The truth, not infrequently, is apt to be so unpalatable that he never forgives the truth-teller nor forgets the damage done to his pride and his feelings, especially if the candid and unvarnished statement comes from an author with whom he has some personal acquaintance. No one but the author knows how much of the harmony of familiar intercourse has been wrecked upon the rock of honest criticism, honestly but inconsiderately sought, and honestly but unwillingly granted.

It is the duty of the editor to accept or reject. That

is what he is an editor for; but it is not necessarily his business to tell the "reason why." If the submitted manuscript is printed and paid for, the reason why is self-evident; if it is declined, no "reason why" ever given would be satisfactory. And the editor is always to blame. He is not disliked so heartily, however, as is the constant contributor or the occasional contributor who, without having the power to reject or accept anything, even his own contributions, is expected to read carefully, to weigh conscientiously, and to give—for nothing—his opinion upon a piece of literary work which is sometimes good, usually indifferent, and generally bad. If he says it is good, he is believed to be saying merely what anybody would say; if he says it is indifferent, he is considered impertinent at least; if he says it is bad, he is not only a fool but a brute; and if he refuses to say anything whatever, he is an impertinent brute and an idiot combined. And all this is brought about through no fault or voluntary act of his own.

There seems to be an impression afloat among amateur authors that nepotism and personal favouritism are strong powers in the editorial sanctums. There is, of course, something in a name. The public likes and demands names in many cases; but the editors are anxious to find new names that are attached to new thoughts and to new gifts; and they prefer, naturally, something good under a name unknown to fame, to something indifferent or bad signed by a name that has already made itself famous or, at least, familiar. And in many instances this work of the 'prentice hand, because it is good work, but rough, is polished and scoured and scraped and patched—by means of the traditional blue pencil and with great patience and infinite pains—until it is fit for use.

This patching and scraping and cutting and fitting, by the way, is another great trial to the practised writer, although he often has to endure it. He does not always see the reason or the necessity for it; he protests against the twisting of what he considers one of his happiest phrases or the absolute elimination of what he knows to be one of his best thoughts. And when one hyper-moral editor, in a description of a railway accident, cuts down fifteen flasks of whiskey to two; and when another very particular editor turns the familiar quotation "Damn the critics who damned the play" to "Dash the critics who dashed the play," the author rebels altogether—if he can afford to!

When *The Boy I Knew* was telling the young readers of *St. Nicholas* how he and his friend, Bob Hendricks, smoked their first cigar, "half a cigar left by Uncle Phil," and how they wished they had n't, the editors asked him to throw away the half of Uncle Phil's cigar. No self-respecting boy, they said, would think of going to his father's box and taking out of it a whole, new "Delicioso," for that would be stealing; but he might be tempted to pick up a stump from the ash-tray, and try that—"if the idea was put into his head!" "But him no buts," they said, paraphrasing Aaron Hill in *The Snake in the Grass;* and the butt was put entirely out of the reach of the innocent boy, who looked around for another butt no doubt. And no doubt he wished he had n't!

On a certain centennial occasion I wrote, by request and without payment, for a daily illustrated journal of New York, an article upon the performance at the "John Street Theatre," just an hundred years before that night, of a fine old comedy presented by a fine old company of comedians. I stated precisely where the "John Street Theatre" had stood; on the north side, between Broadway and Nassau Street, directly in the rear of Mr. Grant Thorburn's famous seed-shop; Grant Thorburn having been in his day a well-known "character" of the town. I added that then there still existed the alley-way leading to the stage-door of the old house of entertainment, along which the performers, professional and amateur—Major André among the latter—used to pass before the Revolution and shortly after the Independence of the United States was declared and recognised. The proof of the article came to me as I had written it, and it was read and returned. But when the paper appeared all mention of "Grant Thorburn's famous seed-shop" had disappeared. The professional blue pencil had wiped it out of newpaper existence. When I asked the reason why, I was told that the matter had been laid before Grant Thorburn's descendants and successors, who had refused to pay for my unconscious and undreamed-of advertisement; and the ellipsis had been the result. This closed my connection with the daily illustrated journal in question. And shortly afterwards the daily illustrated journal in question closed its connection with itself.

A short, so-called, poem of mine was cut out bodily from a longish prose paper by another editor, on the ground of its indelicacy; but it was permitted to stand alone in the columns of *Life*. It was called "The Modest Maples"; and, at the risk of shocking you, I venture to quote it in full:

> The willows wept that the summer was dead,
> As they shrank in the bleak, autumn air;
> And the maples all blushed a rosy red,
> At the thought of their limbs being bare!

What are technically called "Comics," it may be said in passing, bring twice as much in verse as in prose and the manufacturer of such articles naturally works for the better paying market. The "Wail of the Waves," with its climactical play upon words, was originally written as a prose dialogue between a mother and her inquiring son. After it was accepted, and paid for in that form with a small check, a second play upon words occurred to me; it was amended, put into rhyme, and the check was doubled! As an object-lesson it is here appended, as it was finally given to the world:

> "What are the wild waves saying,
> As over the sands they sigh?
> Why do they groan and grumble?
> Is it 'cause they are tied so high?"

> "My child, the wild waves murmur,
> And angry passions show,
> Because some careless wader
> Has stepped on their under-toe!"

Still another of the trials of the editor is the receipt and sometimes the acceptance of stolen goods. The dishonest writer who is not afraid and not ashamed to steal away the brains of other persons and to sell them for profit is hardly so unfamiliar an object in the world of letters as he is supposed to be. He may be a pickpocket or a sneak-thief, merely filching ideas or fragments of plots; or he may be a burglar or a highway robber, out and out, breaking in or knocking down and taking away bodily whole poems, whole essays, whole stories, changing the labels and the trade-marks and disposing of them to innocent parties. No matter how well-read the editor may be, he cannot possibly have read everything; certain clever counterfeits and imitations, now and then, escape the eye of the sharpest detective and are passed upon him, and by him are passed along, to his own no little chagrin, and to the great delight of other editors, when the fraud is discovered.

While I have no knowledge of ever being caught by the issuer of stolen goods, it is only because I have had so little occasion to be deceived in that way. But, although I never posed as a victim to the literary confidence game, a much worse fate befell me once when I was accused of having stolen the goods myself! The case was a peculiar one; and the coincidence was certainly remarkable—if it were a coincidence.

There was told me, at a Boston dinner-table one night, the little story of a little girl who, without her mother's knowledge, was embroidering something for her mother's Christmas. The child—child-like—was very eager to finish it—just to see how it would look; and she fretted herself into a sort of semi-nervous fever in her excited haste. At last her aunt, who was in the secret—and so was the mother, for that matter, although she was to pretend to be greatly surprised—at last the aunt said to the child: "Don't be in such a hurry, Elsie. There is plenty of time. Rome was not built in a day, you know!" "Rome not built in a *day*, Auntie?" came the quick and incredulous reply. "Rome not built in a *day!* Why! God made the *whole* world in *six* days. And surely He did not spend all of *one* day on Rome."

I asked permission to put the tale into print and to give the proceeds to Elsie as a Christmas gift on my own account. Shortly after it appeared in "Harper's Drawer," to Elsie's great pride, there came to the Harpers, from a lady living at the other end of the land, a severe letter stating that she was the mother of the child—whose name was not Elsie; that she had sent the contribution to the *Magazine* many years before; that no notice was ever taken of it then; that some member of the editorial staff had appropriated it now; had slightly altered it—but had not improved it,—and that she wanted pecuniary damages! There was no record of such an article; no one remembered it or anything like it; but in defence of my own reputation for honesty I was compelled to get certificates from Elsie's family proving that the remark was original with Elsie and Elsie's very own.

That some small minds think alike on great occasions all editors know. When Miss Willing's engagement to Mr. Astor was announced some years ago, *Puck* received fifty or an hundred single paragraphic contributions to the effect that Jack asked her and she was willing! And the personal play upon the proper names in every variety of verbal shape was seen in every so-called comic paper in this country. The joke—if it is a joke—was a palpable one which almost made itself; and its manifold appearance can easily be accounted for; but how could Elsie and the other child, separated so far in time and space, say the same unusual thing, under the same uncommon circumstances, and in the same exceptional way? If it was mental telepathy, why was it so long in transmission? Or did the far-away mother dream that her own daughter had said it in some previous incarnation?

This is respectfully submitted to the Society for the Encouragement of Psychical Research.

It is not true, as is generally supposed and as is so often asserted, that manuscript from unknown hands does not receive just care and prompt attention. The greater part of it is the recipient of more attention and care than it deserves. It is read—although not all of it is read; and it has every possible consideration. The first paragraph, in too many sad cases, shows its absolute lack of value to the editor or the public; while in the fewer instances it is read from title to finis, it is conscientiously considered, weighed, and measured; and if the pattern be a pretty pattern and an adaptable one, every effort is made to find a place for it and to make it fit.

Nor is it true, as is also generally supposed to be true, that any amount of personal or professional influence has any weight whatever upon the professional decision of the editor. He prints what he considers good and proper; not what is declared to be good and proper by somebody else, no matter who that somebody else may be and no matter how strong may be that somebody else's alleged "pull." I received once a bulky package of manuscript from an old acquaintance who said, in effect: "You are in the Harper Ring; you have got your wife into the Harper Ring; you have got Harry This and Lilly That into the Harper Ring; and I don't see why you don't get *me* into the Harper Ring too! Here are a couple of articles as good as anything the Harpers generally publish. If the one is too feminine for the *Magazine*, see that it goes into the *Bazar*. If the other is too juvenile for the *Weekly*, find a place for it in *Young Folks* [as the *Round Table* was then called]. Anyway see that they are published and get me into the Harper Ring!" Happily or unhappily, for me, there were on my writing-table at that moment four official notes, one from each of the editors of the periodicals in question, and each one of them declining a contribution of my own! I put them into an envelope without comment and sent them to my correspondent as my only reply. They seemed to prove conclusively that I was not in the Harper Ring, although I had been, for years, on the editorial staff of the *Magazine* as well as a frequent contributor to the other journals; and I hope that they proved, which is certainly the case, that there is not and never has been a Harper Ring.

I started, in 1893, my semi-centennial year, to make a slow and deliberate journey around the world—"My Pilgrimage." I spent a longer or a shorter time each, in London, in Paris, in Venice, in Florence, in Rome, in Genoa,—all of them more or less familiar to me; and also in the, then, to me, new cities of Athens, Constantinople, Cairo, and Jerusalem. And when I felt that I could hold no more, that I had bitten of the fruit of the tree of knowledge of travel all that I could at that time digest, I came home. As a member of that editorial staff of *Harper's Magazine*, with no authority whatever in the so-called "Harper Ring" except over my own particular department, I was asked in every one of these cities as well as on every one of the steamers sailing the Mediterranean, the Bosphorus, the Adriatic, and the Atlantic, to read and accept some sort of a contribution to that publication. In London it was a short history of the trade guilds and an excellent one. In Paris it was a description of the Carnavalet Museum. In Venice it was an account of a trip to the Engadine. In Florence it was the story of Dante's career there,— about which I myself had already written. In Rome it was a series of articles upon the home life of the Italian King and Queen. In Genoa it was a scientific treatment of ancient Italian coins. In Athens it was, of all things, a tale of early Virginia. In Constantinople it was the true account of the adventures of a man who had figured in a romance by Mr. Marion Crawford. In Cairo it was a disquisition upon the folk-music of the Arabs as compared with the songs of the negroes of the Southern States of America. In Jerusalem it was a paper showing the existence of petroleum in the region round about the Dead Sea and the money that was in it to American investors. On the Bosphorus it was a report of the labours of the American missionaries in Turkey. On the Adriatic it was " Rhymed Rules for American Leads in Whist." And on the Atlantic it was just a plain little poem for young readers. I thought I *might* escape this last, but I bet a big cigar that it would happen, and I won my bet! The verses were handed to me as we passed Fire Island on our way to Sandy Hook.

They were each in its line good enough, or so it seemed to me. I took them all—although I did not read them all—and, except the verses, which I presented in person the next day, I sent them, generally at my own expense, to the only man who could accept or reject them, Mr. Alden, the Editor-in-Chief of *Harper's Magazine*, over whom I had no more influence than has any one of his other friends.

The Cairo incident was, perhaps, the most amusing of all; as it was, in a measure, the most disappointing to my personal if not to my professional pride. I had spent some six or seven weeks at Shephard's Hotel, visiting from day to day every nook and corner of the place; studying the mosques; making myself familiar with all the easily reached and all of the out-of-the-way bits of Oriental architecture; haggling in the bazars for scaribs and embroideries and things I did not want and had no intention of buying; mixing freely with all sorts and conditions of native women and men; going, generally uninvited, to weddings and to funerals; drinking queer coffee, queerly made, out of queer little cups; smoking queer tobacco with my queer, newly found friends.

I had sat on the chairs of Shephard's veranda for hours together, watching that wonderful and unfailingly delightful procession of donkeys and camels and tea-carts and dromedaries and artillery caissons and litters and *saises* and sheiks and snake-charmers and Arab hawkers and guides and dragomen and kilted Highland privates and red-coated British officers and English and American ladies in Parisian gowns and Arab women with veiled faces and half-naked babies and all the picturesque paraphernalia, local and personal, of that ancient city. It appeared to me to be the realisation of an *Arabian Night's* dream added to a stray chapter or two out of the Old, or the New, Testament; and I did not know whether I was asleep or awake. One fine morning, and nearly all mornings are fine on the banks of the Nile, on my way from Cairo to the Second Cataract, there came to me an official notification on a dromedary that the Khedive's Minister of War, unsolicited by me, would grant me an interview at five of the clock the next afternoon.

This, I said to myself and to my wife, is fame. My reputation has preceded me. It has won for me recognition these thousands of miles away. And it had! The Minister of War of the Khedive, very black with one eye only and pock-marked, received me in the War Office to which I went in an Anglicised cab, not on foot or on donkey-back, as was my usual mode of procedure. He presented me to a lady whom I assumed to be his First Wife but who was not—a lady as pock-marked, as one-eyed, and as black as he was; he spoke to me most graciously, in pretty poor English and in very good French,—of both languages his First Wife was entirely ignorant. He gave me some very decent five-o'clock tea, which I never drink. And then he informed me that he had sent for me, not because I was a distinguished visitor to Egypt's coral strand, but because he had read a paper of mine in *Harper's Magazine* upon the "Negro Minstrel on the American Stage," and because he himself had made a study of the aboriginal music of his own country. He had written, in French, an exhaustive paper upon the subject which he wished me to have properly translated and promptly published in the periodical of which, as he thought, and as he expressed it, I was the Literary Minister of the banjo and bones! Two short "poems" of mine, perpetrated at Shephard's Hotel, where they had won some little popularity because of their purely local flavour, I thought might, perhaps, have attracted the favourable attention of the noble member of the Khedive's Cabinet, who consequently wished to meet and to thank their author. I had heard dragomen recite them in the streets and it was not impossible that they had found their way into court circles. They were the only examples of original literary composition coming within my knowledge during that twelvemonth, which were not sent to Mr. Alden; but it may not be amiss to set them down here:

> I bought a scarib,
> From an Arab,
> Who was dressed up like a sheik;
> And was willing,
> For a shilling,
> To declare it "real antique."

> A ring with a ruby in,
> Bought I of a Nubian,
> Who was ready to swear to its real ancient date.
> But ways that are Nubious
> Are apt to be dubious—
> The ruby's a bead, and the setting tin-plate!

Still another of the trials of the author is the typesetter, as he is backed and supported by the proofreader. It sometimes seems as if they must do it on purpose, for many of their mistakes are too ingenious to be accidental. An entire volume might be filled with the stories of typographical errors and it would be entertaining if not instructive reading. A number of these, as happening to me or as coming within my ken, may be worth repeating here. The first befell Mr. Brander Matthews. He wrote of a certain collection of short stories, translated from the French, that they suggested in a way *The Tales of a Wayside Inn;* he found himself put into print as declaring that they suggested "*the tail of a wayside hen!*"

I was made to speak once, in print, of " the *manures* and customs of the Mexicans." Their *manners* may be unpleasant. But I did not mean to express it in that blunt way.

In reviewing a book about the British Parliament, I wrote that "the most interesting and comprehensive chapter, perhaps, was that which gives the history of Lord Palmerston's *career!*" The final word of the sentence was printed *cancer*, passing proof-reader and writer both ; and so standing, in the back pages of a copy of *Harper's Magazine*, to this day. It was the subject of much facetious comment in the editorial pages of a leading journal at the time ; the editor, in a perfectly kindly and good-humoured sort of manner, having great fun at my expense and commenting freely upon my familiarity with that peculiar disease, particularly as it was developed in the case of Lord Palmerston. All of which I enjoyed as much as the editor did. The editor is still my good friend ; but my name, by strict orders, has never been mentioned in the journal in question since I said once of its publisher and proprietor that he could afford to keep house upon his professional income because (unless he dined out) his living was not high and he burned his own natural gas ! The fault of this remark could not possibly be laid at the door of the composing-room and I have never been forgiven for it. I am not criticised in his columns, I am not condemned or abused ; I am invariably and absolutely and entirely ignored. And I have never explained that the remark, although it got into print, I did not intend of course to be printed.

The most perplexing and absurd of these typographical errors tried to find its way into the columns of *Harper's Weekly* but fortunately was captured. At the time of the union of the Astor, Lenox, and Tilden Libraries, I wrote a long and hurried paper of several columns concerning the three institutions and their founders. The journal was to go to press early on Saturday and the article was not finished until very late on Friday night. The messenger-boy took it to Franklin Square the next morning before I was awake, and by the time of my arrival at the editorial-rooms, the long, wet galley-proofs, unseen as yet by professional proof-readers, were ready for my inspection.

Printed on different presses and in different rooms, they came down to me naturally in an irregular way, without sequence, without head or tail. I skipped from paragraph to paragraph, from subject to subject, in a most confusing manner, the printer's-devil standing impatiently at my elbow, the typesetters crying for "revise"; and all went swimmingly along until I came to the following remarkable sentence: "New York, perhaps, has never fully realised until this day how greatly it has been enriched by the receipt of the *vest buttons* of James Lenox!"

Why "*vest buttons*"? I had no recollections of writing anything about Mr. Lenox's "*vest buttons,*" or about any buttons of any sort belonging to Mr. Lenox or to his library. And I could not remember, in the haste of composition, what I had written. But I certainly had not mentioned "vest buttons," which could, in no possibility, have any connection with the subject in hand. At last in despair I sent for "copy," when it was discovered that Mr. Lenox's "*vest buttons*" were the "*vast bequests*" of that generous, public-spirited gentleman!

But still I ask, why "*vest buttons*"?

Even since I have been at Princeton, I have found myself quoted as picking up many "*earnest persons*" instead of "*honest pennies*"; as taking a "*dog*" instead of a "*day*" out of my vacation; as being possessed of a coach and four and "a *gold gallows*" instead of "*gold galore*"; as "*aiming from* the train" instead of "*arriving on the train*"; as "*arranging myself*" instead of "*arraying myself*" in a golf-suit; as driving and putting "*gold balls*" instead of "*golf balls*"; as making my cook "*garbage*" instead of "*garnish*" the dish with parsley; as making my dairy-maid "*charm the butler*" when her business was to "*churn the butter*"; and finally, as speaking of a friend as being "*slightly dead*" instead of "*slightly deaf.*"

Many "earnest persons" in Princeton have witnessed these typographical contortions of mine and will vouch for the fact that they are not invented for the occasion.

I can understand the dairy-maid as being willing and ready to "charm the butler"; but again I ask—why "vest buttons"?

One of the most serious of all the trials of an author is the selection of the proper and the "taking" title for an article or a book. *Plays, Players, and Play-Houses* is the sub-title of Doran's *Annals of the English Stage.* Upon this hint I let my 'prenticework speak; and its name, I am sure, helped the sale of *Plays and Players*, and struck the public eye and interest. *The Literary Landmarks of London* appealed to me because of its alliterative latitude and the series of "Literary Landmarks" naturally followed. *The Curiosities of the American Stage* was an accident. It was so named because it was to be the companion-volume to a series of papers which I intended to call "The Curiosities of Books"; but it appeared before "The Curiosities of Books"—which never appeared at all! The "Book" papers were split up into two little books, companions to each other, and known as *From the Books of Laurence Hutton* and *Other Times and Other Seasons*. The name of the latter of these expresses, fairly well, its contents, a collection of papers upon Golf, April-Fooling, Tennis, Christmas Pastimes, Foot-ball, The Feast of St. Valentine, Boat Races, and the like, as they were evolved and existed in the days gone by; but the former is a mistake and a misnomer. The volume opens with a chapter upon "American Book-Plates"—*Ex Libris*—the parent-article, by the way, of a subject which has since developed a library of its own,—and it is devoted to what I considered at the time were the out-of-the-ordinary, and the interesting things, personal and otherwise, which were contained in the books in my own possession,—" Poetical Inscriptions," "Personal Inscriptions," "Poetical Dedications," and the like. I intended its title to be "*Ex Libris*, Laurence Hutton," but I was told that very few persons knew what *Ex Libris* meant and that a book under a foreign name or an unfamiliar name is a dangerous experiment—this was long before the days of the great success of *Quo Vadis*—so I put my *Ex Libris* into literal English, and called it *From the Books of Laurence Hutton*, thereby misleading those who never read it—and they, naturally, are very, very many—into the idea that its contents are "from the books" I myself have written, not "from the books" of other and better men which I chanced to own or to have known. And the author is still regarded by press, by public, and by personal friends, as one of the most self-conscious and the most self-advertising of men.

Portraits in Plaster was an inspiration. The articles upon which the volume was based had appeared in *Harper's Magazine* as "A Collection of Death Masks," notwithstanding the fact that a number of them are masks from nature—before death. "A Collection of Masks from Life and Death" was considered too long and too cumbersome even for a quarto or a folio, and it would not have been what is termed "taking" or easy of notice. For many months, therefore, a better name was earnestly looked for. Mr. Stedman, Mr. Warner, Mr. Matthews, and Mr. Bunner were asked their advice; and many and kindly were the titles suggested—as, "Masks and Faces," by Mr. Warner, but that had been pre-empted by Charles Reade and Dion Boucicault in their famous comedy, already printed and copyrighted in book form; Bunner gave me "Old Mortality's Matrix"; Mr. Stedman, "The New Mask of Death"; Mr. Matthews, "The Mask of Fashion and the Mould of Form"; and others of my literary friends gave me other titles equally happy, but, so it seemed to the publishers, equally impossible. "The New Mask of Death" pleased me best; but I was told that the general reader would not read about death in any shape or in any form if he could help it; and that had to be set aside.

The work was in print, in galley-proofs, announced

LAURENCE HUTTON'S BOOK-PLATE

as "forthcoming," before it had a name at all. When a name was absolutely necessary, the matter was laid before Mr. J. Henry Harper, who, without seeming to give it any particular thought, said: "They are all plaster casts, ar' n't they? And they are all portraits, ar' n't they? You like alliterative titles, don't you? What is the matter with 'Portraits in Plaster'?" And *Portraits in Plaster* it was and is.

A good title is so essential that men have been known to copyright titles and then, some day perhaps, to write books to fit them. The nomenclature of fiction does not seem to be so difficult as is that of more serious works. It is easy to name a novel after its hero, as *David Copperfield*, or after its heroine, as *Anna Karenina*, or after a place, as *The Exiles of Siberia*, or after an incident, as *A Terrible Temptation*, or after some personal characteristic, as *The Woman in White* or *The Man Who Was*. Shakespeare, happy in everything, was happy in his titles, as *The Comedy of Errors* and *As You Like It;* and Mr. Howells has found happy titles in Shakespeare's phrases, as *A Foregone Conclusion*, *A Woman's Reason*, and *A Chance Acquaintance*. The simplest thing of all is some familiar quotation or striking line from prose or verse. *Ships that Pass in the Night* did not a little popularise a one-time popular story, and *Red as a Rose is She* and *Cometh Up as a Flower* were titles not without good effect upon the novel-reading mind.

Next to *Vanity Fair*, the happiest title of the last

century, perhaps, is borne by a volume not so generally known as it ought to be, and written by Oliver Wendell Holmes. A number of his clever essays, contributed from time to time to a famous magazine of Boston, were gathered together and given to the world as *Soundings from the Atlantic.* The play upon words is worthy of the gentle monologist of the Breakfast-Table; but some of those carping local critics of his who were fond of telling us that "Wendell Holmes was not half so bright and witty as was his brother John," went so far as to say that the Autocrat gave *The Atlantic* its name for the sake of having a good name for his book!

CHAPTER X

The American Actor Series—*Literary Landmarks of London*—Colley Cibber—The Grave of Charles Lamb—Joanna Baillie—Butler—Boswell—The False Making of History—Comparative Rates Paid to Authors and Illustrators—*Literary Landmarks of Edinburgh*—Sir Walter Scott—Dr. John Brown.

AFTER the fireplace-heater episode, and after the *Mail* was married to the *Express*—a happy union for both of them,—and after the *Arcadian* died a very natural death indeed, I had but little connection with periodical literature until I went to the Harpers after my marriage in 1885. I devoted most of my working hours to the writing, to the compiling, and to the editing of books, with a decently fair consideration of profit in the way of royalties—semi-annually and regularly paid. With Mrs. Clara Erskine Clement, author of the *Handbook of Legendary and Mythological Art*—a book familiarly and disrespectfully known to the trade as "Leg. Art,"—I made two large volumes entitled *Artists of the Nineteenth Century*, published in 1879. My partner contributed the biographies of the Continental painters, architects, sculptors, and engravers who have figured in the annals of art since 1800. I devoted myself to the exploiting of the productions of the men in similar lines who were of British and American birth. We collected a vast amount of information, which seems to have been valuable, for it still brings us in—at the end of these twenty years—a very comfortable and pleasant sum *per annum*.

In 1881–82 I edited the "American Actor Series" for James R. Osgood & Company, in six volumes. [These were written by Kate Field (*Fechter*), William Winter (*The Jeffersons*), Mrs. Asia Booth Clarke (*The Elder and the Younger Booth*), Lawrence Barrett (*Forrest*), Joseph N. Inland (*Mrs. Duff*), and Mrs. Clara Erskine Clement (*Charlotte Cushman*).]

In the summer of 1882 I began the construction of *The Literary Landmarks of London*, the only work of any lasting worth with which my name is to be associated. It is not valuable as literature, for it is not literature and it does not *pretend* to *be* literature. It is likely to be respectable and enduring only on account of the vast amount of original matter it contains, relating to the homes and to the haunts of the British men of letters in the great British metropolis; and its main value consists in its correction of the many topographical errors made by less careful and less diligent compilers. The story of its origin and conception, and of its construction, may be worth the telling here.

One pleasant day, a memorable day to me, I went to Stoke Pogis, acting as guide to a party consisting of Mr. William Winter, Mr. Howells, Mr. Lawrence Barrett, and Mr. Charles Dudley Warner. We spent many hours in the old churchyard immortalised in the *Elegy*, and containing Gray's grave; and I remember the effect upon us all of Gray's touching epitaph upon the tomb containing his mother's ashes. I had lost my own mother a few months before, dearly loved by the men who were with me. And we all felt the affecting significance of the affectionate words. Barrett's voice broke entirely as he tried to read them aloud; and Winter finished the lines, "Sacred to the memory of the devoted mother of seven children, one of whom alone had the misfortune to survive her!"

On our return to London late in the afternoon, I suggested, in order not to separate the party—we were to dine with James R. Osgood that night at the Criterion—that we mount a 'bus and all ride together. We passed, on the way, a number of memorable houses that I pointed out as we went by, telling the story of their literary association. When we stopped for a moment at the corner of St. James's Street and Piccadilly, I said : " Do you see that red lamp in front of the chemist's shop, a block or so before you? In the room over that shop Byron woke up one morning to find himself famous!" Without a word and with one accord they left the omnibus, hot, tired, hungry, dusty as they were, and stood in front of the dingy, little, commonplace tenement, unmarked by tablet, which is certainly one of the most interesting of all the literary landmarks in the literary capital of the world. On the way back to Piccadilly and to dinner, Mr. Howells, Mr. Warner, and I chanced to walk together. They took my arms and said to me: "You know more about these things than any man alive. Why don't you put on imperishable record what you know and what all the rest of us want to be told? You are alone here and in the world. You are passing through the greatest sorrow of your life. You need something to occupy your mind and to take yourself out of yourself. Write a book about London, and about its associations with all its men of letters, and you will be the happier for it, and do the world some service." They probably never thought of the words again. But during the evening I thought of nothing else; and before I fell asleep that night I had laid out, in my own mind, the plan of the work. I had been making my researches for years, but only for my own edification and for my own pleasure, with no thought of the pleasure or the edification of anybody else.

The story of the writing of that book would make a book as long as the book itself. I devoted three winters in New York to the gathering of my materials; reading and consulting my own library of guides to London, and thousands of biographies, autobiographies, reminiscences, and volumes of correspondence. Every house in which a British author had lived in London, every tavern he had frequented, every club to which he had belonged, every spot familiar to him, was noted; the where, and the when, and the how; the church in

which he was christened or married, or from which,
or in which, he was buried; his tomb and his tenement. And I devoted three summers in London to the
verification of what I had read at home, and to actual
inspection of every spot I have mentioned in my text.
Houses and churches and taverns had disappeared, and
had left no signs; the guide-books differed, or were
silent, as to their sites; streets had been renamed and
renumbered, shortened or lengthened, or wiped out of
existence altogether; and the confusion sometimes
seemed insurmountable. Happily I discovered, in the
reading-room of the British Museum, the first official
insurance survey of the metropolis. It was made
during the 18th century and it contains the shape, and
size, and exact position of the ground-plan of every
house then standing in London and Westminster; and
best of all, it has the original street numbers of each
building. This to me was an indispensable "find"; and
that night, I remember, I did not sleep at all. I was permitted by the authorities to make tracings of this map;
it has a correct scale of inches to the mile; and by
actual comparison with contemporary maps made to
the same scale, and by pacing the streets themselves,
I was able in all doubtful cases to come to very satisfactory conclusions and to prove, in many instances,
that my own previous conclusions and the conclusions
of other investigators were entirely wrong.

Colley Cibber, for instance, according to his own
statement, " was born in Southampton Street, facing

Southampton House." But there were two Southampton Streets and two Southampton Houses! The earlier Southampton House was taken down some twenty years before the date of Cibber's birth. The latter, standing until the beginning of the last century, was on the north side of Bloomsbury Square, facing Southampton Street, Bloomsbury; and Cibber, therefore, first saw the light in that Southampton Street; not in Southampton Street, Strand, as was universally accepted by guide-books and biographers.

The place of Cibber's burial was a greater mystery still. It was generally supposed that he was laid in the cloisters of Westminster Abbey, by the side of his wife; but the records of the Abbey are entirely silent upon the subject. I discovered that he had not died in Islington, as some authorities declared; and a careful search through the files of contemporary periodicals, in the never-failing reading-room of the British Museum, gave me no account of his death or of his grave. That Caius Gabriel Cibber and his wife were buried in the vaults of the Danish church, Wellclose Square, Ratcliffe Highway, was an established fact; and it might be that the bones of the Poet Laureate were placed there by the side of those of his father and his mother. So I decided to go to see the Danish church. Here I met with three great obstacles. There was, in 1884, no Ratcliffe Highway, no Wellclose Square, no Danish church! Ratcliffe Highway, it was remembered, was once the name of the present St.

George's Street; but nobody remembered Wellclose Square. Policemen, postmen, oldest inhabitant, knew nothing about it; and nobody had ever heard of a Danish church. At last I found an aged resident who thought it might be the Swedish church, Princess Square; and thither I went. It was an autumn Sunday afternoon, and I entered to attend the service and to look about me. The congregation, consisting of Swedish sailors, was very small and the exercises were in the Swedish language. A few tablets on the walls attracted my attention; and one, over the pew in which I sat, startled me not a little. Its inscription is to the effect that " Near this spot was interred the mortal part of Emanuel Swedenborg"! This was a discovery indeed, a literary landmark worth finding; and it opened up to me a new field of research.

After the service I spoke to the Swedish chaplain, who told me that his church had nothing whatever to do with the Danish church, and had never had; that the Danish church had disappeared with Wellclose Square, and that a certain board-school, in the present St. George's Street, now stood on their site. His sexton, however, was the son of the old sexton of the Danish church, and could, perhaps, give me the information I sought. This sexton, a middle-aged man, knew nothing, of course; but he volunteered to take me to his father on Tower Hill. And to Tower Hill we wended our way. The elder Dane was very old. He was a shoemaker, using as his workshop the body of a dismantled four-wheeled cab, which sat in a little front garden by his own front-door. The establishment was painted a bright green, and the top and the driver's seat were filled with growing plants. I explained my business to the ex-sexton, present-cobbler, who gave me a cup of tea and asked me if I were acquainted with a brother of his living in Mobile, Alabama. But he knew nothing about the Cibbers, had never heard their name. He referred me, however, to Rev. Dr. Greatorex, Rector of St. Paul's Church, Tower Hill, who had been the rector of the Danish church. And at the end of Dr. Greatorex's evening service, I got from him the whole story. When the chapel was doomed, he, with the Danish Consul, had removed the bodies of the Cibbers, father, mother, and son, with his own hands, had read the coffin-plates, and had placed the fragmentary bits of bone in a vault under the chapel of the then new board-school. And so, for the first time in more than a century—Cibber died in 1752—the matter was settled. And all later biographers have generously given me the credit for the "find."

Another Sunday afternoon I devoted to a pious pilgrimage to the grave of Charles Lamb, at Edmonton. As usual, nobody at Edmonton knew anything. The churchyard is not a small one, and it is entirely filled. The sexton, and the grave-digger, and a few persons wandering about could give me no information. Most of them had never heard of " Mr. Lamb "; and I could not find the sacred spot. Naturally, I applied to the rector; and, as he left the vestry-door, after service, leaning on the arm of a pretty young woman, I approached him, raised my hat, and asked politely, if he could tell me where Charles and Mary Lamb were resting? Really, he could not say! And I, forgetting the day, the place, and his sacred office, cursed that rector for his criminal ignorance. " Great Heavens ! " I said, " you ought to be ashamed of yourself. In your care have been placed the ashes of one of the foremost men in the whole history of English letters. And you don't know where they are! They have made your churchyard and your parish distinguished all the world over. I have come three thousand miles to visit Charles Lamb's grave, and you, the rector of the church, don't know where it is ! You ought to be heartily ashamed of yourself." And I turned upon my heel and left him standing there, speechless and confounded.

Never before, perhaps, since the days of Cromwell, was English priest so spoken to at the porch of his own church. Half an hour later, while I was still groping about in the twilight, stumbling over the mounds in which the rude forefathers of the hamlet sleep, searching in vain for the resting-place upon the lap of earth of one poor youth unknown to fortune but well known to fame, the rector approached *me*, took off *his* hat, and said, " I *am* heartily ashamed of myself; and if you will step this way, I will show you what you have come so

far to see.   Let me assure you that no one will ever
accuse me of such ignorance again."

A well-dressed, intelligent-looking lady, who might
have been a rector's wife, was equally confused as to
the grave of, and even as to the existence of, Joanna
Baillie. It is an established fact that the venerable
lady had lived for a long time, and had died in the
early fifties full of years and of honour at Hampstead.
Her house, an old-fashioned, picturesque mansion,
still stood in 1885 and no doubt is still standing on the
top of Windmill Hill, opposite the Holly Bush Inn,
easily discovered and readily identified. But her present resting-place, among the many mouldering heaps
in the crowded churchyard, could not be found. The
supposed rector's wife, working over a carefully kept
little plot of her own, was finally accosted. The case
was stated as politely as possible, and I was assured
with equal politeness and to my no little amazement,
that "Joanna" was still living, doing "char-work" in
the village, and lodging with her granddaughter in the
rear portion of a High Street tenement. It was explained that another and more widely known Joanna
Baillie, who had been the intimate friend of Wordsworth, and of Samuel Rogers, and the other giants of
her time, was referred to. But it appeared that the
great Joanna must have died before my informant had
come to the neighbourhood, for she had never heard of
her.

Another difficulty met with and never finally overcome, was the establishment of the birthplace of the younger Disraeli, variously stated in the different biographies as being at Hackney in the Adelphi; at St. Mary Axe (pronounced "Simmery Axe"); in Trinity Row, Islington; in King's Road; and in Bloomsbury Square. It was a matter of some confusion, evidently, to Disraeli himself, for he told one friend that he first saw the light in a library in the Adelphi, in London; and his intimate, Montague Corry, afterwards Lord Rowton, once informed S. C. Hall that he had gone with Disraeli late in his life to the mansion now numbered 6 Bloomsbury Square, where the Primrose Sphinx had sat for some time, in deep meditation, in the room in which he was born. But the parish rate-books, most carefully examined by me, prove that the family did not take possession of this house until 1817, when Benjamin was at least twelve years of age. The name Disraeli does not appear in the London directory for 1804, when Benjamin was born; and so the mystery is still unsolved. All this research, naturally, occupied a great deal of time and study although the result, or the lack of result, is dismissed in the book in a few short lines. It was a most interesting study while it lasted, however; as entertaining to me as the working out of a riddle or the solving of an enigma.

Curious was it to trace the workings of the minds of the makers of guide-books who followed each other, for right or for wrong, like a flock of sheep through the same broken hedges, down the same steep places, into the same deep ruts, accepting as facts the statements of their predecessors without any attempt at verification or correction.

It is a well-known fact that the author of *Hudibras* was buried in the yard of the Church of St. Paul, Covent Garden, London. Aubrey put him "in the north part, next the church, at the east end. His feet touch the wall." Anthony Wood, on the other hand, places Butler at "the west end of the said churchyard, on the north side, and under the wall of the church, that wall which parts the yard from the common highway." And to this day the worthies of the parish know not which chronicler is right or if both chroniclers are wrong. The parish books, thoroughly examined by me, say nothing to clear up the mystery.

It is equally well known that a tablet to Butler was placed in the interior of the church "by the inhabitants of the parish" in 1786, all the authorities agreeing that it was on the south side. The exact position of this mural memorial is described in the guide-books bearing date at late as 1884-85; and its inscription is even quoted in full by the most recent of the works in question. Every tablet the edifice contained in 1885 was carefully studied, and there was found no word about Butler. No person connected with the church had ever seen or heard of such a tablet. And then it was discovered that the church had been destroyed by fire nine years after the tablet was erected, and that the tablet was not restored or renewed or rebuilt with the church. The present Landmarker was probably the first person who had thought of it or looked for it in nearly a century.

The guide-books say that James Boswell, the biographer of Johnson, died in 1795 at a certain number of a certain street near Oxford Street and the Regent Circus. And the guide-books are undoubtedly correct. But they are not correct when they point out, or when they used to point out, a house in that street, bearing now the same number, as being the real house of Boswell. It is an old house, clearly dating back to the end of the eighteenth century; but since Boswell's demise the street has been renumbered, widened, extended, and renamed; and the body of Boswell was carried, to be buried at his family seat in Scotland, from a house no longer standing and a block or two away.

Among the many images forced to be broken, often to the iconoclast's own deep, sentimental distress, was the tomb of Goldsmith by the side of the Temple Church. No one knows now where his bones rest. The monument, weather-beaten and weather-stained, looking very much older than it really is, was placed in 1860 " as near as possible to the spot where he is supposed to lie."

Massinger has no personal connection with the stone in the floor in St. Saviour's, Southwark, upon which his name is engraved. Nor are Fletcher or Edmund Shakespeare, the brother of the Immortal, in any way associated, even by conjecture, with the records that "here they rest." St. Saviour's has been peculiarly inventive and destructive in this respect, for even the memorials to Gower have been moved. Stow, in 1603, wrote: "John Gower, Esquire, a famous poet, was there buried, in the north side of that church, in the Chapel of St. John, where he lieth under a tomb of stone, with his image, also of stone, over him." But the tomb of stone and the image of stone were transported, in 1832, to the *south* transept and Gower was left behind.

They show one in the Garrick Club in Garrick Street, Long Acre, Thackeray's chair, still carefully preserved "in the corner in which he loved to sit." But the only Garrick Club that Thackeray knew was in King Street, Covent Garden, some little distance away; and the Garrick Club which the gentle spirit of the gentle-man Thackeray is supposed to haunt so pleasantly was not built until a year after Thackeray's mortal part was laid in Kensal Green.

Most inexplicable of all, perhaps, is the curious error clinging to the single important coffee-house still left in London, intact, as it stood in Johnson's day, "The Cheshire Cheese," in Wine Office Court, Fleet Street. One is still shown Johnson's portrait in Johnson's room over Johnson's table, and Johnson's chair, in the Cheshire Cheese. And Johnson clubs, and Johnson societies, and Johnson worshippers gather there to do honour to the memory of Johnson; while in all the contemporary correspondence and memorabilia, and

Johnsoniana, and Boswelliana, is to be found no allusion whatever to Johnson's association with the Cheshire Cheese! It is the only tavern of his day, in his part of London, of which there is no record of its having been frequented by the man who now renders it famous and keeps it alive.

Thus is history made!

To return, for a sentence or two in this connection, to the emoluments of what is called literary work. One entire twelvemonth was devoted to the "London" book and to nothing else. I was literally in love with the task and it quite absorbed me. My income from my pen, naturally, was confined to royalties, unusually small that year, even for me. And on the 1st of April I received my sole annual literary revenue, a small check from J. R. Osgood & Company, owing to me on "The American Actor Series." The check was too insignificant to merit a deposit in the bank on its own account; there was nothing coming in that month from other sources to be added to it; and it was held over, until certain patrimonial coupons were due. But in the meantime the Osgood House suspended payment, the royalty check was returned with a charge of some seventy-five cents for "protest"; and my total income in 1885 from that particular source amounted to three-quarters of a dollar—on the wrong side of the ledger!

To say nothing of the year spent in its actual production, that "London" book was a long time in paying for itself. The complete Double Index of Persons and Places, with its innumerable cross-references, was a slow, laborious, and expensive performance. I made it, without help, during many brain-wearying and many back-breaking months of dull routine work; and I spent no small sum of money in the salaries of the scribes who copied it and saw to its correct alphabetical sequence, and in the payments to the experts who verified it all, after it was completed. And, moreover, as the work had none of the qualities which would warrant its appearance in magazine form, I have received from it in money value nothing but the semi-annual, but not enormously large, book-royalties.

The Landmarks of Venice, of *Florence*, of *Rome*, and of *Jerusalem* found, on the other hand, two markets. They appeared and were paid for liberally in the periodical before they were sent out to stand or to fall alone between covers of their own. And they impressed upon me, for the first time, the startling fact—startling, I mean, to authors—that, in the matter of periodical literature, at least, the illustrator generally, if not always, is paid more than the writer—and sometimes a good deal more. This I say without wishing, in the slightest degree, to reflect upon the artist. It is not his fault if his work is worth more to the publisher than is mine; it is merely my misfortune. For the articles upon the three Italian cities, and upon the ancient capital of Judea, the editor of *Harper's Magazine* gave me one thousand dollars; a sum with which I was perfectly satisfied. Mr. du Mond, who made the drawings which so enrich the text, received from the head of the Art Department, two thousand five hundred dollars; and he deserved it. But there his share in the profits ceased, while mine continued. For he has no interest whatever in those long-drawn-out, and comforting, royalties upon the books.

This condition of affairs is not at all uncommon. Mr. Frank D. Millet, artist in words as well as colours, spent, I remember, some years ago when he was living in New York, not a little time upon a paper entitled "Cossac Life," based upon his intimate knowledge of Cossac character. He presented it to the editor of *Harper's*, who said he would gladly accept it if it were illustrated. In his sketch-books Mr. Millet found a number of half-forgotten, stray, and various studies of the Cossac and his surroundings; a number of typical faces, male and female; bits of uniform, of harness and of armour, spear-heads, pitstol butts, saddles, headgear and footgear, and the like. From these, with pen and ink, he readily evolved in half, or less than half, the time it took him to prepare his article, all that was necessary to make it acceptable and understandable, in a pictorial way. For his written sketch, as an author, he received an hundred dollars. For his drawn sketches, as an artist, he was to his surprise paid three hundred dollars more. And, curiously enough, he was better pleased with and more proud of that part of the work which had brought him the less financial profit.

The Literary Landmarks of Edinburgh, a later book

than that on London, was a simpler task. Edinboro' is a smaller city, its literary lights are fewer, and the changes and growth of the town are not so great. And above all I had the help and sympathy of almost every individual I questioned. Scotchmen love their heroes and worship them; and know full well where they lived, and died, and were buried. There were two White-Horse Inns in Edinboro'; both of them celebrated, although they were not contemporaries; and of course they are mixed up, in our days, by careless guide-books. One was near the "Foot" of the Canongate, the other near the "Top." The Canongate, by the way, is the name of a dirty, old street, that is very interesting for its associations' sake. In search of one of these White-Horse Inns, the pilgrim, misdirected, of course, went to the wrong end of the Canongate and, of course, he could find it not. But he entered a public-house near where he thought the White Horse Inn ought to be, or ought to have been, and he asked the way to it. To him spoke a miserably clad, wretched-looking, half-drunken man, who said, " Were you in search of Waverley's White-Horse Inn, or of Dr. Johnson's White-Horse Inn?" And then he told him—for the price of a dram—the position of each of them and most of their history. The same man, living in Gough Square in London, in Johnson's very house, would never have heard of Johnson and certainly would never have heard of *Rasselas*.

Another day I was in search of the "Dame's" School

FRANCIS DAVID MILLET, BY SAINT-GAUDENS

"in Hamilton's Entry—off Bristo' Street"—where Sir Walter Scott was taught his letters. There was no sign of it, and I received no satisfactory reply to the questions asked until I went into another public-house —for it was soon ascertained that most of the intelligence of the lower walks of life in Edinboro' was to be found, alas! in the public-house. Here was met a man who had seen better days, although on that day he had sunk to the bottom of days and nights. He had evidently been a gentleman, or something like it, once; and "too much whiskey" was written all over him. He gave the information sought, without hesitation, and then—for the price of a dram—he said suddenly and solemnly: "Do you know that the spot on which thou art standing is holy ground? Here Tom Campbell wrote *The Pleasures of Hope!* Yonder lies Mrs. Cockburn, who wrote *The Flowers of the Forest.* De Quincey was buried over there. Over there Robert Ferguson lived, and yonder once lodged Robbie Burns!" And in each instance, as later research has shown, he was entirely correct.

I was standing one morning in St. James Square trying to make out in which house Burns had lived for a time, when an old man, a plasterer by profession, stopped and asked if I were looking at the poet's window. Naturally, I was curious to find out what, and how much, he knew about it; and I learned that in his boyhood he was a friend of Burns's "Clorinda," who in her old age had shown him the casement out of which Burns had watched for her as she passed; and I gathered that he never went by without casting a glance up at it and—mentally—taking off his hat to the one-time occupant of the room it lighted. The Scotchman never takes his hat off—actually—to anybody but the Duke of Buccleuch, or the Duke of Argyle!

In Buccleuch Pend—a pend is an archway, making a passage under tall houses from street to street—in Buccleuch Pend was once a public-house in which Burns is known to have occasionally refreshed himself. I was anxious to place it exactly; and as no sign of it now exists, I sought information of the present inhabitants of the neighbourhood. One man had lived in that very house all his life, and he remembered hearing a lecture in his boyhood, in which the whole matter was laid bare. The lecturer was still living and to him I went. He told me the story and established the exact site. Then I asked him if he knew the house where Burns and Scott had met for the first and only time. He gave me his ideas and the address of a man who could tell me more. To this man I went and I found in him an enthusiastic antiquary, by profession a book-cover maker. He lived in the famous house himself, he had searched the records himself, and he helped me to identify and to make public for the first time "the spot where Robert Burns ordained Sir Scott!"

All this could have befallen a literary pilgrim in no

other city of the world. They passed me on from man to man, each man giving me the information sought; each man's information being more valuable to me than the last, and each man being as eager to give the information as I was to obtain it.

One of the most gratifying experiences of my life was connected with the making of this Edinboro' book. The Harpers were to have sent an illustrator to meet me there, but he did not come; and I was forced to set myself out in search of illustrations of my own. In the window of an old book and print shop in Bristo' Place, I saw some engraved views of the town which I thought would serve my purpose. In conversation with the dealer, I mentioned that I was commissioned by an American magazine to write an article upon the "Homes and Haunts of the Scottish Men of Letters in the Scottish Metropolis." He said that the Earl of Rosebery had been into his place that very day, and had remarked that he wished somebody would do for Edinboro', in that line, what an American writer had been doing for London. I replied that the wish was very gratifying, because I presumed that I was the American writer in question. "Losh! mon!" cried the little bookseller,—"Losh! mon! you're no' Laurence Hutton! Come with me!" And he led me into a little back-room, and out of a bureau drawer he took two copies of the *Century Magazine* containing articles of mine upon "The Portraits of Mary Queen of Scots." I discovered that he knew all about me. And I felt that this, at last, was Fame, or something like it. My name and work were familiar to a man living three thousand miles away. And I felt that my head was swelling!

On the last night of our stay in Edinboro' that year, with my work there all done, I walked out after dinner to take a last look at Scott's house in George Square and to satisfy myself as to what was meant by the "sunk-floor" in which the young Scott had a "den" full of books. While I was standing in front of the building, smoking my cigar, a gentleman came along and noticed my interest in the place. He stopped and spoke to me, learned who I was, and what I wanted to know, and he said that Scott's house had been changed but that he himself lived next door; and he offered to show me his own "sunk-floor," which I discovered to be, simply, what is called "a front basement" in America, a room a few feet below the street-level. He then took me through his house, presented me to his wife and daughters, and insisted on my taking "a bit of supper" with him. When I mentioned my wife, his wife said she would call on her at once, and regretted that she had not had an opportunity to meet her before. We were to leave the next morning by an early train, and when the next morning came my host and his daughter were at the early train to see us off; he with a book for me to read on the journey, she with a bunch of flowers for the wife. We parted with them as if they were old friends; and all this was because I

PEEP O' DAY, THE HUTTON HOMESTEAD AT ST. ANDREWS, SCOTLAND

was a lover of Sir Walter Scott and a stranger in Edinboro'!

I corresponded with these new-old friends of mine for some years. They wrote to me when their daughter married, and they received my heartiest congratulations. They wrote to me when their daughter died—within the twelvemonth,—and I sent them my sincerest sympathy. We had an intimate fellow-feeling. We loved Sir Walter Scott!

Old Mortality (whom Scott immortalised) was my maternal grandfather's uncle or cousin—I have never been able to establish which,—and his house in Haggisha, in the town of Hawick, is the same in which my grandfather and my grandfather's mother were cradled. Lately there has been a tablet placed upon the front wall of this thatched cottage, stating the fact that Robert Patterson, the prototype of Old Mortality, was born there in 1715.

In the Introduction to *Old Mortality* Scott wrote:

" Robert Patterson, *alias* Old Mortality, was the son of Walter Patterson and Margaret Scott who lived during the first half of the eighteenth century. Here (in the house of Haggisha) Robert was born in 1715."

Later on, in the same Introduction, Sir Walter, speaking of the three sons of Old Mortality, says that one of them, "John, moved to America in 1776 and, after various vicissitudes of fortune, settled in Baltimore." There is a tradition that a daughter of this John Patterson, a famous beauty in her time, became, for a while, the wife of Jerome Bonaparte. The tradition is firmly believed to this day by the descendants of the Pattersons and the Scotts of Haggisha.

Sir Walter Scott and Robert Patterson — although the author never hints it — were distantly connected by marriage. My grandfather, William Scott, who had a brother Walter, always boasted of the relationship, remote as it was, and of his acquaintance, slight as it was, with the Laird of Abbotsford. Herding the cows in his own native parish of Hawick, he often saw there the *Shirra* (Sheriff) riding by the pasture. Having a brother William himself, the *Shirra's* invariable salutation on these occasions was:

"Good-morning, Wully, hoo's Waltaire?"

And the equally invariable reply from the lad was:

"He's brawlie, Sir Waltaire; hoo's Wully?"

This was considered a great joke, and it stood for a good many years, highly respected to the end and seemingly as fresh to each of them as if it had never been uttered before.

Old Mortality was a stone mason, and the people of Haggisha still have his trowel and his spectacles, which I should very much like to possess.

I once wrote of the Old Mortality-Patterson-Bonaparte marriage in the New York *Evening Mail*, but my statement was strenuously controverted. When I was in Hawick — more than thirty years ago now, — I found that while my cousins, the Scotts, had no proofs of the connection, it was a valued and entirely accepted tradition among them.

One of the most precious of my treasures is a slight but original crayon sketch of Sir Walter, by Gilbert Stuart Newton, and from life. This I had admired greatly in the rooms of my friend Mr. Hennell, in London, and I had so expressed myself on many occasions. Without comment from its donor, the little portrait was left at my door, among some other things of much less value which he had promised me; and for it, the very next day, I was offered an exceedingly and ridiculously high price by a collector of such things. Upon taking it to America and comparing it with a very rare print of the original by Gilbert Stuart Newton, R. A., I discovered that, while the resemblance between them was very marked, the print was not reproduced from my drawing; and I felt I had been cherishing something which, charming as it is, is not what it claimed to be, until in reading over the *Recollections* of Charles Robert Leslie I came by accident upon the following paragraph:

"A profile of Walter Scott, in lead pencil, drawn by Newton, I had seen before and I had asked him to give it to me. He had promised that he would when he had made a copy of it. And he now (1834) showed me the copy, and said I might have that or the first. I chose the first, but they are both very like Sir Walter."

Whether mine is the first, or the copy, I know not. But it also is very like Sir Walter.

During my visits to Edinburgh I occasionally saw Dr. John Brown in the streets, always accompanied by a dog or two. After reading *Rab and His Friends* and *Marjory Fleming* I had a great reverence for their author, particularly when I had heard the sad story of his life and of his life's sorrow, so like that of the Thackeray concerning whom he had written so beautifully and tenderly. Once I followed him into a book shop on Princes Street, and lounged about the counter while I listened to his talk. Going out before him, I stopped to speak to a Dandie Dinmont of his who was patiently waiting at the door and looking wistfully for his master to come. The dog responded cordially to my advances and seemed to feel that we had a good deal in common. I was rewarded by a kindly smile of half recognition from the master as I raised my hat to him and passed on. I was very anxious to meet and to know the gentle old man, so beautiful and so kindly in face, but we had no friends in common and I never had the courage or the assurance to feign illness that I might consult him in a professional way, although I was often tempted to do so. At last the opportunity came, which I chronicled in my note-book thus:

"Aug. 16th, 1876. Edinboro'. Called upon Dr. John Brown with Kate Field and Louise Chandler Moulton. Mrs. Moulton had a letter to him from John G. Whittier, and our reception on that account was cordial. His library or study is a small book-lined room with one window. The books were medical and classical

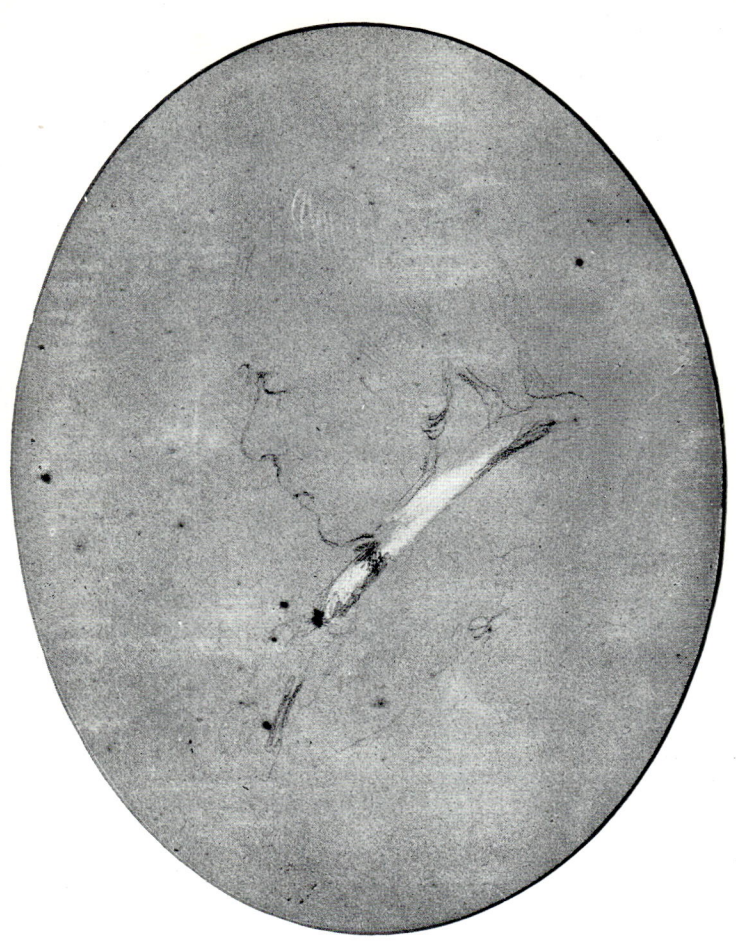

SIR WALTER SCOTT, DRAWN FROM LIFE BY GILBERT STEWART NEWTON

books of reference, histories and general literature; old books in plain bindings, rare prints, and original sketches ; photographs of the leading literary men of the day; of Thackeray, Emerson, Mark Twain, and Dr. Brown on one *carte;* and dogs without end; original Landseers with Landseer's compliments, and original sketches by Leach with Leach's love; the large head of 'Rab' which Edmonston & Douglass have had engraved for the book ; and Marjory Fleming. He spoke very affectionately of Whittier, quoted some of his verses, and had a very high regard for Emerson.

"When asked by Miss Field how he wrote *Marjory Fleming*, he said, ' I did not write her,—she wrote herself.' Marjory's sister had been to see him the day we called. He said he had but one dog now, a terrier, who had gone to the seaside for his holidays and for a change of air. Dr. Brown is a sweet-faced, white-haired, mild-mannered, gentle old man, with a pleasant voice, and with a peacefulness about him that is charming. He has a sad look, however, which may be accounted for perhaps by the melancholy madness which sometimes takes possession of him and which is inherent.

"He remembered my name as that of the man who had sent him from America photographs of Longfellow, Holmes, Emerson, Hawthorne, Bryant, and others, whom I happened to have learned he wished to possess. And he gave me his autograph photograph in return. I never saw him again, but the pleasant memory of that short interview I will carry with me to the grave, and Dr. John Brown of Edinburgh is one of the men I hope to know better in the better world to which he has gone."

CHAPTER XI

The Collectors of Autographs — Begging Letters—The Conscientious Collector and the Pirate—A Dickens Pilgrimage—Mary Anderson.

"AUTOGRAPHISERS," as Dibdin once, and a little disrespectfully, spoke of them, may be divided into four distinct classes—the Buyers, the Beggars, the Stealers, and the Receivers. The first study the catalogues; they order by mail or by wire; sometimes they exchange, and they always pay full prices. They find profit and, no doubt, a certain amount of pleasure in their hunting and angling for letters and signatures. They bag their game, and they catch their fish, ready cooked. It is often the rarest of fish and game. But it is not sport.

The real collector would not exchange a little note in his possession, written on the night of his election to the Century Club, containing the simple words, " Dear Mother Blank, your Boy is a Centurion," and signed " Edwin " (Booth), for the manuscript of Washington's Farewell Address ; nor would he give a familiar letter of Bunner's, full of affectionate personalities and closing, " with love, as always, to the Wife," for the sealed and signed Death-Warrant of Lady Jane Grey.

The mendicant of autographs seems to find pleasure in his methods, and now and then he finds profit; for he has been known to sell the results of his begging to men who are too proud to beg for themselves. But he is generally an honest suppliant, holding his hat in his hand, or, with palm extended, telling you openly that he wants your signature, enclosing a card upon which to write it and a stamped envelope addressed to himself in which to return the card. And he rarely says "Thank you," in reply! Sometimes he demands a little more. If you are are an artist, he asks for a sketch; if you are an author, he asks for a quotation; if you are a man of affairs, he asks for a sentiment; if you are a clergyman, he asks for a text; if you are a doctor, he asks for a prescription; if you are a judge, he asks for a short sentence—in favour of the plaintiff. Not infrequently he tells you how much he admires your work, or your course; he adds that in his part of the community your name is a household word; and in addressing you he spells your name wrong. Once in a while he gets all mixed up, and asks his favourite author what he is painting now; or his favourite artist when he is to publish his next book. Often he is more insidious in his inquiries; and while he says he realises that he is trespassing upon your valuable time—a very popular expression of his—he ventures to seek some indispensable information as to the present address of Mr. Mark Twain for instance; or as to the number and names of the children of Mr. Frank Stockton; or if

*I wish this to carry
My love to my Larry—
God bless him and keep him for life's longest span!
And when finally he greets
And turns up his toes,
May the good God be good to a God damn good man!*

H. C. Bunner

A PAGE FROM THE HUTTON GUEST-BOOK

Demands of Collectors

Miss Julia Marlowe ever played "Meg Merrillies," and if so, when, and who were in the cast; or if Mr. Richard Harding Davis's "Gallagher" was an actual episode in his own life; or if George du Maurier was the real name of the author of *Trilby*, or merely a pseudonym; or if you prefer Dickens to Thackeray, spring to autumn, the mountains to the sea-shore; or if you ride a wheel, and whose make; or if you shave yourself or go to the barber's; or if you believe in the higher education of women; or does authorship pay? He generally encloses a stamp. But he almost invariably forgets to say " Thank you, sir!" And "Thank you, sir!" is so easily said!

A very interesting specimen of the autograph-beggar's literary style, received not long ago, is here given *verbatim*. It reads: " Dear Sir. Among the many important duties that engross your time and thoughts, I would respectfully solicit one moment of your time, and proffer an earnest request that I may possess some autographic remembrance from your hand. I desire much, and would highly prize, such a souvenir from one to whom I am so greatly indebted for many an hour of pleasure and profit that has been afforded me through your very interesting books. Since the critical press and public have long since placed the stamp of their high endorsement upon your refined, instructive, and always excellent work, I feel that my wee tribute of appreciation must seem indeed trifling to you. Yet I am quite sure that in such expression I am but voicing the opinions of thousands of lovers of good literature in our land, who, like myself, have been greatly influenced, instructed, and entertained by your writings. Trusting that the sincerity of my request may kindly excuse whatever inconvenience that shall attend your compliance with it, I remain, Yours very sincerely."

As the request is absolutely impersonal and indirect, its sincerity must be doubted. It is evidently one of very many similar letters sent to the authors of entertaining, instructive, and influential works, whose names were to be read on the title-pages of books found in the circulating library to which the writer had access.

The compliance with the request, it may be added, met with no expression of "Thank you, sir." And why not?

The worst form of autographic beggary is displayed by the young person, hinted at above, who trespasses upon your valuable time with the request to read an accompanying essay, story, or poem; to criticise it freely and fully; to tell the young person candidly what you consider its merits; to point out its short-comings—if any; and to present it to some editor of your acquaintance for immediate publication. By so doing you will make the young person the very happiest of mortals, perhaps you will save a large and dependent family from penury or worse, and you will certainly confer a boon upon the reading-world.

A PAGE FROM THE HUTTON GUEST-BOOK

Stamps are enclosed for a reply. But the "Thank you, sir," as usual, is omitted.

One young person ventured to trespass in this way upon the valuable time of a total stranger because his father, whom the stranger did not remember, had once made an ocean voyage with him; another asked him to read her verses because her favourite uncle bore his first name and spelled it in the same manner; another ventured because he had broken his leg; another trespassed—without apologising for the venture—because she had read in her local paper that the hall of his house was filled with rare portraits and prints; and still another took the liberty because he knew that the stranger was a friend of Walt Whitman, and because he wanted—not an autograph of the stranger—but an autograph poem of Walt Whitman, signed!

Perhaps the most ingenious and the most original of all these schemes for procuring autographs was from a lady in a Western town. She was raising funds for the building and support of a public library, and she had conceived the idea of issuing a volume to be called "The Authors' Recipe Book." Authors from all over the country, the most distinguished of Authors—always Authors with a capital "A"—had been good enough to send her a list of the favourite dishes of their own construction, with their method of making them.

The cook-book was one of the many forms of literature to which the present recipient had never turned his attention. He had no more idea of cooking than he had of milking a cow, or of harnessing a horse, or of setting a hen, or of building a dynamo. He did not even care what was cooked for him, so long as it contained none of the ingredients of tripe and none of the essence of the tomato. But he was asked to contribute a paper—which she would have reproduced in fac-simile —stating what he could prepare—most to his liking— upon a kitchen range, or in a chafing-dish—with his manner of procedure. This quite non-plussed him, until he bethought himself of one particular and peculiar delicacy, in the evolution of which he could safely trust his reputation as an expert. In reply—for which he received no thanks—he said : " Take a long paper-cutter ; attach to the same, by means of rubber-bands and securely, an ink-eraser ; insert the ink-eraser firmly into a marsh-mallow plug, and hold the same over a student's lamp or study-fire until the marsh-mallow begins to sizzle, drops into the ashes, puts out the light, or burns your hand. And eat while hot ! "

To most of these petitions, modest and otherwise, and every one of them actually received, some sort of reply has usually been granted at no little sacrifice of time. But the " Thank you, sir," was rarely returned. In one particular instance, where no reply was possible, there came in due course the very reverse of "thanks." The writer said that she was quite well aware that she was at that moment one of many who preferred similar requests without the slightest claim upon her victim's time or patience. In spite of this too certain knowledge, she ventured (they always venture, you see) to send a few poems. It was imperative desire that led her to cause this trouble; and having been fortunate enough to find acceptance in various places, she would still like to have the dictum of one whose judgment she felt was assured — to wit, catholic and discriminating, etc. All of which was very pretty and very flattering; and the poems themselves were not so awfully bad. Stamps were enclosed for their return, and for the victim's catholic and discriminating dictum, but nowhere was any hint given as to the residence or post-office address of the poetess. She lived, then, somewhere on Main Street, at number 85. And that is all that was known about her. In the course of a few months there came a second letter—this time lacking even the Main Street as a guide, and in an envelope which, as in the former case, had unfortunately been destroyed without a glance at the post-mark. She was deeply hurt, she said, at the neglect, and she was almost ashamed of the marked discourtesy towards a member, if an humble member, of the Guild of Letters. She hinted that if the name at the bottom of her verses had been as famous as that of Mrs. Browning or of Miss Ingelow, the result would have been very different; and she went so far as to insinuate that her silent correspondent had, after the manner of his kind, appropriated her stamps to his own base uses.

Among the most trying of begging letters are those

which are accompanied by printed books, generally with presentation-inscriptions. The volume is, usually, the first venture of some young author, who asks for a published review in the journal with which the recipient is connected; or, failing that, for a personal acknowledgment, with some unprejudiced opinion concerning the work and some kindly advice for future guidance. The book is, not infrequently, privately printed; it is almost always in verse; its value for the critic to whom it is sent is very small; and the "Thank you, sir," in this case, is not always so easily said. If it goes to Mr. Howells, to Mr. Warner, to Mr. Bridges, or to Mr. Woodbury, the response to the gift is worth, in the autograph-market, twice as much as the gift itself.

Certain applications which must, of necessity, meet with a negative answer are requests to an author for the autograph letters he has received and preserved from those of his personal friends who have gone, alas, to that land from which no letters or messages are sent. For weeks after the death of Lowell, of Booth, of Barrett, of Kate Field, of Bunner, of Walcott Balestier, of Lester Wallack, of Celia Thaxter, of du Maurier, concerning whom at the time a certain journalist had said something in print, he was deluged with letters which begged letters of theirs. A few lines of Mrs. Thaxter's, in which she mentioned "The Little Sandpiper," or some of the wild flowers she knew and loved so well, would please a bed-ridden woman who had never seen the sea-shore or heard the murmur of the waves, ex-

DRAWING BY FREDERICK BARNARD

cept as Mrs. Thaxter had written of them and spoken through them in the pages of her books. A youth who was president of the literary society in the high school of his native village said, concerning two notes of du Maurier which had been quoted, that, while he would willingly accept either of them, he would very much prefer that one in which the novelist spoke of Frederick Walker as being in a way the original of Little Billee, and which described the music-teacher in Antwerp, upon whom Svengali was based. And a professional writer, who should have known better, who said he did not want to part with any of the few letters he himself had received from Barrett, would like, for an unnamed friend, a note of the protagonist on paper of The Players Club and signed in full; failing that, Barrett's book-plate—if autographed—would do! Unfortunately there was sent, to the unnamed friend of the friend, a note, consisting of a line or two, accepting an invitation to some little festival, before it was discovered that the friend's friend was a man whom the sender particularly disliked and who was by no means a favourite with Barrett. It may be added that the friend of the friend was one of the few men to say, "Thank you, sir." And that was the way he was found out.

The reverse of these pictures is, perhaps, worth painting here, if only for the sake of the moral it teaches. A young girl—she said she was a young girl— who knew where she lived on the banks of the Hudson and did not neglect to put the address on record—had begun, in her humble way, a collection of autograph notes and letters of literary men. Some of them, already in her possession, were addressed to her father; others had been given to her by her own and her father's friends. Would the present Literary Man kindly, without any trouble to himself, send to her, in the enclosed stamped envelope, a fragment of manuscript, or a line or two of his own, which she could put into the little book she prized so highly? Of course he complied; and he was so overwhelmed with surprise at her grateful acknowledgment that he felt it his imperative duty to thank her for thanking him. He asked what she had and what she wanted. She forwarded her modest list, and from his own accumulation—for he keeps everything of that sort, no matter how unimportant it may seem to him—he was able to give her short, impersonal, notes of Mr. Howells, Mr. Warner, Mr. Aldrich, Mr. Dobson, Mr. Gosse, Mr. Stockton, and their peers, in each of which was nothing that the writer would not be willing that the whole world should read. And thus without materially impoverishing himself he was enabled to enrich her. All because she said "Thank you, sir!"

To the autograph thief may be applied some of the epithets bestowed in *The Book Hunter*, upon the extra-illustrator of books. The Grangerite, says Burton, is a sort of literary Attila, or Genghis Khan, who spreads terror and ruin around him; a monster who

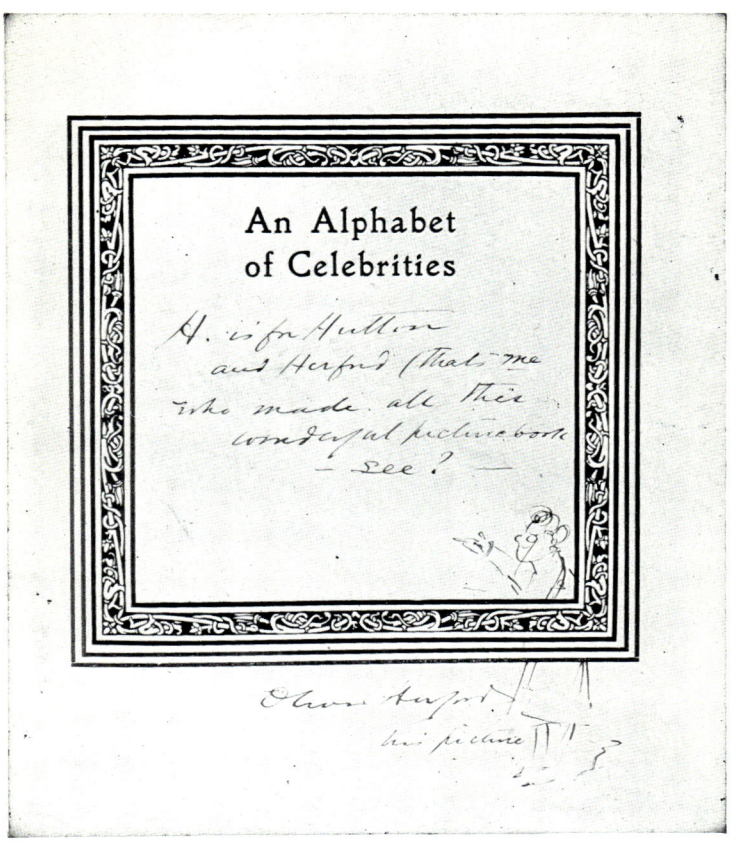

OLIVER HERFORD'S DRAWING IN LAURENCE HUTTON'S COPY OF
"THE JINGLE BOOK"

makes the meat he feeds on. Attila, it will be remembered, a king of the Huns, was called by mediæval writers "the Scourge of God" because of the ruthless and expansive destruction wrought by his arms; Genghis Khan was a Mongol emperor, who slaughtered and tortured and plundered his enemies and sacked and burned their cities. He was particularly distinguished for his treacherous atrocities and his thirst for blood and vengeance.

None but the honest, conscientious collector knows of the ruin and terrors spread around him by the monster who steals autographs, or of the ruthless destruction that follows in the wake of his pen-knife or his scissors, whether he pillages for the sake of profit or simply from the spirit of secret hoarding. In one of the large hotels in New York, not long ago, many and grievous were the complaints made to the manager, to the General Post Office in Washington, to the local sub-station on the next block, to the carriers, and even to the newspapers, concerning the mysterious disappearance of important missives posted in the house. It was noticed that they were all from the pens of personages of consequence in the political, literary, or theatrical world, who were guests of the establishment. And finally, when detectives were employed to ferret out the matter, it was discovered that an Attila of a bell-boy had been in the habit of appropriating letters given him to mail. He opened the envelopes; bartered the stamps for chewing-gum or cream-soda; and, after destroying the body of the documents, he made a comfortable income by selling the signatures to a not very scrupulous dealer who was willing to give a fair price for "good specimens" of the sign-manual of Mr. Speaker Reed, of Mr. Anthony Hope, or of Miss Ellen Terry.

To a certain semi-professional club to which he belonged, a well-known author once presented a complete set of his printed books, writing in each of the volumes his own name with an appropriate sentiment. Shortly after his death, when the literary journals were full of sketches of his life, appreciative critiques of his work, portraits of him at all ages, views of the houses in which he was born and died, fac-similes of his most familiar verses, and the like, the librarian of the certain club found that some still unknown Genghis Khan, in his thirst for autographic blood, had mutilated many of the presentation copies by cutting out the sentiments and the signatures. It was all done, evidently, by the same ruthless, vandal hand; for the instrument used in each case was a very sharp one, and it was applied, invariably, in the same expert manner. This Mongolian, it is to be hoped, was a servant of the institution, not a member; although club-waiters as a rule are not particularly skilful in such matters; they rarely carry about with them keen-cutting blades, unless they are negroes, and then chiefly for attack and defence; they seldom collect autographs for autographs' sake; and they are not apt to value the

A MARK TWAIN LETTER

signature of a poet more highly than that of a publican or a prize-fighter.

From the alcoves of an important university library has disappeared the fly-leaf of a biography of Oliver Cromwell on which Thomas Carlyle had seen fit to put on record the fact that it had belonged to him. The signature (not a very rare one), without the book, was perhaps worth, to the trade, some fifty cents; the book (a common-place edition, poorly printed), without the signature, was perhaps worth to the trade half a dollar; the book, with the signature, was, to the university which owned it, absolutely beyond price.

From a private library was taken, some years ago, an especially-bound copy of *The Prince and the Pauper*, with a peculiarly affectionate, Mark Twainey inscription, from the author to the friend for whom it was bound and to whom it was given. If its author and its former owner could know of what pleasure and benefit it can be to its present possessor, who cannot exhibit it, who cannot look at it, except in secrecy, who cannot sell it, or give it away—without giving himself away with it,—they might be a little more resigned to the ruin and terrors he spread.

Perhaps the worst case of autographic brigandage on record was displayed in the conduct of a young relative of a well-known artist. The artist, a man of unusually interesting personality, died, one day, and was cremated. His enterprising young relative proposed to prepare a memoir of the painter, and he wrote to all the painter's friends for characteristic letters, not too confidential, which might be published in the volume and might show to the world what manner of man was the deceased in his private as well as in his professional character. The letters were freely tendered; the volume was never published nor written; and the letters were sold for the benefit of the young relative. One of his most unfortunate victims, six thousand miles away from the metropolis, received a dealer's catalogue, advertising a number of "exceedingly fine examples" which were written to him—with that fact mentioned, of course—and which were even quoted in part. Time and space did not permit him to utter a public disclaimer; and he still finds himself in the ignominious position of appearing to have sold for money what no money would have bought. He has never obtained redress. And yet the mediæval authors looked upon the king of the Huns as the most distinguished of the scourges of creation.

The truly happy, and, perhaps, the only proper holograph-maniac is the fortunate man who pilfers nothing, who petitions for nothing, who purchases nothing, but who receives in a natural way, and who keeps and dearly prizes, what no money can buy, what no money has bought, what no money will ever buy, unless his heirs, executors, administrators, or assigns put them upon the market long after they have lost to him their earthly charm—to wit, the autographs addressed to him, or written for him, not as autographs but as personal expressions of good fellowship or good will.

Among these may be classed Mr. John Fiske's letters from London in which he tells how he once called on the Leweses, at the Priory, in St. John's Wood, and found George Eliot sitting on the floor—of all things—with hammer in hand and a mouth full of tacks, putting down the dining-room carpet; and how lonely Mr. Fiske himself would have been, in a strange city without his wife and his children, if the fellows were not good to him, and did not often drop in at his lodgings near the British Museum,—the "fellows" being Huxley and Darwin and Spencer and Tyndall. Then there is a long letter from John Brougham, giving the history of his first play at his first theatre; and a few lines from Mr. Thomas Bailey Aldrich, saying: "I've just finished *The Sister's Tragedy*, which I think will like you"; and a note from Mr. George Boughton illustrated with diagrams of pyramids, showing thereby how much more sorry he was to be out when you called than you could possibly have been not to find him at home; and a note from Mr. Edwin A. Abbey, signed by a caricature of himself—all teeth and all eye-glasses,—asking one to dine—at the Star and Garter at Richmond—to celebrate the birthday of a gentleman whose name is not mentioned, but who is represented in a clever pictorial way as a personage writing words with one hand and catching salmon with the other, and is easily recognised as William Black. Added to these there may be little poems by Mr. Austin Dobson, by Mr. Edmund Clarence Stedman, by Mr. Thomas Nelson Page, all saying—which the recipient tries to believe to be true—how much they like him; and all written on the fly-leaves of books of theirs, sent on the day of publication. And then, too, are the bits of sentiment, the scraps of original verse, with all sorts of bad and almost impossible rhymes on one's name, and pretty little sketches of places and persons and things known and loved for their associations' sake, put into guest-books or birthday books by Mrs. Kate Douglas Wiggin, by Mrs. Mary Mapes Dodge, by Mrs. Ruth McEnery Stuart, by Mrs. Custer, by Miss Helen Keller, by Florence, Booth, Barrett, Wallack, by Mr. Frank Stockton, by Mr. Blashfield, by Mr. Henry M. Bacon, by Mr. Beckwith, by Mr. Vedder, by Mr. Zorn—men and women whom the owner of the books likes so much, and men and women whose friendship, and the expression of it, no money—of any amount—can buy.

That money might have bought some of these things has been shown in a curious and gratifying way on several interesting occasions.

One morning some time after the close of our Civil War there called at a literary workshop in New York an aged lady, bearing a personal letter of introduction from Mr. Bryant. She hesitated to occupy any valuable time, and she then proceeded to occupy some sixty minutes of it in the narration of her troubles and trials during the late conflict. She had lived on

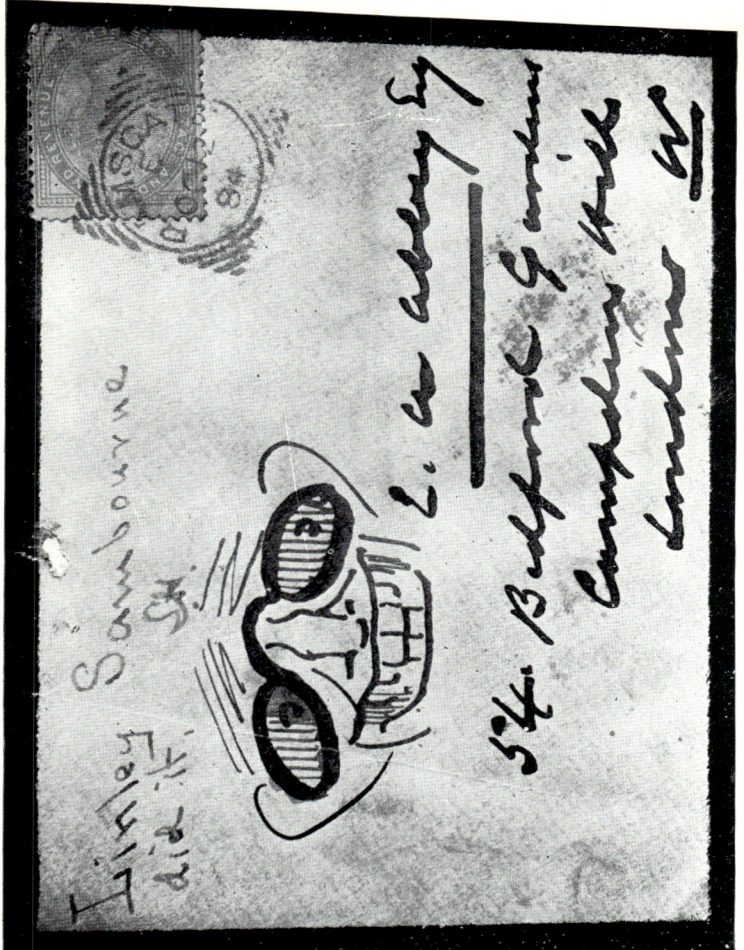

LETTER FROM SAMBOURNE TO ABBEY

the borders; her home was desolate; her possessions were scattered and lost; her income was reduced to a pittance. But, by the financial aid of the ever-generous members of her Guild-of-Letters, so prosperous now in the North, she had a scheme by which she felt assured she could not only help her neighbours on the banks of the River James,—and incidentally herself,—but could do great service to American letters, the country over. The present member of her guild listened as patiently as he could to her plan. He explained to her that he was not a prosperous author, and that he had no acquaintance with authors who were prosperous in that particular way; that the claims upon him were many and great and more than he could meet; and that he must be forced, with no little natural regret, to decline the opportunity to subscribe, which she had so kindly given him. However, as she had kept a cab at the door from eleven to twelve of the clock, at a dollar an hour, here was, if she would condescend to accept it, a dollar-bill to cover the cost of her entertaining visit. She took the money. And an enthusiastic collector offered two dollars and a half for the letter from Bryant.

A friend of Irving's (then Mr. Irving, not Sir Henry) was lucky enough to be the actor's guest some years ago at a breakfast he gave at Delmonico's to Edwin Booth. With the others present at the symposium, this lucky friend put his name upon a menu-card and passed it along the table. It came back to him, in due course, with the signatures of the host, of Mr. Whitelaw Reid, of Mr. Samuel L. Clemens (Mark Twain), of Mr. Charles Dudley Warner, of Mr. Thomas Bailey Aldrich, of Mr. Augustin Daly, of Booth, Barrett, Lester Wallack, John McCullough, Harry Edwards, and William J. Florence, in the order given. Because, as it was discovered long afterwards, the bit of paper contained thirteen names, and because six of the actors there present had signed it in succession, and had all quitted forever the stage of life, a fabulous price was offered for it by the same enthusiastic collector, who would never for a moment have thought of parting with it if it had been his own and had come to him in the same direct and pathetic way.

Irving, dining in a New York house, one December night, expressed much interest in certain proofs of engravings of Mr. John S. Sargent's Players Club portraits of Booth, Barrett, and Mr. Jefferson, which were hanging in the hall. His host saw a way of reciprocating some of Irving's many acts of hospitality and courtesy on both sides of the Atlantic; and he had a set of the three proofs mounted and sent to Irving as Christmas cards. The morning when the reply came —Irving always says "Thank you, sir"—this very same enthusiastic collector was sitting at the recipient's breakfast table, and he was shown the letter. It was a four-page epistle, all in Irving's handwriting—a very unusual performance because he almost invariably dictates to Mr. Bram Stoker, his manager, or to his secre-

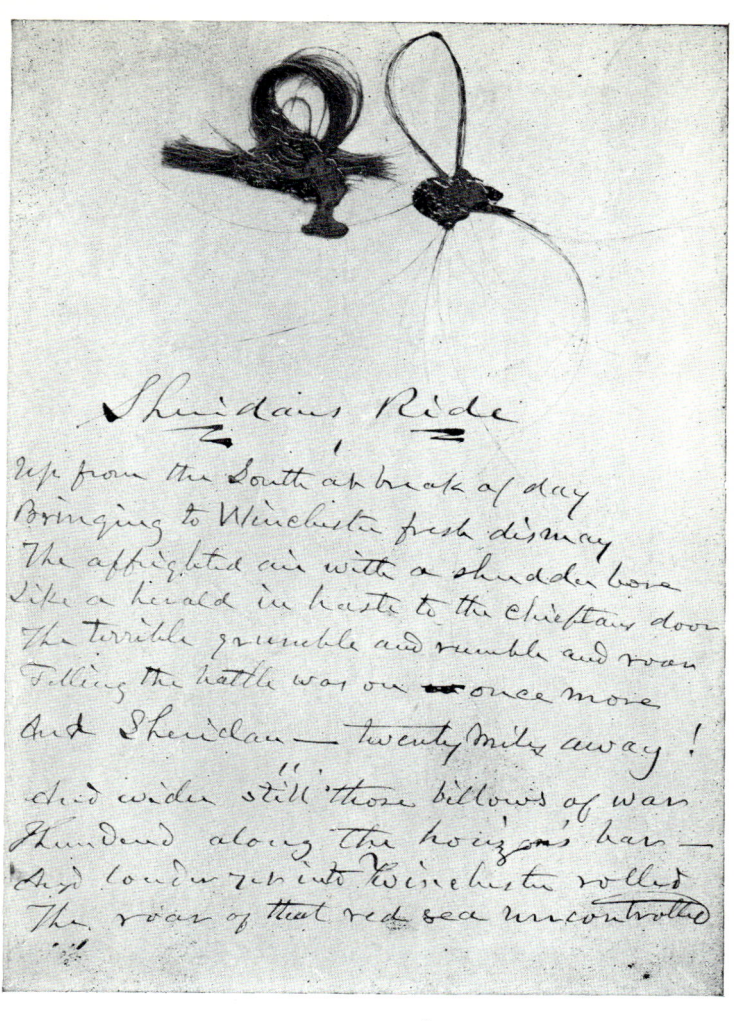

PART OF THE ORIGINAL MS. OF "SHERIDAN'S RIDE"
Attached to the sheet is a knot of horse-hair, as presented in the reproduction

tary,—and it was full of the kindliest, most tenderly affectionate words of appreciation of the two good friends—Booth and Barrett—whom he had lost by death, and of the good friend left to him—Mr. Jefferson, —whom he hoped might long be spared as an ornament and shining example to his profession. It is one of the best "examples" of Irving extant, for the reason of its manner and its matter. And as such the enthusiastic collector offered twenty-five dollars for it down! That same morning's mail had brought the bill for the proofs —one dollar each. And thus, in his efforts to get even with Irving, the donor of the pictures had made an apparent pecuniary profit of seven hundred *per centum* on the investment. But no man can ever expect to get even with Irving.

One or two examples of a sincere appreciation of autographs in humble and unexpected corners of the world may be cited here. The recipient of a post-office notice that a foreign book from an unknown source awaited his personal application and the payment of legal fees, called for it in due season. At the clerk's window he remarked that he was willing to bet fifty cents that the book was not worth the fifty cents charged for it, when the official replied that he would give fifty cents for the wrapper. The piece of brown paper contained, in his own handwriting, the name of Henry Irving. How, under the somewhat anomalous circumstances, it was recognized as genuine, and how it was recognized at all, for Irving's chirography, while "characteristic," is never, even at its best, very legible, is still a mystery.

Opposite the Black Jack Tavern in Portsmouth Street, near Portugal Street, London, stands or once stood a curious, irregular little building which claimed to be " The Original Old Curiosity Shop." No hint is anywhere given in the book itself, as to the exact situation of the home of the Trent family or even as to the neighbourhood in which the Trents lived. But the house in question must have been very familiar to Dickens, lying, as it does, or did, in the direct line of his many walks from the Strand to the Lincoln's Inn chambers of his friend John Forster ; in which chambers, by the way, he placed, and killed, Mr. Tulkinghorn, the family solicitor of the Dedlocks. If there is nothing to prove that it was the dwelling-place of Little Nell, there is nothing to show that it was not ; and on the strength of the might-have-been it was an object of no little interest and reverence on the part of visitors to London, especially of visitors from the United States. Two Americans who had made a particular study of the scenes of the stories of Dickens, who knew, or thought they knew, Tom All-Alone's, the dwelling of Bob Sawyer, the rooms of Mr. Dorrit in the Marshalsea, Tom Pinch's chambers in the Temple, and many more, knew well this alleged Old Curiosity Shop ; and often did they pass it and discuss it and wonder about it, with no thought of entering it ever occurring to them.

At last, one day during what she called a " Dickens

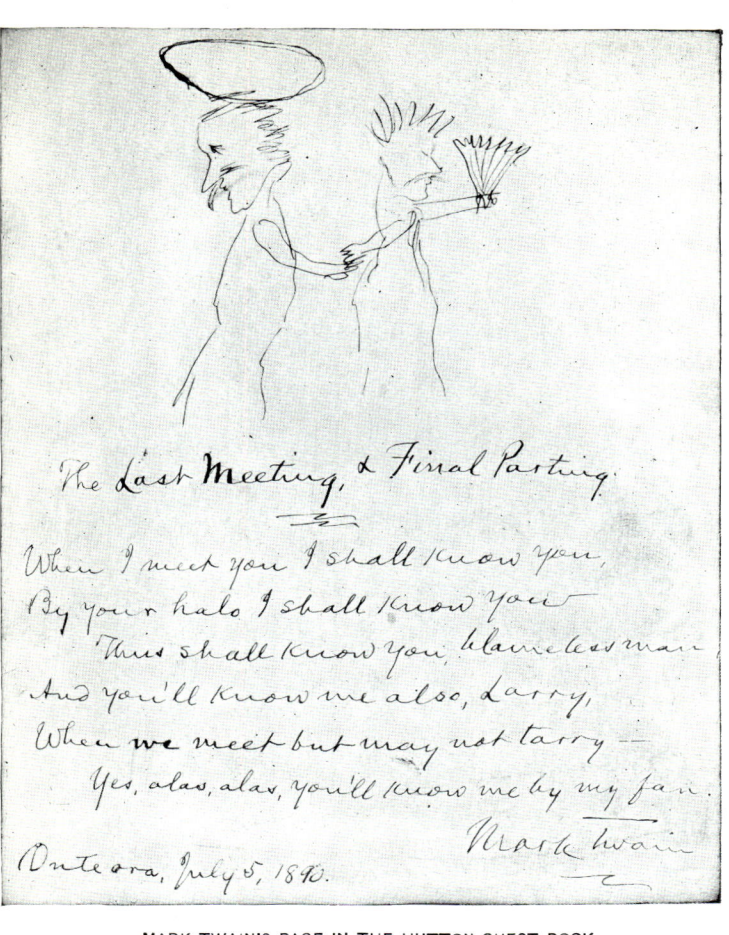

MARK TWAIN'S PAGE IN THE HUTTON GUEST-BOOK

Pilgrimage," they showed it to Miss Mary Anderson, then playing her first theatrical engagement in London. Without a moment's hesitation she opened the door and walked in, her two guides following meekly in her wake. The establishment had sunk in the social and mercantile scale, and had descended to the depths of the rag-and-bottle trade, with nothing attractive or romantic in its interior aspect. The present occupant, an agèd woman typical of her class and peculiarly typical of London, received her visitors cordially enough. She was evidently used to such inspection—especially on the part of Americans,—and quite as evidently she was proud of her surroundings, and of the attention paid them. She, at all events, believed firmly in the authenticity of the legend, and she did not seem to doubt for a moment that she was the direct successor of the famous curator of the emporium. She exhibited in a cheerful, chirpy way, the little that was to be seen, and finally she led her visitors into the sitting-room, which she assured them had been little Nell's own apartment. Here, the hour being five of the afternoon, she produced the inevitable cups, caddy, and kettle, and brewed the never-failing tea. She and Miss Anderson did all the talking; and, in an equally marked manner, they showed how much they were mutually impressed. The young actress, not unknown to fame but hitherto unrecognised by her new acquaintance, told who she was and asked her hostess to be her guest that night at the Lyceum Theatre, writing out, in her big, irregular, scrawling hand, a document which read: "Pass my friend, Mrs. Betty Higden" (that was not the name, but it is the name by which Miss Anderson always speaks of her to this day), "Pass my friend, Mrs. Betty Higden, and party to the stalls to-night."

The pass was never used. A year or two later, making another "Dickens Pilgrimage," Miss Anderson, this time acting herself as guide to an especially conducted party of her countrymen and countrywomen, called again on Mrs. Higden, and found the paper, neatly framed, with a photograph of "Galatea," hanging in the place of honor over the spot where is supposed to have stood little Nell's bed. "So you did not come to see the play after all?" she said, a little disappointed. "Oh, yes! We saw the pl'y. But when we found we 'd 'ave to give h'up the h'order or give h'up the stalls, we give h'up the stalls and kep the h'order. And we pied h'our w'y into the pit!"

Miss Anderson declares this to be the most gratifying indirect compliment she ever received. And for once, and by a plain, ignorant, little cockney-tradeswoman, in a very humble way the "Thank you!" so easily said but so rarely said, was said, most silently but most gracefully.

Thank you, good Mrs. Higden, for saying it!

CHAPTER XII

Mary Anderson in London—Dean Stanley—Westminster Abbey and the Izaak Walton Tablet—Stratford-on-Avon—William Winter—William Black—The Kinsmen.

WHEN Miss Mary Anderson and her brother, Mr. Joseph Anderson, were in London for the first time in their lives, I saw much of them, and did what I could to help them in a social way, almost perfect strangers as they were to the great metropolis. And I was, naturally, deeply interested in what she was doing upon the stage. I had, of course, a "bone" to the Lyceum Theatre in which she was playing, and saw something of them almost every day. During her first engagement in "Pygmalion and Galatea" I was living close by in Craven Street, Strand, busy with my own work, when I happened to mention to her that three of my mother's sisters and the husband of one of them were coming to make me a little visit on their way to New York; and that consequently for a week or two I would be occupied with them. Upon their arrival in the lodging-house, they were met by a note from Miss Anderson asking if Miss Scott, to whom the letter was addressed, not to me, would come with the other Aunts and occupy her box as her guest on some evening which they were to specify. They were old rather than elderly ladies, in deep mourning for the mother who had lately died, and most emphatically they were non-theatre goers. I question if any one of them had seen the inside of a play-house three times in her life. After a good deal of hesitation, they accepted, and went. They were met at the door of the theatre with a great deal of ceremony by Major Griffin, Miss Anderson's step-father and manager; and they were ushered to their seats in the box that had been placed at their disposal. At the end of the second act a servant appeared with ices, with Miss Anderson's compliments; Major Griffin called once or twice during the evening to see if the ladies were comfortable and enjoying the play; and from where we sat—I was with them, of course—we could see Miss Anderson in the wings, waiting for her call; and she never left the stage or entered it without some little smile or nod of recognition to the three dear old ladies who were entire strangers to her.

When the curtain was finally rung down and we were preparing to leave the house, Major Griffin appeared again and said that Miss Anderson would like very much to meet her guests, but, as she could not come to them, would they waive all ceremony and come to her in the dressing-room. To go behind the scenes, to see an actress in her war-paint, was something that had never entered their wildest dreams; but they marched bravely on, across the stage-entrance, and

MARY ANDERSON, WILLIAM BLACK, AND JO ANDERSON

were met by the Star of the evening, with outstretched hand. She distinguished one of them, particularly, by kissing her cheek and saying:

"This must be Aunt Charlotte, for she looks so like his mother!"

These words quite upset Aunt Charlotte, and the rest of my mother's sisters, and won their hearts. They realised that Miss Anderson and I must have talked them over and in an affectionate way; and the next morning, without saying anything to each other, they marched off silently and alone to the nearest photograph shop, to buy a picture of Galatea.

This is only one of the many examples of Miss Anderson's tact and sweetness and thoughtfulness for others.

Going through the Abbey of Westminster on a very memorable occasion with Miss Mary Anderson and her brother, under the escort of Dean Stanley, the historian of the Minster, he showed us a great many rare and curious things, which were not contained in his own volume. He stopped before the mural tablet to Isaac Casaubon, in the South Transept, and said:

"There is only one bit of desecration of the Abbey that I am disposed to forgive. I'll show it to you."

And he laid his beautiful fingers in a caressing way upon the monogram initials "I. W.," and the date "1658," which he had discovered to have been scratched there, with a nail, by Izaak Walton himself. This seemed to bring me as near to Walton—always dear to me—as I had ever come. The Dean was kind enough to permit me to have a tracing made of the letters and the figures, though such things were against the rules of the institution.

Izaak Walton had confessed the deed in one of his letters, and the gentle prelate told us that on discovering the fact, late at night, he could not rest till he had proved for himself that the marks still existed. And with a lighted candle he went from the Deanery, in the silent hours of the morning, to satisfy himself that they were there.

With a deep and affectionate reverence he showed us the tomb of his wife; and pointing to a spot in the same chapel, he said: " In the natural course of events you young people will come here some day and find me lying there."

And there he lies. I never saw him again. But the impression he made upon me then, as before, was that of a character unusually gentle, strong, and sweet.

I went that same year from Broadway, in Worcestershire, to Stratford, to attend the opening of the Shakespeare Memorial Theatre in the town of Shakespeare's birth. Miss Anderson was playing Rosalind for the first time, and the occasion was considered a wonderful one. Low, and Archer, and Abbey, and Comyns Carr, and Frank Millet, and Tadema, and all the artists and dramatic critics in England were present. It was on a Saturday night; and Miss Anderson and her company

MONOGRAM, "I. W.," IN WESTMINSTER ABBEY

At Stratford-on-Avon

were to go early on the next morning to Birmingham, where she was to play on the Monday evening. After the performance and long after midnight, William Winter, who had borrowed the keys of the church, took us into the sacred edifice; and there we had, all alone to ourselves, with the bright full moonlight shining through the stained glass windows, the resting-place of the "Immortal." Winter was our chaperone and guide. It was a night never to be forgotten. We had no business there; but although we realised that, we did not care.

The next day Mr. Winter carried us about the Shake-spearian country, showing us Ann Hathaway's cottage; quoting:

> Ann Hathaway,
> She hath a way
> To make men say,
> "To be Heaven's self Ann hath a way";

taking us to Charlecote Park; showing us the green-wood tree; asking us to stop and "listen to the sweet bird's note, who tuned his merry throat"; "Come hither, come hither, here shall he see no enemy but winter and rough weather"; and the spot on which "the wild thyme grew." Finally, when he left us at the door of our own hotel, Mr. Malcom Bell, an Englishman, remarked:

"I don't know who this Winter of yours is, but he is certainly a man of wonderful Shakesperience!"

It was a year later at Stratford (1883) that we made

William Black a Kinsman. The occasion was a farewell dinner in the Shakespeare Inn to William M. Laffan, who was returning to America after some years' residence in England as the London representative of the New York *Sun;* and the party consisted of Abbey, Parsons, Millet, Laffan, Boughton, Black, and myself.

The printed bill of fare at my plate, which I still preserve and cherish, was illuminated by original signed pencil drawings of the artists present. Mr. Boughton illustrated the soup, Mr. Abbey the fish, Mr. Laffan the cutlets, Mr. Millet the salad and game, Mr. Parsons the joint, and Mr. Black added to the value of the document by a most wonderful landscape, under which he wrote that it was done by that " 'ere Crow" (Eyre Crowe being a well-known British painter not present but an intimate friend of us all) or "Corot,"—William Black.

Black's drawing as a drawing is of but little value as a work of art. But to his many admirers in another line it cannot fail to be of interest as perhaps the only example in existence of his work as a draughtsman.

The story of this dinner found its way into the British and American press and, shortly after, returning to America on one of the Cunard steamers, I was accosted by an enthusiastic young lady who was very anxious to meet me and so expressed herself.

She said that she was familiar with everything I had done and admired it, and then she asked me, in the

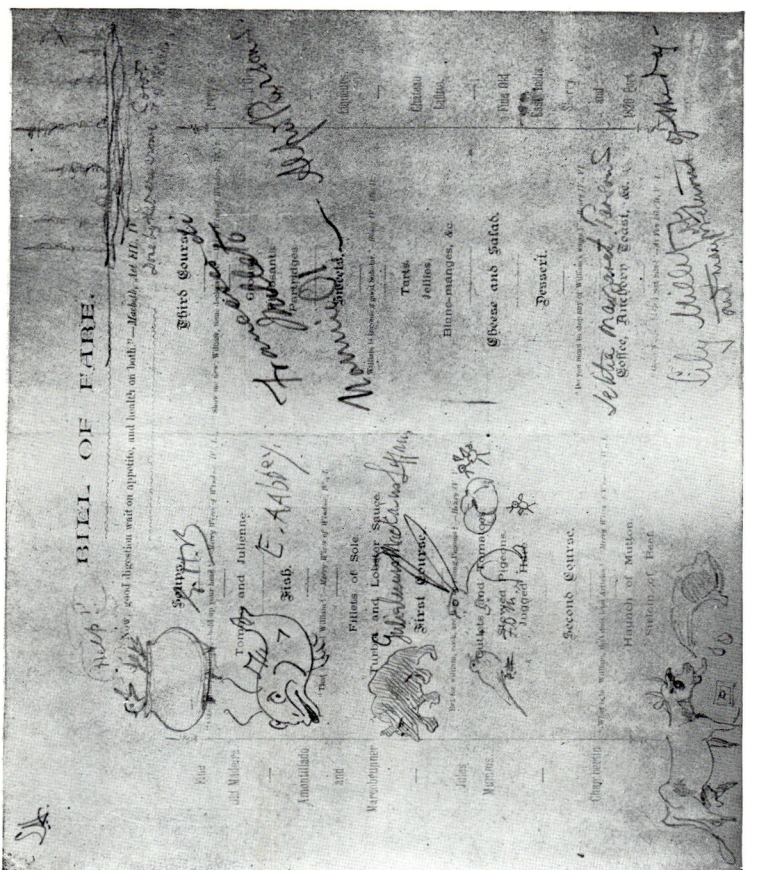

A KINSMEN MENU WITH AUTOGRAPHED DRAWINGS

most impressive voice, what I was doing now. Seeing my name among a group of painters, she had naturally concluded that I belonged to that profession. Such, I felt, was fame!

Another unusual menu card celebrated one of the earliest international feasts of this organisation. It was a composite drawing, Mr. Boughton making a punchbowl into which John Bull, by du Maurier, and Brother Jonathan, by E. A. Abbey, are pouring the wine. On the bottom are a series of bottles and a box of cigars, the work of Linley Sambourne; while at the top, in an illuminated scroll, are the words, "The Kinsmen," from the hand of Alfred Parsons. The original composition, in pen and ink, bears in each case upon his own production the autograph of the artist. The document coming, somehow, into the hands of Osgood, was bequeathed to me.

William Black was an interesting little man with dark hair, a long moustache, very red and weather-beaten cheeks, and a marked Scottish accent. He was shy in the presence of strangers—particularly women, — but was a warm and faithful friend. He lived in Brighton, where he had a large study on the top of his house, facing the ocean. Here he worked hard, writing many hundred words a day, in a very fine hand and on small sheets of paper. His manuscript is legible and unusually free from erasures or corrections. The manuscript of each novel was bound separately and was given to his children, the letterpress copy going to the printers. When he was in the throes of composition he was never interrupted by any member of his household on any account, and no one ever ascended to the floor which he had taken for his own.

He also had a suite of apartments at the foot of Buckingham Street, Strand, from the windows of which he had a glorious view of the Thames, up and down, and as the street is not a thoroughfare he had absolute quiet. The house is a very old one; it is but a few feet from Inigo Jones's picturesque York Water-Gate; it is built upon the site of York House in which Bacon was born; and the present structure is now famous as the one-time residence of Peter the Great. Black's rooms have an interesting history of their own. They were occupied for some time by Clarkson Stanfield, and they were the gathering-place of all the bright men of his particular set. Dickens was his frequent guest then, and he gave the chambers to "David Copperfield." Here David entertained Traddles, the Micawbers, Mr. Dick, and once—very much against his will—Uriah Heep, who, it will be remembered, slept all night upon the sofa. And here "Trotwood" gave that famous and disastrous dinner party to Steerforth which was broken up by somebody falling down-stairs,—that somebody, as Trotwood realised afterwards, being Trotwood himself,—and which ended by Trotwood being disgraced in Dora's eyes by a drunken exhibition in the theatre. Black put George Brand, the hero of *Sunrise,* in the same apartments at No. 15 Buckingham

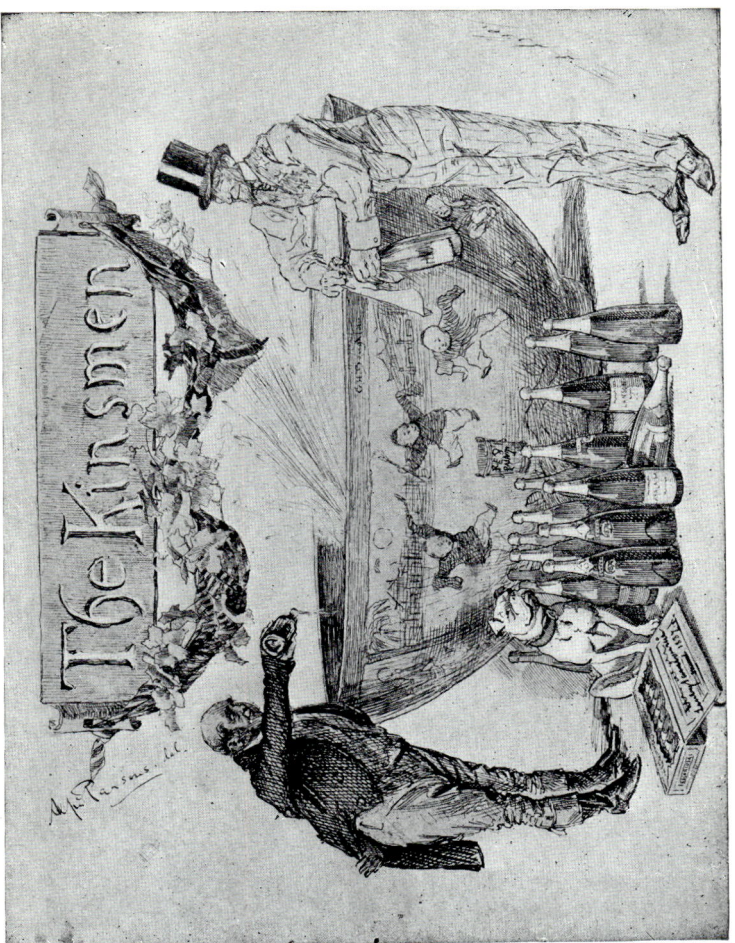

THE PUNCH BOWL COMPOSITE DRAWING

Street. He was not very fond of the association of the rooms with Peter the Great, but cared very much to tell his friends that Samuel Pepys lived across the way, that David Hume, and Rousseau, and Henderson the actor, and Etty the Royal Academician had been his neighbours in the little street, and that Smollett's "Strap" was the keeper of a lodging-house not very far away,—all in the broadest Scotch I think I ever heard, even in the Highlands; and he loved his Scotland dearly.

Black was an enthusiastic fisherman and yachtsman; he spent his holidays in the Highlands or on the water. Many of the salmon killed by his heroes were captured on his own hooks; he had trod his *White Heather;* he had sailed his *White Wings;* and *The Strange Adventures of a Phaeton* and *The House Boat* are based upon his own experiences, although the "Queen Titania" who so often figures as the author's wife is by no means, either physically or mentally, a portrait of Mrs. Black.

My first meeting with William Black was during his visit to America in the middle seventies, and it was pleasantly and peculiarly accidental. I received at the Arcadian Club one day a letter from Mr. Edmund Clarence Stedman, written in the third person, asking Mr. Hutton to meet the Scottish novelist at a supper to the Century Club, then, of course, in the old building in Fifteenth Street. I was much gratified and not a little surprised, for my acquaintance at that time with Mr. Stedman was very slight. I was only trying my 'prentice hand in journalism,—had made no mark whatever,—and could not understand how I should be selected for such an honour. I was still more surprised when I discovered the men by whom I was surrounded: Bryant, Parke Godwin, Stoddard, Huntington, Wm. H. Appleton, Joseph W. Harper, Bayard Taylor, and their peers; and I wondered if among such big guns a pocket-pistol fire-cracker like me was expected to let himself off. I said little, but I listened; and, up to that period, it was certainly the night of my life.

Not till many years afterwards did I discover that the letter which I had found in the *H* box at the club, was intended for Mr. Joseph Hatton, who, naturally, never received it. Stedman would seem to have understood matters at a glance, and he was, of course, too much of a gentleman to let me realise for a moment that I was there under false pretences, though of course through no fault of my own. The joke was on Hatton, and he appreciated it. He calls me " Hatton-Hutton " to this day, addresses me as his " Dear Joseph," and always signs himself " Laurence." It was on that evening, by the way, during the very post-prandial remarks, that one gentleman spoke most feelingly and admiringly and affectionately of the guest of the evening as the author of *Lorna Doone*, dwelling chiefly upon the wonderful merits of that particular work of the man whom they had gathered to meet and to greet. This caused somebody to say in an undertone that what we wanted was a little less Blackmore and a little more Black.

WILLIAM BLACK'S ROOM

Some time afterwards Black and I were together for six weeks at Stratford while he was writing his *Judith Shakespeare*, Abbey making the illustrations. Abbey frequently, in the absence of a professional model, drew me as all sorts of persons and in all sorts of shapes and places; and on one occasion I may be seen with a smooth face reading the Bible at family worship, and on another with myself in a beard. When the day's work was over in Stratford, during that autumn of 1883, we tramped for miles in all directions, coming home to late dinners and to good talk. Black put a great deal of care and thought into his *Judith Shakespeare*. It was, perhaps, by him, the best liked of all the novels he had written, and he was bitterly disappointed that the world who read him did not regard it in the same light. Although he never said so, I have always felt that this particular romance was inspired by the remark of Carlyle to Black once: " You have done good things which are light, my man, why don't you do something serious?" or words to that effect.

During the succeeding winter I received from William Black the following letters:

" PASTON HOUSE, PASTON PLACE,
" BRIGHTON, Oct. 8.

" MY DEAR HUTTON :

" Thank you very much for the ' Literary Notes.' I am glad you like *Donald Ross*. But you don't seriously imagine that I set to work to write a novel in reply to the trivial trash of that ill-conditioned Yankee tourist?

"I was about to write to you in any case. Do you remember my asking you about the games played by the New York street-Arabs, and your saying that Mrs. Hutton was an authority on that subject? I wonder if she would be so very kind as to tell me whether there is a game or dance of distinctly American origin that the children have. The 'Oats-pease-beans' that you mentioned is merely the old English 'Oats and Beans and Barley'—as familiar as 'Round about the Mulberry Bush' or 'Mary-Ma-Tanzie' (Mary May Dance). It would be most interesting to know if the American children had invented for themselves something like 'Poor Mary lies a-dying' or 'Three Dukes a-riding'; but it is hardly likely: these things are handed down from the dark backward and abysm of time, etc.

"WILLIAM BLACK."

"PASTON HOUSE, PASTON PLACE,
"BRIGHTON, Nov. 1.

"MY DEAR HUTTON :

"Thank you very much for your letter and all the information contained in its enclosures—though I am afraid there is not much resemblance between the house-boat described by your correspondent and the little floating palaces of the Thames. I did not happen to see what you said about the *Adventures* [*The Adventures of a House Boat*]. I presume you know that your section of *Harper's Magazine* does n't appear in the English edition.

"Yes, that was rather a merry time at Stratford

PEN-AND-INK SKETCH OF LAURENCE HUTTON BY ABBEY

My wife and I are just back from a more soberly gay week in Dublin which we spent with Miss Anderson and her brother, to bid them good-bye. You should have witnessed a pretty incident that occurred on one of these evenings in *The Winter's Tale.* An ancient and venerable shepherd made his appearance in the Pastoral Scene; and the youthful Perdita was so kind as to come forward and present the poor old man with a cake surrounded by laurel. What significance there was about his taking the cake was probably not guessed at by the audience who only saw an act of compassion and consideration. As to the identity of the ancient shepherd?—but hush!¹ . . ."

"March 20.

"MY DEAR HUTTON:

"Had I learned sooner of your marriage I would have sent my congratulations at the time; but I suppose the happy event has not yet lost all the charm of novelty. I thought there must be something of the kind in the wind, from the demureness of your behaviour at Stratford (which, by the way, quite prepared me for finding you seated at a Bible reading in a recent *Harper's* illustration). I am sure you will be glad to know that your friends over here are much pleased at the step you have taken; and hope that it will have an educational effect on your character, etc.

"WILLIAM BLACK."

¹ The ancient shepherd was, of course, Black himself, making his *début* among the supernumeraries of the cast.

"REFORM CLUB, May 16.

" . . . Very glad to hear you are coming over; there 's a powerful American contingent here at present. I dined with Osgood, Laffan, Abbey, Brisbane, and a lot of them last night.

" Miss Anderson is slowly getting better, but she has to take great care. She sees hardly anybody; does not read nor write; but she goes out for drives and walks, and the spring weather is just now simply delightful. By and by when Jo and Gertrude have fixed on a house [Jo Anderson had married Gertrude, the daughter of Lawrence Barrett] she will live with them. She is in capital spirits, but of course has to avoid the least excitement for fear of bringing back another attack of the nervous prostration. And thank you for the *Harper*. By the way, why does n't the American *Harper* wear an outer garment more nearly suited to the English one?—the latter being more cheerful.

"WILLIAM BLACK."

"June 3, BRIGHTON.

" MY DEAR HUTTON :

" If you have now emerged from that Slough of Despond in which all No 45 Albemarle Street [London] seemed to have got sunk the other morning, I hope you will reconsider your decision about Sunday and come down with the two boys. It will be quite as much rest for you as remaining in London—and you will get a breath of sea air as well.

" There ain't no formalities about this here mansion;

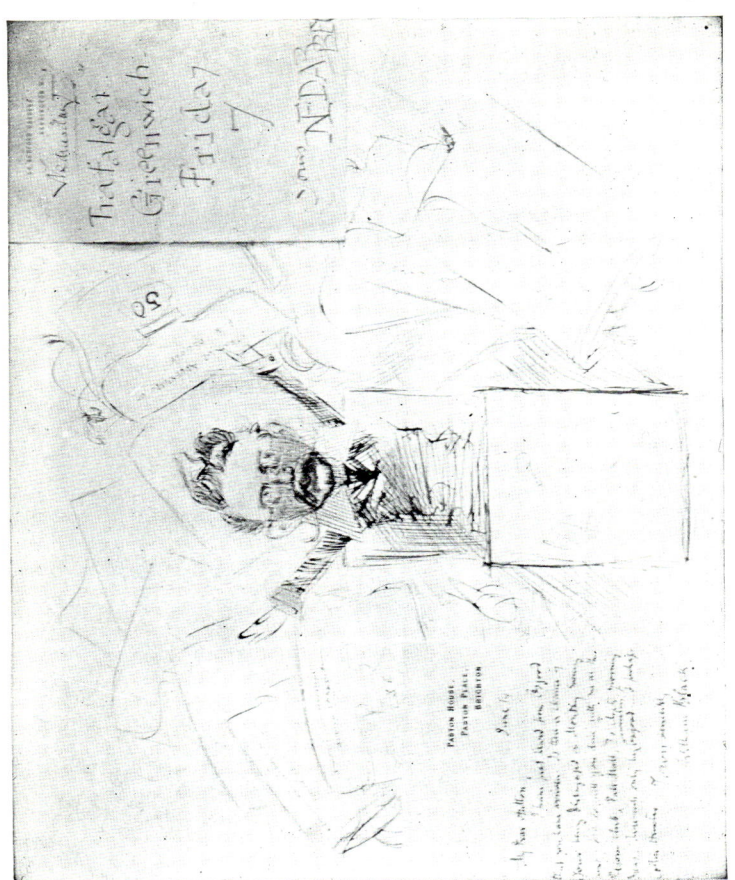

SKETCH OF WILLIAM BLACK BY ABBEY

so even if those mysterious shirts have not turned up, you may put aside that consideration. I do hope you will come. James will bring you down and take you back, either the same night or the next morning, whichever is the most agreeable to you all. Which *we* should prefer I need not say.

"Yours sincerely,
"WILLIAM BLACK."

The initial idea of " The Kinsman " was Lawrence Barrett's; the name was an inspiration of my own. The actor had long contemplated the foundation of a little club in this country upon the lines of the " Green Room " or the " Beefsteak " in London, to which none but professionals should be admitted and only those of the right sort. He wanted to bring together the players, the writers, the sculptors, the painters, into some simple organisation which should be select and fraternal. He, Abbey, Laffan, Millet, and Brander Matthews, with their wives,— such of them as had wives,—chanced to gather in my house in the early part of 1882; and the scheme was then and there discussed and endorsed, but without coming to any definite conclusion. Finally, Matthews suggested that we adjourn to dine with him at the Florence House a few evenings later; and there, about a round table, the unique little society was formally organised. There were to be no dues, no fees, no club-house, no constitution, no by-laws, no officers, "no nothing" but good fellowship and good times. We were to breakfast, or dine, or lunch, or sup, together; each member was to bring to each symposium a guest of his own choosing and of his own profession, whom he felt would be acceptable to the other members,—the simple presence of such a guest making him a member of the club itself without any other form of choice or ballot; and in this way was the society to be increased with no limit except that of the proper fitness of congeniality and talent. All sorts of names were suggested for the organisation, but none of them seemed suitable or sufficiently comprehensive until Barrett, in a neat little speech, alluded to the " amiable and convivial association of the kindred arts about our simple board." And that gave me the cue; " Kinsmen, then, let us be!" And " Kinsmen " we are to this day.

The death of my mother a few weeks later, and a general separation of all parties concerned for many months, postponed all further action until the next year, when in March (1883) the second meeting of the Kinsmen was held at a dinner in my house. Barrett brought Julian Hawthorne, in the absence of Booth and Jefferson, who were travelling and far away; Matthews brought H. C. Bunner; Millet brought Elihu Vedder; Laffan and Abbey were over the water; and my guest was Samuel L. Clemens—otherwise, Mark Twain. The breaking of bread and sipping of beer and claret was their only initiation, and everything was going on beautifully and harmoniously, when a

Rose Meinie.
(From a novel to be written in 1884 by
W. Black, & Illustrated by E. A. Abbey.
A gamekeeper log:)

O wilt thou be my dear love?
            (Meinie and Meinie)
O wilt thou be my ain love?
            (My sweet Meinie)
Were you wi' me upon the hill
It's I would gar the dogs be still,
We'd lie our lone, and kiss our fill
            (My love Meinie)

Aboon the burn a wild bush grows
            (Meinie and Meinie)
And on the bush there blooms a rose
            (My love Meinie)
And wad ye take the rose frae me
And wear it where it fain would lie,
It's to your arms that I would flee
            (Rose-sweet Meinie!)

———

You can present this to Minnie, if you
like — but as your own composition.
            Yours always,
            William Black.

"ROSE MEINIE," WRITTEN BY WILLIAM BLACK

cab brought J. R. Osgood to the door from the Grand Central Station. He was uninvited and unexpected, and he was given to understand that he could dine at the sideboard or at the mantel-piece or at a little table near the window, but that this was a private and particular feast to which, unfortunately, as only a publisher and a friend, he was not eligible. He contended that he was eligible to anything, that we were all his kinsmen not once removed, that he had been an uncle if not a father to every one of us, he drank out of somebody's tumbler, ate off of somebody's plate, sat on the arm of somebody's chair, and before we knew it or could help ourselves — even if we had wanted to — Osgood was a Kinsman in good standing forever. And no more enthusiastic Kinsman ever lived. He entered into the spirit of the thing so thoroughly, made so many suggestions, had so much to say about it, that finally Clemens rose and in a most serious way observed that he had been so much impressed by the remarkable eloquence and flood of advice, expostulation, exhortation, admonition, and guidance, which had come from the lips of the youngest member present —the member of about half an hour—that he felt we must be unanimous in the sentiment that the name of the Club should be changed at once, and that in future it should be called "The Osgood Club." He begged to put that as a motion, and to ask, nay, to urge, with all the native force of which he was capable and from the bottom of his heart, that it be carried *viva voce*.

"This has got to be 'The Osgood Club'!" Osgood was comparatively silent for the half hour which followed.

The next gathering of the Kinsmen was held at the Blue Posts Tavern in London, in June of the same year. Laffan, Osgood, Matthews, Abbey, and I, instituted there and then the initial English chapter. The new members were Comyns Carr, Clarence King, Andrew Lang, Gosse, Parsons, George Boughton, Dobson, Linley Sambourne, and Randolph Caldecott, all of whom entered heartily into the spirit of the thing and in later years added to their number such men as du Maurier, Luke Fields, Tadema, William Podgett, Harold Frederic, Lionel Robertson, Burnand, Anstey, Guthrie, Collin, Hunter, Frederick McMillan, John Hare, Anthony Hope Hawkins, Orchardson, Pinero, Forbes Robertson, Bram Stoker.

Irving, Jefferson, Gilder, and George Parsons Lathrop were gathered into the fold at a breakfast at the Brunswick, New York, in November, 1893; Irving shortly afterwards presented each and every one of his Kinsmen with a perpetual free pass to any theatre in which he may be playing at any time. This pass is in the form of an ivory disk, upon one side of which is engraved the words "Lyceum Theatre," with the autograph of "Henry Irving" in fac-simile. On the other side is engraved the name of the Kinsman whose especial property it is. It is called a "bone," from the fact that in the early days of the British drama admis-

DRAWING BY CALDECOTT

sion checks were made of that material, and to be on the free list at any theatre there to this day is expressed in the terms of the profession as "having a bone."

In the spring of 1884, Edwin Booth became a Kinsman,— in New York,— and he always regretted that he was not the possessor of a "bone." With him that night were initiated Howells, Swain Gifford, William Baird, John A. Mitchell, and Dudley Warner. Our British Kinsmen made Thomas B. Aldrich a Kinsman at the Saville Club in London in 1884, and we initiated the international chapter by electing John L. Toole at The Players in New York in 1894, adding to our number at the time, John Drew, Thomas Nelson Page, Augustus Saint-Gaudens, E. C. Stedman, Stanford White, Francis Wilson, and the Rev. Joseph Twitchell. Among the members whose names I have not recorded, are Charles Fairchild, Bret Harte, Fitzgibbon, Henry James, John S. Sargent, and David Murray.

During our existence we have lost among others by death: Lawrence Barrett, Edwin Booth, Caldecott, Osgood, T. F. Bayard, William Black, H. C. Bunner, Harold Frederic, George du Maurier, Locker-Lampson, George Parsons Lathrop, Sir Arthur Sullivan, Bret Harte, Clarence King, and Charles Dudley Warner: and surely the roll of the Kinsmen is as creditable a list of clever and good fellows as the history of modern clubs can show.

CHAPTER XIII

Alma Tadema—George du Maurier—Charles Reade—George Eliot—Swinburne—Joaquin Miller in England—Locker-Lampson—John Fiske—James Russell Lowell.

MRS. HUTTON'S first meeting with the Tademas came very near proving a serio-comic tragedy. We were spending the summer of 1885 in Broadway, Worcestershire, England, at The Lygon Arms, the leading inn of the place. The Frank D. Millets, then living in Broadway, had entertained us on many occasions and Mrs. Hutton felt that it was our place and our privilege to reciprocate on a certain Saturday, the 8th of August. The Millets, E. A. Abbey, Alfred Parsons, and others of their friends and ours, were to dine with us that night. Great preparations had been made by the hostess of the evening, when Mrs. Millet came in on Saturday morning to say that a telegram had just reached them announcing that Tadema, Mrs. Tadema, their daughter, and Mrs. Williams, Mrs. Tadema's sister, were coming from Evesham to spend with the Millets the week-end, and would Mrs. Hutton forego her dinner, in the circumstances, and dine with the Millets instead, to meet the Tademas? Mrs. Hutton insisted upon her own party: her husband, not

THE KINSMEN "BONE"

THE KINSMEN "BONE" (REVERSE SIDE)

exactly understanding why, but like a good husband—although a new one—willing to submit to the rule of the better half. The result was that the Millets and their guests appeared in the Huttons' apartment at the proper time. Hutton himself, in his innocence, was overwhelmed when his attention was called to sundry bottles of champagne being iced in his hip-tub, in an ante-room to the apartment, Mr. Millet remarking:

"Can such things be! This is the first time in all our experiences in Broadway that we have had anything to drink of more importance than *vin ordinaire.*"

At the proper moment the champagne was uncorked with a great deal of difficulty by a maid who was entirely unused to its manipulation; the glasses were filled when, to her husband's amazement, Mrs. Hutton arose and said:

"I want you all to drink with me to Laurence on his birthday."

Laurence, entirely overcome, for he had forgotten that it was his birthday, happened to glance at Tadema and Mrs. Tadema, when he saw the looks of overwhelming astonishment which they cast toward each other. Before he had time to rise and express his feeble thanks and appreciation of the toast, Mr. Tadema got up and in a few well-chosen words replied. It so happened that his name was Laurence and that it was his own birthday; and, curiously enough, that of his eldest daughter, who had been born also on the 8th of August, and had been named Laurence Tadema, Jr., on that account. Tadema confessed afterwards that he had read *Daisy Miller* and fancied that here in this little provincial English town was a real Daisy Miller, drinking to him whom she had never met before, drinking his health on his birthday, and calling him familiarly and lovingly by his first name.

My own acquaintance with Tadema began in an equally curious way. James R. Osgood, who always expressed himself by a dinner or a luncheon, having discovered incidentally that William Dean Howells and George H. Boughton had never met, invited them with a few friends of his and theirs to dine at the Arts Club in London. In the middle of the symposium it was discovered that Tadema and Whistler were sitting together at an adjoining table. I alone of Mr. Osgood's party was unknown to Tadema. He came forward, leaned over the back of my chair—why *my* chair I never knew,—planted his chin on the top of the little bald spot on my head, and addressed the assembled coterie for some fifteen minutes, the vibration of every word he uttered moving through my entire frame; Whistler with his one eye-glass taking it all in and very much amused. At the conclusion of Mr. Tadema's oration, eloquent and amusing, he went back to his own seat at his own table and I inquired of my host:

"Who is this British Sarony who has been taking these liberties with the top of my head?"

"Why, that's Tadema; don't you know Tadema?"

Of course I knew Tadema the artist, but Tadema the

DRAWING BY ALMA TADEMA

man I never before had met so emphatically in the flesh, and Boughton said:

"Come over here, Tad, and let me introduce you to Laurence Hutton—one of our kindred kind."

And Tad replied:

"I knew he was one of our kind or I would n't have talked into him as I did. You can never fool me about one of the boys."

We were fortunate enough to be in London supping with the Gosses, on the occasion of Alma Tadema's first housewarming in the building in London which has since become so famous. Mrs. Hutton and I, in the natural course of events, drifted apart; she talking to those of her friends whom she knew, and I looking for old friends and acquaintances. Stepping up to Miss Tadema, the eldest daughter of the house, and looking about me at the vast array of celebrities there gathered, I said:

"Now tell me who some of these people are. I know that they are all somebodies, and I recognise a great many faces, familiar either from my personal association with them or from the photographs I have seen in the literary or artistic journals or in shop windows. Whistler I know, of course, and Sir Frederick Leighton, and Charles Dickens (the younger), and Joseph Hatton, Miss Genevieve Ward, and Dobson, and Lang; but there is one man talking to your father now whose face I know perfectly well, but whom I cannot place."

Whereupon an extremely pretty young woman, to

whom I had not been introduced, sought to enlighten me by saying:

"Why, that's *my* father." And I replied:

"Now, Mademoiselle, you have added very much to my curiosity, because I've been trying to place *you*."

"Oh, Mr. Hutton," she said, "you have seen me in *Punch*. I'm Miss du Maurier. And if you don't know Papa, who has just been made a Kinsman and is more proud of the fact than of his membership in the Royal Academy, let me tell him who you are."

And that was the beginning of my very pleasant but short acquaintance with George du Maurier. The pleasant sentiment of fraternity existing among all the members of that unique little association, The Kinsmen, gave us a feeling of belonging to each other which our personal knowledge of each other would hardly have warranted. We dined together in London at one or two of the Kinsmen festivals, and we met in other places in a "how-de-do" passing way. And that was all. I am sure he was a good fellow. But he had no opportunity to make any positive impression upon me in a purely personal way. Two of his letters inserted into my bound copies of *Peter Ibbetson* and *Trilby* I prize very highly. In the first he says:

"I am delighted that you should like the opening of *P. I.* I took much pains with it as it is in contrast with the sordid English life that is to follow. Then he will get back to France again, and the old life, but in a new and unsuspected way.

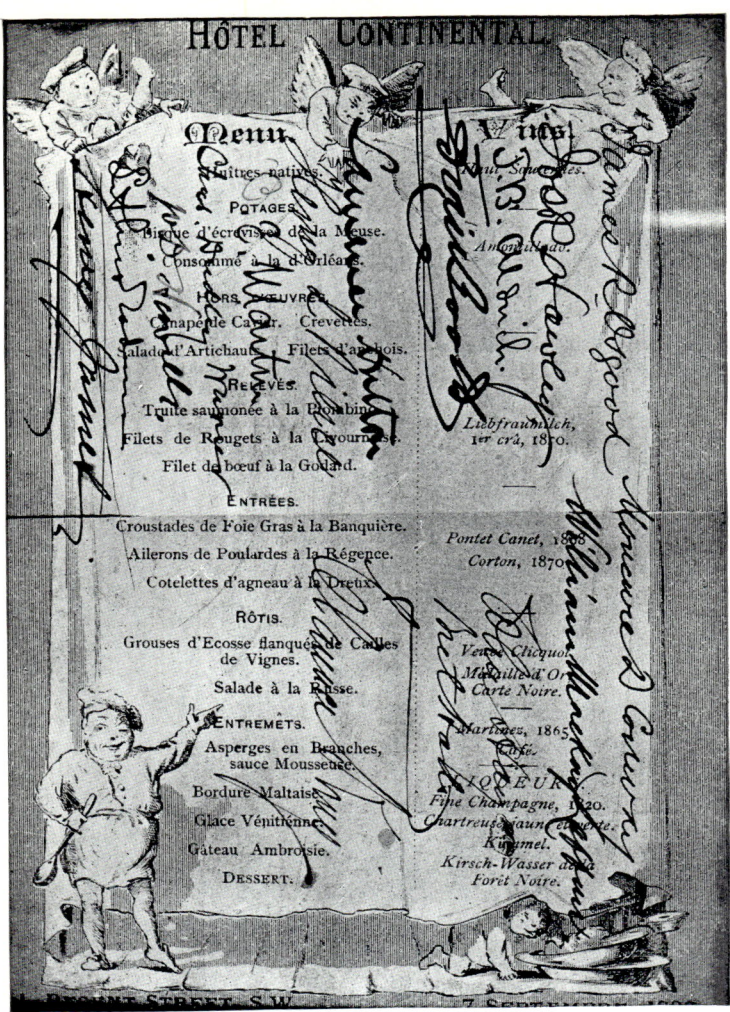

AN AUTOGRAPHED KINSMEN MENU

"Barring that I have beautified the principal people and elongated them by a foot or so, the first part is almost autobiographical, and the old Major, whose real name was du Quesne, is a portrait." (This is dated June 2, 1891.)

On the 18th of January, 1893, he wrote:

"I am delighted that you like the beginning of *Trilby*. It makes me hope that you will like it all through as it was all written *of a piece* with a galloping pen after having carefully made it all out in my head.

"Taffy is made out of two or three people. Van Trump is only there for the strength. 'Little Billee' is what I imagine Fred Walker might have been in similar circumstances, and the villain is founded on a certain Louis Brassin whom I knew in Antwerp and Dusseldorf, a great pianist but monstrously increased and bedeviled. I am glad you like the girl. The drawings cost me much pains and I have n't finished them yet,—one hundred and twenty in all."

A propos of these letters, there appeared in *The Critic*, in 1893, the following paragraph:

"Mr. Laurence Hutton had a shock not long ago. Among his many literary treasures is a copy of *Peter Ibbetson* in which is bound an autograph letter from du Maurier, telling who the different characters in the story are, or rather from whom they were drawn. Mr. Hutton wanted to flaunt this interesting volume before the eyes of a friend, and went to the shelf to get it, when lo! it had disappeared. High and low he searched, but could not find it. Weeks passed by, and he had given it up for lost. The subject came up in the presence of a visitor. 'I know where the book is,' she said, and straightway walked to the bookshelf marked 'Fiction' and took it out. The trouble is that Mr. Hutton classifies his books, and the du Maurier should have been on the shelf with 'Presentation Copies,' instead of which it got among the fiction. Believing that his system is infallible, Mr. Hutton had not thought of looking for the book there, though he looked everywhere else. The moral of this is that when one loses a book, he must look for it in the likely as well as the unlikely places, if he would find it."

Since then the Hutton library has little printed inscriptions on every group of volumes, "Please do not return the books to the shelves." Any one knows how to take a book out, but no one but the owner knows just where to put the book back.

I wanted to possess a copy of the *Trilby* that first appeared in *Harper's Monthly*. The issue for March contained a take-off on Whistler and was immediately suppressed, although the numbers already issued before the complaints from Whistler came to hand could not be recalled. I said to one in authority at *Harper's*:

"I want a copy of that issue."

"You can't have it, it has been suppressed."

"But I'll buy it."

A Means of Possession

"We can't sell even one more; but — damn you — you know where they are!"

I did, and the result of my knowledge is the cutting that is pasted in the back of my copy of *Trilby*.

Another case of possession that was very similar was when I once wanted an original drawing from the Century people, and could not prevail upon them to either give or sell me a copy. But a day or two following I received the picture with a courteous note explaining that the Century Company would be very glad indeed if I would accept the drawing as a loan for a period of one hundred years.

And yet again, a third time, has this experience of possession befallen me.

I once wanted very badly to bring out to the Golf Club in Princeton the Rules and Regulations of the Club of St. Andrews, printed in due form, and upon which all the rules of golf, from the beginning of golf, are based. I found a copy of the Rules one day in a little book-shop of the town of St. Andrews in Scotland. Expressing my desire to purchase it, the owner said:

"You know they are not here for me to sell or to give away; but I am going into the other room for a minute and I see no reason why you should n't take them!"

The *Trilby* bit was cut from page 142 in the volume as it was published by the Harpers in 1894, and is as follows:

"Then there was Joe Sibley, the idle apprentice, the

king of Bohemia; *le roi des truands*, to whom everything was forgiven, as to François Villon, *à cause de ses gentillesses*.

"Always in debt like Svengali, vain, witty, and a most exquisite and original artist; and also eccentric in his attire (though clean), so that people would stare at him as he walked along — which he adored! But (unlike Svengali) he was genial, caressing, sympathetic, charming, the most irresistible friend in the world as long as his friendship lasted—but that was not forever!

"The moment his friendship left off, his enmity began at once. Sometimes this enmity would take the simple and straightforward form of trying to punch his ex-friend's head; and when the ex-friend was too big, he would get some new friend to help him. And much bad blood would be caused in this way — though very little was spilt. And all this bad blood was not made better by the funny things he went on saying through life about the unlucky one who had managed to offend him — things that stuck forever! His bark was worse than his bite—he was better with his tongue than with his fists—a dangerous joker ! But when he met another joker face to face, even an inferior joker—with a rougher wit, a coarser thrust, a louder laugh, a tougher hide—he would just collapse, like a pricked bladder!

"He is now perched on such a topping pinnacle (of fame and notoriety combined) that people can stare at him from two hemispheres at once; and so famous as a wit that when he jokes (and he is always joking) peo-

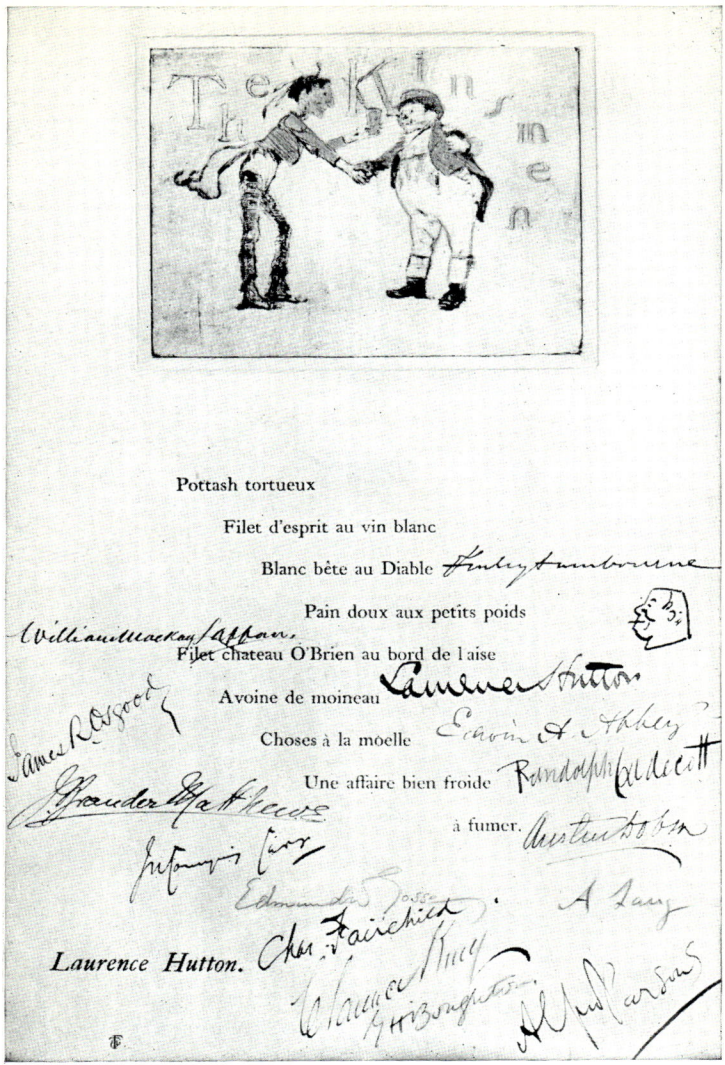

AN AUTOGRAPHED KINSMEN MENU

ple laugh first, and then ask what it was he was joking about. And you can even make your own mild funniments raise a roar by merely prefacing them, ' as Joe Sibley once said.' The present scribe has often done so. And if by any chance you should one day, by a happy fluke, hit upon a really good thing of your own —good enough to be quoted—be sure it will come back to you after many days prefaced, ' as Joe Sibley once said.' "

And a little farther on some more cutting was done with the result that the following was eliminated:

"Joe Sibley, equally enthusiastic, was more faithful. He was a monotheist, and had but one god, and was less tiresome in the expression of his worship. He is so still,—and his god is still the same,—no stodgy old master, this divinity, but a modern of the moderns! For forty years the cosmopolite Joe has been singing his one god's praise in every tongue he knows and in every country—and also his contempt for all rivals to this godhead—whether quite sincerely or not, who can say? Men's motives are so mixed! But so eloquently, so wittily, so prettily, that he almost persuades you to be a fellow worshipper. *Almost*, only!—for if he did *quite*, you (being a capitalist) would buy nothing but ' Sibleys ' (which you don't). For Sibley was the god of Joe's worship, and none other! and he would hear of no other genius in the world!

"Let us hope that he sometimes laughed at himself in his sleeve—or winked at himself in his looking-glass, with his tongue in his cheek!

"And here, lest there should be any doubt as to his identity, let me add that although quite young he had beautiful white hair like an Albino's, as soft and bright as floss silk — and also that he was tall and slim and graceful; and, like most of the other personages connected with this light story, very nice to look at, with pretty manners (and unimpeachable moral tone).

"Joe Sibley did not think much of Lorrimer in those days, nor Lorrimer of him, for all they were such good friends. And neither of them thought much of Little Billee, whose pinnacle (of pure unadulterated fame) is now the highest of all — the highest probably that can be for a mere painter of pictures!"

The Harpers sent to Whistler the following apology:

"Pursuant to an arrangement made with Mr. J. McNeill Whistler by our London agents, Messrs. Osgood, McIlvaine, & Co., the publishers of the English edition of *Harper's Magazine*, the following letter is published:

"August 31, 1894.
"Dear Sir :

"Our attention has been called to the attack made upon you by Mr. du Maurier in the novel *Trilby*, which appeared in our *Magazine*. If we had had any knowledge of personal reference to yourself being intended, we should not have permitted the publication of such passages as could be offensive to you. As it is, we have freely made such reparation as is in our power. We both agree to stop the future sales of the March number of *Harper's Magazine*, and we undertake that, when the story appears in the form of a book, the March number shall be rewritten so as to omit every mention of the offensive character, and that the illustration which represents the Idle Apprentices shall be excised, and that the portraits of Joe Sibley in the general sense shall be altered so as to give no clue to your identity. Moreover, we engage to print and insert in our *Magazine* for the month of October this letter of apology addressed to you.¹

"Assuring you again of our sincere regret that you should have sustained the least annoyance in any publication of ours, we are,

"Yours respectfully,

"HARPER & BROTHERS."²

Another interesting episode of letter-writing, which it can now do no harm to make public, fell under my notice during my connection with *Harper's*. In a long letter, dated "Dec. 18th" merely (without the year), that is now in my possession, Charles Reade speaks freely of the books of a contemporary writer, in which he compares her work with his own. He says:

"In *Daniel Deronda* everything is sacrificed to bulk. It is *parvum in multo;* but my stories are *multum in parvo*. You might as well estimate the precious metals by superficial area and pay what you pay for a bag of

¹ The note of apology appeared in the English edition of the *Monthly*, according to the expressed wish of Mr. Whistler.

² And on the same back cover of *Trilby* with these two clippings Mr. Hutton has pasted the suppressed print of the Idle Apprentices that appeared in the fatal March, 1894, issue.

feathers. Even in the case of *The Woman Hater* this applies. The bulk of *Daniel Deronda* entails on the publisher a greater expense of paper, that is all. The book will not sell any the more for all that verbosity. Consider what follows :

"1. George Eliot has a fine mind, but is a novice in fiction and cannot tell a story well. *I* can, thanks to so profound a study of the art.

"2. She lives with an anonymous writer, and they have bought the English press and humbugged the English public. But they cannot humbug the American public. She is not so popular in the United States as I am, and never will be.

"3. If by any cabal she can attain higher prices in England than I can, it is no reason why injustice should cross the water. The American public prefer me ; and I ought to profit by the preference.

"4. *Daniel Deronda* is below her average : it is a wind-bag. To use the words of Milton, it is ' Bulk without spirit vast.' It is a bungling, ill-constructed story with an ignoble heroine and an unmanly hero, and a lot of romantic, greasy Jews that the Anglo-Saxon despises, varnish them how you will. That dreary waste of words leaves on the mind not one really powerful situation, not one new and salient idea, not one great lesson of virtue, wisdom, justice, or public policy. It is given a lining of a pretentious kind, and its verbosity will land it in the trunk-maker's shop in two years at farthest."

CARICATURE OF CHARLES READE

When I had an opportunity and a good one, I did not meet George Eliot,— a fact that I have always regretted. During his first visit to London, John Fiske was asked to take a cup of tea at the Leweses' and suggested my going with him, but as I was absolutely unknown to these people — much as I wanted to know them—and as I had n't been invited, I did not do so.

Charles Reade I knew only by sight and by some very slight correspondence. He objected strongly to having his portrait painted, and he is said never to have sat for a photograph. I have a lithograph of a pencil drawing of Reade, and an original coloured caricature by *Sem*, whereon Charles Reade wrote in 1877 that he was " glad there is no photo of me, for it would be enough sight worse." And I have, also, a scrap of paper upon which he had written for Miss Kate Field, in response to a request for his signature :

"Damn Autographs,
                    "CHARLES READE."

I saw a good deal of John Fiske the first time he was in Europe. I met him by appointment on his arrival in Liverpool, and the next morning we went to Chester, the traditional thing for all strangers in England to do. We were to spend some days in that part of the world; but John felt that he could not wait, so I telegraphed to my landlady in Craven Street, London, that I would be there late that night with a friend. After long delays—the day being Sunday—we reached

Craven Street about midnight. The whole thing was new to Fiske, and immensely interesting; the porters, the cabs, the dingy, dirty, silent streets,— all appealed to him. At the door we were met by the whole force of the establishment: the typical London landlady made familiar by Dickens, the boy in buttons, the slavey — begrimed as she always is — who carried our portmanteaus to their proper places. Then, to his delight and to my satisfaction, we found on the table in the sitting-room cold beef, crisp salad, chunks of old Cheshire cheese, knobs of bread, and pints of stout. John felt that it was the realisation of the dream of his life. He was at last in London, which meant so much to him and to all those who are familiar with the literary men among whom he had lived all his life. He could not go to bed; he was too excited for that; and as the night was clear, I suggested a walk. It was about two o'clock in the autumn morning when we sallied forth.

Going to the bottom of Craven Street, then nearly cut through to the Embankment,— John silent and absorbed,— I told him nothing. I simply answered his questions. He asked:

"What's that stream, Laurence?"

"That's the Thames, old man," and we stood looking at it in absolute silence. Then we walked westward a bit.

"And what are those buildings across the river, over there?"

"The Lambeth pottery works; and beyond, Lambeth Palace."

And again we stood perfectly silent, and gazed. Making a little detour, I then showed him the window in Whitehall Palace out of which Charles stepped to his execution; the statue of his son, then pointing to the spot where the scaffold stood, but since removed; and a little farther along I showed him the Church of St. Margaret, in which Sir Walter Raleigh is buried.

"And beyond?" he asked, "the big building?"

"John," I said, "that is the Poets' Corner end of Westminster Abbey."

He clutched me by the arm, and literally ran towards the spot as if afraid that the thing which had been there so many years would not wait until he reached it. After a long reverent pause, he said:

"I want to go home now."

And neither of us spoke again until the next morning at breakfast.

The month which followed was one of great delight to me, simply in watching his own delight and appreciation and thorough understanding of all he saw in and out of London. After a few days he knew the streets of the town even better than I did,— I, who had been making a study of them for a quarter of a century.

Our visit to Stratford was in that year or a later one, I cannot remember which. It gave great pleasure to us both. There he saw his first smock-frock, and tasted his first home-brewed ale. His great pleasure was in his talks with the Warwickshire old men and old women, whose curious dialect became at once familiar to him. And he was particularly impressed with many of the quaint sayings and phrases which seem to show the survival—if not of the fittest—of something he thought well worth surviving. And never did he question the fact that Shakespeare wrote Shakespeare's plays.

Paris did not appeal to Fiske so much as did London; but in a way it exhibited to me very strongly his extraordinary possession of what is called the gift of location. We arrived in Paris late one evening, long after dark. The rain was falling in torrents, and the streets were deserted as we drove to our little hotel in the Rue de Rivoli. When we had climbed to the top of the house, it was discovered that John had left his umbrella in the train. Such things were never lost in France, he was told, and he would find it safely enough when he went for it. We two had adjoining bedrooms, and when I awoke the next morning—the sun shining brightly—there was no Fiske. By the time coffee was ready, he marched in with his umbrella in his hand. He had walked directly to the station, through streets with which he was absolutely unfamiliar and had never seen except through the dripping panes of a cab window. How he went and came without asking a single question, he never could explain. To him it was a matter of course; to me it was a most remarkable performance.

A curious incident which pleased Fiske very much related to the spelling of my surname. We had gone together one morning, in London, to get our letters, and for me there was none. I gave my name carefully, but there was nothing. I felt sure that there must be some correspondence for me, and was inspired to ask the cockney clerk if he were looking under *H*. Immediately, a great mass of mail matter was produced. It seems he had been searching in vain for *Hutton* in the box of *U*.

For years after that John Fiske in writing to me always dropped the initial *H;* and I heard him one night in a public lecture in Baltimore speak of the occurrence *a propos* of some eccentric linguistic matter which he wanted to illustrate. After I had returned to America that year, he wrote:

"11 CRAVEN STREET, STRAND,
"October 8th, 1873.

"DEAR UTTON:

". . . After leaving you I proceeded to Windermere and stopped at Cloudsdale, Crown Hotel, Bonness, during three days, making excursions to Coniston, Furness Abbey, Patterdale, etc. Then I proceeded to Ambleside, Grasmere, and Keswick, thence to Carlisle, and thence to Edinburgh, where I spent several days. The weather was superb, and I never enjoyed myself so much anywhere else in my life, I think. I believe I must have explored nearly every corner of the town, besides climbing all the high places to get a comprehensive view of it. I was positively enchanted with the town. From Edinburgh I went to Stirling and had a gorgeous day, with a cloudless American sky, for the grand view from the ramparts of the Castle. I saw the Trossachs, Loch Katrine, and Loch Lomond under a brilliant sun. But at Glasgow there arose a fiendish yellow mist, and there descended rain and sleet and devilish little did I see of the Clyde. As we entered the Isles of Bute it cleared up, and the sail through the Crinan Canal was jolly. But from Crinan to Oban we had three hours of a heavy gale with fearfully rough sea. The waves broke several feet above the tops of the paddle-boxes, and twice the floor of the saloon rose up and hit me on the head. We had at least one hundred passengers and they were mostly seasick within fifteen minutes, but I escaped without any nausea. It was so rough that I doubted if the steamer would start for Staffa next day, and so kept on to Ballachulish. Tried Glencoe next day in the most horrible rain I ever saw, went back to Oban, and took coach through the Pass of Brander, and by Loch Awe and Glenarchy to Tyndrum, and thence through Inverary and Glencoe back to Ballachulish, and thence to Fort William. This took me through some of the grandest moorland in Scotland, and I enjoyed it hugely. Weather sunny, with showers. Then on a superb day I went by the Caledonian Canal to Inverness, seeing the Fall of Foyers *en route*, and this day I enjoyed most of all It remains in my mind as the climax of the whole journey, which altogether was the grandest journey I ever made.''

In the same letter Fiske speaks of stopping in Ipswich at the Great White Horse, "where Mr. Pickwick had the romantic adventure with the middle-aged lady in yellow curl-papers, and it's a jolly old place."

"LONDON, December 8, 1873.
"MY DEAR UTTON :

"I am a great fellow to answer letters, you will say. Here it is December 8th, and yours of November 2d, still unanswered. This morning I made up my mind to make a clean sweep, and so I have been at it all day. I will try to plunge at once *in medias res*, and give you a general notion of things.

"*Imprimis*, I left Craven Street October 11th, and moved to 67 Great Russell Street (opposite British Museum) where I still hang out. The *heft* of the time since then has been employed at hard work on my book. That is, I get up at 10 A.M. (say) and work till 5 or 6 P.M., and then dine out on invitation, or dine alone at Kittner's or some shilling roast-beef place. I have found a great deal of work still left in my book, and if I get through with it in four weeks more I shall be lucky. Half of Vol. I. went to the printer ten days ago, but no proofs have come in yet. Macmillan is going to publish it (*Outlines of Cosmic Philosophy*) in connection with J. R. Osgood & Co., but we don't expect to get it out before next September. Proofs will have to chase me by mail all over the Continent, so that the printing will be slow. I have become quite friendly with old Macmillan, and have had several very gay times at his house. I have seen Spencer so many times that I can't count 'em all; have lunched and dined with him five or six times, and met him elsewhere, and had him drop in here several times. I have dined twice with 'Uxley,— once at Spencer's, once at the X Club, and shall again dine with him twice this week,— at his own house, and at the Royal Society Club. Have also lunched or dined, or both, with Tyndall, Lewes, Frankland, Hooker, Darwin, Froude, W. K. Clifford, and M. D. Conway. . . . And have seen George Eliot and had a long talk with her, and see no reason in the world why she should n't have her photograph circulated about. She is n't a blooming beauty, but she is not particularly homely, and is certainly a most remarkable and attractive woman in conversation. I enjoyed the afternoon with the Leweses very much, and shall go there again.[1] Of all the men I have seen I like Darwin the best. He is a dear, good, gentle, modest, charming old grandpa. I never saw such a delightful man in all my life. Next to him I think I like Huxley; he is such a keen, clear-thinking fellow that it is a rich treat to talk with him; and he is a thoroughly white-souled and genial man too. Have

---

[1] Blackwood, the publisher, in George Street, Edinburgh, has the only portrait of Mrs. Lewes (George Eliot) in existence, done for Blackwood in crayon by Lawrence, an American.

also enjoyed Spencer very much. I have n't seen Stevens again, but have seen his brother several times, and dined with him at some droll antiquarian club, in Lincoln's Inn Fields. I don't like Froude. He appears like an insincere and treacherous chap. I don't think half so well of his history now that I have seen him. I can well believe him capable of suppressing or perverting facts to make out a case. . . . All the other coves mentioned I like, more especially Lewes and Tyndall.

"I am going to 'preach' to Conway's congregation these next two Sundays (December 14th and 21st) — subject 'Darwinism.' It is thought there will be a good audience, and that I shall get some fun out of it.

"I believe this is about all that I have in the way of news that can be well detailed in a brief epistle. As you may imagine, if I had you over here, with a pot of beer between us, I could tell you a number of good incidents. Which leads me to inquire, Why don't you come back again? Eh?"

John Fiske never did anything in moderation. He never took a short walk or drive; always a long one. He either smoked to excess or not at all. He has been known to sleep from a Sunday to the following Tuesday night. In eating, working, singing, playing, in everything he went to excess. All one summer at Petersham I remember he played casino, at every available hour and in every possible place. He once went out by appointment to Jamaica Plains to listen to the music of a very accomplished pianist. The engagement had been made for a certain hour on a certain afternoon. Fiske arrived on time, but, as he entered the music room, was told that he would have to wait a few moments for the lady whose music he had come to hear. In her absence he sat himself down to the piano and began to play the music, which appealed to him, and for four hours he sat there playing and utterly oblivious to the fact that he had come to listen and not to exhibit himself. He went on and on, and as dark came, he went away without even offering his hostess an opportunity to utter the sounds which had brought him so far away from home, she apparently being as well content as he was.

Fiske's memory for dates, facts, and figures was remarkable; and his exceptional powers in that line may account, in a great measure, for the quality and the quantity of his work. When I visited him one summer in Petersham to join in a "grand loaf" as he called it, I was told that he had nothing to do but the writing of one chapter in one of his books. For this he had not a note. It was all in his head, and the transcript was to him as nothing at all. The finished manuscript when I saw it was in a very perfect condition, with no blots or erasures, written neatly in his clear, round hand, and without pause or a break, all at one short sitting.

Another instance of his wonderful memory was exhibited one night, when I quoted from *Our Mutual*

Friend, which I had just been reading, the description by Dickens of a heap of nuts at a village fair as being "long exiled from Barcelona, and yet speaking English so indifferently as to call twelve of themselves a pint."

Fiske replied, " It was fourteen of themselves."

" I think it was a dozen, John," said I, " and I 've just been reading it again."

"I never read it but once, many years ago, in the Household Edition published by Houghton about 1866. It was in the last volume, on the left-hand page, about a quarter of the way from the beginning; and if you have that edition and will look it up you will find that they called themselves fourteen."

And so they did!

One morning in New York he said suddenly, *a propos* of nothing, seemingly:

" Do you know what you and I did eleven years ago to-day at this very hour?"

Concerning where we were or what happened to us eleven years before I had no idea.

Then he reminded me how we had started from Craven Street to a restaurant in Soho Square. How our attention had been attracted by an odour of sausages and baked potatoes in a little shop in the Haymarket. How we had stopped and partaken of that frugal repast, which he had pronounced the best he had ever experienced. And then he repeated *verbatim* what we had said to the buxom cook and what the buxom cook had said to us, as if it were all a matter of yesterday.

Mrs. Hutton said to him one night at our table:
"What are you talking about, you two?"

It seems we were discussing old times, of which he was very fond, and she asked:

"How far back do your old times go? How long have you known each other?"

"The first time that I saw Laurence was on a day in one of the sixties, in October, when Harriet Brooks brought him up to us while we were living in Oxford Street during the first years of our married life. I remember it was the day we bought the double baby-carriage for Maud and Harold, who were so near of an age and who looked so much alike that by strangers in the street they were often taken for twins. I remember that Laurence had on a green plaid silk necktie with fringe at the ends, and that I thought it one of the most beautiful examples of that sort of decoration I had ever seen."

Mrs. Hutton when she first knew John Fiske, and then very slightly, asked him at dinner a question about Pierre Marquette in his *American History*, to which he made absolutely no reply, but looked at her in a blank, far-away manner, rather to her disgust. I, who knew the man, knew what was coming. He spoke but little after that until perhaps an hour later, when, standing and swaying back and forth in front of the library fire, he broke out upon the subject and deliv-

JOHN FISKE WITH TWO OF HIS CHILDREN
(From a discolored photograph)

ered to us, alone as we were, a lecture of many minutes in length, in reply to the question she had put: most entertaining, most instructive, every word the proper word, and in the proper place, times and localities accurately described,—and then he sat down upon the piano stool, playing *Songs without Words* for another hour. Mrs. Hutton declared that she did not understand that peculiar exhibition of genius, although she was very ready to confess that what she had heard was well worth the waiting for.

She once met him by chance, later in his life, at the door of a certain public hall as he was going in. She spoke to him, concerning her interest in his subject, and he remarked seriously, that he hoped " the ladies would enjoy the lecture he was going to deliver, because it had taken him seven years to write it."

The Latin motto in John Fiske's library in Cambridge was *Disce ut semper victurus, Vive ut cras moriturus*, the translation of which is, roughly: " Work as if you were to live forever; live as if you were to die tomorrow." These words he wrote on the picture of himself in his workroom, which is now in the collection at Princeton.

Two young Americans came to us in London once. It was their first trip abroad. They were interested in everything, and because I had studied and knew my London, they were interesting to me. They wanted to know, and they knew what they wanted to know and why they wanted to know it; and it gave me great pleasure to take them about and to show them the things that most appealed to me.

One day we devoted to the lower Thames, going by the river from Westminster down to Greenwich, I pointing out as we sailed on the penny-boat everything that had any literary or artistic or historic interest or tradition. At the Charing Cross float there came aboard two ladies of my acquaintance to whom, after asking their permission, I introduced my two American boys in a perfectly informal manner. The names of none of them meant anything to the others; and as we passed under Waterloo Bridge, I remarked:

"You know, you fellows, or if you don't know you ought to know, that this is the Bridge of Sighs,

> 'One more unfortunate,
> Rashly importunate,
> Gone to her death.' "

One of the ladies said:

"Is it really the Bridge of Sighs? I never before realised which of the two bridges it was. And, as you know, Tom Hood gave my husband the original draft of the poem."

This naturally excited the attention of the two young men in question. As we went on, personally conducting the boys, I discovered that the ladies had drawn up to us and were equally eager to be personally conducted. London Bridge, the Tower,—all these things were absorbed and gazed at, until we came to a quaint, very old-fashioned, tumbled-down, river-side public-house on the left bank of the Thames. As we were going past the scene, I said:

"That is the Three Jolly Fellowship Porters, of *Our Mutual Friend*, in which John Rokesmith met with his disastrous adventures."

The same lady said:

"Oh, let us go ashore. I have tried many times to discover its identity, but without success. I shall never forget how Dickens took my husband and me all through it one day, many years ago."

My young friends could not contain themselves any longer.

"For gracious sakes! who is she? Friend of Tom Hood; friend of Charles Dickens; and a young American woman! For gracious sakes! who is she?"

She was Mrs. James T. Fields, and her companion was Sarah Orne Jewett.

Joaquin Miller was an American of whom I saw much in London. He tells this characteristic story of Swinburne. Swinburne is very susceptible to boredom, it seems, and suffers a good deal of it at the hands of inquisitive strangers who intrude upon him out of mere idle curiosity and take up a good deal of his time, giving nothing in return. One of this kind of bores, an American and friend of Miller, was anxious to be taken to Swinburne's house. Miller was under obligation to Mr. Lion-hunter, and did not like to refuse him. He knew Swinburne's peculiarities, and dreaded the result; still he went and sent his card to Mr. Swinburne—" Joaquin Miller and Friend." After a little delay the maid-servant returned, but in such evident confusion that Miller knew at once matters were not smooth upstairs, and that she had a message she did not like to deliver. This, with some persuasion, he got out of her, and it was to the effect that Mr. Swinburne would be very glad to see Mr. Miller, but his " friend " might go to hell !

Miller would not be unlikely to send precisely such a message as this himself, under similar circumstances ! His eccentricities are very marked.

[1] " Brought up on the outer skirts of civilisation with all of the Border training and with the true ' poetic temperament ' we read about, which chafes at social rules and laws, it is natural enough that he should not appear as the city-bred people in ladies' drawing-rooms, and that he should lack the ease and grace which only long association with cultivated people can give, still it is evident to the closer observer that there is much affectation in his queerness and a little straining after effect. His wearing several diamond and red- and green-stoned rings on the forefinger and little finger of both of his hands, his placing the three diamond studs in his shirt bosom so close together that they are all apparent even with a high-buttoned waistcoat, the great gold chain he wears and his constant use of a toothpick throughout a full-dressed Arcadian dinner,

[1] Extract from an old journal of 1870.

are no doubt evidences of a lack of easy refined education, for which he is not responsible, perhaps, but his abrupt speech, his familiarity with ladies, the absurd and fulsome compliments he pays them, his kissing of their hands in crowded parlours, and his brushing of their foreheads with his fingers, are all marks of what he considers 'genius,' which are studied by him to make himself conspicuous by his eccentricities. He is very fond of ladies' society and of the sensation he creates among them and of the attention he receives. He goes among them and gushes and rhapsodises, and talks sentiment, and wishes he was dead, and calls himself the loneliest man in the world, and gets the female sympathy which he seems to crave.

"If a low-strung, unromantic man should enter this charmed female circle of which Miller is the centre, he immediately relapses into boorish silence and goes into his cell. He does not shine among men unless they are molly-coddle men who molly-coddle him, or unless they are men of his own temperament, whose eyes roll in fine frenzy constantly and who are always filled with inspiration and celestial fire.

"Among the Swinburne and Rossetti set I can imagine him happy and contented. Among the short-haired, prosaic, critical men who go to Arcadian dinners he is not himself at all. Among men he says little and drops none of the pearls of poetry and sentiment that he is apt to spue out fully in the society of the softer sex. He told Mrs. Brooks that 'Tennyson

was a dear old peanut.' He said that little Gretchen
Brooks was pretty enough to set in a ring. After he
had been in the house of Mrs. Brooks three minutes on
his first visit, he crawled across the library floor on his
hands and knees to bite Marjory Brooks on the leg.
When Mrs. Brooks sent upstairs to ask her sister-in-
law, Mrs. Hendricks, to come down, he interrupted by
saying he did not want her, he did not want to see
anybody else. Mrs. Brooks told him she did not care
whether he wanted to see anybody else or not. She
wanted her sister to see him. He said he wanted to
get married; wanted a fireside and children. But he
wants a young wife and one with money. He told of
a delightful flirtation he had had with a queer sort of
girl who fascinated him by her odd ways, but whom he
discovered to be a lunatic and who, even during the
time of his companionship with her, was under the care
of a keeper. He said he liked lunatics. He asked
permission to call on Mrs. Brooks in Boston, said he
would not take her address then (he called here first December 12, 1875) for he would certainly lose it, but she
would see his arrival noted in the Boston papers and
could send him her card or a note then. He told a
very pretty story of Prentice Mulford's love-making,
which may or may not be true, but which he told in a
most charming manner. His reputation for veracity in
such matters is none of the best! I cannot give the romance in his own words (more 's the pity) and may
not remember, after the lapse of a few weeks, all of the

incidents as he gave them. He is very fond, it seems, of wandering about the low quarters of London in search of adventure and in the study of character. His evenings and his late nights, many of them, were thus spent in this London stay. In this way he became familiar with St. Giles and St. Giles became familiar with him. He knew personally the rough element of that neighbourhood and won to a certain degree its confidence and respect, by his good humour, good deeds, and interest in them. Himself a Bohemian of the Bohemians, he was more at home in the society of the lawless London beggar and thief than in the drawing-rooms of Mayfair and Hyde Park which were thrown open to him. In one of these excursions of his in the Seven Dials way, with Prentice Mulford, they fell in one evening with the prettiest little beggar maid he says he ever saw. She was a child of about fourteen years of age, evidently unused to the profession, in fact not of the profession, and one who would have made the fortune of any painter by her beauty and the picturesque effect of her dress and action. She had a companion of about her own age but less interesting. Both men were greatly struck at once by Josie — such was the Cinderella's name — and entered into conversation with her. Miller had been in the way of picking up these London waifs on the streets when they particularly interested him, and taking them to his lodgings, where he had them washed, no doubt to the disgust of his landlady, and after he had got out of them all he wanted in the way of characteristic speech he let them go with a shilling or so in their pockets. He offered Josie a shilling, two shillings, half a crown, to go home with him and have tea. Josie was willing to accept the shilling, but her mother was alone with a sick brother and she could not leave her so long. The temptation of half a crown was too much for Josie, however, and finally she went to Miller's lodgings with her cousin, was washed,—and he says she needed it,—and had the first good meal in many days. She told her story. Her father had been a humble tradesman in the provinces, had been unfortunate in business, had taken to drink, had been compelled to leave his native town, had come to London, had gone from bad to worse, dragging his family with him, until he was only a care and a disgrace to them, contributing nothing to their support.

"After tea Miller went home with the children, discovered that the story was true, made the acquaintance of her mother, and finally, after some time, adopted the child, introducing her to the kindly friends who had been interested in him and who, for his sake, and then for her own, became interested in her. She was given some education, and during the Vienna Exposition while he was at the Austrian capital on business, he received a letter from Mulford asking permission to marry the girl, then eighteen years old or less. Miller consented, and Josie became Mrs. Mulford.

" Mulford himself is the shyest man I think I ever

met, in this respect presenting the most marked contrast to his friend Miller. I met him first at Mrs. Brooks's reception; noticed, in a common chair upon which he seemed afraid to sit, this queer man with a wistful, far-away look in his eyes, who seemed to know nobody and whom nobody seemed to know. His stillness in that crowd where everybody seemed to talk to everybody was peculiar and attracted my attention to him. A little later when Miss Booth said she wanted to introduce me to Prentice Mulford, I knew that the timid little fair-haired, light-eyed person must be the man. He seemed to be unhappy there, to want to get out of it and not to know how.

"Until I began to see more of him and to know him a little better, I could make but little out of him. But he can be, when he feels at home, the most amusing of men. He has a great deal of dry and original humour, a quaint and peculiarly Western phraseology, and a timid, halting manner of speech that is almost an impediment and yet is not an impediment, that is very attractive. His speech and conversation are full of surprises. His art comes out so unexpectedly to his hearers and seemingly to himself that it is most refreshing on that account. How far it is spontaneous, I cannot say. Certainly of all the band of Western humourists I have met and heard—and I've met them all personally except Mark Twain—[it will be remembered that this was written in 1870], Mulford is the brightest in genial talk with people with whom he is at home, and the best after-dinner speech-maker. He is delivering a series of Sunday-evening talks here in one of the uptown halls for an admission of ten cents with but doubtful success, and his struggle for his daily bread is no doubt hard and never-ceasing."

Some time in the seventies I walked over from the Piccadilly side of London with Mr. Henry James, Jr., to lunch with C. P. Cranch and his family, who were lodging opposite Bloomsbury Square. We were met at the door by Mr. Cranch and his daughter, and we saw that Mrs. Cranch, standing in a bow-window, was in earnest conversation with a gentleman, whose back was turned our way. In a moment or two Cranch said: "Come here, Jim; I want you to know two young countrymen of ours and friends of mine." "Jim" came forward, and, to our surprise, "Jim" was James Russell Lowell! I had never thought that any man alive could call him "Jim." My companion must have known him before; but it was my first meeting with the man whom I regarded, even then, as the First Citizen of America. He was quite as charming in his manner as I had found him in his books; one of the most entertaining and agreeable persons I had ever met, and one of the handsomest men, physically, I think, I ever saw. I cannot remember anything of his conversation, except that I told him that only a fortnight or so before I had dined at his own house, Elmwood, with the Ole Bulls, who were his tenants; and that I had smoked a cigar in his library, and had looked at the backs of his books, finding no little satisfaction in reading, among the many titles, works of all kinds which were in my own collection. He replied that he did not care so much for his books as for his trees; and could I tell him how they were looking, and how they were feeling? " I 'm sure they miss me," he said. " They seem to droop when I go away, and I *know* they brighten and bloom when I go back to them, and speak to them, and shake hands with their lower branches!" He spoke seriously and tenderly, and I was rewarded with a very appreciative and responsive smile when I replied, " They half forgive your being human."

I next met Mr. Lowell half a dozen years later, when Booth was playing at the Adelphi Theatre, in London. I was sitting in Booth's own box, with his wife and daughter. Between the acts the usher announced " The American Minister," and I arose to slip out and make room for the new-comer, presuming, of course, that I had been entirely forgotten; but he stopped me in the dark passageway, held out his hand in his cordial manner, and asked, " How are the dear Cranches?"

Lowell was associated with one of the most curious experiences of my life — curious because it cannot be explained.

I remember distinctly going to a large dinner at the Savage Club, in London, as the guest of Harry Beckett, the actor. I remember distinctly sitting between

Beckett and Samuel Phelps, at the lower end of one of two long tables, far away from the raised platform upon which the guests of honour were placed. I remember that it was at the time of an unsuccessful movement to erect a monument to Lord Byron in Westminster Abbey, and that the members of the Savage Club had subscribed largely for the testimonial, and were greatly chagrined at the opposition raised in influential quarters. I remember that the Prince of Wales was to have presided at the feast, but was absent, and I remember wondering afterwards what would have happened if he had been in the chair. I don't remember who *did* preside, but I remember that the several speakers alluded to the Byron matter, and very bitterly. And I remember when Lowell arose to speak that those of us who were not near enough to catch his words crowded forward to the dais in order to miss nothing of his wonderful eloquence. And I remember with absolute distinctness that this, in part, is what he said, clearly, solemnly, and most impressively: " The Dean and Chapter of your great Abbey of Westminster have refused a resting-place to the pedestal of a statue of one of the greatest of your poets, in the ground which is polluted by the rotten ashes of the mistresses of your kings!" I remember perfectly the effect of these words, the profound silence which followed, the catching of breaths, the looks of astonishment, and then the sudden outburst of enthusiasm and wild cheering.

I remember all this as if it happened yesterday. And yet I am assured that it never happened at all. I am told by Mr. Charles Eliot Norton that he never heard of Lowell's having made such a speech, that he hardly thinks he could have made such a speech. Beckett and Phelps are dead. I can find no one who ever heard of such a dinner; I can find no record of it in any of the London journals. I could not have invented it. I did not dream it. How do the psychologists account for it?

CHAPTER XIV

Longfellow—Emerson—Whittier—Celia Thaxter—Louisa M. Alcott—Kate Field—Helen Keller—Charles Dudley Warner —Certain Treasures—Thackeray Drawing of Thackeray— Fitz-Gerald Book-Plate—Signatures with the Hat—The Names of Literary Men—Bret Harte.

WHILE I was never a lion-hunter, I have been a worshipper of heroes all my life, and I have worshipped chiefly at the shrines of the heroes of the pen. I find it even now, after half a century's experience of men and things, very hard to believe any evil of the personal character of the writers in whose books I see nothing but what is good. By their printed works I know and judge them all. Dickens, in my youthful mind, was possessed of all the virtues of Tom Pinch, of Traddles, of old Sol, of Esther Somerson's Guardian, and of the Cheerible Brothers; and to me the elder Dumas was Athos, Porthos, and d'Artagnan, put together and combined in one.

I have been disappointed once or twice, but not of my own free will, and if we make believe hard enough, we will find men, and even heroes, to be what we think they ought to be and not what we want them to be.

One of my earliest heroes was Mr. Longfellow, and

when I went to Cambridge for the first time, in the middle of the sixties, I thought of it not as the seat of a great university, but as Longfellow's home. I wanted to see Craigie House, not the Washington Elm. I longed to meet the "village blacksmith" and the "youth who bore the strange device," rather than all the faculty of Harvard College put together. I hung about Craigie House, but at a respectful distance, for hours, getting an occasional glimpse of the beautiful white head at a window, now and then seeing the grand old man walking about his garden, and once I met him face to face near his own gate. He looked as if he thought I were somebody else, somebody whom perhaps he knew, but I had not the courage to lift my hat.

In later years I met him personally, saw him seated in his own library, sat near him at Elmwood, and heard him talk about music to Ole Bull or about the drama to Booth or Barrett, but I never said much to him nor he to me, and to him I was only one of a countless number of young men who crossed his path, neither making it pleasanter for him nor getting in his way. I was too afraid of stepping on his toes to try even to step over the hedge of our very slight acquaintance.

His life was very simple and very beautiful. Everybody loved the man, even if they did not admire the poet, and his position in Cambridge was without parallel.

I remember once riding from Boston to Cambridge in a horse-car which chanced to pass his door. It was comfortably filled after it left Harvard Square with men who were his neighbours or his friends: as he entered, to go from his own house to some point farther along, every man rose and every head was uncovered! It was simply, unostentatiously done, and as a matter of course; and as a matter of course, but very sweetly and very kindly, he accepted it. He refused the seats which were offered to him by the seniors of the party, but he took that of a small boy who was with the rest and with his hat in his hand, and holding the little chap — who accepted it as a matter of course too — between his knees, he talked to him until his destination was reached. This was a spontaneous tribute to worth and genius and to grey hairs, which could have occurred in no other land under the sun and perhaps to no other man in the world at that time.

A little story of Mr. Longfellow's fondness for and attitude toward children, and of their devotion to and affection for him, which came under my own observation, may be worth telling here.

Arthur Brooks, a lad of seven or eight, was sent by his mother one morning with a note for Miss Longfellow. The poet opened the door for the boy and took him into his own study while the answer was being written. The two entered into pleasant conversation; and Arthur was asked what books he was reading. *Jack and the Bean Stalk* was at that time the subject of his absorbed attention. He had bought the volume — highly coloured and in big type — at a certain toy store in town, and he enjoyed it thoroughly. The price he mentioned incidentally was five cents. *Jack and the Bean Stalk* was also a favourite with his host, who had not read it for years and was exceedingly anxious to see it again. The boy rushed home in a state of great excitement, fished a five-cent piece out of his family safe on the mantel — he would not permit me to lend him the money; it must be his own money,—and he hurried away to the Square to purchase a fresh copy of the tale. This, without taking anybody into his confidence, he carried at once to Craigie House, rang the bell, and asked to see Mr. Longfellow, to whom the work was duly presented. It was received with all the dignity Mr. Longfellow could assume, and the donor was thanked as heartily as if the gift had been a first folio of Shakespeare's plays, the recipient saying:

"Now, Arthur, if you will write your name and mine upon the cover" (it could boast no fly-leaf) "you will add greatly to its value in my eyes and I will keep it among the treasures of my library."

The inscription was printed in big, scrawling, capital letters, "Arthur H. Brooks to his friend Mr. Longfellow." And Arthur was escorted to the door with much ceremony, the happiest and the proudest boy in Cambridge that day.

The Longfellows were, and justly so, the reigning family in Cambridge; their friendship was a patent of nobility in that university town; and no woman's social status was established until she had exchanged calls with Miss Longfellow or her sisters. This dignity was thrust upon them. They were quiet, unassuming, dignified young ladies, who demanded nothing from their neighbours, and who put on no airs. I remember once that Booth, who was playing an engagement in Boston, sent me a card to his box for a matinée performance, so that Mrs. Brooks, in whose house I was stopping, might bring her children and some of her young friends to see *Richelieu* the next afternoon. She included the Longfellows in the invitation; but the regret came saying that unfortunately papa had asked some people to lunch, and of course they could not accept. There was no hint as to who were the expected guests, but we read in the papers the next day that the Marquis of Lorne and the Princess Louise had lunched with Mr. Longfellow and his daughters. Who but an American woman, and one of an assured position, would speak of a Governor-General of Canada and a Princess of the Blood Royal of England as "some people"!

A curious effect of the benignity and purity of Mr. Longfellow's presence upon the actions of a man who was forced to say what he did not mean and what he should not have said and would not have said anywhere else, is shown in a little incident that came to my knowledge. This particular man always stood up straight. But on this occasion he felt that he had to stand up so very straight, that he fell over backwards!

I was spending the Christmas holidays of 1875 or

1876 with the Brookses, in Cambridge, who were invited by the Longfellows to "see the New Year in" and took me with them. A very small party were assembled, and all the Longfellow servants had gone to a ball. We talked quietly until nearly midnight, Mr. Longfellow joining in the conversation, and walking backwards and forwards between his study and the parlour in which we were sitting. At last some one suggested lemonade, and as all adjourned to the dining-room, lemons and sugar were provided, rolled, squeezed, and pounded by the different members of the company, Mr. Longfellow superintending it all and showing great interest in the operation. Water was boiling in a great kettle hanging on the crane in the fireplace and, when all was ready and the decoction complete, Mr. So-and-so—I won't mention his name—was asked to try it and to pronounce judgment upon it. He was an unusually shy, reticent, pure-minded, gentle, clean-spoken man, and we all waited anxiously for his verdict. He raised a great spoonful of the smoking stuff to his lips, swallowed it at a gulp, and said, with the utmost deliberation, "It is not only damned hot, but it is as sour as hell!"

Violent profanity in the presence of the Pope of Rome or the Archbishop of Canterbury would not have been more unexpected or more untimely. I shall never forget the horrified look of his wife, or his own startled expression when he realised the strength of his words. There was an instant of awful silence, and then shouts of laughter. The old poet beamed with unsurpassed amusement, and taking the spoon in his own hand he tried the potation and said, in his gentle way, "Mr. So-and-so is quite right; quite right!"

I don't believe Mr. So-and-so ever uttered another oath in his life, before or since, and why he lost control of himself in that marvellous way and on that particular occasion, he was never able to explain.

My only meeting with Emerson was a very casual one, and the occasion was the famous Greek play at Harvard in 1881. He sat by the side of Longfellow, and near them were grouped Agassiz, Dr. Holmes, Eliot, Howells, Higginson, and Aldrich. As he left the hall on Longfellow's arm, some one spoke to him, and asked how long he was to stay in Cambridge, and where he was staying.

"I am visiting my dear old friend here," he replied, patting Longfellow on the hand, "Mr.—Mr.—Mr.—"

He had forgotten Longfellow's name! He was very feeble in body, and his memory had almost entirely failed. But he was very beautiful to look upon and so like my own father in face and action that I was startled by the resemblance. It seemed as if my father had come back to me, and was as he would have been had he lived so long.

With Miss Longfellow I walked to the door of Craigie House, behind the two magnificent old men, but I did not enter; and I never saw either of them again.

The only time I ever saw Whittier was at the Isle of Shoals, where he was the guest of Celia Thaxter. The ordinary person, present in Mrs. Thaxter's drawing-room, thought the necessary thing to say was how much they admired Whittier's work. He had heard the remark innumerable times, and considered of no importance any reference as to what he had done or as to what he had written. He told us in his gentle way that such remarks reminded him of what had been said to him a few days before in Portsmouth by a lady who had admired and spoken of his little verses called *Poor Lone Hannah*. "And" he said with a twinkle of his old eyes, "I had n't the courage to tell her that Miss Lucy Larcom wrote that particular poem."

He was particularly pleased at the story I told him *a propos* of such blunders, of a young woman who professed to a literary stranger her profound admiration for Sir Walter Scott. He asked her how she liked *Ivanhoe*, and she liked it immensely. He asked her what she thought of *The Lady of the Lake*, and she thought it just sweet. Then he said:

"And now tell me what you think of Scott's *Emulsion*."

To which she replied that she thought it the best thing Scott had ever written.

The funeral of Celia Thaxter must have been a most picturesque and pathetic picture. As being part of it I did not see it; but those who watched the black coffin, covered with wild flowers, carried over the rocks from her cottage to her grave, on the little island of Appledore, one very sad grey day towards the end of August, 1894, speak of it as one of the most impressive sights they ever witnessed. The simple service was held in the parlour so intimately associated with her for so many years, and in the presence of her own people and a very few near friends. The clergyman read certain lines of her own, repeated the Lord's Prayer, William Mason played one or two of her favourite airs on the little piano, and that was all. The bearers, her two brothers, J. Appleton Brown, Childe Hassam, Dr. Stedman, Dr. Warren, Coswell—who had been in the employ of the Leightons as fisherman and general factotum for thirty-five years,—and I, carried the casket, followed by her sons and their wives. And with our own hands we lowered it into the open grave. The sky was dull and sorrowful; the many servants and guests of the hotel stood about the burial plot in groups, the sea was moaning on three sides of us and close to our feet; and the birds seemed to sing sad songs. Each person present who was near to her, beginning with her oldest son, strewed the flowers she had loved over what was left of her; and we walked silently away.

She had been ill but a day or two. We saw her on the Friday, bright and cheerful, listening to the music of Mr. Mason, surrounded by her worshippers, laughing now and then her clear, ringing laugh. As she entered the dining-room that evening, I met her with my hands filled with the letters and papers which the mail had just brought. She caught me by the lapel of the coat as I passed without noticing her, she turned me half around, gave me a little pat, and said:

"Here is that Mister Laurie Hutton, full of business as usual."

And I never saw her again.

On the Sunday morning, early, with her pain relieved, she sat up in her bed and asked her daughter-in-law to open the shutters that she might see the light. And without warning, she went at once to where Light is.

Celia Thaxter's life and personality were absolutely unique. She was carried to her island home as a child, and for many years she knew nothing else. Her brothers were her only playmates, and her only playthings were the shells on the beach. The children were as wild and as unartificial as were the waves and the winds, the sea-birds and the ocean plants. She knew a fisherman or two, and a dun cow. It was a wonderful school for a poet of nature, but a poor school for a woman of society or of the world,— and this latter she never became. So long as she lived she went but little into the world, and almost the only world she knew was the small fraction of the world which came to her. Nature was her only teacher until she became a woman, and her intercourse with her fellow-beings, and her study of the literature of the ancients, or of her contemporaries, had but little influence upon her work. She was, as a writer, as unique as she was as an individual. And unique — that hackneyed, much-abused, often misapplied word — is the only word which describes Celia Thaxter, the poet and the woman.

I had spent some portion of the summers of ten years at the Isle of Shoals, and my wife had been going there for upwards of a quarter of a century. Naturally, we knew Mrs. Thaxter, and knew her well; although never intimately. We did not belong to the set, and did not altogether care for the set, of men and women who were frequenters of her daily and nightly levees. The atmosphere of the place, when she was not alone in it, seemed to us to be artificial. There was inflated, "high-falutin" gushing, ultra-sentimental, up-in-the-clouds, far-away talk, which the talkers themselves often did not understand. Every one appeared strained and unnatural, to be always on intellectual parade. And there was always an element of the critical present which contributed nothing, which absorbed everything, and which looked phenomenally wise, particularly when the flights of fancy rose so high that they were lost in the mists of unintelligibility, — as was usually the case. The hostess was generally surrounded by a dozen young women of all ages who adored and worshipped her; and by commonplace droppers-in from the hotel. For all that, Mrs. Thaxter's guests were sometimes the most brilliant men and women of the day, and what was said there was often well worth listening to. Hawthorne, Lowell, Whittier, William Hunt, were among her intimate friends, drawn towards her by feelings of genuine respect and affection. She had a personal magnetism which was not to be resisted; and old and young, the ignorant and the educated, came under its influence.

The strongest head in the world would have been turned, and the simplest nature spoiled, by the flattery and adulation so openly bestowed upon Celia Thaxter for so many years. And the occasional trace of her artificiality of manner which sometimes repelled strangers, is not altogether to be wondered at. These affectations, however, were reserved for the crowd, and for the crowd of a certain kind. When she was among natural persons, she was as natural as any of them, and then her full charm was apparent, and then the true Celia Thaxter appeared. She was a handsome woman with a sweet, strong face, simply dressed always, but most effectively, in some Quakerish garb of grey stuff with soft veiling material about her own throat. Her hair, during the later years of her life, was quite white; and her manner was invariably cordial and cheerful. The room in her cottage, in which she held her court was as unique as everything about her. The walls were crowded with water colours, original drawings, autographed photographs, copies of the famous masterpieces of art, and medallions. And upon the shelves, and mantels, and piano, and tables, were by actual count two hundred little glass vases filled with the flowers from her marvellous little garden outside, making a mass of bright and delicate colours arranged in harmonies as flowers have never been seen, perhaps, before or since. Here, with her knitting or her painting, in a certain corner she sat every forenoon and every evening, chatting or listening to the talk about her, or better yet, to the songs-without-words played so sympathetically by William Mason, one of the oldest and most cherished of her friends. Her greatest interest in life was her flowers. She was in her garden (not so large as the ordinary grass plot of a city backyard) at three or four o'clock every morning, watering, cherishing, petting, and communing with her plants. Celia reigned not only in the little society of intelligent people she drew around her, but also in the hearts of the fisher-folk who inhabited the little group of islands known as the Shoals. Among them she was a queen indeed; and as good and as great a queen as ever won and held the devotion and esteem of her subjects. They were a colony of simple, hard-working Swedes, to whom she was physician, patron, pastor, friend. She nursed them when they were ill; named their babies; shared their joys and sorrows. And it is pleasant to think that two of these Swedish girls, Mina, and the Nicolina whom she has almost immortalised in verse, were with her at the last and caught her in their arms as she died.

This is not the place to speak of Mrs. Thaxter's position as an author. Of that the world will judge for itself. But as to Mrs. Thaxter's powers as a reader, I must say a word or two. Her *Little Sandpiper* she recited with rare skill and feeling, and I have seen her auditors literally moved to hysterics as she related the story of the *Murder at Smutty Nose*—which I consider one of the strongest pieces of prose in the English language.

I never met Miss Louisa M. Alcott but once and that for a few moments only, at the house of Miss May L. Booth, of *Harper's Bazar*. The occasion was a large reception given to Miss Alcott who was, naturally, the centre of observation and the one object of attention. All the writing men and women of Miss Booth's acquaintance were present, and I merely exchanged a word with the lady, as I entered the rooms, and passed on to make way for the next new-comer. Late in the evening I found myself upon a sofa by her side, and alone; and I had the pleasure of half an hour's cosy commonplace uninterrupted chat with her, talking to her as if she had been anybody else and upon the ordinary topics of the day. When Miss Booth approached to present some very belated visitor, Miss Alcott said, to my great satisfaction:

"Oh, don't take this young man away. He is the only person who has not mentioned *Little Women* to me to-night!"

I was taken one evening by Oliver Lay, in the early sixties, to call on Kate Field, then living with her mother in Twenty-sixth or Twenty-seventh Street, west of Sixth Avenue, in New York. She was writing editorials for the *Herald* on a salary of five thousand dollars a year, which was considered, in those days, an enormous price; and she was looked upon as the most promising young woman in her profession in America. For thirty years or more we were excellent friends, meeting in all parts of the New World and the Old. We spent six weeks with her in Paris during the year of the Exposition of 1878. We saw much of her in London before and after that. She knew my wife before I did, and all our relations with her were most pleasant and intimate. She was a woman with a good deal of brain and a great deal of heart—sympathetic, loyal, and very generous. On many points we did not agree; but upon no subject did we ever quarrel. I have known her to put herself to no little trouble and expense to help those who had no claim upon her; and I have known her to demand a good deal of help from those upon whom she had no claim. She was a curious admixture of sentiment and assurance. She was an indefatigable worker, quick and ready with her pen and her tongue. She was blessed with a good deal of practical common-sense, and yet she did many foolish things. She made many warm friends, and she antagonised friends whom she could not afford to lose. She was ambitious, self-assertive, and self-advertising; but she was the soul of honesty and honour. She had a feminine side, with all her masculinity and angularity, and there was a gentleness and sweetness about her which the world did not suspect. She was bitterly treated, but I never heard her speak bitterly. She fought a hard fight against the world, and she fought it alone. She never hit a man when he was down, and she never hit a false blow. She said what she thought, without regard to the ultimate effect of her speech upon herself. She had a good deal of tact, and yet sometimes she was utterly tactless. She was a stanch friend, and never a cruel enemy. She made many mistakes. She had a hard life and not a very successful one; but she never lost her self-respect, and she never forfeited the respect of those who have known her. She lived alone, even as a young and not unattractive girl; she went about the world alone and unattended; yet she never laid herself open to reproach or insult; and no word against the purity of her private character has ever been uttered.

She was one of the cleverest, most self-contained, most self-sustaining women of her generation in any country, and hers was one of the most contradictory individualities I have ever known. But the good always, and largely, predominated over the bad. She never had a home. She died alone as she lived alone. And I am sure she died like the brave woman that she was.

Kate Field's innate sense of honour, honesty, and justice, was shown in a most characteristic way in her last will and testament, executed in Washington in the midsummer of 1895. After arranging for the disposition of her body, which was to be cremated and placed between the coffins of her father and mother at Mount

Auburn, Cambridge, she made certain personal bequests to those who were nearest to her by blood or by affection; to Mr. S. W. White of Brooklyn she left the "Walter Savage Landor Album," as payment of a loan of five hundred dollars, and to Mr. John E. Searles of New York, a drawing by Gainsborough, in payment of one thousand dollars, invested by him in *Kate Field's Washington* shortly before she was forced by ill health to suspend its publication. These were all she had of money or of sentimental value, and with her all she paid as far as she could her great debts.

Among the interesting women I have known, Helen Keller has a prominent place. We first met her in the rooms of Mrs. Mary Mapes Dodge. I cannot give expression to, nor can I altogether explain to myself, the impression she made upon us. We felt as if we were looking into a perfectly clean, fresh soul, exhibited to us by a person of more than usual intellect and intelligence, freely and without reserve. Here was a creature who absolutely knew no guile and no sorrow; from whom all that was impure and unpleasant had been kept; a child of nature with a phenomenally active mind, one who knew most things that were known to men and women of mature age and the highest culture, and yet who had no thought of evil in her heart, and no idea that wickedness or sadness exists in the hearts of others. She was a revelation and an inspiration to us. And she made us think and shudder, and think again. She had come straight from the hands of God,

HELEN KELLER AND HER DOG
(Copyright 1902, by Emily Stokes)

and for fourteen years the world and the flesh and the devil had not obtained possession of her.

Physically she was large for her years, and more fully developed than is the every-day girl of her age. Her face was almost beautiful, and her expression charming to behold, in its varying changes, which were always bright. Her features were regular and perfect. And she moved one to tears even when one was smiling with her.

Speechless, sightless since she was a year and a half old, remembering absolutely nothing of sight or of sound, she has been taught in some miraculous way (to me as marvellous as the science of astronomy) to express herself rapidly in the sign-language, and even by the vocal organs. Her voice in the beginning was harsh, and mechanical, and metallic, but distinct; and her articulation still is slow, but clear. She has no sense of the sound she utters, but she utters it plainly enough. Her teacher, Miss Sullivan, told her (by the sign-language) that I had written a book about Edinburgh, and she said, "Edinboro must be a pretty city," giving it the proper pronunciation, "Edinboro," with which those who are ignorant of Scotland are, as a rule, so rarely familiar.

She had been taught to hear by the touch. She placed her forefinger on the lips of the speaker, and with her thumb and little finger on the throat and vocal chords she caught what was said, and repeated it in her turn.

She seems to have a sixth sense. She receives and understands somehow what of course she cannot hear. The devotion she has for her teacher is beyond all words; her absolute dependence upon that teacher is inexpressibly touching; and when some one spoke of this, and wondered what would become of Helen in case of any separation, the child, hearing nothing of course, turned to the teacher, and pulling her face towards her own, kissed her on the lips, as if to say she could not think of it. This to me was the most startling of all her actions—almost an evidence of psychological impression. She had perceived, through some unconscious movement of the teacher's hand, which she held, the teacher's own inmost feelings at the suggestion of this idea—perhaps a new one even to her; certainly one never before entering the head of the child. Miss Sullivan told us that, with no conscious movement, no intentional or perceptible "talking with her fingers," she could make the child follow her own thoughts, do what she wished her to do, go where she wished her to go, perform any of the acts of "mind-reading" which the professional psychologists exhibit on the stage, or in an amateur way. The teacher, however, was not aware of anything like phenomenal thought-transference. She could not control the child except by the power of touch. She repeated the story of Helen's first experience of death, of her first notion that anything like death had ever come into the world. They had entered a cemetery with her—a word of which she knew nothing, a place concerning the significance or the use of which she knew nothing, when the child suddenly began to weep and to ask what it all meant. This, however, the teacher ascribed to nothing more than the child's phenomenal perception of the unexpressed feelings of those about her. Death, and the idea of death, she never then seemed to have grasped. All sad thoughts and lessons had been kept away from her. She was familiar with history, as she was familiar with all literature. She knew that men and women are now, have been, and are not; but with their going away, and where to, and why, she had not concerned herself. No doubt she thought, simply, that they had gone back, for a time, to the sightlessness which still possessed her; back to the absence of the sense of hearing from which she suffered—although not unpleasantly,—back to the condition of want of speech from which she was just emerging.

She had read, of course, all the books for the blind which had come within her reach; and her teacher had read to her the standard works, not only in English, but in other tongues. Speaking of Edinburgh, she was perfectly familiar with Scott's association with the beautiful old city, and she told me, vocally, that she had "read" *Ivanhoe* and *Quentin Durward*. She knew Mark Twain's works, and laughed at the mere mention of his name. She knew Mrs. Kate Douglas Wiggin's stories, and when we told her of Mrs.

Wiggin's approaching wedding she quoted, out loud, "Patsey's" remark about somebody that "she'd be married the first chance she got." She asked the happy gentleman's name; girl-like, she wanted to know if he was good-looking, and she was pleased to hear him so reported. And then she said, vocally always, "What a queer combination, the doubling of the double 'g's'—Riggs-Wiggin!"—thus exhibiting, with all her deafness, some miraculous sense of sound. She said she loved Mrs. Wiggin and wanted to meet her. She also loved Mark Twain, and she laughed heartily at some little characteristic story of the gentle, serious humourist, which her teacher translated to her. It reminded her of a scene in the *Old Homestead;* and then we learned that she had "seen" the comedy, and knew all about it. When I told her of its presentation at Keene, New Hampshire, where the scenes are laid, and that the spectators there were disappointed in it, and said "it was not acting, but just a lot of fellows going about doing things," she was greatly pleased, and spoke of the difference in the "point of view"— the phrase being her own.

She laughed at everything. She smiled with every one. Everything was pleasant to her. Everybody was good. God grant that she may never find out the innate cussedness of things and of men!

When one asked her if she thought she saw and heard in her dreams, she replied, at once and with strong emphasis, "I am sure I do." But nothing that she had dreamed could she remember to tell us. It was all forgotten when she awoke, she said.

Mrs. Dodge's little grandson, to amuse her, put into her hands a toy engine and car, when she immediately asked, "Where are you going to on the train?" She was given a little bronze figure of a bull, and was told it was by Barye. She did not recognise it as Barye's work, and said so. And she was right. Then she was handed another piece of sculpture, and she said at once, "That's a Barye lion." And again she was right.

She already wrote an excellent, strong, clear, characteristic hand. The letters were firm and upright, and there was no blot or blur. Her composition was better than that of most women twice her age. She had three type-writing machines, containing different combinations of characters, upon each of which she expressed herself as regularly, as orderly, and as rapidly as could any professional worker on that instrument; and no one seeing her "copy" would for a moment imagine under what dreadful difficulties it had been made.

To a Miss Herrick to whom she was introduced she spoke of the great poet who bore the same name. Her familiarity with literature and history was far beyond that of any child of fourteen of whom I ever knew or heard. And her memory of what she had learned was as phenomenal as is anything about her miraculous career. Her powers of concentration then as now were of course heightened and intensified by the isolation of her surroundings. She is not distracted or attracted by disturbing sights and sounds, as other mortals are; and the time we spend in seeing and in listening are spent by her in thought.

Helen came to see us at our own house a week or so later. And there she met, by a prearranged plan of ours, Mr. Howells and "Mark Twain"—for the first time, and to her own great pleasure and theirs. She was prepared to see Mr. Clemens, but Mr. Howells was a delightful surprise to her. They both talked to her—through the teacher and through her own delicate sense of touch on the lips. "Mark" told her stories, serious, comic, and curious, and she understood and appreciated and enjoyed them all. She asked how he came to adopt his *nom de plume*—the words are her own. He repeated the already well-known tale. Told her that "Mark Twain" meant a depth of twelve feet, and that it was used because the sound of the word "Twain" "carried farther" than the words "two fathoms." This she comprehended at once. Then he added that it had been the pseudonym of another pilot, and that he, Mr. Clemens, took it and used it when the original had gone into port and did not need it any more. And Helen added, "And you made it famous!" He said, in his serio-comic way, that it was not inappropriate to him, because he was sometimes light and on the surface, and sometimes—"Deep," interrupted the child. She felt his hair and his face in a tender, inquisitive way—the only one of us whom her curiosity prompted her to examine in that manner—in order to satisfy herself as to how he "looked." A few of the violets we had given her she selected and put, herself, into the proper button-hole of his coat. He was peculiarly tender and lovely with her—even for Mr. Clemens —and she kissed him when he said good-by. Ten minutes after she supposed he had gone, and after their adieus had been made, he came into the dining-room where she was taking a cup of tea, and put his hands on her head in passing; and she recognised at once the mere touch of his fingers on her hair, although she did not know that he was still in the house. She recognised every one of us by the touch, although there were but two of us whom she had ever met before, and them but once. As she sat on the sofa we approached her, in turn, and she knew us all, even Mrs. Hazlehurst, whom she called, at once, by an entirely unfamiliar and uncommon name, though she had simply met her as she entered the room.

We all talked to her in turn. She asked about my dogs, and I repeated some of the rhymes I had written about them, foolish and silly enough. But she understood all the jingle and all the plays upon words, and she said, "Why, you are a humourist too." I wish she were right.

When Mrs. Hutton said to her, "I believe you like to talk to strangers, Helen," she replied immediately, "But there are no strangers here." And she said once, *a propos* of nothing—"How many books you have!" She had come directly from the library door to her sofa. She had not been told that it was a library. She had had no intimation that there was a book in the room.

In the dining-room I "showed" her a quaint little wineglass in the shape of a thistle. She felt it, recognised at once the flower it represented, and hesitated to accept it when I told her that I wanted her to carry it home, in remembrance of me. And when I explained that it was one of a set brought from Scotland years before, and dearly prized by my mother, that but one of them had ever been given away, and that one by the mother to the wife that now is, and long before there was any thought of such a thing in the minds of any of us, she drew my face to hers and kissed me—twice. I felt that I had received a benediction.

She was peculiarly affectionate and demonstrative in her disposition. And she bestowed her innocent kisses upon persons of all ages and of either sex as freely and as guilelessly as the ordinary girl of fifteen would bestow a harmless innocent smile.

She came to us again, just before the last Christmas, to meet Miss Ellen Terry, by especial request of both of them ; and, naturally, they were mutually delighted and impressed. A number of her friends and ours dropped in during the afternoon, and the child was peculiarly happy among us all. Mrs. Hutton had bought for her, as a Christmas gift, a little plaster cast, which she recognised as a lioness, admiring the freedom and action of its movements. When the author of *Timothy's Quest* entered, I said, "This is a literary lioness, Helen, but you can only look at her; she belongs to Mr. Riggs." When the author of *Hans Brinker* came I said, "Helen, this is the biggest literary lioness in the whole show." With a smile, and a caress for Mrs. Dodge, she replied, at once, "All the lionesses in *your* menagerie are very gentle!"

When she was presented to Mrs. Sangster, whom she had never met before, she said, "But your name should be Songster, you sing so sweetly."

After the guests had gone their different ways Helen staid behind "to talk them over"; and thus she summed up Miss Terry: "Her voice is soft, gentle, and low, and full of pathos. She is quite as divinely tall as I had pictured her, but not so slender. She is full of tender sympathy. I am not at all disappointed in her. And when I spoke to her of her children she kissed my hand!"

At Sir Henry Irving's invitation she went to the theatre to see *Charles the First;* and before the performance she was carried by Mr. Stoker to the dressing-room, where she saw the mimic King and Queen, entirely equipped for their parts. She examined, carefully, every detail of costume, wig, and "make-up"; and then, from her seat, she listened to the story of the pathetic play, as it was told to her by Miss Sullivan, through the medium of the sign-language, communicated in some miraculous manner from hand to hand.

On her way to the theatre she had told the teacher that she did not care for Charles; that she did not admire his character; that she thought he was foolish and selfish, if not actually in the wrong. On her way home from the theatre she confessed that she had seen him in an entirely new light, that now she not only pitied, but loved him!

The teacher interested and impressed us almost as much as did the pupil. Greater love, greater devotion, greater patience never were known. A whole life has been given up to one beautiful, unselfish object, with no hope of reward here. And, if the theory is true that in the next life we are to carry on the work we have done in this, what reward can she have hereafter? In the world to which she is going there will be no blind, no deaf, no dumb to teach, no helpless to care for; the fruit of knowledge will grow upon every tree, and all the souls will be protected and saved.

During the ten years that have passed since that first meeting with Miss Sullivan and her pupil, they have been closely allied to us in many ways. *The Story of My Life* Helen has herself told; and she has noted in her modest way her wonderful, almost phenomenal progress and development. Certain little examples of what she has said and done to us, and before us, in our social circle are perhaps worth repeating.

After the Princeton house was finished and furnished in 1899, she was very anxious, as she said, to "see it." Familiar as she was with the old home, she was natur-

A Peculiar Sensitiveness

ally greatly interested in the new. Under Miss Sullivan's guidance and with me as prompter, she examined the library thoroughly, being told as she touched them what the various objects were and how they looked to eyes that could see. When she came to a certain cast hanging on the wall, I asked Miss Sullivan not to tell Helen the name of the original. Miss Sullivan replied that this she could not possibly do, in view of her own ignorance regarding the matter.

Helen felt every feature, wonder and uncertainty expressed in her face; and her fingers dwelt particularly on the lower part of the image, returning thereto and lingering about the chin. Finally she exclaimed:
"Why, it looks like Lincoln!"

And it *was* Lincoln, taken from the living face before the beard, with which she herself was so familiar, had been allowed to grow. It was the first time she had "seen" Lincoln without the hair upon his face. This recognition is all the more remarkable when it is considered that many persons with all their faculties have not been able to identify the cast. And then Helen said: "O that I could see the bare chin of Grant. So much is expressed in the chin; and I seem to know Lincoln better than I did before."

Helen's peculiar sensitiveness to all vibration was shown, one day, in a most startling manner. She had knocked in some way two empty glasses at the table and made them ring. Apparently unconscious of anything unusual or remarkable, she placed her fingers on each tumbler to break the sound, doing precisely what some one else, with all his normal senses, had done, of course without her knowledge, under similar circumstances and at the same table a few minutes before.

Vibration to her is noise. She will ask, "What is that noise?" *feeling* the noise even before the noise is heard by those of natural hearing about her.

When a group of young persons of Helen's own age were invited to meet her one bright summer afternoon in the gardens of the home in Princeton, they amused themselves for a time on the bowling-green and elsewhere about the lawn, doing things with balls and golf-sticks and bows and arrows which naturally were beyond the power of Helen, with all her wonderful facility of amusing herself as do other girls and boys. Some one, seeing her sitting alone for a moment, took her hand and said:

"You and I, Helen, seem to be out of all this play."

And Helen replied:

"Oh, but you know that I am like a music-box. *My* play is shut up inside of me; and there is plenty of it!"

Here follow a few of her personal letters, taken at random, most of them written after the publication of her book, and none of them appearing in it.

In a letter to Mrs. Hutton, when the latter was in Venice in 1895, Helen writes:

"Please give my kindest love to Mr. Hutton, and

Mrs. Riggs [Kate Douglas Wiggin] and Mr. [Charles Dudley] Warner too, although I have never had the pleasure of knowing him personally. As I listen Venicewards, I hear Mr. Hutton's pen dancing over the pages of his new book. It is a pleasant sound because it is full of promise. How much I shall enjoy reading it!"

" From the regions of eternal snow and ice [she had just been reading about Dr. Nansen and his wonderful vessel, the *Fram*] I descended into the fair forests and mountain glens of Scotland, where dwelt the *Lady of the Lake* in the days of old. I think it is a great poem, full of startling, splendid passages, and with an air of romance all through it; but I cannot help being glad that the poem belongs to the past and not to the present, and that the endless wars and struggles which it celebrated are over for ever; for I see, through the shadowy veil of romance that Scott has drawn over those times, the ruin and desolation and sorrow which were as much a part of those struggles as the heroic exploits of Roderick Dhu and his warriors."

" Dear me, what a bother money is. I really think it would be a perfectly lovely world if we did n't have to think about money. Why, we can't even live without it, which seems very strange indeed, especially when we think how beautifully Nature manages without spending a cent. The trees and flowers have put on the loveliest Spring suits, and they have n't cost them a penny. Happy trees; happy flowers; I would that we were like them."

"WRENTHAM, August 27, 1903.

"DEAR UNCLE LAURENCE:

"The other day we went on the trolley to visit the Wayside Inn of Longfellow's tales, and passed through Wayland, where the first public library in Massachusetts, and the second in the United States, was built in 1850. The Inn was extremely interesting. Nearly all the old furniture was gone; but we saw the 'bar' and the old-fashioned ball-room and the room in which Lafayette slept one night; also the one in which Longfellow had thought out so many of his verses. On the doors and walls were inscriptions and verses which painters and poets had written. The picture of 'fairy Mary, Princess Mary' from which Longfellow copied some lines in the tales was there; also the swords and guns of the Hessian soldiers."

"CAMBRIDGE, October 16, 1903.

" . . . We returned to Cambridge the 1st of October, and my work is now under way. I have this year two Latin courses, *Tacitus* the first term with Professor Morgan, and *Plautus* with Dr. Moore. The other two are English literature of the nineteenth century and Shakespeare. The plays we read this year are *Othello, Hamlet, Henry V., Antony and Cleopatra,* and *Winter's Tale*. I have been re-elected vice-president of my class and made Honorary Member of the

HELEN KELLER MISS SULLIVAN, MARK TWAIN, AND LAURENCE HUTTON

'English Club,' and the 'Classical Club.' I have entered upon my Senior year, and I am looking forward with gladness to the end of my college work. I do not mean that my college life has not been happy. There have been discouragements, it is true, and hard work which has tasked my powers to the utmost, but I feel that it has been worth while. I am glad I came. I shall be glad to go. I am better prepared for what the future holds of activity for me, and the fact that work is open to me is a precious thought. I am most grateful to the college for what it has done for me, and to the friends who have given me this splendid opportunity to try my strength with others.

"I am now writing a little essay on Optimism, and I hope it will be finished in time for the Christmas sale. I was very unwilling at first to undertake any extra work this year, but it was urged that the essay would help on the sale of my book. I think I wrote you that it was not selling very well. Mr. Bok and others think the book has not been properly advertised, and they advised this way of calling attention to it.

"Last August I wrote a short article called 'Looking Forward,' for the November number of *The Ladies' Home Journal* with the same object in view."

"CAMBRIDGE, November 4, 1903.

"At last I have finished the essay on Optimism! Dear me, what troublesome children of the mind these essays are! I have worked from sun to sun, and half the night to boot, and at times I have positively thought that if I kept on long enough I should become 'a proverb of industry' in New England. The proofs are coming every day, and I think the essay will be out this month. There is to be a picture of me in my cap and gown in the book, and you may see for yourself how very important I feel."

"CAMBRIDGE, December 8.

"To-day I received letters from Dr. Hale, Mr. Mitchell, editor of *Life*, and President Roosevelt, and each had a kind wish for the little book. . . .

"I have had an interesting letter from a 'bronco buster' in Nevada. His spelling is a miracle of ingenuity; but I don't know that it is any queerer than Shakespeare's. The man has read my book, and says it reminds him of a great drove of cattle which he herded once, and he goes on to describe a blind steer which got on as well as the rest of the herd. He calls me 'little broncho' and says that 'Miss Sullivan's ideas are all right'; that 'a colt must lurn by expereances.'

"I am getting many letters from England now. You will be glad to hear that *The Story of My Life* has reached its seventh edition there."

"Thinking of those whom we love is almost like having them with us. Every thought flash we send out to them seems to bring a pleasant word or smile in

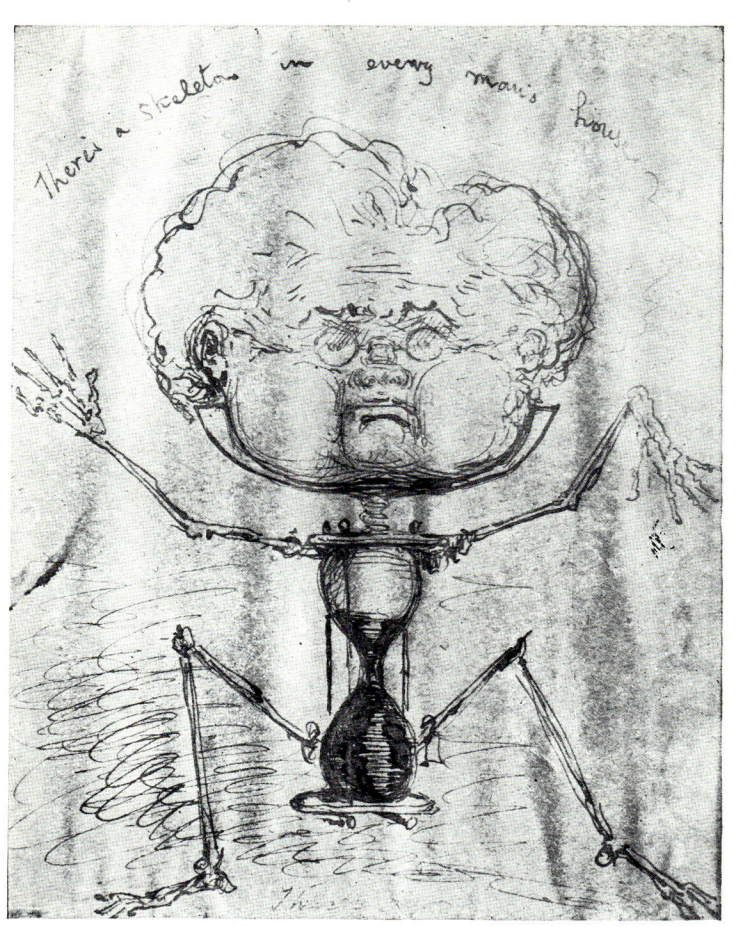

A CARICATURE OF THACKERAY BY HIMSELF

response, and all our day is brightened, and the hardest tasks are easy. . . ."

"I think Greek is the loveliest language that I know anything about. If it is true that the violin is the most perfect of musical instruments, then Greek is the violin of human thought."

". . . Now I feel as if I should succeed in doing something in mathematics, although I cannot see why it is so very important to know that the lines drawn from the extremities of the base of an isosceles triangle to the middle points of the opposite sides are equal: the knowledge does n't seem to make life any sweeter or happier, does it? On the other hand, when we learn a new word, it is the key to untold treasures. . . ."

". . . The *Iliad* is like a splendid youth who has had the earth for his play-ground. . . ."

The average writer of books, going into a book-room, no matter how large or how small the collection, is apt to cast his eye immediately upon one of his own volumes. The first time Charles Dudley Warner came into my library, he walked directly to a certain shelf and picked out his own *Backlog Studies* — then just published. He looked over it, and saw that it was pencilled and interlined. He had marked in many books, himself, the passages that appealed to him: but it had never occurred to him that anybody had ever cared enough for what he had written to *mark* him.

We happened to be talking that night about Dickens, the man rather than the writer, as to whether he was a good man or not: and Warner turned to his own little volume in question and read three or four lines among them which I had designated: "I don't believe that the world has a feeling of personal regard for any author who has not been loved by those who knew him most intimately."

I knew Warner most intimately; and my feeling for him was one not only of personal regard, but of absolute love. In society he was quiet but most sympathetic and appreciative. He was one of the best of listeners. While I can remember thousands of words he had written, I can hardly remember one word he said, although he never said a word that was not worth remembering.

I saw him first, of all places, in the crowd on Epsom Downs, on a certain Derby Day many years ago, where he had gone and I had gone to make copy for our respective newspapers. He had no interest in the horses, and as I had no interest in the horses, we were there simply to study and to reflect the crowds; he doing it, naturally, in a way which was much better than mine.

One of the most treasured of my possessions—if it is authentic—is a pencil drawing of Thackeray, supposed to have been done by Thackeray himself. I cannot, unfortunately, speak with authority in the matter. It

EDWARD FITZ-GERALD

is done in pen and ink, it represents Thackeray with a big head—which Thackeray certainly had,—with a small body in the shape of an hour-glass, and with human bones for legs and arms. It bears the inscription on the top: "There's a skeleton in every man's house," and it is signed in a hand very like Thackeray's with Thackeray's own name. It was given to me over a quarter of a century ago by Mr. John Crerar of Chicago, who founded the Crerar Library, and whom I know to have been a friend of Thackeray. The tradition, which I fondly hope to be true, is that Thackeray, during one of his visits to America, drew it and gave it to Crerar, who gave it to me. The story is that the hour-glass and its flowing sand represented the hurry in which Thackeray was always, in a social way, during his sojourn in the United States. He had so many engagements to luncheons, to dinners, and to suppers; he was so much in demand; he had so few moments to spare between this house and that; that he was literally haunted by the fact that he was a slave to time. He had only twenty minutes, or half an hour, or an hour, between invitations; and the skeleton in the house of the friends who were so kindly disposed toward him was his hurry to get from one entertainment to another.

Mr. Crerar, and every one who could give me any information regarding the drawing, has gone to join Thackeray in the country where Art is long: and I have been unable to verify what I want to feel in my heart to be Thackeray's caricature of himself.

In my collection is one of the rarest and most highly prized of British book-plates,—that of Edward Fitz-Gerald, prized not only because it is Fitz-Gerald's, but also because it was designed and drawn by Thackeray. The figure, queer in itself, is said to have had for its model Mrs. Brookfield; but this is a very uncertain supposition. The face, indistinctly rendered, is not unlike that of Mrs. Brookfield; but, while Mrs. Brookfield had wings no doubt, they were not visible in the flesh. A few years ago a collector of *Ex Libris* came to me in great tribulation because he had not succeeded in buying, at an auction sale, the Thackeray-Fitz-Gerald book-plate, the price being far beyond his limit. He said:

" I suppose you know the plate?"

" Yes," I said, " and I possess a copy which is emphatically It! It was given me by Harry Edwards, the entomologist and actor, and an intimate personal friend of the author of *Omar Khayyam*. It contains the following inscription in the handwriting of Fitz-Gerald himself:

"Done by Thackeray one day in Coram ("*Joram*") Street in 1842. 'All wrong on her feet,' he said: I can see him now.
"E. F. G.
"March 19, 1878."

While I fail somehow in my appreciation of Fitz-Gerald's great work, which is in spots sometimes beyond my comprehension, I have a great respect for the man. This book-plate of his with its autograph en-

THE FITZ-GERALD BOOK-PLATE, DRAWN BY THACKERAY

dorsement, and an etching of a drawing of Fitz-Gerald, in his old age, by Charles Kean, I would rather possess, almost, than the original manuscript of *Omar Khayyam* itself.

A literary curiosity that I have is the card of autographs that was sent me with a new hat.

I had been wearing for a long time what my friends considered an exceedingly shabby hat, but one which I considered was good enough for me, when on Christmas Day (1891) there came to my address a castor bought, by subscription, by a number of my friends, and carrying with it a paper containing many words in prose and verse, relating to the hat and to the head it was intended to cover. As a specimen of ingenious good-fellowship these autograph inscriptions are perhaps worth preserving, not because of any wonderful intrinsic merit of their own, but on account of the great variety of talent displayed in so many various ways. Mr. Drake had no opportunity to make his mark upon the paper until after it was framed, so he set his seal upon the mat.

I was stricken speechless by the gift. My only reply was a circular note complaining that the hat was without the narrow band of crape which I always wore, and asking for the further subscription of fifty cents each to remedy the deficiency.

The reference to "Dunlap" has a double meaning, the hatter, and William Dunlap, the earliest historian of the American stage, who gave his name to a literary organisation of stage lovers and book lovers who founded a society for the reprinting of obsolete, obsolescent, and current affairs. Nearly all the men, notably Mr. Jefferson and Mr. Bunner, who made the play upon the name "Dunlap" were active members.

Mr. Jefferson contributed this additional poem on a separate sheet:

A HAT FOR HUTTON

Bombasties Furioso 't was who said,
"A hat can do no harm without a head."
But Laurence has a head that 's done much good,
With brain developed, be it understood.
This is the kind of Hat I 'd choose for him,
Bell-crowned at the top, curly as to brim,
Black and stately as an old gondola,
Smooth and silky as a young Angora;
Smooth and shapely in its bold exterior,
With his virtues writ in the interior.
Worn by him alone—for none should share it,—
If this Hat will fit him let him wear it.

J. JEFFERSON.

Writing men seem to think that there is a good deal in a name, and perhaps it is true. Names that are not commonplace somehow seem to carry books and magazine articles; and men who are still known familiarly to their personal friends as "Jim" or "Jake" are known to the world by some more euphonious name which as certainly belongs to them and which they have made more famous than they could ever make "Sam" or "Bob." The first edition of Bayard Taylor's *Views Afoot*—we are told on the title-page—was the work of James B. Taylor; Brander Matthews was christened

SILHOUETTE OF H. C. BUNNER
(By courtesy of Keppler & Schwarzmann)

"TWO GHOSTS OF LAST SUMMER"
MARK TWAIN AND LAURENCE HUTTON

"James"; Hopkinson Smith was christened "Frank"; and Rodman Drake was "Joseph."

One night when there had come to us the news of the death of a very well-known and exceedingly popular American author, he was discussed in a most feeling way in a monologue talk of an hour or two by Mark Twain. To my surprise nobody seemed interested in the conversation, although it is very seldom that Mr. Clemens does not have an attentive audience, no matter what his subject may be. When our guests were gone, Mrs. Hutton asked Clemens why he had disappointed so many who were ready to hang on his words, by talking about the personality of an unknown man of whom they had never heard and in whom they could have no possible interest, when it suddenly struck the two of us, who knew what we were talking about, that Bret Harte—who was the subject of the theme—could not of course be identified with the "Frank" Harte about whom so much had been said. He was "Frank" to Clemens, and always will be "Frank" to Clemens, just as he was "Frank" to everybody in the old California days, and when he first came to the East. He began to write as F. B. Harte, then as Francis B. Harte, then as Francis Bret Harte, and he is going down to posterity as "Bret Harte," and as nobody else.

Of Bret Harte I have seen more or less for the last five years. My first introduction to him was peculiar. I had never seen him to know him, although I had been interested in him for a long time and had read and thoroughly enjoyed everything he ever wrote. I knew him as a clever writer long before I knew anything about him, and before he was famous. I take a little satisfaction to myself in having discovered him for myself; and in having been one of the most ardent admirers of his peculiar style before it was the fashion to be so. I picked up a country paper somewhere in which was his *Miggles*, and read it with the most intense delight, and made up my mind that the author of that sketch was a wonderful fellow who, if he lived, would make his mark. That he has made his mark there can be no question now, and even if, as some of his critics say, he is not destined to last or to be read by the next generation, he certainly is read in this as very few living American writers are read; the fact that he has received from the Scribners the highest price ever paid for a single novel (*Gabriel Conway*) in this country, is proof of the popularity and the high value publishers, who are the best judges of public taste, put upon him. Shortly after the announcement of a new edition of his *Condensed Novels* in 1871, I went into Dutton's book-store to get the volume, sat down in a quiet corner to look through it, laughed heartily over the clever burlesque of the style of popular story writers, and said to Clapp, who stood by me, "That Bret Harte is a wonderful fellow." Mr. Clapp said, "Indeed he is that; and this is the gentleman himself," presenting a quiet little man who had stood by looking at me, but whom if I had even seen I had not noticed, as Mr. Bret Harte!

A Hat for Hutton

Bombastes Furioso 'twas who said,
"A Hat can do no harm without a head,"
But Laurence has a head that's done much good,
With brain developed to it — understood.
This is the kind of Hat I'd choose for him,
Bell crowned at the top, curly at the brim.
Black and stately as an old gondola,
Smooth & silky as a young Angola,
Smooth and shapely in its bold Exterior
With his Virtues writ in the interior,
Worn by him alone — for none should share it —
If this Hat will fit him let him wear it —

J. Jefferson

December 25th 1891

LETTER BY JEFFERSON, SENT WITH A NEW HAT FOR LAURENCE HUTTON

Whether Mr. Harte looked upon this as an intentional bit of flattery on my part, I never knew. I tried to assure him of my utter innocence of his presence. At all events, from that time on, we became excellent friends, although never intimates; and my association with him ever since has always been of the pleasantest. He was amazing in conversation; told a good story with much of the dramatic effect that makes his writing; was full of anecdotes and ready to see anything marked or peculiar or characteristic in the people about him, and to improve upon it in the repetition or description of it. Like all writers he is open to flattery, and nothing in his life probably pleased him more than the praise given by Dickens to his early poems and sketches, as described by John Foster in Dickens's *Life*. He told me one day of Mark Twain's *Jumping Frog* story and of the first time Mark Twain ever told it. He had heard it in some far Western bar-room among the stories of like character that are so often told at such places; had remembered it, but had been attracted more by the manner of the man who told it than by the yarn itself. This he attempted to imitate in repeating the story to Harte, and was not a little surprised at the delight with which the frog's adventures were received by Harte. He had no great opinion of it, but, at Harte's suggestion, published it and made by it his first reputation in his peculiar vein. How many good things are told by people and done by people who are utterly unconscious of the good thing they are guilty of until the world discovers it and points it out. Harte told me that nothing ever surprised him more than the marvellous success (marvellous to him) of his spurt, *The Heathen Chinee*. He had written it in a minute, had thought nothing of it, had thrown it aside, when it was picked up by somebody by chance, and put in a corner of the magazine to fill up a space, for want of better "copy." Probably no "poem"—to dignify it with that title—ever written has made so great a sensation in its way or in so short a time, as that. I don't believe there was a journal in the United States at that time of its first appearance, literary, religious, or scientific, that did not copy it. It was repeated by everybody, quoted by everybody, set to music, translated into foreign languages, and became almost a classic. It did more to make Bret Harte than anything else that was ever written by him, and yet he thought so little of it himself that he did not think it worth putting into print.

CHAPTER XV

Authors Club—Kipling—Tile Club—Vedder—Henry James—Mark Twain and Cable—Mark Twain's Story of Mrs. Stowe—Mark Twain and Corbett—Stockton—Stoddard—George William Curtis—Thomas B. Reed—H. C. Bunner.

WHEN the Authors Club was in its comparative infancy, a select little party of its members found themselves in its rooms in West 23d Street one night, sitting about a fire that would not burn. A heavy snow was falling, and the weather was bitterly cold. A motion to adjourn to a neighbouring hotel was carried unanimously; and thither we went in pursuit of light and warmth and spirituous cheer. The great bar-room was crowded, and it was with no little difficulty that we found a place to seat ourselves. At last, two gentlemen at a table in a far corner courteously made room for us. We gathered from their conversation that they were strangers in New York, and that they had been to hear John Fiske lecture on the "Nebular Hypothesis" that evening at the Cooper Institute. Their discourse was so intelligent that Mr. Stedman hazarded a few remarks, saying that we were all friends of the lecturer; and the talk became general. They seemed to be pleased with us, and we were interested in them. They consented to take a parting nip with us, and as we all rose to leave the room Mr. Stedman ventured to tell them who we were. "This is Mr. Conant," he said, "of *Harper's Weekly*. This, Mr. Julian Hawthorne. This, Mr. George Parsons Lathrop. This, Mr. Richard Grant White, the Shakespearian author. This, Mr. George Cary Eggleston, of the *World*. This, Professor Boyesen of Cornell. This, Mr. Bunner, of *Puck*. This, Mr. Laurence Hutton, the historian of the Stage; and I am Mr. E. C. Stedman." The strangers looked at us for a moment in solemn silence; when the elder of them said—"I am Bismarck, and my friend is the Pope of Rome!" And without a word of "good-night," or a glance behind them, they hurried out into the storm.

To this day, no doubt, they are convinced they had fallen into the nest of a gang of bunco steerers, and they are still congratulating themselves on their escape.

A group of short story writers once happened to gather in the Century Club, when the subject, not unnaturally, turned upon short stories; and the question was raised as to which was the best short story of modern times. Somebody said, "Wait a bit; let us write down our answers without discussion or collaboration": and when the pads upon which the responses appeared were read, it was discovered that the six best short stories, in the opinion of the experts, were six different short stories—all of them written by Kipling! They were *Wee Willie Winkie; Ba, Ba, Black Sheep; Without Benefit of Clergy; The Man Who Was; The*

SIGNATURES SENT WITH A NEW HAT TO LAURENCE HUTTON

Man Who Would be King; and *The Ship that Found Herself.*

Mr. Gilder, about this same time, gave a lunch at the old University Club to Kipling, to which I was invited. Another engagement made me late and I entered the room as the party was breaking up. I was introduced to Mr. Kipling, with whom I exchanged the traditional few formal words, and we drifted apart: but a moment or two afterwards he placed himself on the arm of the chair in which I was sitting and said:

"I did n't realise, Hutton [not *Mr.* Hutton], when I met you a moment ago, who you were. Dear old Wolcot Balestier, your friend and mine, tried so hard and so many times to bring us together in London and elsewhere, and now he is gone, and I can't understand it at all. He died so suddenly and so far away; we had so much to say to each other, and now I have got to wait so long before I can say it."

This was not meant for the world; but for one listener. After patting me on the shoulder as if he had known me twenty years, he went to the window and looked out on Madison Square, saying nothing, as I afterwards noticed, for several minutes.

When Kipling lay a-dying, as we all supposed, in New York a year or two later, and finally recovered, I wrote to him:

"I am so glad, Dear Man, that you did not go to have that talk with Wolcot, for he can afford to wait better than we can."

The famous Tile Club of New York used to have its meetings in a queer old place in the rear of West 10th Street, opposite the Studio Buildings. The men, all of them artists, met irregularly in a simple way to exchange ideas. All the bright young sculptors and painters, in colour and in black and white, were members of the then simple little association. One man was the host of each evening. Each man on every night did something in his own line. The results of the work, all of it educational and improving, went to the host of the occasion. O'Donovan once selected Abbey as the subject of a *bas relief* which afterwards came into my possession, and which seems to me to be worth preserving.

The Tile Club entertained, naturally, all of the distinguished strangers of the kindred professions who came to this country.

One night there chanced to be sitting on a settle in a corner three of us, Stanford White, Arthur B. Frost, and myself, waiting for dinner—always a simple one—to be announced; when there entered an old friend of two of us but a total stranger to the third. Placed in a row, and with red moustaches, we three looked not unlike; and the stranger, curiously enough, looked like all three of us. He stood in front of us, gazed upon the group, examined White carefully and me carefully, and then gazed in a most inquiring and interested way at the man he had never seen before. He looked again at White, and again at me, and at the other man.

THE TILE CLUB PORTRAIT OF EDWIN ABBEY

Then he walked to a little mirror in the corner and looked at himself; and he came back and gazed at me and White once more, and he said to the inoffensive, silent, wondering replica of all of us:

"For the Lord's sake, here's another chimpanzee!"

Frost, astounded, gasped out:

"Who is it?"

"Arthur," I said, "it's Vedder. Don't you know Vedder?"

And without other introduction the two chimpanzees threw themselves into each other's arms; perfectly familiar with each other's works and admiring them, but up to that time absolutely unknown to each other in a personal way.

During the early days of the American Copyright League a meeting was held in my library in Thirty-fourth Street. Many of the men most prominent in the movement were present. Mr. Richard Grant White presided, the minutes of the previous meeting were read and approved, and unfinished business was in order. Various suggestions were being made when a guest, sitting in a corner of the room by the window, suddenly arose and addressed the assembled authors. He had attracted very little attention, and it was only noticed that he had been absorbed apparently in a book on his lap. The Chairman, not recognising him, turned to me in an inquiring way, and I whispered:

"Mr. Henry James."

Every head was turned in his direction, surprise was

on every face, and the scene was as effective as is that in Bulwer's play *Money*, when the entire *dramatis personæ* push back their chairs to gaze upon Alfred Evelyn as the unexpected heir of the will.

For ten or fifteen minutes the speaker, known to every man present by his work, unknown in a personal way to most of his hearers, talked of things *a propos* of the matter in hand, in a manner absolutely to the point and carrying much weight. He made as great an impression as a speaker as he had ever made as a writer; and for the first time, after a long residence abroad, he was brought into intimate contact with the men of his own guild in his own country.

A party of Boston and New York men once met by appointment in Hartford as guests of Mark Twain on the occasion of Mr. George W. Cable's first appearance as a public reader. We had an early dinner and we occupied in a body seats on the platform, where we were arranged behind the speaker's desk, and, to the tremendous self-consciousness of some of us, in a row of chairs like a group of negro minstrels. Mr. Clemens had to introduce the speaker to his audience and thus, so far as I can remember, he did it. He said:

"A complete stranger myself to Mr. Cable personally, though a great admirer of his books, I appear before you as his sponsor to-night, if he needs one. The original idea was that Mr. William Dean Howells of New York was to introduce Mr. Cable of New Orleans to the Hartford audience, when it occurred to the Committee that Mr. Howells was himself a stranger to Hartford and did not know Hartford, nor did Hartford know him. So Mr. Thomas Bailey Aldrich, of Boston, was brought from Boston to introduce Mr. Howells of New York, who was to introduce Mr. Cable of New Orleans. But some one was necessary to introduce Mr. Aldrich of Boston, so Mr. Gilder of New York was asked to introduce Mr. Aldrich of Boston, who was to introduce Mr. Howells of New York, who was to introduce Mr. Cable of New Orleans. Then the same objection arose. No one knew Mr. Gilder of New York, so Mr. John Boyle O'Reilly of Boston was asked to introduce Mr. Gilder of New York who was to introduce Mr. Aldrich of Boston, who was to introduce Mr. Howells of New York, who was to introduce Mr. Cable of New Orleans.

"Once more an awful problem arose in the minds of the committee. Mr. John B. O'Reilly, of Boston, had never been in Hartford before, and only knew it as a place of five minutes for refreshments on the New Haven Railroad. The question once more arose, who would introduce Mr. O'Reilly of Boston? And for a time no proper person appeared on the horizon. After some deliberation—for the matter was getting serious—we decided to dispense with an introduction altogether which would occupy another evening at least, and to let Cable speak for himself. I have, however, here present on the platform all these distinguished gentlemen from our suburban cities, which will account for the menagerie behind me. And this, ladies and gentlemen of Hartford, is Mr. Cable of New Orleans."

Mark Twain is very fond of telling stories about his children. One day little Elsie Leslie was dining with the Clemenses at Hartford, and there were present several grown people, with whom she talked in a perfectly easy way. Jean Clemens, then very young in years, was surprised to see a child so self-possessed in the presence of strangers, and of her elders, and was annoyed that she herself could not converse as well, and as much, as her visitor; but there seemed to be no subject introduced on which she had any knowledge. At last her chance came. Some mention of *Tom Sawyer* was made, and Jean piped up:

"I know who wrote that book; it was Mrs. Harriet Beecher Stowe!"

Such, again, is fame!

Mrs. Stowe, a near neighbour of theirs at Hartford, was allowed, in her feeble old age, to go into the Clemenses' green-house and help herself to flowers,— often to the disgust of the gardener, as she carelessly pulled up bushes by the roots while picking the roses. However, Mrs. Clemens gave directions that she was to do as she pleased.

A new and very taciturn gardener was working on the place one day when Mrs. Stowe came in. She saw that his face was unfamiliar, and saw that his manner was unpromising; so she set herself to conciliate him, and to give him a hint as to who she was, by asking if he had ever read *Uncle Tom's Cabin.*

" Tried to! " said the man.

And there the matter rested.

Among the very kind and touching letters we received, when our engagement was announced in 1884, was the following:

"HARTFORD, December 22, 1884.

" MY DEAR HUTTON:

" I must not venture to write to Miss Mitchell, so I want to ask you to be my messenger to her and congratulate her upon the good fortune which God has bestowed upon her and which she without any doubt comes as near deserving as anybody could. *I* think she has done exceedingly well, and I rejoice with her beyond the power of words to express.

"And now I am relieved of a burden which has long been secretly oppressing my heart. Months ago, fully aware of the relations existing between you and my daughter [Jean, then aged three or four], I was shocked and grieved to discover that she had transferred her affections to a kitten. I would have written you and exposed her treason, but I *could* not break your heart; and so I lingered, hoping that you or the kitten would die, and so disburden me of my shame and sorrow. I tried to think of other ways out, but none occurred to me. Yet Providence takes the thing in hand, and lo! by a simple turn of the Supreme wrist, everything is lovely and the goose hangs high. How wonderful *are* the ways of Providence, when you come to look at it. Good-bye. We all send our very warmest congratulations.

"Sincerely yours,

"S. L. CLEMENS."

He was once granted a special interview in the Madison Square Garden at a benefit given to the fully trained prize-fighter, Mr. Corbett, just before a great battle for the championship belt. Great was the contrast between the two men as they stood face to face, the one in evening dress, and the other in the costume of the ring; the one elderly and not particularly robust in a physical way, the other as magnificent a specimen of the purely animal man as could well be seen. Clemens, in his drawling manner, said, as he shook hands with his *vis-a-vis:*

"Well, Mr. Corbett, you look as if you could do it, and for your sake I hope you may. But I want you to understand that if you come out the victor, I shall challenge you myself, and you will have to stand up with bare knuckles in front of me!"

Corbett replied, very quickly:

"That, Mr. Clemens, is an entirely unfair proposition, because if I lick you—which is not impossible— I'll be only the champion of America, *but* if you lick me, you'll be not merely the champion of America but Mark Twain too; and the odds are too great against me!"

As we stepped out of the training-tent to take seats in the arena, Clemens said:

"There is one thing about that man: he will fight with his head."

A letter he once wrote to us is as follows:

"December 29, Midnight.

"DEAR MRS. HUTTON:

"Thank you ever so much for the invitation. If I live I'll be there; — otherwise — but that is further along.   "S. L. CLEMENS."

There had been in the early days at John Wood's gymnasium a silent, homely, quiet little man taking his nightly exercise, who appealed to me because of the dry humour of his occasional remarks. We were both rather strong in the arms while rather weak in the rest of our anatomy and we could do together the same gymnastic stunts, between which we would sit on the mattresses or a spring-board, and talk about all sorts of things; I giving my immature impressions, and he expressing himself in his terse, snappy, unforgetable way. We drifted apart, not knowing each other's names, and only seeing each other occasionally at the time in the Institution of Physical Culture, as its proprietor called it.

Years afterwards, when I had read and enjoyed *Rudder Grange*, and *The Lady or the Tiger*, I met one night at Mrs. Mary Mapes Dodge's, the author of those delightful tales. He was introduced to me as

Mr. Frank Stockton; he remembered me, and I remembered him at once as the quiet little man with whom I had swung Indian clubs and put up weighted dumb-bells twenty or more years before.

In those early days he was associate editor of *Hearth and Home*, and absolutely unknown to fame. How he has made himself famous, all the world knows. Mrs. Hutton in her journal tells the story of her own first meeting with the Stocktons:

"Frank Stockton and his wife dined with us. They are nice people; so gentle and unassuming. They took a house at Dunster for six weeks, then went to Broadway, in England, which was a great come-down after the land of the 'Doon.' Mr. Stockton told a funny darky story of an old negress who said she had one foot in the grave, while the other was shouting 'Glory Hallelujah!' He said, *a propos* of Mrs. Mary Mapes Dodge, that her personal physician called on her once, when she sent him word she 'was too ill to see him.' I repeated her remark to me at Onteora, that 'Champagne was a bottled Sermon on the Mount, it made every one blessed,' which he thought extremely happy."

Frank Stockton was once invited by a lady, who called herself a society lady, to a most elaborate luncheon. He discovered that he was the only person of his own sex at the table, and he realised to his own modest regret that he was the hero of the occasion. Everything went off very well and to everybody's

PAGE FROM THE HUTTON GUEST-BOOK, WITH PORTRAIT OF MRS. HUTTON BY CARROLL BECKWITH

satisfaction, until the end of the symposium, when there was presented to him, first, a dish of ice-cream in the moulded form of a lady and a tiger. He quickly realised that this was a test case; that his hostess and her friends meant him to establish the fact as to whether it was the tiger or the lady; and to his own subsequent great satisfaction, he had presence of mind enough to say that he did not eat ices; and so the momentous question was never settled.

Richard Henry Stoddard was very much my senior in years; nevertheless, I saw not a little of him in the Century Club as well as in my own house and in his. Toward the end of his life, when his eyes began to fail him, I was able to act sometimes, in a sort of irregular, informal way, as his amanuensis. Although he had very little schooling and no college education, I was always singularly impressed with his strength and simplicity of diction, and with the unusual extent of his vocabulary. He spoke sometimes for hours almost in monosyllables, never failing to put the short right word in its proper place, and where it had the most effect. One night he wrote for me, in his old, feeble handwriting, twelve lines which he called a *catch*, in which he had only two words of more than one syllable and those were pure Anglo-Saxon. This was at the Century Club, December 7, 1888.

A dinner was given to him by the Authors' Club in New York in 1897, at which were present all the distinguished men of letters that could be gathered together.

It was a great event. He spoke very beautifully and very suitably, himself; and at the end of the dinner, when everything that could be said about him had been said by his many friends, and in the most charming way, I found myself called upon to reply to the toast of Mrs. Stoddard and Mr. Lorimer Stoddard, their son. I was entirely unprepared, and nothing was left me to add to the previous remarks; happily I was inspired, in speaking of Mr. Lorimer Stoddard, whom I had known since boyhood, to say that perhaps the boy who had just made a success as a playwright and an actor was, after all, the very best bit of work which Mr. Stoddard had given to the world; and it seemed to me that his must be a happy lot. Other men are proud of the fact that they are their father's sons, but Lorimer had done things which made his father proud of him. This touched the old man greatly, and when at the close of the symposium I went up to speak with Mrs. Stoddard—who with a number of ladies was sitting in the gallery of the hall—she said nothing, but kissed my cheek, and that was reward enough. I prompted the old man in his speech, and sat behind him. At the close of it he was overcome with exhaustion, and almost fell into my arms.

A propos of Stoddard and his lack of schooling and early education, I have been struck with the fact that a great number of American writers, early and late, of more or less distinction, have received no college training. Poe spent but one session at the University of

A Latch

I said to Fate— Let be,
Since I am done with thee:
Or heap upon my head
The ashes of the dead,
And hustle out of sight
The thing that once was Me.
For he was husbed [?] white,
And he is poor and old,—
Yes time his grave was made;
Then mattock fetch, and spade,
And let the bell be tolled:
And so, sweet Fool, good night

The Century   R H Stoddard
Decr 27th, 1888.

For my old friend Laurence Hutton
With best wishes. R H S

A LETTER FROM R. H. STODDARD

Virginia, and he was expelled by court-martial from West Point at the end of six months. Bryant was only one year at Williams; Stedman left Yale in his Sophomore year; Cooper left Yale as a Junior; William Winter's university career was confined to the Harvard Law School; while Mark Twain, Howells, Aldrich, Stockton, George W. Cable, R. Watson Gilder, Walt Whitman, Whitcomb Riley, Bunner, Hopkinson Smith, Charles Henry Webb (John Paul), Bret Harte, Joaquin Miller, Thomas Russell Sullivan, Artemus Ward, Edward Eggleston, Hamilton Gibson, John Burroughs, Harold Frederick, Howard Pyle, Thomas Janvier, James Parton, Buchanan Read, E. L. Youmans, Bronson Alcott, Charles Brockton Brown, Horace Greeley, Fitz-Green Halleck, Thomas Paine, Audubon, Rodman Drake, Bayard Taylor, John G. Whittier, John Howard Payne, George William Curtis, and Washington Irving, never went to college at all!

Of George William Curtis, in the later years of his life, I saw something, but not much—not nearly so much as I would have liked. I had read his earlier works in my boyhood as they first appeared, and I had inherited from my father, from whom I also inherited my love of *Trumps* and *Prue and I*, a very complete collection of the first editions of Curtis's books. This pleased and touched him, because, he said, he questioned very much if he possessed them himself. He made me very happy by writing on the fly-leaf of his *Washington Irving* a line of presentation in which he called me his "*confrère*"; and he pleased me almost as much once in print, when he said of some unimportant little essay of mine that he had discovered in it a touch of the manner and the sentiment of Charles Lamb. But unwittingly, one night, he was the cause to me of deep embarrassment and distress. The Harpers had given a farewell dinner to Mr. Charles Parsons, for so many years the conductor of their Art Department, at which were present the heads of the house, the editors of the periodicals, many contributors, and all the regular members of the editorial staff. Everybody had something to say in praise of Mr. Parsons, whom we all respected and revered. I was notified that I would be called upon to make a little speech; and I had prepared myself with great care, revolving certain little compliments in my mind.

After the coffee came the talk, more or less formal Mr. Harper spoke, Mr. Parsons replied. Mr. Charles Dudley Warner made a charming speech, and Mr. George William Curtis in direct succession came after him, saying things most beautiful, most kindly, most affectionate, most true, as no man but Mr. Curtis—the prince of orators—could have said them. And then, to my horror, was my own turn. I felt absolutely crushed. Everything I had thought of had gone from my mind and memory. I was, in a minute, to follow Mr. Curtis, and I had nothing to say, except to repeat what I had had no thought of repeating, that once, when asked who would be likely to take Mr. Curtis's

A NOTE FROM CHARLES READE

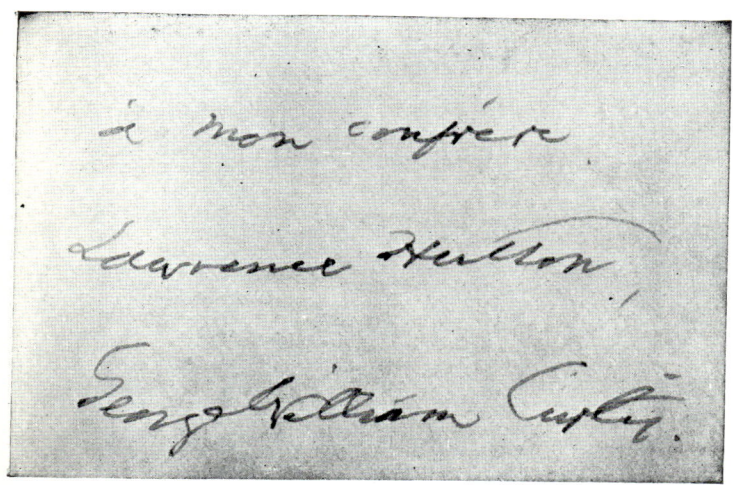

INSCRIPTION IN BOOK FROM GEORGE WILLIAM CURTIS

A Decision 427

place in the "Easy Chair," I had replied, that "plenty of men might succeed him but that nobody could take his place."

That night we walked up Fifth Avenue together from Delmonico's to the house of the friend in the upper part of the town with whom he was stopping. Mr. Curtis then told me a pretty little story I had never heard and which I have never heard since. Perhaps it is unwritten history.

Many years before, and after he had been with the Harpers for a long time, he received in midsummer a letter from the publisher of a magazine about to be started in a distant city, offering him—Mr. Curtis—the position of editor-in-chief at a salary quite double that which he was then receiving. He showed the letter to one of the original members of the Harpers firm and a founder of the house, with the remark that he had decided not to accept the offer, but that he felt that Mr. Harper ought to know that the offer had been made.

Mr. Harper replied to this effect:

"Don't decide rashly, George. This is a great compliment to you, and a very serious matter. Take the letter home with you and sleep over it for a night or two, and talk it over with Mrs. Curtis. We don't want you to go, but we can't afford to keep you for the handsome sum which these men are able to offer. Think it over carefully, and let me know your decision on Monday morning."

On the Monday morning Mr. Curtis laid upon Mr.

Harper's desk the unsealed letter containing his definite reply,—a polite refusal. Mr. Harper said :

"Is this final, George?"

"It is final. I have been with you a long time, I have been very happy here, I feel that I belong here, you have been very good to me, and I cannot go."

Mr. Harper said nothing, sealed the letter, stamped it, and gave it to a messenger to post. Mr. Curtis started to go up to the editorial room, when Mr. Harper overtook him, led him up to the cashier's desk, and said:

"Dating from the 1st of January last, Mr. Curtis's salary is to be increased an hundred per cent."

And Mr. Curtis's voice broke a little as he told me the tale.

Mr. Thomas B. Reed I had met occasionally, and casually, before we were thrown together for a month or six weeks during a cruise to the West Indies in the *Kanawah*, the steam yacht of Mr. Henry H. Rogers. The party was a small one, including Mark Twain, Dr. Clarence Rice, Mr. Augustus Payne, Mr. Wallace Foote, and of course Mr. Rogers himself.

Naturally, in our cramped but luxurious quarters, we were drawn very closely together, and upon Mr. Reed was enforced an intimacy with all of us which he could not have avoided if he had wished, and which to me was most agreeable. He asked me one day how far Theodore Parker—a man for whom he had great admiration—was known and read, if known and read at all, among the graduates of the University with which I was connected; and then he spoke of the ephemeral reputation of the great men who are great only during their own short lives, and in the minds of the few who really appreciate their greatness. He said that Parker's writings must have been familiar to Lincoln, as the famous Gettysburg Address clearly proved. And then he quoted, with his wonderful memory, a speech of Parker's delivered at an anti-slavery convention in Boston ten or twelve years before the outbreak of the Civil War, in which the clergyman said that ours "is a Government of all the people, by all the people, for all the people. A Government on the principles of eternal Justice, the unchanging law of God, for shortness' sake I will call it the idea of Freedom."

Reed thought that this suggested to Lincoln the great sentence with which his name will ever be associated: "A Government of the people, by the people, for the people, shall not perish from the earth." And he added that perhaps Parker himself based his own thrilling statement upon a speech made by Daniel Webster when Parker could not have been more than twenty years old, to the effect that "the people's Government is made for the people, made by the people, and is answerable to the people." His dates and his quotations were all from memory and spontaneously uttered in the course of unpremeditated conversation, and they all seem to have been correct.

Returning abruptly to Parker he said, in his epigrammatic way and with the familiar twinkle in his eye, that Parker to his mind was "of indubitable courage and originality, because he was almost the first man who attempted to raise hell with Hell, in public!"

Later, writing home from Jamaica Bay, I said:

"Since we shipped some Jamaica rum on board, of very fine and ancient quality, the ex-Speaker has made us occasional punches in the concoction of which he is said to be famous, and of the nature of which he is extremely proud. The results are good and not harmful, but the great charm of it all lies in watching the face of the manufacturer during the operation. He looks very much as Pickwick must have looked under similar circumstances. In appearance he is a sort of cross between Pickwick and Ben Butler, although unlike either of them in character and in disposition, except that he has some of the simplicity of the one and all the acuteness and originality of the other."

Still later, I spoke of a wet day upon one of the little islands, and of the spectacle of Pickwick-Reed in a very bright yellow so'wester cap and gown, suggesting the advertisements of Scott's Emulsion, to which naturally, with a good deal of laughter, his attention was called. He himself thought that it was all very funny until the sun came out—hot!

To any sort of personal display "Mr. Speaker"—as we called him—was particularly averse. On the occasion of the inauguration of Professor Wilson as President of the University of Princeton, Mr. Reed was one of the guests of the institution. He marched calmly and majestically with the other dignitaries of the nation in the procession, capped and gowned, but refusing utterly to wear the bright-coloured hood to which he was entitled, on the ground that it would make him look like a Knight of Pythias!

With Mark Twain, Mr. Edmund Clarence Stedman, and Mr. Samuel Elliot, he was our personal guest during those same inauguration performances, remaining with us for a short time, and going from us almost directly to Washington, to die in a few days. It was, therefore, the last visit he ever made; and almost the last letter he ever wrote was to me, thanking Mrs. Hutton for the care she had taken of him:

"25 BROAD STREET, 13 November, 1902.
"DEAR MR. HUTTON:

"I heard from Mr. Elliot that you had reformed and become a man. It is a good thing to try, especially if you keep it up. I have tried the beginnings of it myself, but cannot speak as one having authority about the prolongation thereof; keep on, and tell us what you think of it.

"I wish I could express the pleasure which the visit to your home gave me, as well as all the rest. It will always be a delightful memory to recall the way in which Mrs. Hutton personally conducted me and moved me without jostling me at all, in this direction and that.

"I pride myself on my skill in finding it out, for no less skilful a man than myself could ever have known it. Do give her the assurance of my personal regard and good wishes.

"I am glad to hear that Mrs. Clemens is on the road to health for that means so much to Mark.

"With best wishes for yourself,
"Truly yours,
"T. B. REED."

Just before that memorable yachting party broke up, there was given at my house a dinner to some twelve or fourteen men. There were present, besides the house-party, Mr. E. C. Benedict, Mr. Richard Watson Gilder, Mr. J. Henry Harper, Colonel Harvey, Mr. George Armour, Mr. Allison Armour, Mr. Cleveland, and others. The Ex-President and the Ex-Speaker sat facing each other, one at the head and one at the foot of the table; and as Mr. Gilder afterwards wrote: "It was the greatest affair at which I ever assisted. It was so much more than amusing; it was so deeply instructive, and at the end so thrilling and so ennobling. It was your tact and right feeling that made the climax, that impromptu outburst of Cleveland. He was never more himself, never more afire with righteous fury, never more wise or nobly convincing. Indeed, the whole occasion was a great treat: I may say, a remarkable and unique event. How many scores of dinners, public or private, have I not assisted at: yet I can think of none of its kind that surpassed it in substance or that equalled it quite."

With such men and with such speakers, perfectly free to express themselves, absolutely sure that everything said was said in a confidence that would be respected—that the reporter was pre-eminently absent,—the dinner could not help being a "remarkable and unique event."

The two great statesmen, representing everything that was good in the two great rival parties, holding each other in the highest regard and respect, had never, perhaps, been so closely together for so many hours—for we were at the table from eight o'clock till long after midnight,—and it was a little startling to some of the onlookers, listening naturally with all their ears, to see how nearly alike the two men spoke and thought upon all great public and moral questions.

I told Mr. Reed more than once during that famous voyage of ours that if I could shut my eyes and my ears to the material differences in their personal appearance, and in their utterance, I would suppose the President was speaking the words that I heard; and he said to me just as the voyage was coming to a close, after one of our long talks:

"What are your politics, anyway? You came on board this boat a month or two ago and avowed yourself, openly and defiantly, a Democrat,—no Mugwump, but a Democrat,—and this to a party made up exclusively of Republicans. What are your politics, anyway?"

I said:

"Mr. Speaker, since I have been with you and have imbibed your views and impressions, I have come to the conclusion that I must be a sort of Grover-Cleveland-Thomas-B.-Reed-demi-Republicrat."

Henry Bunner was a man I would have nothing to do with for years. It was a case of reciprocal Dr. Fell. We did not like each other, and we neither of us could tell the reason why. We met constantly at the theatres—we were both enthusiastic "First-nighters"—but we never looked at each other if we could help it, and, of course, we never spoke. We had many friends and acquaintances in common, and very often we escaped an introduction by the merest chance, or by the most elaborate mutual avoidance. He always thought of me, when he permitted himself to think of me, as "Play-bill Hutton," because of my interest in, and my collection of, theatre-programmes; and I never allowed myself to think of him at all. The reason why I cannot imagine now. At last, one night we were thrown violently at each other. It was in 1878, at a large reception. I knew almost nobody. Bunner knew everybody. He saw my situation, which was trying—an outsider among a large party of intimates,—and too loyal to his hosts, and instinctively too much of a gentleman to see a man neglected in that house, or a stranger in any house wandering about forlorn and

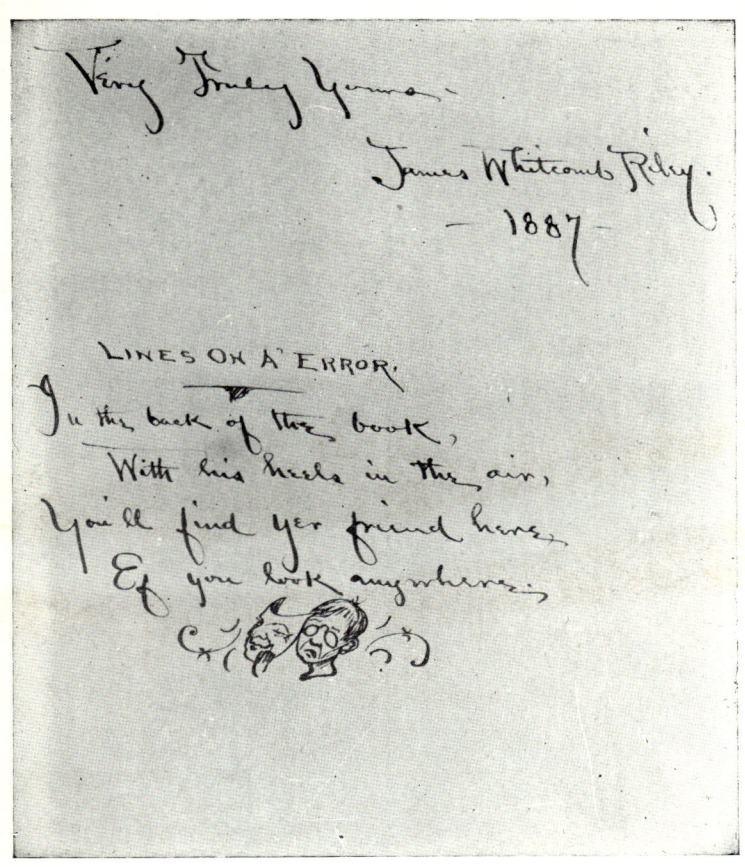

A PAGE FROM THE HUTTON GUEST-BOOK

alone, he came up and asked me if I would smoke a cigarette and take a glass of sherry in the dining-room. I replied, promptly, that I would—if there were no cigars and no whiskey! And from that moment we were friends. We never passed each other by again.

When my mother died, and I lived alone for some years, I never dined alone at home. James O'Brien, at one time steward of the Arcadian Club, had taken a lease of the restaurant in the Westmoreland Hotel, on the corner of Fourth Avenue and Seventeenth Street, in New York, and there, when I had no other engagement, I took my evening meal. Bunner began to drop in now and then, and later more regularly. Finally our nightly meeting became an established custom; a large round table in the bay-window was reserved for us—always—and one of us was very sure to be found at it; usually both of us. When this fact became generally known, many of the bright young journalists of his acquaintance made it their trysting-place after dinner, if not at dinner; and good was the talk that round table heard. Mr. Brander Matthews, who lived in Eighteenth Street, not far away, would look in after his (then little) daughter had gone to bed; and among the men we saw and heard there were Mr. Clarence C. Buel, Mr. John Moran, Mr. James L. Ford, Mr. Edgar Fawcett, Mr. Henry Gallup Paine, Mr. Francis Saltus, Mr. Munkitrick, Mr. George Edgar Montgomery, Mr. William J. Henderson, Mr. Ripley Hitchcock, Mr.

Julian Magnus, Mr. A. E. Watrous, and many others who have since made good names for themselves.

All this came to an end for me when I married in 1885, and for Bunner when he married shortly after.

Bunner and I went often together to the theatres during this period; we were members together of the Authors Club, of the International Copyright League, of The Kinsmen; and in common we had many tastes and interests. He read me in advance all the poems afterward collected together as the *Airs from Arcady*. We talked for hours over *Love in Old Clothes*, the best, perhaps, of his tales, and a little bit of work which cost him infinite care, and thought, and labour. He was then helping to establish the edition of *Puck* in English —now a power in the land—and working hard at it. He was very quick of insight, and remarkably ready of utterance and expression, even in verse. I remember stopping one day into the *Puck* office, then in a cross street off lower Broadway, to lunch with him by appointment. As we were going out of the editorial rooms the printer's devil entered with a process-picture of a commonplace young woman, to illustrate which Bunner was asked to contribute a "stickful" of text— and at once. He lighted a fresh cigarette, stepped up to somebody else's desk, and, more rapidly than I could have copied them out, set down sixteen or twenty rhythmical lines which would scan and would parse, and were very fair "poetry"—as such things go. He did not sign them; and he said lightly that that was an every-day occurrence and of no moment.

Bunner was equally ready with his occasional poems of dedication, inscription, or the like. In our Guest-Book he transcribed the following impromptu lines:

TO LARRY HUTTON

> You may write it LAURENCE, all you please,
>   Your name to Fame to marry;
> But you 're only whistling down the breeze,
>   For folks will call you LARRY.
> And if the reason you inquire,
>   I 'll tell you all I know;
> Why is Joseph Jefferson, Esquire,
>   Called Jo?
>
> You may spell your LAURENCE with a U,
>   Till it 's Scotch as a green glengarry,
> But other folks are naming too;
>   And your name they say is LARRY.
> And if you 're curious in the least
>   To know what that comes from;
> Why was T. Bowling, late deceased,
>   Called TOM?

H. C. BUNNER.

October 19, 1893.

He and Mr. Telford and I spent together, at the Westmoreland and in Bunner's rooms, the last evening of my single life. He had heard that luck would be insured if the groom, on the occasion of his marriage, would wear "something old, something new, something borrowed, and something blue," He urged, therefore, my appearance next day in a pair of socks procured especially by him for me. One was absolutely unworn, the other had seen service and was darned. But they were both *blue*. And I *must borrow* them. Mr. Telford, I remember, loaned me a necktie for the same purpose; and both of those dear boys were married, when their time came, in something blue that was borrowed from me.

Mrs. Bunner I knew as Miss Alice Learned long before she was his wife. Happy was the day for him, and happy for her, when she became Mrs. Henry Bunner. We sent to her at New London a travelling-clock as a wedding gift, to which I attached a card bearing these lines:

> For Old Times' sake
>   Will you and H. C. B.
> At this time take
>   The Time from mine and me?
>
> Time is, Time was,
>   Let Time be old or new,
> The Times for us
>   Are High Old Times with you."

To this, in similar verse, Miss Learned replied:

> I lack the time, in spite of time from you,
> To write the heartfelt thanks I feel are due.
> But every passing hour, while time endures,
> Shall speak to me and mine, of you and yours.

And he and his and I and mine had many happy times together for many years. There never was a break, or the shadow of a break in our friendship. He was very strong in his likes and in his dislikes— often without good reason. And I like to think now that, when we came to know each other, he always liked me, whatever his reason may have been. A more disinterestedly loyal man to his friends I never met, nor a man more devotedly attached to his own family. He was always sympathetic, always ready to help, always full of encouragement, never sparing of his words of praise for the work of others. His laugh was hearty and contagious, and how quick was his appreciation of everything that was good all the world who reads can tell. He was an excellent listener, and he was an admirable talker upon all sorts of subjects, grave and gay. He had an unusual knowledge of books and of their contents, particularly of the works of the poets, ancient and modern. He quoted readily, correctly, appropriately, and at length; and if one wanted to remember a line or a sonnet of any of the half-forgotten men of the period of the very beginning of English verse, Bunner could always say where it was, whose it was, and exactly what it was, and why.

As in the case of many of the brilliant men with whom I have been lucky enough to have come into intimate contact, I have, unfortunately, let most of Bunner's best talk fly up the chimney. I dreaded to appear as a chiel among them taking notes, and the happy thoughts, the flashes of wit, the bright turns of expression, the bits of epigram and of wisdom I would now give much to have preserved went out into the thin air long ago, and melted away.

One of the most touching and pathetic incidents in his career is the story of his Lost Joke. It was in the old days of our Westmoreland *café* life, when, in my absence, Bunner found but one man at the table—a fellow of a peculiarly clear mind. He asked Bunner some simple question, as "Did you come up-town in the Fourth Avenue or Sixth Avenue Line?" To which Bunner replied in an equally commonplace way, as, "No, I walked." Bunner, at the end of many years, could remember neither the question nor the answer nor the nature of them; but the words he uttered, whatever they may have been, were received with shouts of laughter. Bunner did not know why, and he never knew why. He saw nothing funny in them—at that time or later. And he entirely forgot what they were and what prompted them. But his interlocutor pronounced it the best thing that Bunner had ever said, and he laughed over it until he wept, and then he laughed again. It was to him the acme of humorous expression. He was too diffident to repeat it, whatever it was, because he thought that Bunner said it intentionally, and wanted him to say it in his turn, and so, somehow, commit himself; and he never told it; and he died; and Bunner never discovered the joke on his own account. He was very miserable at the thought that his most sublime effort of wit was unrecognised by himself, and went into the ear of the only man who ever heard it and who ever appreciated it, and was there kept for ever from Bunner and the rest of the world. And poor Bunner could not even think what it was about.

It is a subject for a tragedy, but it has never been written.

We had "high old times" with the Bunners some eight or nine years later in London. It was their first visit to the Old World; and I had much pleasure in taking them about the town I loved so well, although my own pleasure, I am afraid, was greater than his. He had developed symptoms of a rabid Anglophobic nature, and the present-day Englishman seemed to be stepping upon every sensitive nerve in his system. He had succeeded in fretting all the skin off his mental body, and he was never so happy as when he could taunt some Englishman into rubbing salt into his wounds. He left St. Paul's Cathedral in disgust because upon the monument to Cornwallis there was every allusion to that person's worth, his valour, and his victories, and no reference whatever to the important fact (to us), but not creditable (to him), that he had surrendered his sword to Washington at Yorktown! At Westminster, Bunner rebelled against the great crowd of men in the Abbey who were nobodies but princes or royal dukes. He was impressed, however, at standing so close to the mortal parts of so many immortal men, and he was subdued and respectful as we sat in the Poets' Corner. "There are some good and great Englishmen, after all, Harry," I said.

"Yes," he replied, "there are three classes of Englishmen whom I can endure—the Irish, the Scotch, and the dead!"

Bunner was a poor correspondent, not fond of writing or answering letters, even after he learned to dictate. But when he did write, he wrote as he talked and as he felt, directly from the heart. Some of his personal notes to me, covering a period of nearly twenty years, may serve to show to those who knew him only as the editor of *Puck* and as the author of the *Midge* and of many pieces of charming verse what sort of man this Bunner was to his friends:

"NUTLEY, August 28, 1891.

"I am just back from Canada, and I don't care who calls me an Englishman so long as nobody calls me a French Canadian. That would call for bloodshed.

"All the same, Quebec is the delight of my liver, and the hostelry of Dennis O'Hare is the Home of my Heart. That is where 'the whole house, sorr, is mohogany; and none but the gintry lives in this quarter. No, sorr—onless *this* house—only gintlemen, sorr!'

"I have brought you a little copper-plate, torn from a book, of William Charles Macready, in armour, mighty prodigious; the old *Albion* print of Ellen Tree, as *Ion*, in all her legs; and a picture of Napoleon, not in your collection, I think. It is a hand-painted print published about Waterloo time, showing N. B. mounted on a prancing charger, leading on his troops to ignominious defeat.

"The Missus joins me to-morrow. She is at New London gathering in the children.

"Why can't you and Mrs. Hutton leave the inclement heights of Onteora, and come and frivol with us for a space at Nutley? You shall have all the rooms you want, and every opportunity to loaf or to work, as may please you.

"Please, Mrs. Hutton, make him say yes! . . . Now what is the matter with finishing up the season at Nutley? If you want to be busy I can be busy too. Give our love to your Lady, and suggest to her this means of breaking off the Onteora habit."

"February 5, 1892.

"It is an elegant gilt-edged joy to catch *you* on an unanswered letter; but coming across this sheet of paper reminds me that I sent you its fellow some time in August or September, a few days after my return from Quebec, telling you I had picked up three agèd prints in that city, which I thought would please your fancy, and that they were lying in the office waiting to know whether they should go to you to Thirty-fourth Street or to Onteroarer.

"Since then various events, including seven grips under our humble roof, have conspired to make me forget the three gems of art. One is Miss Ellen Tree, in a dress-reform skirt; one is W. C. Macready, thirsting for somebody's gore; and the third is a Napoleon, which will give your collection the jim-jams. I will mail them to you.

"I was very sorry that we could n't hit it off with Mr. [Ripley] Anthony. The more so, that I had seen his picture at the Academy, and had taken a great shine to it. But I 'm afraid our style of pen-work was a little too stiff for him. In fact, if a man does that kind of work, he can't do anything else. But *he* can paint; there is no doubt about that!

"How are you all? We are well and I am working. I have a sort of a novelette on hand, two or three short stories, and some other stuff; but of course I am away behind with everything since that grip hit me.

"I bought me *The Literary Landmarks of Edinburgh*, and I read them too. What are you going to Landmark next? You can't do much with New York, but you can do something with the suburbs—Sunnyside, Yonkers, Long Island Sound, Roslyn, etc. It would probably not be used as a hand-book by a throng of eager tourists, but it would make mighty interesting reading. And it would give you a chance to become as familiar with the outskirts of the city you live in as you are familiar with the outskirts of London and other second-hand towns. And when you push your way up the Passaic Valley, where Irving, and Hoffman, and their crowd used to sport, and where Frank Forester lived on a desert island, you might push a little farther, and come and see a fellow named Bunner, who lives up that way, in the House of Spare Bedrooms. He is said to be of an amiable and thirsty disposition.

"Mr. Samuel Pepys was cut for the stone, at Mr. Turner's, in Salisbury Court, on March 26, 1658, and he never missed an annual opportunity of reverting to the agreeable subject. It may interest you to know that January 16, 1892, was the first anniversary of my swearing off on cigarettes; and that whereas in January of 1891 my trousers were 32 waist measurement, they are now 34, and I take great comfort in a pipe.

"We've vaccinated a baby to-day. We keep a pig, two dogs, two cats, and we are contemplating a donkey; the dogs are mixed in their ancestry, but they do not bite.

"With our united love we are yours,

"H. C. B. & Co."

Under date of November 19, 1893, he wrote:

"I am in for anything to do Irving honour, in The Kinsmen or out. I think he ought to get a laurel wreath, in silver, or some such enduring tribute this trip; for his 'Becket' is one of the biggest things I ever saw, and, besides, he deserves great credit for being an Englishman, and yet conducting himself white; which must be the toughest job in the way of acting that any man ever undertook. Nor have I any objection to doing a little of the work—what little I *can* do as a hard-worked suburban.

"I wish, also, you would think very thinkingly about doing something for Brander, and in a general way, too; not through any one club, or through the college, or through any magazine gang. He has been good to all sorts of people, and they ought all to have a chance to get back at him. As far as I know, he has never had any sort of dinner given to him—outside of private affairs, I mean—except that little one we gave him at the Brunswick, almost ten years ago.

"We ought to do something very good, and not in the least bit *cliquey*, for him. To do that, I will work all you please, and will, if necessary, come into town to do the work.

"Love from ourn to yourn."

This led to the very successful dinner given to Mr. Matthews at Sherry's in the month of December, 1893. Mr. Charles Dudley Warner presided; Mark Twain, Mr. Stedman, Mr. Howells, and Professor Sloane, then of Princeton, spoke. And Bunner himself, who read a tender and characteristic poem, was as happy over it all, and as proud, as if he had been the guest of the occasion.

"NUTLEY, February 3, 1894.

"In compliance with the terms of the circular, just received, concerning the supper of The Kinsmen, I enclose you my check for 'Four Dollars without wine.'

I am glad that I am not required to send wine with the check, for I doubt if I could find any dry enough to pass the United States Post Office, as permissible mail matter."

I saw Bunner a week or so before he went to California, when I was more than shocked at his condition. He never had enough physical strength to support his active brain, and he was very feeble, although in many ways he was the same old Bunner. We parted at the little station at Nutley, and as the train passed on he waved a cheerful " God be with you." But my vision was blurred, and I saw him dimly through my tears.

We met for the last time but a little while before the end came. He had not lost his indomitable spirit, and he was full of hope. He told me the plots of stories he intended to write, spoke of his plans for future work, and, as he himself expressed it, he was determined to " pull through."

I wonder when and how soon we are to meet again?

INDEX

A

Abbey, Edwin, caricature of, 303; illustrations of, 321; Tile Club likeness of, 414

Abbey, Westminster, with Booth in, 74; the stone to Newton in, 188; tomb of Queen Elizabeth in, 190; statue of Disraeli in, 195; Mary Anderson and Dean Stanley in, 313; effect on John Fiske of, 345

Actors, the standing of, 62; anecdotes regarding, 63, 65; children of, 65; Booth's opinion on the art of, 85; reminiscences by, 115, 116; article on, 142

Alcott, Louisa M., meeting with, 381

Aldrich, Thomas Bailey, near neighbours, 12; friendship of Uncle John with, 13; Barrett-Aldrich anecdote, 13; Marjory Daw, 13; joke about the Washington portrait, 83; as charter member of The Players, 86; as originator of the name, 87; joke on the trials of Job, 163; letters by, 303

American Actor Series, editing of, 262; royalties on, 275

Anderson, Mary, Dickens pilgrimage of, 309; in London, 311; courtesy of, 312; in Westminster Abbey with, 313; at Stratford with, 314; a pretty scene, 323

Articles, first published, 32; on Lester Wallack, 106; magazine, 133; fate of, 136; on actors, 142

Art of story telling, Mark Twain's opinion of, 6; Kipling's art of, 412

Authors Club, a meeting at the, 411

Autographs, collectors of, 289; begging letters for 291, 292; demands for famous, 296; the stealing of, 299, 301; valuable, 304; Bryant's, 305; Irving's, 306; Mary Anderson's, 310; with new hat, 405

B

Baillie, Joanna, a strange ignorance about, 270

Barrett, Lawrence, Aldrich's bon-mot regarding, 13; as charter member of The Players, 86; fondness of Booth for, 88; shock to Booth of the death of, 89; as author, 94; illegibility of writing by, 95; antecedents of, 95, 96; characteristic of, 97, 98, 99; portrait by Millet of, 98; illness of, 99; family relations of, 100; friendship of Laurence Hutton with the family of, 100; naming of

Barrett (*Continued*)
the Millet baby by, 101, 102, at Maidenhead, 103; effect of Lord Houghton's reminiscence on, 104; article on, 143; price of death mask of, 180; coincidence of letter by, 180; sentiment regarding mask of, 181; at Stratford with, 182; at Stoke Pogis with, 263; request for autograph of, 297; naming of The Kinsmen by, 325

Beethoven, the two masks of, 172; place in the British Phrenological Society of, 173

Behind the scenes, 61

Bentham, mention by Combe of, 178; posthumous fate of, 179

Black, William, caricature of, 303; as Kinsman, 316; personality of, 317; the apartments of, 318; first meeting with, 319; the writing of *Judith Shakespeare* by, 321; Carlyle's remark to, 321; letters from, 322, 323, 324

Bonapart, Napoleon, recognition by the extraordinary man, 54; explanation of the recognition, 56; interest of O'Reilly in, 164; the Antomarchi mask of, 165; the last hours of, 166

Booth, Edwin, engagement of Ward by, 66; off and on the stage, 68; letter about his wife's illness, 70; last portrait of, 71; first meeting with, 71; at Saratoga with, 72; daily companionship with, 73; in the cloisters of Westminster, 74; sense of humour, 74; nonsense verse by, 75;
generosity of, 76, 77, 82; friendship with Black Betty, 79; *Pinafore* pun, 80; Marjory Telford and, 81; sympathy of, 81, 82; as man and as actor, 83; tribute by Jefferson to, 83; opinion on the art of the actor, 85; tribute to his father, 86; devotion to The Players, 88; shock of Barrett's death to, 88; last engagement of, 89; article on, 143; first meeting with Ben Caunt of, 212; effect of Lincoln mask on, 212; taking of the masks of, 213; gift of Burke mask by, 216; obituary of, 230; as Kinsman, 329

Boswell, James, burial-place of, 273

Boucicault, Dion, perfection of the mask of, 193; successful plays of, 194

Brougham, Lord, cast of head of, 149; the extraordinary nose of, 208

Brown, Dr. John, meeting with, 286; personality of, 287

Bruce, Robert, cast of head of, 149; exhumation of, 152, 153

Brunel, Junior, builder of *Great Western*, 162

Bull Dog, origin of Princeton, 148; likeness to Aunt Jane, 149

Bunner, H. C., early acquaintance with, 434; dinners with, 435; poems by, 436, 437; marriage of, 438; lost joke of, 440; letters by, 442–446

Burke, Edmund, gift by Booth of mask of, 216

Burns, Robert, cast of the head of, 149; exhumation

Index

Burns (*Continued*)
of, 152, 154; the window of, 279; Scott and, 280
Burr, Aaron, explanation regarding mask of, 168; the personality of, 169; an unfortunate resemblance to, 169; suggestion to Bentham by, 178
Butler, burial-place of, 272

C

Cable, George W., at Hartford, 417
Calhoun, John C., possession of mask of, 167; the making of the mask of, 170
Canova, mask of, 179
Carlyle, Thomas, introduction to Owen of, 163; possession of Cromwell mask by, 173; cast of hand of, 226
Caunt, Ben, 151; mask of, 211; alleged association with Byron, 212
Cavour, price of mask of, 180; discovery of the mask of, 184
Chalmers, Rev. Thomas, finding of the mask of, 180
"Charley," first acquaintance with, 25; his devotion, 26, 28; association with "Andrew," 27
Cheshire Cheese, The, false association with Johnson, 274
Chopin, cast of hand of, 229
Cibber, Colley, contradiction of evidence regarding, 266
Clay, Henry, interest of sculptors in mask of, 167
Cleveland, Grover, at dinner with, 432
Coleridge, Samuel Taylor, mask of, 159; interest by Ernest Hartley Coleridge in mask of, 160; resemblance of Ernest Hartley Coleridge to, 161; uncertainty regarding mask of, 168
Combe, George, printed lectures of, 152; possession of the Cromwell mask by, 173; burial-place of, 174; mention of Bentham mask by, 178
Criticism, spirit of, 122; professional and domestic, 140; instance of, 141; impersonal, 142, 143; sarcastic, 145; stupid, 147
Cromwell, Oliver, cast of head of, 149; the two masks of, 173; wax mask of, 174
Curran, John Philpot, cast of head of, 149; personality of, 216; likeness by Lawrence of, 217
Curtis, George William, acquaintance with, 425; courtesy of Harpers to, 427
Custom-house, duties exacted by, 178; damage done by, 178

D

Dante, examples of casts of, 189; inaccuracies of guide books regarding, 190
Dickens, Charles, 2; style of, 29; readings by, 32; as actor, 35; a scene from, 37; as a reader, 39–42; Christmas Carol, 43; letters, 44; as a man, 44; as a poet, 44; lasting qualities of, 45; as a religious man, 47; quotations from, 48–50; explanation of Tom All-Alone's, 52; the extraordinary man and, 56; Owen's friendship with

Index

Dickens (*Continued*)
162; a pilgrimage, 309;
No. 15 Buckingham
Street, 318; the nuts of
Barcelona, 353; Mrs.
Field's acquaintance with,
357; as a hero, 368
Dickens, the younger, discussion regarding Tom
All-Alone's, 38; dinner
with, 38; friendship with,
39; at Osgood dinner, 332
Disraeli, Benjamin, fate of
the mask of, 195
du Maurier, George, request
for autograph letter by,
297; Laurence Hutton's
meeting with, 334; letters
by, 335; the Whistler,
trouble with, 338
D'Urfey, Tom, mural tablet
to, 55

E

Early reading, 28; fact and
fiction, 29; *David Copperfield*, 43; *Pendennis*, 43; a
course of, 123
Edwards, Harry, accident to
mask of, 196; pursuits of,
196; interest in portraits
in plaster of, 197
Egyptian Princess, mummy
hand of, 229
Eliot, George, letter of Fiske
regarding, 303; Charles
Reade's opinion of, 342;
Fiske's comment on, 350
Emerson, Ralph Waldo,
meeting with, 373
Errors, typographical, 253,
255; guidebook, 272
Ex Libris, 257

F

Farragut, Loyal, 129
Fiction, mothers in. 124

Field, Kate, Dr. John Brown
and, 287; personality of,
382; the bequests of, 384
Fisher, Clara, 116; newspaper verse about, 117
Fiske, John, size of the head
of,170; story of Voltaire by,
179; letters by, 303; first
visit to England, 344; at
Stratford, 346; in Paris,
346; letters from, 348;
peculiarities of, 352; Latin
motto of, 355
Fitz-Gerald, Edward, bookplate of, 404
Florence, William J., as Captain Cuttle, 36; death of,
36; as charter member of
The Players, 87; versatility
of, 109; the last joke of,
110; friendship with Mrs.
Kendal, 110; the pallbearers of,111; Guest-Book
verse by, 111; last visit to
The Players, 112; tribute
to women by McCullough
and, 114; article on, 143
France, Henry IV. of, exhumation of, 152; cast of
face of, 154
Franklin, Benjamin, mask
of, 200; authenticity of
mask of, 201; burial-place
of, 202
Frost, Arthur B., at Tile
Club with Vedder, 414

G

Garrick, David, coloured
print of, 55; allusion by
Lord Houghton to, 104;
Rogers account of, 105;
mask of, 206
Gilbert, Mrs. G. H., as Hester
Dethridge, 122
Goethe, cast of hand of, 224
Goldsmith, Oliver, burial-place of, 273

Index 453

Gower, John, burial-place of, 274
Grant, General, anecdote of Jefferson and, 91; the mounting of the mask of, 170; the two casts of, 175
Great, Frederick the, 151; unusual detail of the cast of, 170; royal dignity of, 171

H

Hands, collection of casts of, 223; Voltaire and Whitman, 223; Lincoln, Thackeray, and Goethe, 224, 225; Duke of Wellington, 225
Harte, Bret, talk by Mark Twain about, 407; popularity of, 408; and Mark Twain, 409
Haydon, injuries done to the mask of, 177
Hood, Tom, *The Bridge of Sighs*, 356
Houghton, Lord, reminiscences by, 104
Hunt, William, cast of hand of, 228
Hutton, John, financial relations with, 18, 23; Saint-Gauden's likeness of, 19; death of, 27; study of fiction with, 29; dedication to, 60; interest in casts of, 150; the hero of, 179

I

Irving, Henry, Mr. Sherry's likeness of, 21; as Dombey, 36; generosity of, 66; Jefferson's message to, 93; autograph letter by, 307; Kinsman "bone," 328

J

James, Henry, at Copyright League meeting, 415
Jefferson, Joseph, as successor of Booth in presidency of The Players, 83; tribute to Booth, 84; as charter member of The Players, 88; letter regarding the death of Booth, 90; forgetfullness of, 91; anecdote of Grant and, 91; Fourth of July verse, 93; verse on himself, 93; identification of Laurence Hutton by, 94; story of "Billy" Florence by, 110; greeting of Mrs. Maeder by, 118; obituary of, 232; verse by, 406

K

Kean, Edmund, mask of, 206; burial-place of, 207
Keats, John, expression of cast of, 176; opinions regarding the mask of, 177
Keller, Helen, the hand of Whittier and, 227; cast of hand of, 227; first meeting with, 384; education of, 386; Mark Twain and, 390; letters by, 397
Kingsley, Henry, funeral of, 130, 132
Kinsmen, The, initial idea of, 325; "bone," 328; membership of, 329; du Maurier at, 334
Kipling, Rudyard, basis of the *Recessional*, 11; the short stories of, 412; meeting with, 413

L

Lamb, Charles, enjoyment of the taking of mask of

Index

Lamb (*Continued*)
Wordsworth, 176; ignorance of clergyman regarding, 269
Landlord, the crazy, 103
Lawrence, Sir Thomas, likeness of Curran by, 217; mask of, 217
Leopardi, personality of, 185; portraits of, 186
Life, the literary, anecdote of, 135; remuneration of, 136; anecdote by Mrs. Wiggin of, 137; trials of, 138; methods of, 233; certain details of, 236; duties of, 240; curiosities of, 244; demands made by, 248; typesetters' part in, 253; partnership in, 261; fame attending, 281; an instance of fame in, 317
Lincoln, Abraham, effect on Booth of mask of, 212; taking of the two masks of, 213; Mr. Volk's description of, 214; cast of the hand of, 224; finding of the cast, 225; Helen Keller's recognition of death mask of, 395
Lincoln, "Bob," 129
Liszt, obtaining the mask of, 216
Literary Landmarks of Edinburgh, The, 277; details of the collecting of notes for, 279, 280
Literary Landmarks of London, The, 156; origin of title, 256; first suggestion regarding, 264; the writing of, 266; difficulties of research for, 267
Literary Landmarks of (The), Venice, Florence, Rome, Jerusalem, 276
Longfellow, Henry W., acquaintance with, 369; tribute to, 370; Arthur Brooks and, 371; the daughters of, 372; New Year's party with, 373
Louise, Queen of Prussia, authenticity of mask of, 170; the beauty of, 171
Lowell, James Russell, first meeting with, 364; his love for his trees, 365; an improbable event, 366
Lynde, Francis Stetson, 23

M

Mabie, Hamilton W., 23
Mail, The Evening, connection with, 58; staff of, 119; letters to, 123
Malibran, Madame, authenticity of mask of, 183; false mask of, 222
Man, an extraordinary, 51; recollections of Dickens, 52; recollections of the Duke of Wellington, 53; recognition of Napoleon's face, 54; his explanation, 56
Marat, mask of, 204; burial-place of, 205
Mark Twain, opinion of story telling, 6; at the Irving dinner, 22; as charter member of The Players, 87; saying about mothers by, 186; Kinsmen initiation of, 326; Helen Keller and, 391; Bret Harte and, 407; George W. Cable and, 417; stories about the children of, 418; letters from, 419; Corbett and, 420
Mason, William, friendship of Celia Thaxter and, 380
McClellan, General, meeting with, 128
McCullough, John, as Othello, 62; phonograph rendering

Index 455

McCullough (*Continued*)
of "The Ravings of," 113;
mental affliction of, 113,
114; tribute to women by,
114; article on, 143; in the
"scullery" with, 198; belief in Shakespeare of, 199
McElligott, Dr., method of
teaching, 15; method of
reporting, 16
Mendelssohn, Felix Bartholdi,
death of, 171; contemporary allusion to taking
of the mask of, 172
Miller, Joaquin, eccentricities of, 358, 359, 360; meeting of Josie with, 361
Millet, Frank, portrait of
Barrett by, 98; naming of
the son of, 101, 102; McCullough leaving the studio
of, 113; relative sums paid
to, 277; dinner at Broadway with, 331
Mirabeau, mask of, 204;
burial-place of, 205
Montague, Henry J., death
of, 107; personal charm of,
108; anecdote of the topical song, 108; the last
spoken words of, 109
Moore, "Tom," biography of
Sheridan by, 156; authenticity of the cast of, 159
Morris, Clara, first appearance of, 122
Mulford, Prentice, love affair
of, 362; characteristics of,
363

N

Napoleon, the Third, peculiarity of the mask of, 163;
interest of O'Reilly in, 164;
morning walks of, 164;
mounting of the mask of,
171
Newspaper fakes, 120, 121,
122; London Letters, 131

Newton, Sir Isaac, 151; uncertainty regarding mask
of, 168; bust by Roubiliac
of, 187; burial-place of, 188

O

O'Reilly, John Boyle, personality of, 163; joke by
Aldrich on the name of,
163; interest in Napoleon
masks, of, 164
Osgood, James R., at Maidenhead, 103; interest in articles on *Portraits in Plaster*, 151; as a Kinsman,
327; dinner given by, 333
Owen, Sir Richard, life mask
of, 162

P

Paine, Thomas, authenticity
of mask of, 209
Palmerston, Lord, perfection
of the mask of, 193; price
paid for mask of, 194; typographical error regarding, 253
Partnership, A Literary, 261
Pius IX., purchase of mask
of, 184; funeral services of,
185
Plaster, Portraits in, origin of
title, 258
Players, The, 62; gift by
Booth to, 82; origin of, 86;
the naming of, 87; inauguration of, 88
Plays and Players, 60; origin
of title, 256
Portraits in Plaster, 148;
dearth of literature on,
151; difficulties of research
on, 152; lectures of Combe
on, 152; sentiment regarding, 181; enthusiasm of
collecting, 184; processes
in making of, 189; occasional misrepresentation of,

Portraits (*Continued*)
199; Washington's objection to, 203; negro type of, 217; process of, 218; opinion of Laurence Hutton regarding, 219; collecting of, 220; method of exhibiting, 221; money value of, 222; anecdote about money value of, 222; origin of the title, 258

R

Reade, Charles, letter by, 342
Recipe Book, The Authors', 293
Reed, Thomas B., on the yachting trip, 429; last letter of, 431; meeting with Cleveland, 432
Robespierre, authenticity of mask of, 204
Root, Elihu, 23
Rossetti, Dante Gabriel, opinions regarding the mask of, 214; cast of hand of, 226
Russell, Horace, 23

S

Sailor, anecdote of old, 146
Saint-Gaudens, brooch likeness of John Hutton, 19; opinion on mask of Clay by, 167; opinion regarding Lincoln mask of, 213; finding of the hands of Lincoln by, 225; hand of Stevenson by, 227
Schiller, story of the cast of, 172
School days, end of, 17
Scotch, nomenclature, 125; local information, 280; specimens of wit, 284
Scott, Sir Walter, proportion of the face of, 191; death mask of, 192; the last drive of, 193; *Old Mortality*, 283; relationship with, 284; crayon likeness of, 285; anecdote about the writings of, 375
Shakespeare, William, Lord Houghton's connecting link, 104; the mounting of the mask of, 170; fondness of Barrett for, 182; cast of the bust of, 190; controversy regarding likeness of, 191; description by John Aubrey of, 192; belief of actors in, 199; the burial-place of, 315; the country of, 315
Sheridan, General, cast of head of, 149; confusion with Richard Brinsley Sheridan by Mr. Kruell, 158
Sheridan, Richard Brinsley, 155; circumstances of the death of, 156; cast of the hand of, 156; Savile Club legend regarding, 157; confusion with General Sheridan by Mr. Kruell, 158; uncertainty regarding mask of, 168; place in British Phrenological Society of, 173
Sherman, General, as charter member of The Players, 87; death mask of, 99; Barrett's last request regarding mask of, 180; shaking hands with, 182
Stedman, Edmund Clarence, opinion of Dickens's verse, 44; dinner given to Black by, 320
Sterne, Lawrence, uncertainty regarding mask of, 168; circumstances of the death of, 210
Stevenson, Robert Louis, cast of hand of, 227

Index 457

Stockton, Frank, at the gymnasium, 421; meeting with, 422; a test of, 422
Stoddard, Richard Henry, acquaintance with, 423; dinner to, 424
Stories, plots for, 3, 4, 5
Stowe, Harriet Beecher, anecdote about, 418
Sweden, Charles XII. of, 152; exhumation of, 155
Swift, Dean, authorities on, 199; death mask of, 200
Swinburne, callers on, 358

T

Tadema, Alma, first meeting of Mrs. Hutton with, 330; a curious misunderstanding, 332; first meeting of Laurence Hutton with, 333
Tasso, the original mask of, 186
Terry, Ellen, desire to preserve Mr. Sherry's *chef-d'œuvre*, 21; opinion of Eleanor Duse, 21; Helen Keller and, 392, 393
Thackeray, William Makepeace, 2; "that-reminds-me" style of, 29; inscription in *Christmas Carol* by Dickens to, 43; friendship with Owen of, 162; mounting of the cast of, 170; finding the mask of, 207; cast of the hand of, 224; attitude of the hand of, 225; chair in Garrick Club, 274; caricature by, 403; book-plate by, 404
Thaxter, Celia, at Appledore with, 209; startling presentation of the mask of, 210; request for autograph of, 296; the funeral of, 376; life and personality, 377; the writings of, 381

Tile Club, members of, 414; incident at, 415
Titles, selection of, 256; Shakespeare as source of, 259; appropriate, 260

V

Vedder, Elihu, at Tile Club with, 414
Verse, inspiration of, 10, 11; by Laurence Hutton, 9, 31, 243, 252
Veteran, a young, 59; experiences of, 61
Voltaire, anecdote regarding mask of, 179; cast of hand of, 223

W

Wallack, Lester, his reminiscences, 105; family relations of, 107; fondness for Harry Montague, 107; last letter of, 108; death of, 108; burial-place of, 108; article on, 143; "leading old man" in company of, 196
Walton, Izaak, monogram of, 313
Warde, Frederick, as Iago, 62; as Othello, 64
Warner, Charles Dudley, photograph of hand of, 228; acceptance of manuscript by, 235; suggestions to Laurence Hutton by, 264; first meeting with, 402
Washington, George, portrait of, 83; cast of the head of, 149; original cast of, 202; the process objected to by, 203
Webster, Daniel, possession of mask of, 167; the making of the mask of, 170

Wellington, Duke of, leaving the Horse Guards, 53; funeral of, 54; acquaintance with the extraordinary man, 56; cast of hands of, 225
Whistler, James McNeill, the caricature in *Trilby* of, 338; Harpers' apology to, 341
Whitman, Walt, mask of, 214; personality of, 215; cast of hand of, 223; first meeting of Laurence Hutton with, 224

Whittier, John Greenleaf, cast of hand of, 227; meeting with, 374; anecdote told by, 375
Wiggin, Kate Douglas, anecdote by, 137; Helen Keller and, 392
Winter, William, about Stratford with, 315
Wordsworth, William, "trying-to-look-pleasant" expression of, 176; the taking of the life mask of, 176; the funeral of, 177

jd 4-29-71